The Interplay of Influence
News, Advertising, Politics, and the Mass Media

T H I R D   E D I T I O N

Kathleen Hall Jamieson

UNIVERSITY   OF   PENNSYLVANIA

Karlyn Kohrs Campbell

UNIVERSITY   OF   MINNESOTA

Wadsworth Publishing Company

Belmont, California

A Division of Wadsworth, Inc.

Communications Editor: Kristine Clerkin
Editorial Assistant: Nancy Spellman
Production Editor: Angela Mann
Managing Designer: Carolyn Deacy
Print Buyer: Barbara Britton
Art Editors: Kelly Murphy, Nancy Spellman
Permissions Editor: Robert Kauser
Designer: Al Burkhardt
Copy Editor: Jennifer Gordon
Cover Designer: Bruce Kortebein/Design Office
Cover Illustrator: Robert Hunt
Signing Representative: Jonelle Calon
Compositor: G&S Typesetters
Printer: Maple Press

*This book is printed on acid-free paper
that meets Environmental Protection Agency
standards for recycled paper.*

1   2   3   4   5   6   7   8   9   10—96   95   94   93   92

Library of Congress Cataloging in Publication Data

Jamieson, Kathleen Hall.
    The interplay of influence : news, advertising, politics, and the mass media /
Kathleen Hall Jamieson, Karlyn Kohrs Campbell. — 3rd ed.
        p.   cm.
    Includes bibliographical references and index.
    ISBN 0-534-14106-4
    1. Mass media—Influence.   2. Mass media—Audiences.   3. Mass
media—United States.   I. Campbell, Karlyn Kohrs.   II. Title.
P94.J34   1992
302.23—dc20   91-12894

To Our Grandmothers—

Myra Moore Hall Zabel
and
Hinke Douma Kohrs
who loved us, indulged our eccentricities,
and nurtured our dreams.

Contents

CHAPTER **4**

Influencing the News Media   98

CHAPTER **5**

Ratings and Revenues: The Audience in Mass Media Social Systems   125

CHAPTER **6**

What Is Advertising?   157

CHAPTER 7

Persuasion Through Advertising   179

CHAPTER **8**

Influencing Advertisers   210

CHAPTER 9

How to Influence the Media   234

CHAPTER 10

Political Versus Product Campaigns   252

CHAPTER **11**

News and Advertising in the Political Campaign   263

Preface

In the mid-1970s, when we first began thinking about writing this book, the mass media looked and sounded the way they had for decades. There were three networks offering news. Live news was national, not international. If we wanted to watch the news or a favorite program, we had to adjust our schedules to the times they were aired. There were no VCRs. No way to zip through ads existed either. The NAB was a powerful self-regulator of the broadcast industry. The Fairness Doctrine was alive and well.

What we thought other books about the mass media had missed was a sense of the ways in which news, advertising, and politics interact, hence the title *Interplay of Influence*. We also concluded that a rhetorical perspective on this interaction would help readers to fathom and respond to the realities that the news, advertising, and politics shaped and presented.

A decade and a half later, new technology, changed regulation, and a proliferation of broadcast channels have made the interactions among news, advertising, and politics more complex and increased the subtlety of the persuasive strategies used by politicians, advertisers, and journalists. But the principles governing these interactions have changed very little.

Accordingly, this third edition is a chronicle of how things have changed and how they have remained the same. Simulcasts and Simulsats, VCRs and Camcorders, multiple channels and multipolar international politics, the demise of the Fairness Doctrine, and the retrenchment of the NAB are among the topics that were not on the horizon in the mid-70s but that are central to the mass media today. But now, as then, industries engage in self-regulation to forestall external regulation, the need to reach a purchasing audience drives commercial broadcasting and newspaper publishing, and newscasters prize drama, conflict, and novelty.

We thank our colleagues whose adoptions of *Interplay* have made this third edition possible and whose hard-headed critiques have improved its content. Our increased emphasis on technology and politics in this edition reflects their advice. We also thank those at the University of Minnesota and the University of Pennsylvania whose good will and intelligence encourage and stimulate us. We thank the following reviewers for their helpful suggestions—Jane Banks, Syracuse University; Gina Daddario, State University of New York at Cortland; Kathryn Ingle, University of Virginia; and James L. Rogers, University of North Texas. Finally, we thank Robert and Paul with whom we carry on an endless interplay of influence.

Kathleen Hall Jamieson
Annenberg School for Communication
University of Pennsylvania

Karlyn Kohrs Campbell
Department of Speech-Communication
University of Minnesota

The Mass Media: An Introduction

Many Americans wake up to the sounds of music and news on a clock radio, wash and dress to the "Today" show or "Good Morning America," breakfast with the morning paper, commute to the patter of a favorite disc jockey, dine with the evening news, relax with prime-time television, and doze to the strains of music on the clock radio. Americans, on the average, have their television sets on more than seven hours each day and listen to radios more than eighteen hours each week, report reading some part of a daily newspaper four days a week, and about fifteen books each year. The mass media are undeniably a central part of life in the United States.

This book is about the influence of the mass media, specifically television, radio, and newspapers. Many books on this subject already exist, but this book considers not only how the media influence all of us, but how the media are, in turn, influenced by others—individuals, groups, government agencies, politicians, and other mass media. We hope to show that media persuasion works two ways: the media persuade us, but we and others can and do influence the media. This book is neither a history of nor an attack on media; it is a study of the communication and persuasion that take place through them.

Our perspective is rhetorical, focusing on how news, advertising, and political uses of the mass media shape conceptions of reality and influence attitudes and behaviors. We examine how consumer choices, individual and group protest, and regulatory mechanisms influence the mass media. As students of rhetoric, we know that any choice has an influence; whatever decisions newspeople, advertisers, or programmers make, the result will be a world view shaped by those decisions.

We are not, then, looking for evidence that media personnel make choices—that is an inevitable part of using symbols. Rather, we examine patterns of choice. The decisions of newspeople, advertisers, and programmers are significant, as they fall into systematic patterns that consistently present a particular view of

How Much Americans Say They Watch

According to a Gallup survey made in August 1990, 97 percent of Americans watch television on an average weekday. The typical American admits to watching 4.1 hours a day during the week, and 3.5 hours a day on the weekend; 17 percent watch more than 6 hours a day. The better educated and those with higher incomes claim to use television less frequently, yet television viewing is reported as 3.1 hours in households with more than $50,000 a year in income and 3.4 hours in college-educated households. The average U.S. household has 2.25 television sets (less than a third have only one set, and 14 percent have four or more sets). Sixty-two percent have cable. Almost 60 percent have a VCR.[a]

[a]George Gallup Jr., and Frank Newport, "TV's Stale Aftertaste," *Star Tribune*, 7 October 1990, p. 7 F.

Rhetoric

The faculty of discovering, in any given case, the available means of persuasion.
Aristotle

That art or talent by which discourse is adapted to its end.
George Campbell

The use of language as a symbolic means of inducing cooperation in beings that by nature respond to symbols.
Kenneth Burke

Rhetoric Is Unavoidable

Even if a given terminology is a *reflection* of reality, by its very nature as a terminology it must be a *selection* of reality; and to this extent it must also function as a *deflection* of reality.[b]

[b]Kenneth Burke, *Language as Symbolic Action* (Berkeley: University of California Press, 1966), p. 45.

"reality." We hope to make explicit the assumptions underlying their choices. A rhetorical perspective is controversial in regard to news because we are used to thinking of the news as "objective," as a report of what occurs. But a rhetorical perspective is natural and common for political and product advertising and for analyzing politicians' efforts to influence the public by manipulating news coverage; these efforts are obviously and intentionally persuasive.

Because of our rhetorical perspective, we focus our attention on mass media messages that are most significant in terms of audience beliefs and attitudes: news, editorials and commentary, and advertising. Because these messages are all

---

Participation/Identification

To *participate* is to take part, to join in, or to share with others. To participate is to be actively involved. Participation refers to the active role of the audience in creating meaning and sharing experience. When participation occurs, source and audience jointly create the message.

To *identify* is to associate or affiliate yourself closely with a person or group or with their values. In this process you see yourself as like someone else, imagine yourself in another's position, or empathize with others' problems and rejoice in their successes.

---

part of political mass communication, this book ends with a discussion of news and advertising in political campaigns. The primary news channels in our society are television and newspapers, so most of our illustrations will be drawn from them. We pay particular attention to television, now the most pervasive and influential mass medium.

The ideas developed here are based on three fundamental assumptions. First, we assume that all communication is reciprocal, jointly created by the source and the audience. No one can commit an act of communication alone. It is an *inter*act (inter = between) or a *trans*act (trans = through, across) that comes into being because the participants cooperate in creating meaning and sharing experience. For this reason, participation and identification are key concepts in our analysis.

Second, we assume that each mass medium has unique resources for communication and influence because of the characteristic ways in which we receive, perceive, and interact with it. Each is a special kind of channel with distinctive capacities for inducing our participation. As a result, we contrast the communicative potentials of the various media.

Third, we assume that the nature and impact of mass-mediated messages cannot be separated from the economic and political system in which the mass media function. The mass media reflect certain cultural values and assumptions precisely because mass media outlets are large corporations supported by advertising and constrained by governmental and internal regulation and public pressure. For this reason, we explore the commercial bases of the mass media and detail the forms of regulation and the influences bearing on them.

This book is organized to examine news, advertising, and political communication, in that order. In each instance, we examine the media, first as persuaders who influence their audiences, then as entities influenced and regulated by citizens, groups, and government. In the case of the news, we look first at what news is, then examine its influence, and finally look at how the news media are influenced.

We then look at the ratings and revenues in all of the mass media before exploring the nature and types of commercial messages. We study the ways in which advertising persuades as well as the ways in which advertisers can be influenced. The final sections on political communication synthesize material from news and advertising, as both are involved in political communication.

However, continuing our earlier format, we look first at how people are influenced politically through and by the media and then at how the media are, in turn, influenced by politicians and their supporters. We hope that these chapters will provide an understanding of how mass media influence and are, in turn, influenced.

The mass media are so familiar, so much a part of our everyday lives, that we all feel we know and understand them. But it is precisely because they are so familiar that we need to study them. Familiarity, for example, may blind us to the distinct kind of communication that takes place through the mass media, and especially to the processes by which they influence us.

One important distinction between mass communication and other forms of communication in the United States is their commercial basis: *the primary function of the mass media is to attract and hold a large audience for advertisers*. They also inform and entertain, of course; but informing and entertaining are only means to the end of providing a mass audience for advertisers.

Let us look in more detail at some of the ways in which mass communication is unique.

Distinctive Characteristics of Mass Communication

Mass communication is affected by its context—the industrial, affluent, mass society—and mass communication differs in important ways from other forms of communication. It differs not only because it is commercial, but also in terms of its audience, its messages, and its sources.[1]

The Audience

The audience for mass communication is *large*; it is a mass audience. This means that the audience is made up of so many people that it would be impossible for them to meet and interact face to face. The members of the audience are also *anonymous*; that is, audience members know others are watching, listening, or reading, but they do not know just who the others are. Note that the mass audience is thus the opposite of a *group*, which is defined as a small number of people who can meet and talk face to face, who come to know each other, and who develop attachments to each other. Finally, the mass audience is *heterogeneous*; it is made up of all sorts of people. The mass audience is so varied because nearly everyone has access to the media—you can read or watch or listen whether you are old or young, rich or poor, educated or uneducated, in a city or on a farm.

There are television sets in 98 percent of U.S. households, radios in over 99 percent, and most Americans can afford a newspaper, a magazine, or a paper-

---

1. The distinctions outlined here are those described by Charles Wright in *Mass Communication: A Sociological Perspective*, 3rd ed. (New York: Random House, 1986), pp. 6–9.

Anonymity

Dr. Ruth Westheimer, the pixieish sex therapist, was launched to fame by a sex advice show on New York radio. She now also does a national call-in show for NBC and a TV talk show on the Lifetime Cable Network. "Radio was crucial in giving me the opportunity to talk about sexual matters in an explicit way," she says. "Not only the power of the medium, but the anonymity it provides."[c]

　[c]*Time*, 4 November 1985, p. 75.

The National Village

A young man, dubbed by the press "the mystery boy," was found crying and confused in a bus terminal in Cheyenne, Wyoming, October 26, 1985. He had neither identification nor money. Police and social workers struggled to learn anything that would help them identify the young man. On October 28, newspapers around the country printed his picture. The next day the questions were answered. The youth was Gordon Vanderberg, a convicted felon who had been treated for mental illness and a hearing impairment in New York and Los Angeles. "Basically, the media solved this mystery," police detective Marty Luna said. . . . "They did a fantastic job of blitzing his picture all over the U.S. . . . It's like the whole country was one small town. When they get the word out, you're going to find somebody who can solve these puzzles."[d]

　[d]*Washington Post*, 30 October 1985, p. A 2.

---

back book. This saturation of the mass media reflects our affluent society; although there is an admission fee, nearly all Americans can pay it. The print media require literacy, which narrows their audience somewhat, but electronic media can be consumed and enjoyed by nearly everyone. The audience for mass communication is, then, large, anonymous, and heterogeneous.

The Mediated Message

The messages of mass communication are also distinctive. In general, they are *transient* or ephemeral, here today and gone tomorrow, intended and useful only for the immediate moment. Most mass communication is tied to a particular time, place, and set of events. Morning newspapers report what happened yesterday; the episodes of soap operas and prime-time series are quickly forgotten; paperbacks are read and thrown away. In this respect, mass communication is the opposite of communication in the fine arts or in what is sometimes called high culture. We expect to savor and cherish great paintings and sculptures; we read, reread, and study great books and plays; we listen over and over again to great pieces of music.

Obviously, some high culture is transmitted through the mass media. We can listen to opera "Live from Lincoln Center"; in the summer, we can tune in to the

Boston Pops concerts; we can watch productions of great plays; and we hope to see repeated broadcasts of some mini-series, documentaries, and interviews.

But these are exceptions. The vast majority of mass communication is tied to the daily and immediate; it is temporary and forgettable—a characteristic not only of radio and television, but also of newspapers, even though they are not as ephemeral.

Mass media messages are *transmitted rapidly*. Most audience members receive them at approximately the same time, as illustrated by television. Television critics agree on at least one thing: that the best television is live coverage of sports events, such as the World Series and the Super Bowl, and of breaking news stories, such as the student demonstrations and subsequent military response in Tiananmen Square or an earthquake's interruption of the World Series in San Francisco. No other form of communication reaches so many so quickly, and it is a given of newspapers, radio, and television that nothing is staler than yesterday's news.

Because nearly everyone has access to them, the messages of mass communication are *public*; they are addressed to everyone and they are created to be intelligible and acceptable to all. Newspapers are written in ordinary language with words chosen for their commonality and familiarity. Television and radio censor themselves to try to avoid giving offense to anyone. (Obviously, they do not always succeed!)

Once again, there are exceptions. Some media are specialized (sometimes called segmented or minority media). In contrast to *TV Guide*, *People*, and the *Reader's Digest*, some magazines aim at smaller, well-defined audiences: *Ebony* at African-Americans; *Guns and Ammo* at hunters and gun enthusiasts; *Electronic Media* at those interested in electronic programming. Similarly, although there are radio news networks that blanket the country, there are also Spanish-language stations and stations aimed just at those who love top-40 or jazz or classical music. Note, however, that all of us have access to these varied outlets, and because of their public nature, even such specialized media must take some care to avoid giving offense.

The pornography battle illustrates this problem: groups object to pornography precisely because all of us, including children, may be exposed to it. This issue is complicated and difficult, but it is the public character of pornography that arouses the most serious objections.

In summary, the messages of mass communication are transient, rapidly transmitted, and public.

The Source

The sources of messages in the mass media are also distinctive. Because sending such messages is costly and complex, the sources must be *organizational* or institutional. Historically, the sources of mass communication have been large organizations, such as radio and television networks, newspaper chains, publishing firms, and conglomerates owning different media or a variety of industries including one or more mass media outlets. Of course, there are variations in size. Some stations are independent; some newspapers are family firms; some magazines are produced by small, cohesive groups. But even in these smaller versions, mass communication is the product of an organization.

Production and distribution require a division of labor, highly trained specialists, and elaborate and expensive equipment. For this reason, very few individuals, as individuals, have direct access to the mass media. Those who speak or write through them represent teams, organizations, groups, or the public. In this sense, mass communication is *impersonal*, produced by a unit of people with varied skills.

The sources of mass communication, then, are organizational and, in that sense, impersonal or anonymous.

These characteristics of audiences, messages, and sources differentiate mass communication from other kinds of communication. But there are areas in which these distinctions blur. How is one to classify an outdoor concert by a rock group using sophisticated sound equipment to produce music for an audience of tens of thousands (which may also be sold as a record or marketed as a video)? What of a filmed theatrical production or operas and concerts televised live? Obviously, mass communication is part of and related to other kinds of communication. Although we can indicate distinctions, we must also acknowledge similarities and interrelationships.

Interpersonal and Mass Communication: Relationships

Mass communication is part of the whole process of communication going on all of the time in our lives. People watch television in their homes, and what they see and hear is affected by family attitudes and the comments of friends and relatives. Despite the importance of the mass media, we still hear live speeches, and we still talk to each other in small groups face to face at parties, in classes, at the grocery store, and in city council meetings.

All of these contacts influence our experience of and our reaction to mediated messages. But the messages in the mass media also affect our communication with family and friends. Mass communication needs to be studied, and for purposes of study we have to try to isolate it, but mass communication is not really separable from other kinds of communication.

Mass Media Use

The relationship between mass communication and other forms of communication is evident in our use of the mass media. With the exception of films shown in theaters, mediated messages are consumed by individuals alone or in small groups: a family or group of friends around a television set, a carpool of fellow workers listening to a radio program, a bus rider reading a newspaper.

Thus, the mass media reach large, anonymous, heterogeneous audiences with rapid, transient, public messages generated by impersonal, organizational sources; however, most mass communication occurs in intimate, personal, small-group settings.

Some worry that our experience of the mediated message is displacing our desire to experience the real thing. Scholars debate whether low voter turnout is prompted in part by the would-be voter's sense that he or she has already participated fully in the campaign by watching it in ads and televised news.

Similarly, Philadelphia Orchestra music director Riccardo Muti notes that:

> Recording is changing the way some people view our art. With the continuing refinement of compact discs, and the promise of video discs, some people are beginning to suggest that electronic media could replace the live concert experience. We must never let this happen.[2]

Impact of Mass Media

Mediated messages have not simply entered our lives; they have changed our patterns of living. The impact of television has been the most dramatic: Americans spend more time watching television than doing anything else except sleeping and eating!

The effect of all of this is the subject of much controversy. One recent study gathered ongoing reactions from television viewers; the research led to the following conclusions:

> Television viewing is a passive and relaxing, low concentration activity. Viewing is often driven by the wish to escape or avoid negative affective states. Viewers tend to feel passive and less alert after viewing. Heavier viewers feel worse than light viewers generally, and particularly when alone or during unstructured time.[3]

Television has also changed the way we get information. More and more of us get most of our news from television rather than from newspapers, and most of us think that television news is more trustworthy than news from other sources.[4]

But our attitudes toward television and the other mass media are mixed. We Americans fear the power of the press and the power and influence of the mass media generally, as reflected in such books as *Amusing Ourselves to Death* and *The Electronic Nightmare*.[5]

Some of our fear and distrust arises from a belief that the mass media are monolithic, controlled by ever-fewer people, and speaking with a single voice. Such attitudes reflect an understanding of the power held by those who control our access to information. Patterns of ownership that increasingly concentrate media outlets in fewer and fewer hands are also a source of concern. Despite such concentration of power, the mass media present a varied picture.

---

2. *Philadelphia Inquirer*, 17 October 1989, p. 11 A.

3. Robert Kubey and Mihaly Csikszentmihalyi, *Television and the Quality of Life: How Viewing Shapes Everyday Experience* (Hillsdale, N.J.: Lawrence Erlbaum, 1990), pp. 171–173.

4. Burns Roper, "Changing Public Attitudes Toward Television and Other Mass Media" (New York: Television Information Office, 1977).

5. Neil Postman, *Amusing Ourselves to Death: Public Discourse in the Age of Show Business* (New York: Viking, 1985); John Wicklein, *The Electronic Nightmare: The New Communications and Freedom* (New York: Viking, 1981).

Kinds of Mass Media

Some mass media are international in scope, some are national, and some are segmented, addressing a specialized audience. A few form an elite of opinion leaders. The electronic media may be independently owned and unaffiliated, part of a group with common ownership, affiliated with the networks, or owned and operated by the networks. Newspapers may be independently owned or be parts of chains or media conglomerates.

Finally, each medium has unique qualities because of its technology, its structure, and its function.

International Media

A medium is international if it regularly and predictably carries its messages across state boundaries. The *International Herald Tribune*, for example, is an international newspaper available throughout Europe as well as in the United States.

Broadcast signals don't see national boundaries. Increasingly, national broadcasting is becoming international as satellites make it available to people in different countries and time zones. In summer 1989, the Cable News Network (CNN) signed a five-year agreement with the Soviet Union that enabled CNN to transmit its 24-hour-a-day news on the Soviet satellite Intersputnik to the Indian subcontinent as well as Southeast Asia and Africa. Since CNN was already carried on Pan Am Sat to Central and South America and to Europe and the Far East on Intelsat, this meant that CNN International was beamed to most of the countries on earth. Specifically, the service was available in eighty-five foreign countries and the United States.[6] The first subscribers to the service were international hotels.[7] Existing cable systems in the Baltic Republics, the Ukraine, and Uzbekistan also pick up the news service.

The fall of the Berlin Wall in autumn 1989 offered other prospects for transnational broadcasting. In late 1989, the 24-hour-a-day music channel, MTV Europe (a partnership of the Mirror Group of Newspapers, Viacom International, and British Telecommunications), reached 10.8 million European homes. The channel began exploring the possibility of bringing its service to Eastern Europe with the fall of the Wall. In March of 1989, MTV Europe had moved into Hungary where it reached 112,484 households. Cable was used to reach 60,000 households in Yugoslavia. Terrestrial transmission brought the music to 40,000 homes in Belgrade. Those owning satellite dishes could receive MTV Europe in Poland and Czechoslovakia.[8]

In October of 1990, MTV, the cable music video channel, announced that it had signed an agreement with the Soviet television company Gostelradio to pro-

6. *Electronic Media*, 4 December 1989, p. 38.
7. *Washington Post*, 10 August 1989, p. C 10.
8. Sean Kelly, "MTV Sets Sights in Eastern Europe," *Electronic Media*, 4 December 1989, p. 34.

vide the main Soviet television channel with a weekly hour of MTV programming. Of particular note is that this will be the first time that any regular program on Soviet television has been commercially sponsored. Such U.S. companies as Wrangler and L.A. Gear have signed contracts to sponsor the programming, which will be in English with music videos primarily from U.S. and European rock performers.[9]

The ability of mediated messages to cross national boundaries changed the face of politics in the 1970s and 80s. Underground radio stations originating in a suburb of Paris carried a message that was dubbed to tape recorders. These dubbed cassettes passed through the underground to Iran where the transmitted words of the Ayatollah Ruhollah Khomeini helped inflame a revolution against the Shah of Iran.

In summer 1989, satellite transmission carried the pictures of demonstrating students building a Goddess of Democracy in Tiananmen Square. Countries around the world beamed back evidence of international support for the student movement. Days later the same satellite feeds were used by Beijing police to identify and capture dissidents. Had it not been for television, the students might, in the words of columnist David Broder, "have escaped into anonymity."[10]

The emergence of global media in global markets is comparatively recent. In the early 70s, only twenty-four nations had earth-based broadcasting facilities. By that decade's end, more than 135 nations were using the Intelsat global satellite system full time.[11]

As the 1980s drew to a close, satellite transmission was changing our conception of the world and of international affairs. The Soviet protest over the U.S. invasion of Panama was not delivered first to a U.S. embassy or to the White House. Instead a Soviet leader called the Moscow bureau of CNN.[12]

But more efficient forms of protest are not the only by-product of the new informational age. To deliver satellites into space, previously inconceivable forms of technical and economic cooperation are emerging. In 1989, the White House agreed to allow China to use its "Long March" rocket booster to launch U.S.-made satellites. One U.S. communications satellite already has been launched under that agreement. In July 1990, President George Bush approved a plan to launch U.S.-made commercial satellites atop Soviet rockets from a space center in Australia.[13]

Similarly, in July 1990, McGraw-Hill became the first large U.S. media company to publish a Russian-language newsmagazine—*Business Week/USSR*—in the Soviet Union. In 1990, *Business Week/USSR* will publish two issues; in January

9. Bill Carter, "MTV to Provide Programming for Soviets," *New York Times*, 12 October 1990, p. 4 C Y.

10. David S. Broder, "The Limits of Modern Technology," *Philadelphia Inquirer*, 18 June 1989, p. 7 C.

11. James F. Larson, *Television's Window on the World: International Affairs Coverage on the U.S. Networks* (Norwood, N.J.: Ablex Press, 1984), pp. 2–3.

12. Jonathan Alter, "Ted's Global Village," *Newsweek*, 11 June 1990, p. 49.

13. John Burgess, "Bush OKs Use of Soviet Rockets for Satellites," *Philadelphia Inquirer*, 9 July 1990, p. 3 A.

1991 it will become a monthly. The magazine will include translated articles from *Business Week* and *Business Week International.*[14]

Informational barriers have fallen more rapidly than economic barriers. This is the case in part because television's images do not require that the audience be either literate or multilingual. Words are not needed to caption the exploding shuttle Challenger as a tragedy, to comment upon the significance of Egyptian leader Anwar Sadat's embrace of Israeli Prime Minister Menachem Begin at Camp David, or to explain the meaning of the Pope kneeling in prayer at Auschwitz, with two prison-garbed survivors at his side. And whereas customs officials can intercept goods or books moving illegally across national boundaries, blocking a satellite feed or a fax is more difficult.

At the same time as unprecedented amounts of international information are available, state control of the media is waning. Those long denied free access to political information are eager consumers. In 1988, Mexican newspapers and radio, but not the government-dominated Televisa, gave opposition candidate Cuahtemoc Cardenas coverage. The result was that the public turned to other channels, and Televisa's once dominant evening news ratings plummeted.

Similarly, when the Congress of People's Deputies met in 1989, the Soviet audience was 25 percent larger than it had been for any previously televised event in Soviet history. Across the Soviet Union's twelve time zones, 200 million viewers watched as Mikhail Gorbachev's glasnost took on new meaning. For the first time the Soviet deputies deliberated before a national public. "Something is really turning over in our national consciousness," commented the chief of Soviet broadcast news. "The deputies are realizing the people are watching them, the voters can see them live, and the level of discussion is rising. There's never been anything like this—people watching how the leadership is changing."[15]

But by the summer of 1990, the Soviet audience was following a pattern observed earlier in the United States. Soviet viewers preferred World Cup Soccer to live coverage of the 28th Congress of the Soviet Communist Party.[16] (A similar pattern holds in the United States. Like their Soviet counterparts, U.S. viewers in 1988 preferred entertainment to politics—they emptied the shelves of video stores during televised coverage of the major party nominating conventions.)

Through the first half-decade of Gorbachev's rule, the Soviet state retained control of radio and television. On May 21, 1990, the Supreme Soviet passed a law dictating prison terms for "intentional defamation" of the president. The draft of the law was introduced after hundreds of booing marchers carried caricatures of Gorbachev as they filed by the reviewing stand on May Day in Kremlin Square. State-owned television simply edited the scenes from the coverage.[17]

Soon the censor will not stand between the event and the media report of it. On July 15, Gorbachev issued a presidential decree ending the Communist Party's

14. Deirdre Carmody, "Business Week Publishing Russian-Language Edition," *New York Times*, 20 July 1990, p. D 5.

15. Francis X. Clines, "Soviet's Big TV Hit is Politics, Live and in the Raw," *International Herald Tribune*, 1 June 1989, p. 6.

16. Bill Keller, "Moscow's Party Congress is No Party," *New York Times*, 8 July 1990, p. E 3.

17. Celestine Bohlen, "Insulting Gorbachev Now Illegal," *New York Times*, 22 May 1990, p. A 10.

grip on the broadcast media. The development of political pluralism and democ-ratization "called for cardinal change in the nature of the country's television and radio broadcasting," he said. Any party or public organization with the financial and technical resources can now open a television or radio station. No longer will the air waves be monopolized by "this or that party, political current or group." As important is the affirmation that state-run broadcasting "should be permitted in-dependently of political and social organizations and should provide impartial and all-round coverage of the processes taking place in the country." [18] In 1991, in the face of economic crises and threats of secession by constituent republics, Gorbachev threatened to reinstitute controls on the electronic and print media.

State control has been predicated on the presumption that the power of tele-vision to shape our perspective on the world is profound. In March of 1985, a split screen on ABC's "Nightline" brought the U.S. audience a tense exchange between South African foreign minister Roelof Botha and Bishop Desmond Tutu, the for-mer from Capetown, the latter in his church in Johannesburg. One analyst noted that the positioning of these two adversaries side by side provided "a striking pic-ture by [giving] Tutu the parity on TV that he and his fellow blacks are denied in their South African homeland." [19]

The split screen isn't the only technological change with political repercus-sions. Careful analysis of the tapes of Romanian leader Ceauşescu's execution re-vealed evidence that he had not been summarily executed but probably had first been tortured; magnified portions of the tape played in slow motion carried the evidence to the world.

From the tape showing Ceauşescu's execution to scenes of crowds dancing atop the Berlin Wall, international television has fashioned common global expe-riences. At the same time it has provided a clearer sense of the problems we share. For weeks in spring 1990, stories about the pollution of the air and water in East Germany heightened our awareness of the fragility of the ecostructure. Within the same period, international news carried a U.S. government study's warning that inadequately stored waste produced by the manufacture of nuclear weaponry was posing an environmental hazard that would require costly response.

In what political scientists are calling a "multipolar world," the news the world sees will not necessarily reflect the perspective of the superpowers, or focus on their special interests, such as have dominated international news from the end of World War II to the present. Moreover, the United States will be the object of news coverage that has not been edited by U.S. or Soviet gatekeepers.

The trend has already begun. "CNN World Report" is a global newscast that draws material from 3-minute English-language pieces provided each week by almost ninety participating networks around the globe. The material is aired unedited. [20]

18. Gary Lee, "Soviet Leader Cites Progress on NATO Issue," *International Herald Tribune*, 16 July 1990, p. 1.

19. Howard Rosenberg, "Getting South Africa Down in Black, White," *Los Angeles Times*, 20 March 1985, p. 1.

20. Alter, p. 50.

The emergence of a global village is changing the ways in which we think about ourselves and the world. What was once called "foreign" news is increasingly called "international" news, and those who habitually refer to the United States as America are increasingly aware that is a label we share with our neighbors to the north and south.

National Media

For our purposes, a medium is considered national if it has a large audience in all regions of the country. It is not government owned; there are no state-owned mass media in the United States. The Public Broadcasting Service, though partly funded by the federal government, is an independent corporation. The United States Information Agency, an agency of the federal government, may not broadcast its material in the United States except by special act of Congress.

National media include the major television networks (the Public Broadcasting Service as well as the three commercial networks), the major radio networks, the major wire services—Associated Press (AP) and Reuters—magazines such as the newsweeklies *Time*, *Newsweek*, and *U.S. News & World Report*, and such general interest magazines as the *Reader's Digest*, *TV Guide*, and *People*; the *Wall Street Journal*, the *New York Times*, and the *Christian Science Monitor* also are distributed nationally.

In March 1989, the *Wall Street Journal* had a daily circulation of 1,931,410, the largest daily circulation of any newspaper in the United States and about one-third of the weekly circulation of *Time*.[21] Even the largest newspaper chains tend to be somewhat regional in character, and most chains encourage local autonomy in news gathering and editorial policy.

In mid-1982, the Gannett newspaper chain began publishing a national newspaper, *USA Today*, a newspaper modeled on television's notions of news. The stories in *USA Today* are brief, extensively illustrated, and written to emphasize "the human interest angle." By 1989, *USA Today* had eclipsed the *New York Times* and the *Christian Science Monitor* in daily circulation by reaching over 1.3 million individuals daily.

Competitors to national network news are also emerging. In the summer of 1986, the Associated Press and CONUS Communications instituted a television news feed service called TV Direct. The service provides video-formatted AP news photos and video feeds of Washington events to television stations across the country. AP serves nearly 6,000 broadcast stations nationwide; CONUS is a news cooperative of television stations. The Cable News Network (CNN) based in Atlanta is a 24-hour-a-day national news operation now available in hotels throughout the world.

Specialized Media

Specialized media, also called segmented or minority media, are aimed at and limited to a geographically defined audience—*New York* and *California* magazines, for example—or by interest, for example, *Stereo Review* or *Flying*.

---

21. Audit Bureau of Circulation Report, March 1989.

CASE STUDY
Altering News Norms—The Influence of CNN

Prior to the advent of CNN, if you or I wanted to learn what had happened in the world on a given day, we would either have to locate an all-news radio station or wait until early evening to tune in to a network news broadcast. People interested in world affairs adjusted their time to that of the networks. Meals and social activities were scheduled around network news time. The availability of 24-hour-a-day news changed all that. News is now available at our convenience.

The sheer quantity of news coverage dictated some other changes in the ways in which news was programmed. Instead of a single "star" anchor, CNN developed a cast of anchors; focus on the personality of the anchor decreased. The result was subtle but evident in the difference in public perception when Mary Alice Williams moved from CNN. The sorts of national publicity that followed in the wake of Roger Mudd's departure from NBC did not ensue. Williams was one of many; the news had not been built around her in any special way.

A second difference in patterns of anchoring and reporting emerged. Women and minorities were more likely to appear in those roles on CNN than on the other networks. This pluralization of the news also was reflected in the use of tape and reporters from around the world.

By broadcasting around the clock, CNN ensured that without disrupting "commercial" programming, it could "go live." At 2:32 P.M. EST, CNN led the other networks by four minutes with the report that shots had been fired at President Ronald Reagan. Moreover, it could stay on the air with a live report as long as the news producer wished. CNN, for example, aired twenty-nine straight hours of coverage on the attempted assassination, Hinckley's motives, and Reagan's progress.

Live coverage makes us more aware of the extent to which most broadcast news is packaged by the conventions of editing discussed earlier. In the twenty-nine hours of CNN coverage of the assassination attempt, "CNN's viewers got the story in the jumbled way that a journalist receives fragments of information before transforming them into an orderly, polished report. The 'process' of gathering news determined the form in which the news was delivered. With CNN's unlimited time, the story could unfold at its own pace. With all those 'ragged edges' exposed."[e]

As the tanks moved in on the demonstrators in Tiananmen Square, CNN reporters could no longer sustain the calm, controlled tone that ordinarily characterizes edited news. Neither we nor they could be certain what was happening. CNN audiences around the world were encircled by the tensions and tragedies of the moment. Those who received their information in the 2-minute, predigested packages of edited news could not experience this story in the same way.

In its first decade, CNN established the importance of the function it served. CNN was the only network on "live" on January 28, 1986, when the space shuttle Challenger exploded. For hours in 1987, audiences followed CNN's coverage of efforts to rescue Baby Jessica. That programming drew the highest rating CNN had received up to that time—a 6.6.

In the summer of 1989, CNN's coverage of Tiananmen Square riveted audience attention on the ongoing struggle of the Chinese students to democratize their coun-

[e]Hank Wittemore, *CNN: The Inside Story* (New York: Little, Brown, 1990), p. 192.

try. In May 1989, those watching CNN's coverage of Tiananmen Square heard anchor Bernard Shaw confirm the extent to which live coverage had affected world affairs:

> I am being told that the Chinese government has closed the city of Beijing and no journalists are being allowed. . . . Unbelievably, we all came here to cover a summit, and we walked into a revolution. . . . Now we are being told that if we don't stop transmitting, the Chinese government will take our equipment. It will be interesting to see what happens. . . . President Bush is being quoted by reporters covering him in Maine, and it's being relayed to us. He is saying, "Word of the news blackout is very disturbing."

By 1990, we routinely expected to see CNN LIVE imprinted on newspaper photos of breaking news.

As we noted earlier, CNN's "World Report" has modified the ideology underlying news as well. In the 3-minute segments aired unedited from around the globe, we see the play of competing ideologies at work. The differences were evident in news stories following the invasion of Kuwait by Iraq. From the Palestinians came stories noting that the U.N. sanctions against Iraq created a double standard, pointing out that when U.N. resolutions had condemned Israeli actions, U.N. sanctions had been effectively blocked by a U.S. veto in the Security Council. Small countries dependent on Arab oil focused their stories primarily on the economic impact of the embargo; some declared they were being used as pawns in a U.S. game. One story from the Philippines emphasized the economic hardship imposed on that country by the inability of its nationals working in Kuwait to continue sending payments to their families at home. Only on CNN could audiences around the world hear the 76-minute speech that Iraq's leader Saddam Hussein sent to the United States to be broadcast to the public.

Because CNN broadcasts around the globe, it has become a vehicle for airing the competing claims of various nations and their leaders. Voices previously unlikely to be heard by U.S. audiences have received air play. In September 1990, for example, CNN carried a speech by Jordan's King Hussein appealing for moderation by all sides in the Kuwait–Iraq crisis. King Hussein warned that the world was slipping into war in the Middle East just as it had slipped into World War I. Within days, the Saudi ambassador to the United States was on CNN delivering a rebuttal to Hussein's speech. The appropriate analogy, argued the ambassador, was the role Hitler's aggression played in starting World War II. One index of power is the ability to have one's message heard; by that measure, CNN has empowered countries and leaders that otherwise would play a smaller role on the international stage. In short, CNN has accelerated the emergence of a multipolar world.

At the same time, it had become a medium of information for world leaders themselves. Message after message from Saddam Hussein to the world indicated that he had been following world reaction. The presumed channel: CNN. And in August 1989, the *New York Times* reported a presidential aide noting that President Bush was considering ways to respond to the threat to American hostages in Lebanon while in his study "watching CNN." The president's press secretary, Marlin Fitzwater, told the reporter, "CNN has opened up a whole new communications system between governments in terms of immediacy and directness. In many cases, its the first communication we have."[f]

---

[f]Quoted in Wittemore, p. 302.   (*continued*)

In 1982, Cable News Network (CNN) began 24-hour transmission to Asia. This photo shows the logo that introduced CNN broadcasting in Japan in June of that year. (© 1982 Cable News Network, Inc. All rights reserved.)

On January 28, 1986, CNN was the only network covering the launch of the Challenger. (© 1986 Cable News Network, Inc. All rights reserved.)

In 1990, an oil spill in the Galveston, Texas, shipping channel drew national attention. (© 1990 Cable News Network, Inc. All rights reserved.)

In October 1987, CNN received its highest ratings to that date for its live coverage of the rescue of Jessica McClure. (© 1987 Cable News Network, Inc. All rights reserved.)

Because of its on-the-spot coverage of the bombing of Baghdad as the war in the Persian Gulf began, scores of CBS, NBC, and ABC affiliates dumped their network coverage in favor of CNN. For example, WCCO, a CBS affiliate in Minneapolis, routinely interrupted the "CBS Evening News" to switch to CNN, and in a close three-way ratings race for number 1, WCCO's ratings clobbered its NBC and ABC affiliate rivals during the opening week of the Iraq War.

CNN's dominance of news coverage of the opening days of the war may be a turning point in television news, shifting power from ABC, NBC, and CBS and toward CNN. "The gulf crisis is a defining event," said S. Robert Lichter of the Center for Media and Public Affairs in Washington, D.C. "It's as if history is conspiring to help CNN." Larry Gerbrandt of Paul Kagan Associates, cable television analysts, agreed:

From May into June 1987, CNN provided live coverage of the Iran–Contra hearings. (© 1987 Cable News Network, Inc. All rights reserved.)

On May 19, 1989, Chinese authorities terminated live CNN transmissions from Beijing. (© 1989 Cable News Network, Inc. All rights reserved.)

On April 22, 1990, Earth Day was celebrated around the globe. CNN coverage suggested the extent to which environmental concerns were shared by those in otherwise distant places. (© 1990 Cable News Network, Inc. All rights reserved.)

"No one will ever doubt their advertising line again—that CNN is the most important network in the world. This is the greatest journalism story of the decade."[8]

EXERCISE: Examine the CNN pictures on pages 16 and 17. What is memorable about each? What is newsworthy? What facets of the news story does each picture feature? What difference, if any, does it make that the events captured in these pictures were broadcast live?

EXERCISE: How was our understanding of each of the pictured events changed by the presence of live coverage? Are some events more newsworthy than they otherwise would have been? How are traditional news norms altered by the ability to transmit images from around the globe? What effect will such coverage have on politics? On the conduct of world leaders? On issues of concern?

[8]Adapted from Bob Wisehart, "Amid the Chaos, CNN Establishes a New World Order," *Sacramento Bee*, 20 January 1991, pp. D1, D4.

CONUS

Stanley S. Hubbard, owner of KSTP-TV, the ABC affiliate in St. Paul, Minnesota, established a satellite news-gathering service to compete with the networks. CONUS, an acronym for Continental U.S., is a consortium of some seventy network-affiliated and independent local stations. The key to the system is a fleet of mobile vans (costing $200,000–$300,000) with uplinks to satellites via dishes and capable of reaching more than 700 U.S. television stations.

At a Gannett Center for Media Studies conference, Adam Clayton Powell III, formerly with CBS News, commented: "To get them [live shots] 10 years ago meant about 17 technicians and borrowing a truck from the television network of the kind they used to cover football games and setting up microwave towers—all expensive and time consuming. Now you can do it with three and sometimes even two persons."[h]

[h]Burton Benjamin, "Technology and the Bottom Line Create Profound Challenges," *New York Times*, 17 August 1986, p. 1 H.

Specialized media are defined by their special audiences, such as *Ms.* magazine, aimed at women with feminist leanings. Such an audience may be relatively small but spread throughout the nation. By contrast, local media are defined entirely by geography, aimed at an audience located in a particular area. They can be as small as the *West Central Minnesota Daily Tribune*, directed at those who live in Willmar and the surrounding area, or as large and prestigious as the *Philadelphia Inquirer*.

Elite Media

A third way of differentiating among the media is to recognize outlets or programs having a national impact, although their audience may be relatively small and geographically limited. These media are opinion leaders; they are an elite group that affects the decisions made in other media. The *New York Times* falls into this category. Herbert Gans, for example, writes that "The *Times* is treated as the professional setter of standards. . . . When editors and producers are uncertain about a selection decision, they will check whether, where, and how the *Times* has covered the story; and story selectors see to it that many of the *Times'* front-page stories find their way into television programs and magazines."[22] An elite medium is trusted, respected, and used by other journalists. The *Wall Street Journal* is an elite medium because of its pre-eminence in the financial community and because it covers stories in depth.

Some television programs also fall into this category, such as the "MacNeil/Lehrer Newshour" shown weeknights on the Public Broadcasting Service. To a lesser extent this is also true of the network programs "This Week with David Brinkley," "Meet the Press," and "Face the Nation," aired on Sundays. Clips from

22. Herbert Gans, *Deciding What's News: A Study of CBS Evening News, NBC Evening News,* Newsweek *and* Time (New York: Pantheon, 1979), p. 180.

Elite Media

"Fortunately, because almost everyone in the know realizes that the *Los Angeles Times* is available to the First Couple [the Reagans] every morning over breakfast, they worry about what we say and how we write it. That means that people return phone calls and read our copy and then return our phone calls. It helps."[1]

In response to 1986 data showing a 14.3 percent rise in daily readership of *USA Today* and a decline of 16.7 percent in readership of the *Wall Street Journal*, Thurman Pierce, of J. Walter Thompson USA, said: "The *Wall Street Journal* is like the *New York Times*. People [advertisers] want to be in there because it is the *Wall Street Journal*. It is the premier showcase in its medium; it is a prestige environment to be in."[1]

[1]Eleanor Randolph, *Los Angeles Times* Washington bureau, personal interview, 22 February 1982.
[1]*Advertising Age*, 28 July 1986, p. 64.

---

these programs, featuring prominent international and national political leaders, often appear on Sunday evening newscasts or in Monday's papers. Some specialized magazines with unusually prominent and authoritative authors function in a similar way, as, for instance, the journal *Foreign Affairs*. Most elite media are specialized media that have a national impact because they act as opinion leaders for other mass media. David Broder's column in the *Washington Post* is an example of opinion-leading political analysis; the *Congressional Quarterly* is the definitive outlet for information on Congress; the *New York Review of Books* contains authoritative commentary on books.

Major News Carriers

Classifying media as international, national, specialized, or elite focuses attention on the size and location of their audience and on relationships among the media. But equally important are the technology, patterns of ownership, and organization that exist in each medium.

Television

In 1990, there were 1,449 television stations in the United States. Of these, 1,100 carried commercials.[23]

Television is divided into VHF (very high frequency, channels 2 through 13) and UHF (ultra high frequency, channels 14 through 88). In April 1990, there were 549 commercial VHF television stations on the air and 550 commercial UHF.[24] It is also divided between commercial and noncommercial (educational) stations.

---

23. *Electronic Media*, 16 April 1990, p. 66.
24. *Broadcasting*, 16 April 1990, p. 14.

Independent Television Stations

In 1988, there were 310 independent television stations, up from 83 in 1976 and 135 in 1981. That growth has resulted as the government has allowed more UHF stations to go on the air.

In 1987, independents held a 22 percent share of the television audience, but the costs of programming ate up 47 percent of their budgets, according to a study by the Association of Independent Television States.[k]

[k] Geraldine Fabrikant, "Good Signs for TV Independents," *New York Times*, 22 January 1988, p. 25 Y.

About 85 percent of the commercial television stations are affiliated with a network. The majority of nonaffiliated television stations are UHF stations with limited coverage areas and audiences.

Until 1986, when someone said "the networks" they were referring to ABC, NBC, CBS, and, occasionally, CNN. But in that year the Fox Broadcasting Company began developing the Fox network. By 1990, Fox had 129 affiliates and was running ads in the major trade weeklies declaring

> The Problem: NBC, ABC & CBS are losing Audience. "Married with Children": The Face of television has changed. The Reason [the ad then inserted a photo of the Neanderthaloid slob who is the protagonist of this unorthodox program. In the photo, he is seated on a couch, holding a sledge hammer and staring blankly into space. On his lap is a large mutt. His bedroom slippers are threadbare.] The ad then concludes: "Scary, isn't it?"

One of the few hits of the 1989 season was Fox's offbeat cartoon program "The Simpsons," which boosted Fox's Sunday night ratings 21 percent over the previous season.[25] NBC's Entertainment President Brandon Tartikoff explains Fox's strategy this way:

> Fox is after the 18–34-year-old demographic. Why? Because that is the most fickle group of people on the planet today who have any sort of disposable income. They don't have lifelong habits formed, they haven't always bought a Buick, they haven't always drunk Yuban coffee, they haven't always used Tide. If you come in with a brand new splashy advertising campaign for a Nissan car or for a new brand of toothpaste, you've got a real buyer there.[26]

In 1991, Fox plans to offer a nightly news service. The news feeds will contain international, national, business, and entertainment news. When this plan reaches fruition, local news will change. Most Fox affiliates are UHF, a station type that has not traditionally aired local news.[27]

---

25. *Electronic Media*, 9 April 1990, p. 43.
26. "Tartikoff Talks," *Broadcasting*, 4 June 1990, p. 40.
27. "Fox Affiliates Get the News," *Broadcasting*, 11 June 1990, p. 31.

A&E

Jointly owned by Capital Cities/ABC, NBC, and the Hearst Corporation, A&E went on the air on February 1, 1984, the result of a merger of the ARTS (owned by ABC and Hearst) and the Entertainment Channel (a venture of Rockefeller Center and RCA). It had 9 million subscribers and a solitary advertiser: Ford. In 1989 it had 37 million subscribers, reaching about 41 percent of U.S. households, and 350 advertisers. Its revenues surpassed $50 million and will show a modest profit of about $4 million, according to Paul Kagan Associates, a cable analyst.

To persuade cable systems around the country to carry A&E, an effort was made to make A&E part of the fabric of every community in which it operated. A National Cable Library project was initiated, and working through local cable systems, A&E offered to set up video libraries, composed of tapes of its programming, in local libraries.

The A&E network succeeded by being relentlessly frugal. It produced little original programming, instead acquiring programs, mainly from the BBC. In 1984, 60 percent of its shows came from the BBC; in 1989, less than 40 percent did. By combining dance and opera with slapstick comedy and historical documentaries and programs about war, A&E attracts the viewers advertisers seek. A&E claims to offer advertisers the best demographics in television: people 35 to 45 years old, with four years of college, and average annual incomes of $40,000 to $50,000.[1]

[1] N. R. Kleinfield, "A&E: A Cable Success Story," *New York Times*, 16 April 1989, p. 31 H.

No organization may own more than twelve stations in each service category (AM, FM, or television). An organization or entity may own twelve television stations only if those twelve do not reach more than 25 percent of the nation's television homes. However, if a broadcaster buys an interest in a station that is more than half owned by minorities, that broadcaster may own up to fourteen stations in a service, but only if at least two of the stations are controlled by minorities and if the total owned do not reach more than 30 percent of the nation's television households.[28]

As a medium, then, television is divided into VHF and UHF channels, into commercial and educational stations, and into stations owned by the networks and stations owned by other corporations. Finally, it is divided into network and non-network stations.

Television is changing rapidly because of the growth of cable and low-power television and the possibilities created by direct satellite transmission.

In 1982, cable television had 27 million subscribers, more than one-quarter of all television homes in the United States; by mid-1986, 42 percent of all television homes subscribed. As of November 1, 1989, cable television penetration stood at 57.1 percent of all U.S. television households. In real numbers that meant

28. *Broadcasting/Cable Yearbook 1989*, p. A-3.

BET

The Black Entertainment Network, a 24-hour-a-day, Washington-based operation, is the nation's first and only television network aimed at an African-American audience. The network is owned by Robert L. Johnson, its founder and president, and by Tele-Communications Inc., the Great American Broadcasting Company, and HBO, the cable unit of Time Warner, Inc. In 1989, it was carried on just 1,825 of the nation's 7,500 cable systems and ranked 20th out of 42 basic services in terms of subscribers (with 23.8 million) and was 15th out of 20 networks in revenues, with a projected $22.4 million in 1989. Offered as part of the basic cable package, its revenues come from advertising and subscriber fees. On average, its shows were being watched by about 114,000 in prime time, less than 10 percent of the audience for TBS, the leading basic service. Still, BET is growing; its revenues have tripled since 1985.

Johnson attributes some of BET's problems to a lack of industry support linked to racism. Some cable operators, he said, "absolutely undervalue the black consumer markets." For example, BET was not available on a full-time basis in Harlem or the rest of Manhattan. Both operators that serve Manhattan—Manhattan Cable TV and Paragon Cable Manhattan—cited a limited number of channels as the villain and said BET will get more air time as soon as their channel capacity is upgraded. Industry analysis also noted that Johnson has lacked the resources to market the network properly so "there is poor understanding of exactly what BET is and what it wants to become," said Larry Gerbradt, an analyst at Kagan Associates.[m]

[m] Christopher C. Williams, "A Black Network Makes Its Move," *New York Times*, 17 September 1989, p. 4 F.

News Programming Increases

"Cable is at the heart of the news explosion—on a macro and micro level. Increasingly, cable systems, alone and in consort with broadcast outlets, are venturing into the world of hyperlocalism, starting news operations that provide a video version of the community newspaper. On a national level FNN and CNBC are battling for preeminence in business news."[n]

[n] *Channels/Field Guide 1990*, p. 44.

---

that approximately 52.6 million homes out of a total of 92.1 million having televisions subscribed to cable.[29]

More than half of the subscribers take at least one premium service, such as Home Box Office (HBO). In fall 1989, HBO had 23 million subscribers. Its main competitor Showtime had 9.8 million.[30]

29. "Cable TV," *Electronic Media*, 11 December 1989, p. 38.
30. Geraldine Fabrikant, "Viacom to Sell a 50% Stake in Showtime TV Service," *New York Times*, 18 October 1989, p. D 22.

Shopping by Television

In 1986, Home Shopping Network Inc., which has captivated bargain-hungry consumers by offering discounted merchandise through cable television, expanded into broadcast television by agreeing to purchase nine UHF stations in major markets for an estimated $150 million. The stations Home Shopping is acquiring are in Newark (New Jersey), Smithtown (Long Island), Boston, Baltimore, Philadelphia, Cleveland, Houston, San Francisco, and Los Angeles. "We hope to become the fifth major TV network," said Roy M. Speer, chairman and chief executive of the company, which is based in Clearwater, Florida. In addition to buying stations, the network has been attempting to sign other stations as affiliates.

To maximize their use of UHF stations, most of which have limited range and small viewerships, Home Shopping hopes that they will be carried by cable operators in their areas. Until last year, cable operators were required to carry local broadcasters' signals, but a federal appeals court in 1985 struck down the "must carry" rule. Under new regulations issued in 1986 by the FCC, cable systems must carry a certain number of local stations, depending on the size of the system, at least until 1991. However, the long-term status of the regulations remains in doubt.°

°Richard W. Stevenson, "TV Shopper's 'Fifth Network,'" *New York Times*, 30 September 1986, p. 36 Y.

Cable systems with many channels offer the possibility of diversified programming. Channels presenting only children's programs, news, sports, comedy, and first-run movies now exist. A sports network, ESPN, gained viewers in 1989 while ratings for NFL broadcasts on the other networks remained virtually unchanged. Its contract with the NFL permitted ESPN to televise one game per week during the second half of the regular football season. Nine percent more viewers watched the games on ESPN than had in 1988.[31]

Some cable systems provide nonprofit channels that give local and minority groups and individuals access to the airwaves. Some channels are free of advertising; others cluster ads at the end of a half-hour of programming. Still others, such as in-house home shopping channels, provide two-way interactive systems allowing viewers to purchase products by calling 800 numbers. Interactive technology raises the threat of invasion of privacy, as the system can be used to accumulate intimate and otherwise inaccessible information about users.

Cable also has pioneered what some tout as the future in message delivery—pay-per-view. In 1990, between 13 and 18 million U.S. homes were capable of receiving pay-per-view events. Pay-per-view occurs on channels that carry programs to homes that have agreed to subscribe. To this point, movies and boxing have been the types of programming most frequently carried on a pay-per-view basis.

31. Thomas Tyrer, "Cable Gains, Broadcast Flat in This Season's NFL Ratings," *Electronic Media*, 11 December 1989, p. 6.

In 1992, NBC may change all of this by offering full coverage of the 1992 Summer Olympics to cable viewers on a pay-per-view basis. This will provide 600 ad-free hours of sports coverage from Barcelona, Spain, in a package costing approximately $150 per home. The partnership of NBC and Cablevision Systems Corporation will originate the programming.[32]

In 1984, Congress essentially deregulated cable. The legislation specified that cable rate deregulation would occur in 1987. Subsequent complaints about rate increases and poor service have led to calls for re-regulation. In 1989, Congress released a Government Accounting Office report stating that between December 1986 and October 1988, basic cable service charges increased from $11.23 to $14.48, a 29 percent increase.[33]

The Public Broadcasting Service (PBS) was once the only service dedicating itself to educational television. In 1990, PBS was programming 15 to 20 hours per week in prime time and 120 hours per week at other times. Between 1985 and 1990, PBS's prime-time ratings dropped 30 percent. Cable had begun to provide alternative educational television.

Television's future depends in part on technology: direct satellite transmission to homes without the use of cable; the costs of laying cable; the carrying capacity of fiber optics cable; the potential for using existing telephone lines; the sophistication of interactive systems for purchasing programs and products. Low-power (low-band, very-high-frequency) television offers such opportunities.

Direct Broadcast Satellite (DBS) transmits television programming directly to antennas at subscribers' homes. By 1993, NBC, Cablevision Systems Corporation, Rupert Murdoch's News Corporation, and Hughes Communications plan to have a 108-channel DBS service in place.[34]

In the past, low-power stations have served almost exclusively as boosters or translators, making signals available to communities that can't receive regular transmissions. Low-power stations that originate programming are experimental. In Washington, D.C., a low-power station beams Spanish-language programs to one particular area, an example of low-power television aiming a weak signal at a specific audience. The spring 1990 FCC list showed 757 licensed low-power television (LPTV) stations; the commission has granted construction permits for another 1,713.[35]

However, over-the-air pay television systems soon may compete with cable systems, especially in urban areas. In 1982, the Microband Corporation of America urged the Federal Communications Commission to allow three such "wireless cable" systems in each of the nation's fifty largest television markets. (In fall 1989, Microband filed for bankruptcy.) In summer 1990, fifty wireless systems served about 250,000 subscribers. Wireless cable, also known as multichannel, multi-

32. Bill Carter, "NBC to Offer 600 Hours of Olympics, at a Price," *New York Times*, 12 February 1990, p. D 10.

33. Stuart Brotman, "ViewPoint: Scenes from a Marriage," *Emmy*, vol. 12, no. 4, pp. 1–3.

34. Laura Malt, "Wireless Cable Industry Sees Fortunes on Rise," *Electronic Media*, 9 July 1990, p. 24.

35. *Broadcasting*, 16 April 1980, p. 14.

point distribution service (MMDS), sends multiple channels of programming by microwave transmission rather than by cable. In its early years wireless cable suffered from poor signal reception and limited offerings, often of only one channel. By summer 1990, however, noise had been reduced, and the development of California Amplifier's new Beambender had made it possible to circuit the signal around objects that once had blocked it. Additionally, the Senate Commerce Committee supported legislation that would require cable programmers to sell their programming to wireless operators. HBO has already begun to do so.[36] The costs of MMDS and the time required to build the transmitters and antennas are far less than for laying cable. Because of its potential, large corporations are moving into this area.

Future development also depends on regulation and patterns of ownership. For example, the Federal Communications Commission (FCC) formerly banned telephone companies from controlling cable systems in their service areas and television networks from controlling cable systems anywhere in the country. In 1981 these network regulations were modified, and all three networks are competing aggressively for control of cable television systems and programming. However, television networks and their affiliates still cannot own cable systems in areas they serve. Whether telephone companies can get into the cable business is still at issue. In July 1990, however, the Bush Administration endorsed the idea, thereby increasing the likelihood.

One other factor has changed the ways in which we view television. The advent of the VCR has made it possible to rearrange television's schedule to suit our own. According to Nielsen Media Research in May 1990, VCR penetration had increased to 69.4 percent of television homes.[37]

Radio

Radio best illustrates media specialization and segmentation. It was once dominated by national networks comparable to those we now associate with television. There were originally four national networks—ABC, CBS, NBC, and the Mutual Broadcasting System—but what remains are primarily news services. Today, however, radio has become largely a segmented medium. At the end of 1981, there were about nineteen specialized or regional radio networks. Some of them provide 24-hour-a-day adult popular, top-40, jazz, classical, or country and western music. Two things have contributed to the proliferation of networks: one is an increase in the number of radio stations from about 4,000 in 1968 to nearly 10,000 ten years later, and to 10,688 in 1990;[38] the second is an effort to reach specialized audiences (see Chapter 5 on ratings and revenues). For example, only 41 of the nearly 9,300 commercial radio stations in the country play classical music, yet most of these are profitable. Because there is recognizable public demand for classical music and there are advertisers eager to reach the upscale audience such

36. Malt, p. 24.
37. *Electronic Media*, 30 July 1990, p. 28.
38. *Electronic Media*, 16 April 1990, p. 66.

Formats in Radio

Those who program for radio and who buy time on this medium think of radio formats in these terms:

contemporary hits, top-40, contemporary	album-oriented rock
	classical
adult contemporary	country
oldies (1955–87)	talk
black (75 percent or more of audience)	news
	Big Band
Hispanic/Spanish	middle-of-the-road
urban (majority of audience is non-Caucasian but a large segment is Caucasian)	jazz
	religious
easy listening	gospel

---

programming attracts, the number of classical music stations has remained nearly constant in recent years.[39]

At least twenty-three national radio networks are currently in existence, compared with just four in 1968 and nine in 1974. Though music, news, and sports constitute the bulk of network fare, the radio dial is increasingly filling up with daily, weekly, or monthly "long-form" programming, from music/variety series like NBC's "Live from the Hard Rock Cafe" to national talk/call-in shows, many inspired by the phenomenal success of Mutual Radio's "Larry King Show."

Advertisers want their commercials to reach particular consumers, and to compete with other stations for these consumers, stations need the resources of networks—particularly programming they could not afford to produce themselves. Some networks are regional, such as the New York Yankees baseball network. Others are national but aimed at a particular ethnic group, such as the National Black Network formed in 1980 with ninety affiliates and an estimated daily audience of 300,000. Although radio is generally considered a local medium, this claim is open to dispute. About one-fifth of all radio stations in the United States are now fully automated, using syndicated pretaped programming services. As a result, although programs may be beamed from a local station, the programming can originate elsewhere.

One unusual network, National Public Radio (NPR), took to the air in October of 1970. Beginning with 90 affiliates, it had grown to 377 affiliates by 1989. NPR produces more than fifty-five hours a week of original national programming from its Washington, D.C., headquarters, and more than half of that is news and public affairs, including its well-known news programs "All Things Considered" and "Morning Edition."

39. Jeremy Gerard, "Classical Stations Do Their Best to Survive," *New York Times*, 16 October 1989, p. D 11.

Competition Among Newspapers

Among the 1,526 cities with a daily newspaper, only 44 had at least 2 separately owned newspapers, and those 44 included 19 cities where newspapers were published under joint ownership agreements.[P]

[P]*Facts about Newspapers* (Reston, Va.: American Newspaper Publishers Association, 1988), p. 4.

A comparable public network, American Public Radio, was formed in 1982. Many stations carry programming from both NPR and APR. In 1989, APR had 355 affiliates. Total listenership for public radio, NPR plus APR, is about 11 million per week. The most popular of public radio's shows is NPR's "All Things Considered," which airs nationally during afternoon drive time and attracts 4 million listeners a week.

Along with a small number of noncommercial radio stations, such as the Pacifica Radio Network, APR and NPR are among the few sources of in-depth news on radio; most news coverage on commercial radio is limited to a headline service.

Newspapers

There were about 1,688 daily newspapers in the United States in 1984 with a combined circulation of 63,340,320. By 1990 that number had dropped to 1,626.[40] Competing with them for readers and advertising dollars in 1985 were 7,047 weekly newspapers, some distributed free of charge, with a combined circulation of 39,085,341.[41] Almost 95 percent of daily newspapers subscribe to a major wire service, with the result that much of the news they print, especially on national and international events, originates with the wire services.

Chain ownership of newspapers has been on the increase. About three out of five of the nation's daily newspapers now belong to chains, and the twelve largest chains now account for about two-fifths of the 63 million newspapers distributed daily in the United States. The largest in terms of circulation is Knight-Ridder, but the largest in terms of the number of newspapers owned is Gannett, a chain of about ninety-three newspapers, each of which is locally and independently edited. There are also some relationships between newspapers and television. In 1953, more than two-thirds of all television stations were owned by newspaper publishers; today, however, only about one-quarter of all stations are owned by newspapers.[42] Despite chain ownership, reliance on wire service materials, and ownership of other media outlets, however, newspapers are basically local media.

40. *Electronic Media*, 16 April 1990, p. 66.
41. *National Weekly Newspaper Rate Directory, 1985/86.*
42. An FCC ruling affirmed by the Supreme Court in *National Citizens Committee for Broadcasting v. F.C.C.* (1978) limits divestiture orders to only "the most egregious cases" and balances the need for diversity with the value of "stability and continuity of ownership," particularly when the ownership is local (3 *Media Law Reporter*, 2409–2425 [1978]).

Magazine Circulation for First Half of 1990 [q]

Rank	Circulation
1 *Modern Maturity*	22,443,464
2 *Reader's Digest*	16,396,919
3 *TV Guide*	15,837,064
11 *Time*	4,258,604
13 *National Enquirer*	4,019,187
17 *Playboy*	3,436,471
18 *Newsweek*	3,227,522
19 *People*	3,176,166
23 *Cosmopolitan*	2,714,639
25 *U.S. News & World Report*	2,319,591
50 *Soap Opera Digest*	1,388,930
75 *Scouting*	975,927
100 *Homeowner*	778,319
125 *Stereo Review*	609,885
150 *Audubon*	447,775
175 *Crafts*	352,411
200 *The Kiwanis Magazine*	283,000

[q]Audit Bureau of Circulations.

Magazines

Under the impact of television, both radio and magazines became specialized or segmented media. Because advertisers could reach the same mass audience more cheaply and quickly via television, many well-known mass circulation magazines went out of business—*Look* and the *Saturday Evening Post*, among others. More recently, magazines targeted at special audiences have sprung up. Some of these are *Motorcyclist* and *Fantasy and Science Fiction*. There are only a few national magazines, and three are newsweeklies: *Time*, *Newsweek*, and *U.S. News & World Report*. *Time* is owned by Time Inc., *Newsweek* by the Washington Post Company. These examples are typical because many magazines today are owned by chains, large corporations, and conglomerates—in part because it is very costly to start a magazine and because the survival rate for magazines is low. On the average, only 10 percent of new magazines survive beyond their first year; nevertheless, as of summer 1990, there were 3,100 consumer magazines in existence.[43]

The degree of specialization in this medium can be seen in a closer look at some of the mass circulation magazines. Many publish special editions designed to permit advertisers to reach specific audiences. *Time*, for instance, publishes

---

43. Samir Husni, associate professor of journalism at the University of Mississippi, cited by Deirdre Carmody, "Magazines: Perception Vs. Reality: Just How Bad Is Business?" *New York Times*, 2 July 1990, p. C 6.

regional editions, editions aimed at special groups, and an international edition. One edition goes primarily to college students, another to 1,414 of the most affluent zip code areas within metropolitan markets, and still another to about 600,000 business and professional people. Similarly, *Sports Illustrated* publishes four regional editions and a special homeowners' edition limited to slightly over a half-million subscribers located in zip code areas with the highest concentration of home ownership. Other magazines, such as *Cosmopolitan* and *Good Housekeeping*, publish Spanish-language editions. In other words, although mass circulation magazines exist, many of them publish special editions with advertising aimed at distinct audiences.

Magazines have several advantages over television for advertisers. According to data collected by the Magazine Publishers' Association, better-educated and more affluent people are more apt to read magazines than to watch television. A magazine becomes a trusted and familiar source reflecting an image the subscriber can identify with. In addition, some advertisers now banned from television, like cigarette manufacturers, must rely on print outlets.

T O   S U M   U P

These are some perspectives for examining the existing mass media. Despite the power and wealth of concentrated mass media ownership, few media are national in scope. Instead, most outlets aim at specialized audiences based on location, age, sex, income, education, ethnic background, or other variables important in determining a person's interests. The mass media speak with varied voices to varied audiences.

Selected Readings

Barrett, Marvin, ed. *Broadcast Journalism, 1979–1981: The Eighth Alfred I. Dupont-Columbia Survey.* New York: Everest House, 1982.

Brown, Les. *Les Brown's Encyclopedia of Television.* Expanded edition. New York: Everest House, 1982.

Kubey, Robert, and Mihaly Csikszentmihalyi. *Television and the Quality of Life: How Viewing Shapes Everyday Experience.* Hillsdale, N.J.: Lawrence Erlbaum, 1990.

Lichty, Lawrence W., and Malachi C. Topping. *American Broadcasting: A Source Book on the History of Radio and Television.* New York: Hastings House, 1975.

Schudson, Michael. *Discovering the News: A Social History of American Newspapers.* New York: Basic Books, 1978.

Wicklein, John. *The Electronic Nightmare: The New Communications and Freedom.* New York: Viking, 1981.

Wright, Charles. *Mass Communication: A Sociological Perspective.* 3rd ed. New York: Random House, 1986.

What Is News?

Just what is news? Despite many efforts, no neat, satisfactory answer to that question has been found. Some deaths are news, but many more are not. Some strikes draw headlines; others are ignored. Some protests become lead stories; others go unnoticed; still others are deliberately disregarded. The best answer seems to be that news is what reporters, editors, and producers decide is news.

That answer contradicts traditional notions that news is "out there," that reporters "just cover the story," that news is "what's happening." Instead, that answer says that news is selected, even created, by newspeople. It claims that news is not just "the facts," but also rhetoric—messages influencing how readers and viewers perceive reality. It would be surprising if this were not the case.

News is gathered, written, edited, produced, and disseminated by human beings who are part of organizations and who have beliefs and values. Organizations, such as networks, have functions and goals as well as relationships to government, to regulatory agencies, to advertisers, and to the vast audiences they seek to attract. These beliefs, values, functions, and interests are bound to influence the messages these networks publish and broadcast.

On a more complex level, this answer suggests that newsgatherers and news organizations are persuaders who shape our views of reality, who induce us to believe one thing rather than another. We examine this controversial argument in the next chapter. Here, however, we treat the simpler claim. We examine the concept of "hard news" or "spot news" (everyone concedes that "soft news," such as feature stories, is not objective) in order to set up a model of the news story. We explore the criteria governing what newspeople define as news, the constraints influencing what actually will be covered, and the conventions controlling how a news event will be presented.

Hard News Defined

■

Hard news is the report of an event that happened or was disclosed within the previous twenty-four hours and treats an issue of ongoing concern. The crime story is the model for hard news.[1] A violent crime (murder, armed robbery, rape) is an event, a definable happening. It occurs between individuals (perpetrator and victim). It is dramatic, conflict-filled, and involves extreme physical action and emotional intensity. It disrupts legitimate order and threatens the community. Ordinarily, what happened can be told in a short, simple story, and information about the event can be verified by official sources such as the police or the district attorney. The crime scene or its effects are usually visual, easily reduced to tape or photograph, and it is part of the regular beat of a reporter.

A typical crime has all the qualities of a newsworthy event: it is (1) personalized—it happened to real people; (2) dramatic, conflict-filled, controversial, violent; (3) actual and concrete, not theoretical or abstract; (4) novel or deviant; and (5) linked to issues of ongoing concern to the news media. These characteristics reflect the qualities of mass media messages discussed in Chapter 1.

1. Hard news is personalized, about individuals. Mass media news must be accessible to, and interesting for, a mass audience. Consequently, news stories must be clear, simple, and attention getting. Hard news is personalized and individualized because such stories create audience identification. We care more about the reactions of a tornado victim than about statistics on the force of the wind, and we want to see the person who faced down the tank in Tiananmen Square. The human connection allows us to imagine ourselves in the situation or to create meaning out of what is puzzling and complex. Unlike stories about destruction of the ozone layer or the spread of nuclear weapons, stories about individuals have causes and consequences on a manageable scale. Individuals can act or speak in a time span that fits the news media, and it is easier to visualize a person than an idea, a process, or a structure.

An interview can personify an abstract idea (an economic theory becomes Reaganomics) or clothe an idea in living flesh (Representative Pat Schroeder, a Democrat from Colorado, voices the view that businesses should provide unpaid leave with job guarantees to employees after the birth or adoption of a baby or in response to serious family illness). The personal and individual character of hard news reflects the fact that most news stories are researched through interviews and human sources.

Interviews not only personalize, but allow reporters to draw on the expertise of others, an important advantage for reporters who are usually generalists, not

1. Crime itself is the third largest category of news subjects covered by newspapers, occupying from 2 to 7 percent of the total news space. The selection process in crime news, particularly in large metropolitan newspapers and broadcast outlets, is such that only the most dangerous offenses are reported—primarily murder and manslaughter, crimes committed by individuals, not institutions (Sanford Sherizen, "Social Creation of Crime News: All the News Fitted to Print," in *Deviance and Mass Media*, ed. Charles Winick [Beverly Hills: Sage, 1978], pp. 208, 215). Coverage of particularly sensational crimes helps to sell newspapers.

C A S E   S T U D Y
Focusing on the Individual to Make News

In spring 1990, newspaper readers read that *Outweek* had published gay rights activists' statements that a number of prominent and presumed heterosexual celebrities, newspersons, and politicians are gay. Gay rights activists Michael Petrelis and Carl Goodman held a news conference in Washington, D.C., in May 1990 to read out the names of twelve individuals in public life whom they claimed are gay. Using the opportunity provided by live television, a gay author "outed" a gubernatorial candidate in a northeastern state on a talk show.

Billboards advocating the re-election of Republican Senator Mark Hatfield were altered to read "closeted gay . . . living a lie . . . voting to oppress." And immediately after his death, supermarket tabloids carried stories claiming that business tycoon Malcolm Forbes had been gay. *Outweek*, whose national circulation is 40,000, published a detailed account of what it reported to be Forbes's activities.

Outing is controversial within the gay community. The National Gay and Lesbian Task Force, the Human Rights Campaign Fund, and the Lambda Legal Defense and Education Fund oppose outing, calling it blackmail and psychological terror. Proponents of outing argue: "If I say someone is straight, I have not revealed anything private. But if I say he is gay, there is the impression that I have." Outing for such activists is a claiming of "role-models."[a]

By featuring supposed revelations about individuals who are of ongoing news interest, those favoring outing capitalize on news norms. *Revealing, uncovering,* and *exposing* are words of honor to most reporters. But other news norms argue against coverage. Those listed as gay—including television and film stars Richard Chamberlain and John Travolta—have denied it, and those sources listing them have provided nothing that sustains the tests of proof. Additionally, even in an age obsessed with the private lives of public figures, some find such publicizing an invasion of privacy.

In the column "Press Gallery" published in the weekly *Roll Call*, a publication focused on the actions of Congress, two reporters framed the issues raised by the Petrelis and Goodman press conference this way: "Reporters were skeptical, since, among other things, Petrelis and Goodman gave no proof of the listees' alleged sexual preference. Another problem for the reporters was trying to figure out why they should be reporting this exceedingly private information or misinformation." The reporters concluded: "PG [Press Gallery] contends that in almost every case, a politician's sexual preference, fidelity, bizarre boudoir behavior, or other personal peccadilloes are not fair game unless the politician is stupid enough to invite scrutiny. . . . We also agree . . . that rank hypocrisy also qualifies a Member for disclosure."[b]

But press behavior was not that clear cut. The *Philadelphia Inquirer* and NPR among others named Mark Hatfield as the senator whose billboards were being defaced. Some sources, *Roll Call* and the *Washington Times* among them, covered the press conference but published no names. Some outlets, the *Washington Post* and the *New York Times*, remained silent.

[a]Michael Matza, "Outrage," *Philadelphia Inquirer*, 28 June 1990, pp 1, 8 E.
[b]"How the Media Should Deal with the 'Outing' of Alleged Homosexual Members," *Roll Call*, 4 June 1990, pp. 14, 16.

specialists. The news is personalized and individualized by heavy coverage of the president, of congressional leaders, of the wealthy, powerful, and prestigious, and of sports, stage, screen, and fashion celebrities. These are the "stars" of the news who, like the star hired to lure us to a film, are intended to draw the mass audience to the news channel.

The emphasis on individuals may create distortion. In finding a spokesperson, the news media will generally choose the more flamboyant, articulate, and theatrical characters who are willing to take that role, not necessarily the most thoughtful or most central figures. Critics claimed that it was the media who legitimized the civil rights leadership of Stokely Carmichael and H. Rap Brown, men without large or obvious constituencies. The women's movement made a deliberate effort to avoid traditional hierarchy and had no "leaders," but the media turned individuals like Kate Millett into leaders against their will.[2]

Defining hard news as personal, as about individuals, means that it is not about processes or the exploration of ideas; it is the story of a group or a movement only to the extent that a group or movement can be personified by one member's testimony. The focus on individuals simplifies and clarifies. It creates audience identification; it reflects journalistic reliance on human sources and on the interview.

2. Hard news is dramatic, conflict-filled, and violent. Mass media news must gain and hold audience attention. Presenting hard news as drama is a way to structure a story to do just that. Drama begins with what is called an inciting action, an event that disrupts normal routines (this is the event that becomes the "news peg," discussed in the next section). Conflict escalates in a rising action to a climax, the high point of tension, which is followed by an unraveling or resolution. Such structure, as illustrated by jokes, plays, novels, and television series episodes, is beloved by audiences and can evoke intense participation and identification.

The typical news story is organized dramatically to identify a problem, to describe it in a narrative of rising action, to locate the protagonists and set them against each other (usually in short interviews), and to create some sort of resolution. This format gives coherence to data, and it makes an item a story in the most literal sense, a story that is likely to gain and hold an audience. Hard news is exciting, and the essence of excitement is drama.

Conflict is an intrinsic element in drama; drama's rising action unfolds through increasingly intense conflict. Conflict disrupts routine and is thus novel and unusual (another criterion discussed below). Conflicts are newsworthy events and reporting conflict is a way to create interest. The presidential election campaign that runs for more than a year is treated as a horse race or a sports contest in part so that it can be divided into specific events—primary victories, caucus defeats, slugging it out in debate, going one-on-one with hecklers during a speech—filled with the drama and conflict characteristic of hard news. News coverage emphasizes conflict by interviewing and quoting opposing sides on an

---

2. See Kate Millett, *Flying* (New York: Alfred A. Knopf, 1974), pp. 92–93; Gaye Tuchman, *Making News: A Study in the Construction of Reality* (New York: Free Press, 1978), pp. 140–141.

issue; such interviews not only allow a reporter to remain detached, they also create an impression of fair and balanced coverage.

This focus on conflict creates imbalance in the reporting of both international and domestic affairs. Reporting of foreign affairs tends, for example, to stress conflict while government officials stress accommodation.

Violence is the most dramatic form of conflict, and it is nearly always treated as newsworthy. The attraction of violence explains the relatively heavy coverage of crime news and its capacity to sell papers. A violent event is likely to be a matter of community concern, of great interest to many people. This is particularly true when the vulnerable have been the victims of violence.

The McMartin case is illustrative. In August 1983, a mother reported that her young son had been molested by Raymond Buckley at the Virginia McMartin Preschool. What followed were "lurid news reports of children being raped and sodomized, of dead rabbits, mutilated corpses, and a horse killing, and of blood drinking, satanic rituals, and the sacrifice of a live baby in a church."[3] Six years later, after a 30-month trial, a Los Angeles County jury rejected nearly all of the child molestation charges against Raymond Buckley and Peggy McMartin Buckley.

In the wake of the verdict, the media that had covered the charges and trial engaged in self-examination. David Shaw, who covers the media for the *Los Angeles Times*, wrote a four-part series on that paper's coverage. The series concluded that the paper had consistently favored the prosecution. In Shaw's judgment, the media's role was "pivotal and sometimes distorting."

Some alleged that it was the news media that had "pressured authorities to push the case."[4] The first report on the case was aired on KABC-TV on February 2, 1984. Ongoing reports by KABC-TV were promoted by newspaper ads placed by the station showing a battered teddy bear. The first KABC report combined drama, violence, and disclosure. More than sixty children, it said, "have now each told authorities that he or she had been keeping a grotesque secret of being sexually abused and made to appear in pornographic films while in the preschool's care— and of having been forced to witness the mutilation and killing of animals to scare the kids into keeping silent."[5] The news norms of drama, conflict, violence, and disclosure coupled with the desire to be first and to stay competitive prompted KABC to downplay such other journalistic norms as two-sidedness and balance.

3. Hard news is action, an event, an observable occurrence. Hard news relates the details of a specific occurrence that is the occasion for a news report, the "peg" on which the news story is hung. An event is concrete and discrete; ordinarily it can be explained clearly in a limited time or space. A single event is more likely to be intelligible and to be a novel, dramatic event involving specific individuals. Many events can be photographed or taped, an important consideration for both print and television journalism.

Despite the myth that hard news involves fast-breaking, unforeseen events, news organizations typically cover events that can be scheduled in advance, so reporters and camera crews can readily get to them. As a result, newspeople tend

3. Robert Reinhold, "McMartin Case: Swept Away by Panic About Molestation," *New York Times*, 24 January 1990, pp. 1, 18 A.

4. *New York Times*, 24 January 1990, p. A 18.

5. Ibid.

to cover news conferences and briefings, speeches, announcements, ceremonies, and other scheduled events. This is one reason that pseudo-events (events staged just for media coverage)[6] and what are called photo opportunities are an effective way to manipulate news coverage.

The need to know about the unexpected in advance explains why reporters are tempted to ask participants to recreate what happened when faced with a situation like a riot. In his study of a California newspaper, Mark Fishman found that journalistic concepts of newsworthy events coincided with what he called "bureaucratic phase structures," the ways various bureaucracies punctuate processes in order to divide them into stages—arrests, indictments, verdicts, and sentencings in crime news. He found that journalists depended on such definitions for the meaning and relevance of what they observed, for determining which events were newsworthy, which accounts were suspicious or reliable, what was controversial, and what constituted the sides and terms of a controversy.[7]

Hard news is the story of an act or an event. This single, isolated event is simpler to communicate and easier to understand than a process or an idea. It is likely to be dramatic and novel and to involve individuals. However, the emphasis on events reveals a contradiction at the heart of newsgathering: the desire to cover events as they happen and the need to cover events that are scheduled in advance.

4. Hard news is novel, deviant, out of the ordinary.   Hard news reports what happened today, not what happens every day. Although novel events are more likely to be covered if they are part of a current theme in the news, hard news is the opposite of the routine and accepted.

One study of the mass media concluded that all mass media content is entertainment, in the sense of behavior "outside the expected limits of routine behavior."[8] Even news stories are entertainment designed to attract and hold a mass audience. For example, during the times surveys are conducted by television rating services, local television news programs air "lurid and titillating news features, most often those with a sex or violence angle that can be heavily promoted, ideally as a weeklong series."[9]

The problems with this entertainment requirement—related to the novelty criterion in our scheme of things—are suggested by Tom Wicker: "The dull, the routine, the unexciting, is seldom seen as news, although . . . the dull, routine, unexciting management of rates and routes for the railroads, truckers, and airlines may affect far more Americans in their daily lives than some relatively more glamorous presidential directive or congressional action."[10]

Reporters, chosen partly for their nose for what is new and unusual, have a low tolerance for the long haul of a complex story that may take years to develop.

6. Daniel Boorstin, *The Image: A Guide to Pseudo-Events in America* (New York: Atheneum, 1962).

7. Mark Fishman, *Manufacturing the News* (Austin: University of Texas Press, 1980), pp. 63–70, 134.

8. David Altheide and Robert P. Snow, *Media Logic* (Beverly Hills: Sage, 1979), p. 19.

9. Tony Schwartz, "Ratings Sweeps Boost Lurid Side of the News," *New York Times*, 25 November 1980, p. C 17.

10. Tom Wicker, *On Press* (New York: Viking, 1978), p. 44.

The Scramble for Local News Ratings

A promotional announcement on NBC's owned and operated (O&O) Channel 4 in New York City, shown immediately before "L.A. Law," said that coming news items on the 11 P.M. news included the death of a "star" of the show; subsequent announcements changed that to "familiar face." The announcement referred to the suicide of David Rappaport, who was under four feet tall and appeared as an aggressive but sympathetic lawyer on several episodes of the series during the past two seasons.

A network news executive, who asked for anonymity, said, "It was unseemly but effective," and commented that such incidents demonstrated the increasing interplay between entertainment and news programs at both the network and local levels, and the declining enforcement of news standards.

Both the promotion and its placement were calculated to hold the "L.A. Law" audience for the news program. The tactic worked—the 11 P.M. news broadcast had a 19.3 rating and 37 percent of the audience, an increase of more than 30 percent over the preceding week. In New York, each rating point represents about 72,000 homes with television. The jump in ratings was particularly significant because it took place during May, a sweeps month, when ratings determine how much stations will charge for advertising.[c]

[c]Jeremy Gerard, "Station Uses Suicide Report to Hold Viewers," *New York Times*, 5 May 1990, p. 13 Y.

Ratings and Revenues: Local News Versus Prime-Time Entertainment

In 1989 in Los Angeles, a television trend-setter, KHJ, an independent station owned by the Walt Disney Company, announced that it would introduce in January 1990 the nation's first 3-hour local newscast, from 8 P.M. to 11 P.M. Once KHJ has expanded its nightly news from two 30-minute programs to three full hours, there will be 14.5 hours of local news daily on seven VHF television stations here, the most hours in any market in the country (according to Willis Dugg, president of Audience Research and Development, Inc., a Dallas television news consulting company).

The increasing hours of local news programming is motivated by the quest for advertising profits, especially because many sponsors think news programs attract affluent viewers. Local news can be profitable even when less than 4 percent of households are watching (according to Steve Cagle, a vice president at Frank Magid Associates, a research and consulting firm in Marion, Iowa).[d]

[d]Michael Lev, "Local News is Challenging Prime-Time Shows," *New York Times*, 17 July 1989, p. 29 Y.

This well-known media emphasis on novelty tempts protesters to invent ever more extreme ways to dramatize their cause in order to obtain coverage.

Those protesting the development and use of nuclear power illustrate this problem. Their concerns were dramatized in 1978 with the accident at Three Mile Island, and they received substantial press coverage. Since that time, however,

---

Ad Too Violent and Inflammatory

A 30-second ad urging viewers to call their senators and ask them to vote against $400 million in aid to El Salvador has been rejected by television stations throughout the country. The ad is polished and powerful. As a spot of blood grows on a check being written to the Internal Revenue Service, there are sounds of rifle shots and photographs of the six Jesuit priests murdered by the Salvadoran military in 1989. As the blood grows, a voice says, "Your tax dollars are putting America into the red. Tell your senator, 'vote no' on aid to El Salvador. Keep America out of the red."

The ad was produced by a coalition of peace organizations and may signal a new vehicle of expression for cause-oriented organizations that are finding it increasingly difficult to attract the attention of either the news media or the U.S. public.

All network-affiliated stations in New York and Washington rejected the ad for various reasons, some on the grounds that it was too violent. (A Planned Parenthood study of network "entertainment" discovered that elementary schoolchildren see 12,000 acts of violence a year on television programs.)

The program manager of a Los Angeles station, WJLA, rejected the ad and explained: "We make it our policy to not air material which is intended to inflame or incite unreasoned public responses rather than reasoned debate."[e]

[e] "Ad That Was Too Bloody for Most TV Stations Debuts in Twin Cities," *Star Tribune*, 25 September 1990, p. 1 B.

---

press interest has been low, although these protesters believe that their concerns continue to be legitimate and work on nuclear plants continues. Even the disaster at Chernobyl in 1986 did not help them, once it was established that the construction of that plant had few similarities with plants in the United States. As a result, protestors become more desperate to attract journalistic attention. For example, one antinuclear protestor, participating in a demonstration marking the 36th anniversary of the first nuclear test at the Nevada Test Site, knelt in front of a bus carrying workers to the test site and poured red fluid from a baby's bottle. As sheriff's deputies lifted her from the road, she screamed: "This is the blood of the future! This is the blood of our children!"[11]

Resource-poor groups often have to depend on deviance and disruption in order to get coverage in the media. In her study of newspaper access, Edie Goldenberg concluded that "the more a group's political goals deviate from prevailing social norms, the more likely the group is to gain access to the press, other things being equal."[12] Elsewhere she writes "that the intensity of a conflict is a good predictor of coverage, . . . that 'unruly groups,' those who initiate violence or strikes, are relatively successful as compared with those that do not."[13] As these comments indicate, the emphasis on novelty in hard news is closely related to its focus on

11. "Actor and 71 Others Arrested at Nuclear Test Site," *New York Times*, 28 January 1987, p. 13 Y.

12. Edie N. Goldenberg, *Making the Papers* (Lexington, Mass.: Lexington Books, 1975), p. 28.

13. "An Overview of Access to the Media," in *Women in the News*, ed. Laurily Keir Epstein (New York: Hastings House, 1978), pp. 55–56. Goldenberg also cites the work of William A. Gamson, *The Strategy of Social Protest* (Homewood, Ill.: Dorsey, 1975), in support of her claims.

drama, conflict, and violence; the novelty of a large demonstration is likely to be overshadowed by the violent acts of a few.

Similarly, the news media are more likely to cover a protest group representative who is flamboyant and theatrical, regardless of who has the largest following.

In 1990, a feminist group known as Guerrilla Girls gained the attention of the *New York Times* with its consciousness-raising posters and gorilla masks. On Sunday June 17, 1990, both appeared in that paper.[14] The Guerrilla Girls are social critics of the ways in which female artists are treated. The women in the group remain anonymous. Their prime weapons are sarcasm and humor. After conservative Senator Jesse Helms protested federal funding of a photo exhibit by Robert Mapplethorpe, the group put out a poster saying, "Relax, Senator Helms, the art world is your kind of place!" The poster supported that statement with such claims as: "The number of blacks at an art opening is about the same as at one of your garden parties." Another poster asked: "How many women had one-person exhibitions at NYC museums last year?" A list followed:

Guggenheim	0
Metropolitan	0
Modern	1
Whitney	0

Another poster promulgated a tongue-in-cheek "code of ethics for art museums." The code included the commandment: "Thou shalt provide lavish funerals for Women and Artists of Color who thou planneth to exhibit only after their death." The novelty of the title "Guerrilla Girls," the play on *guerrilla* apparent in wearing gorilla masks, the anonymity of the group members, and the use of humor are all novel. As such, they invite media coverage.

5. Hard news reports events linked to issues prevalent in the news at the time. News coverage follows certain issues at various times, such as the issue of civil rights in the 1960s, women's liberation for a period in the 1970s, and gay rights in the 1980s. For example, when the United States began its space program, each launch received detailed news coverage. Much of this coverage concerned whether or not NASA was ready to launch the rockets involved in the Mercury, Gemini, and Apollo programs and whether flights that included astronauts were safe. However, as years passed without disasters, the space program generally, as well as the shuttle launches begun in 1983, came to seem routine, and newspeople began to treat them perfunctorily.

As a result, television and print reporters did not know of the imminent danger to the Challenger space shuttle, due to the likelihood that the seals—called O-rings—in the solid-rocket boosters might malfunction because of the cold weather at launch time. They had grown accustomed to successful shuttle flights and relied on NASA's assurances that all was well.

The assumption that shuttle flights were routine and safe produced a kind of reporting that put pressure on NASA to launch Challenger on January 28, 1986, despite unsafe conditions. Richard G. Smith, head of the Kennedy Space Center in Florida at the time of the Challenger explosion, argued that snide news stories

14. "Waging Guerrilla Warfare Against the Art World," p. 31

about aborted launches had created "98 percent of the pressure" to go ahead with the ill-fated Challenger flight.

What Smith was referring to included statements by newscasters, such as those by Dan Rather on CBS Evening News. Rather referred to news about one delay as "the latest on today's high-tech low comedy," and later said that because of postponements, the launch was now known as "Mission Impossible."[15]

Initially, news coverage followed the events involved in the development of the space program. As that program became successful, it was seen as no longer newsworthy. As a result, reporters did not continue to probe questions of safety and were caught unaware by the Challenger disaster. What became newsworthy were delays, launches aborted for reasons of safety, and these delays became an ongoing story of implied incompetence, a news perspective that may have contributed to the disaster itself.

Stories about ongoing issues generate audience identification and create the comforting sense of a pattern in the complexity of modern life.

The coverage of individuals who are certifiably newsworthy reflects this concern for continuity in the news. The newsworthy are those who have made news in the past, such as elected officials, athletic champions, and film, television, or rock stars. For example, a presidential candidate labeled a "front-runner"—a status conferred on those who win early caucus or primary votes—becomes more newsworthy and consequently gets more news coverage.

Some themes are woven into the very nature of newsgathering in the United States. These include: (1) Appearance versus reality. This reflects an emphasis on conflict and the "objective" role of skeptical newsgatherers who uncover hypocrisy. (2) Little guys versus big guys. This theme reflects an emphasis on the personal and individual by taking a particular interest in the underdog or outsider or exposing corrupt and self-interested actions by the powerful against the powerless. (3) Good against evil. The essence of drama, this theme is related to crime as a news model and to investigative journalism as a norm for reporting and the reporter's role. (4) Efficiency versus inefficiency. This is usually an attempt to uncover waste and mismanagement, illustrating the emphasis on politics and government in the news. (5) The unique versus the routine. Reflecting a stress on novelty, this is illustrated by the human interest stories appearing at the end of most newscasts or in syndicated newspaper columns. These themes all presume that there are identifiable forces at work in the world, and that they usually are in conflict. News coverage influences us by defining what the sides are and what each side means.

Themes provide continuity in the news and help make some sense out of a welter of happenings. They increase the potential for audience identification. Some themes reflect the journalist's role and the concept that reporters have of their function in this society.

These five criteria—ongoing issues or themes, discrete events, novelty or deviance, drama-conflict-violence, and a focus on individuals—define what newsgatherers consider newsworthy. As the following study of a protester's hunger strike illustrates, those who meet these criteria are likely to obtain news coverage.

15. Neil Hickey, "It Exposed TV's Failures—as Well as NASA's," *TV Guide*, 24 January 1987, p. 3.

C A S E   S T U D Y
When Is a Hunger Strike Newsworthy?

Rick Hoye, a 28-year-old junior majoring in international relations at the University of Minnesota, began a hunger strike June 6, 1980, to dramatize his contention that the university's Board of Regents ought to reverse its earlier vote and order a boycott of Nestlé products on the campus. Prior to the hunger strike, Hoye headed a campus chapter of the Infant Formula Action Coalition, a group that had worked unsuccessfully to pass the boycott for over a year. Fifty student groups supported the boycott. In February 1980, the University Senate, a body composed of faculty and students, had passed a resolution advocating a boycott. In June 1980, the Board of Regents voted eight to three against a boycott. That vote followed the recommendation of University President C. Peter Magrath, who contended that it was inappropriate for a public university to become involved in such a boycott.

The proposed boycott of Nestlé products was designed to protest Nestlé's manufacture and promotion of infant formulas in underdeveloped countries. Because mothers use formula in unsanitary conditions and dilute it with impure water, they increase the likelihood that their infants will suffer from malnutrition or contract diseases. By breastfeeding the infants instead, mothers could minimize these risks.

To dramatize the hunger strike, Hoye pitched a tent outside Morrill Hall, the building housing both the Board of Regents meeting room and the office of the university's president. A large sign at the side of the tent read:

UNIVERSITY OF MINNESOTA

NESTLÉ BOYCOTT

HUNGER STRIKE BY RICK HOYE

DAY _____ WEIGHT _____

After thirty-four days, Hoye ended his fast when a committee of the Board of Regents listened to his case. Although the university did not subsequently boycott Nestlé products, Hoye's strike was a qualified success. His dramatic "visualization" of the process of starvation drew more press coverage to his cause than had his two years of previous work. With press attention came attention from the university's Board of Regents. One of the regents, who had supported the boycott, learned of Hoye's hunger strike not through administration channels but by reading about it in a newspaper.

With press attention came access to university officials. The *Minneapolis Star* noted, for example, that "after a *Star* reporter called [President] Magrath's office Tuesday, he talked to Hoye for the first time since the fast started, and then returned the call."[f]

With press attention came the opportunity to address a committee of the Board of Regents.

With press attention came increased public awareness of the issue.

[f]*Minneapolis Star*, 3 July 1980, p. 11 A.

Staff Photo by Regene Radniecki

Hoye to end fast

Rick Hoye told a committee of the University of Minnesota regents Thursday that the university should be involved in ending world hunger by supporting a boycott of Nestlé Co. products. Hoye, 28, who began fasting June 6 after the regents voted against boycotting Nestlé products, plans to end the protest at 1 p.m. today. The university student, an international relations major, lost 40 pounds and will begin eating on the advice of his doctor to avoid permanent damage to his health. Hoye and other Nestlé critics object to the company's marketing of infant formula in underdeveloped countries.

The *Minneapolis Tribune*, 11 July 1980, p. 1 B. (Reprinted with permission of the *Minneapolis Tribune*.)

The media could have dismissed Hoye's strike as a stunt; instead, they treated it sympathetically. "He is not a nut, or a publicity-crazed radical out to topple the university administration—not even the Nestlé administration," wrote Joe Kimball of the *Minneapolis Tribune*.[8] And the *Star*'s associate editor Harold Chucker wrote, "Despite their snorts and grunts, the cynics—some of them, anyway—have a grudging admiration for the idealist. They see themselves at a younger age when they, too, believed anything was possible with the right kind of protest or demonstration."[h]

Why Did Hoye Receive Media Attention?

The cause he advocated had a following—a body of committed supporters. Groups on campus had endorsed the boycott. The campus senate, a representative body, had endorsed the boycott. The proposed boycott had met opposition. The Board of Re-

[8]Joe Kimball, "Student 'Sticks Neck Out' With Fast," *Minneapolis Tribune*, 4 July 1980, p. 5 B.

[h]Harold Chucker, "Young Idealist Shouldn't Repeat Cynics' Mistakes," *Minneapolis Star*, 24 July 1980, p. 8 A.

(*continued*)

gents had voted it down; the president opposed it. This opposition gave the story conflict, and with the conflict came a recognizable cast of characters. The president would speak for those who opposed the boycott. By staging a dramatic hunger strike, Hoye invited the media to see the conflict as ongoing and to pit him against the regents and the president.

Because Hoye had headed the coalition, he was a credible spokesperson for those on campus advocating boycott.

Because Hoye was an international relations major, his interest in world hunger seemed consistent with his reason for being a student.

Because Hoye had seen mothers feeding their infants contaminated formula in Guatemala and Honduras in 1978, his concern about the issue could be grounded in his personal experience.

Because the hunger strike could be tied to the argument that the infant formula contributed to malnutrition and disease, the dramatic act could not be casually dismissed as a gimmick.

Because Hoye suffered the effects of the fast—nausea, vomiting, light-headedness—and because his doctor warned that he risked permanent damage to his health, the media could not report the story one time and then abandon it. Once covered, the story demanded a follow-up. Would he starve to death? Would his health be damaged? Would he give up? The nature of Hoye's protest involved reporters in a dramatic narrative. One story demanded another and another until the full drama was played out and Hoye either got what he wanted or abandoned the strike.

Hoye apparently had nothing to gain from the strike personally. He would not benefit personally if Nestlé products were boycotted. This was not a way to be elected to an office, for example. Thus, his action appeared disinterested and selfless. The tent, the sign, the physical evidence of weight loss, the sign's daily report of weight dramatized and made concrete an issue that was otherwise abstract. By making it concrete, Hoye made the issue attractive to and usable by the mass media.

What Were the Risks Involved in This Dramatic Act?

Hoye's hunger strike, rather than the reason for the strike, might have become the focus of media coverage. Since Hoye no longer headed the coalition, he might not have been seen as a representative of or a spokesperson for the boycott. The significance of Hoye's act would be reduced if he was not perceived to represent those favoring the boycott.

Perhaps the relation between the tent and the hunger strike or between the hunger strike and the boycott would not have been recognized clearly.

Follow-Up

Hoye's action was part of a national effort led by Boston-based INFACT (Infant Formula Action Coalition). INFACT instigated a seven-year boycott of Nestlé products, which eventually prompted the large company to limit its marketing of possibly damaging infant formula in less-developed countries.

This case study has illustrated one student's use of the principles governing what makes news. The next section of this chapter examines other factors that influence what will be covered.

What Is Covered and Reported?

■   Newsgathering is affected by access, costs, and limitations of time and space. News stories must attract and hold an audience and avoid offending advertisers, audiences, and media owners. These factors influence what choices newspeople make and ultimately determine which stories will be printed and aired.

External Constraints

Some of the factors influencing news coverage lie outside the event or medium itself. These are external constraints. If an event is to be covered, reporters must know it is to happen; if it is to be videotaped, there must be enough advance notice to get a camera crew to the scene. The event must happen early enough to let reporters meet their deadlines, and the cost of the coverage must seem reasonable. In addition, coverage is affected by competition from other media and from other newsworthy events.

Access   News organizations struggle to impose order in the midst of chaos. Reporters often have little or no idea when or where the news will break: when or where a crime will be committed, a riot will break out, one country will attack another. Thus, reporters are assigned to beats so they can monitor the goings-on in places where newsworthy events often occur—the police station, city hall, the State Department, the House of Representatives, the Supreme Court, the White House. The chance that an event will be covered is increased if it is part of a reporter's regular beat, or if official sources that are regularly consulted call it to her or his attention. For instance, one study of 2,850 stories appearing in the *New York Times* and the *Washington Post* found that such routine channels accounted for 58.2 percent of the articles.[16]

Many newsworthy events fall between the cracks of assigned beats. Reporters may be assigned to substantive beats, such as energy or the environment, to overcome this problem. In addition, there are general assignment reporters who are dispatched to cover breaking stories or who try to ferret out newsworthy events. The beat system is really a pattern of access for reporters. It is a method by which reporters survey the scene to learn what is happening and by which they develop "informed, reliable sources" of information. Modern news organizations rely heavily on officials in government bureaucracies. Events on regular beats or confirmed by official sources tend to be covered and reported; events outside these beats or denied by official sources usually go unpublished.[17]

Many news stories could not be written without the help of confidential sources. Jack Nelson, Washington bureau chief for the *Los Angeles Times*, notes that such sources help uncover information others try to conceal from the public,

---

16. Leon V. Sigal, *Reporters and Officials: The Organization and Politics of Newsmaking* (Lexington, Mass.: D.C. Heath, 1973), p. 121, Table 6-1.

17. See David Halberstam, *The Powers That Be* (New York: Alfred A. Knopf, 1979), especially p. 434, for numerous examples of the powers of President Lyndon Johnson to suppress news stories from correspondents in Saigon.

and that some of the most important exposés have been developed this way, including the Pentagon Papers, the My Lai massacre, and the Watergate stories. Specifically, the Pulitzer-Prize-winning My Lai stories of Seymour Hersh were made possible by the confidential involvement of three Army officers, a member of Congress, and two congressional aides.[18]

Although beats and official sources are efficient ways for reporters to obtain and check information, this system limits some kinds of coverage. For example, because early events in a developing social movement fall outside this system of beats and sources, they tend to go unnoticed by the news media. Only as movements increase in size and scope and seek press coverage will reporters be assigned to cover them. Examples are the South Africa divestment movement, the antinuclear disarmament movement, feminism, and gay rights.

Cost   It costs money to get the news to the public. Because a note pad, pencil, and tape recorder cost far less than a camera crew, it is cheaper to gather news for a newspaper or magazine than for television. The more costly a story, the more important it must be before it will be covered and published. Dan Rather, then a CBS reporter, wrote about this constraint and about how it affects investigative reporting: "A newspaper can commit a so-called 'investigative team' to a story and tie up the time and salaries of maybe a half dozen reporters. But that's all. If a television network commits to that kind of assignment, the cost can quickly run into six figures and above." [19] Such costs explain why investigative reporting is more common in the print media.

The competitors to national network news mentioned in Chapter 1 have influenced newsgathering decisions. The video news services offered by CONUS, as well as by TV Direct (a joint venture of CONUS with the Associated Press), the Cable News Network, and other similar services, are comparable to the national and international news wire services. As a result, many independent (unaffiliated) stations are using material from various satellite services to report on world and national news. The networks have responded to such competition. In addition to establishing satellite links that allow their affiliates to share locally produced news stories with one another, the major networks have offered to help their respective affiliate stations pay for satellite vans that are like mobile television stations.

In return for subsidies, a network has the right to use its affiliate's van when a significant news event occurs in the affiliate's area. These vans, with their satellite dishes, enable local stations to cover national and international news; as affiliates' vans are used by the networks, they will extend the coverage of the networks as well.

Similar factors influence the coverage of foreign news. In order to cover and report foreign news, a newspaper or network must support a foreign correspondent and, for same-day coverage, incur the cost of transmitting videotape or photographs by satellite. Such costs were important in the coverage of the Viet-

18. William E. Porter, *Assault on the Media: The Nixon Years* (Ann Arbor: University of Michigan Press, 1976), p. 227.
19. Dan Rather, *The Camera Never Blinks* (New York: William Morrow, 1977), p. 234.

nam War, and they are one explanation for the small amount of news we receive from Africa and Central and South America, despite the frequency of newsworthy events. However, once an expenditure has been built into the system, the more likely it is that the persons and equipment will generate news stories—no matter how newsworthy the events. For example, a network or newspaper maintaining London correspondents is more likely to report news from Great Britain and to seek British reactions to events in the United States than is a network or newspaper without a London correspondent. However, as the heavy coverage of the Iranian hostage crisis illustrated, the number of stories is also related to relevance for the U.S. audience.

Stories that are written but not published ("overset") are not as costly for newspapers as for television. An unused set of stories costs a newspaper its overhead plus the reporter's salary. An unused taped segment can cost thousands of dollars. Consequently, although a newspaper assignment editor stores "overset" for possible use on a slow news day or in Sunday's larger paper, a television producer must be more certain that what is assembled can be and probably will be aired. Yet more television stories are gathered for use on the evening news than are actually aired. To cover their costs, networks try to find other places for these segments. A segment that does not air on the ABC Evening News may air on tomorrow's "Good Morning America" or be fed to affiliates for use on their local news shows.

Time and Space   Like a newspaper, a network evening newscast has a certain amount of space to fill. Television time can be increased by adding news bulletins or special reports, and newspaper space can be increased by adding extra pages, a special section, or even a special edition, but to do so is costly. On days filled with newsworthy events, some stories that might otherwise be printed or aired will be omitted.

On the other hand, because a certain amount of time or space must be filled on a predictable basis, what is newsworthy on a day barren of interesting events will be different from what is newsworthy on an action-filled day. Yet because we receive a newspaper of a certain number of pages or a half-hour news telecast, we are likely to conclude that the events covered on the two days are of comparable importance. A publisher or producer has yet to announce "there was no news today, so the next twenty-one minutes or the next eighteen pages are empty." As commentator David Brinkley observes, "there are days, as we all know, when material of any kind is scarce, and we have to use what we can get, including some we know is not great, but air time has to be filled." [20]

What is covered and published is influenced by factors outside the story itself. These include access, cost, available time or space, and the number of newsworthy events to fill them.

---

20. David Brinkley, "A Question for Television Newsmen: Does Anyone Really Care?" in *Television Today: A Close-Up View; Readings from TV Guide*, ed. Barry Cole (New York: Oxford, 1981), p. 139. The amount of prepaid advertising affects the number of pages in a newspaper. The more advertising, the larger the "news hole."

Internal Constraints

The characteristics of the medium itself may influence whether or not an event is covered and, more important, whether a story is printed or aired. These characteristics of the medium are what we call internal constraints. Some of these constraints are a necessary part of the medium; some are conventions.

Use Available Footage   Television news coverage is also unique because television can replay its own past from tape and film archives, storehouses of the conventions and commonplaces that are television's memory. In the archives are televisual bits of the lives of famous persons who engaged in dramatic events during television's lifetime. The information stored in television's memory is different from that in the morgues of the nation's newspapers. For example, when Representative and former Senator Claude Pepper (D-Fla.) died in summer 1989, the broadcast networks called up the peroration of his stirring appeal to the House to pass catastrophic health insurance. Print obituaries recounted events from his entire career and included tributes from the people who had known and respected him.

Cover Visual Events   For both print and television journalism, the ability to tape or photograph an event is an important determinant of coverage and publication. The effort by a Connecticut television station to show portions of a figure-skating championship on its evening newscast illustrates the intense pull of the visual. ABC-TV had bought exclusive rights to show the 1981 World Figure Skating Championships held at the Hartford Civic Center on its "Wide World of Sports." The Hartford station (WFSB) sued the local sponsors to stop their enforcement of a ban against all television cameras except ABC's. The case is an interesting test of First Amendment principles versus property rights to copyrighted material. However, of more interest here is the admission by the Hartford station's vice president for news that the event would have merited "only a brief mention in the sports roundup *were it not for the visual quality of the skaters gliding gracefully across the rink.*" [21]

Television has a strong preference for visual events, but newspapers also try to accompany stories with attention-getting photographs. The 1984 famine in Ethiopia was widely reported in the newspapers beginning in late 1983 and early 1984. But it was not until late October and early November 1984, when pictures of the victims began appearing on network television news, that massive efforts were mobilized to help the starving people of that country. On October 23, 15.5 million viewers of "NBC Nightly News" saw televised coverage of the famine. In the seven weeks following the NBC broadcast, Catholic Relief Services, one of the two charities mentioned by name in the NBC broadcast, reported 91,000 pieces of mail offering help, including $13 million in contributions. [22]

---

21. Jonathan Friendly, "Exclusive TV Rights vs. Covering the News," *New York Times*, 14 March 1981, p. 21. Italics added.
22. *New York Times*, 16 December 1984, p. 9.

Why the United Nations Isn't News

The United Nations is still making news, but U.S. journalists are not reporting it. "The U.N. is not a visual story," said Tom Ross, the senior vice president of NBC News. "It was when Khrushchev was pounding on the desk, but on the current scene, it really is not a dramatic and visual story."

"It's not the sexy news, it's not the bite," said John Tessitore, the director of communications for the United Nations Association of the United States.

What still grabs headlines are visits to the United Nations by prominent world leaders like President Bush and President Gorbachev of the Soviet Union and by controversial figures like Yasir Arafat, chairman of the Palestine Liberation Organization.

The United Nations is also a casualty of increasingly advanced communications technology. With sophisticated satellite equipment and more correspondents overseas, there is less need to cover a U.N. report on world famine when pictures of emaciated children can be beamed back from Africa in seconds.[1]

[1]*New York Times*, 22 October 1989, p. 9.

The reason for the long delay in securing and transmitting the story to television news was that the Marxist government of Ethiopia had put up roadblocks to stop the reporters. Journalists were denied permission to enter the country to get the story. The photographer and reporter who brought back the dramatic tape aired by the BBC, and picked up by NBC and others, cajoled their way into the country. An acting official had inadvertently given them access to the refugee camps.

Politicians respond by feeding the media's appetite for compelling visuals. The results occasionally are comic. In August 1989, President George Bush's speechwriters conceived the idea of having Bush dramatize his antidrug speech to the nation by holding up a bag of crack purchased by narcotics agents near the White House. The attorney general asked drug enforcement officials to make the buy. The *Washington Post* reported the results:

> The first time, the alleged drug dealer never showed up. On the second try, the undercover Drug Enforcement Administration agent wore a body microphone that didn't work. Then the cameraman who was supposed to be videotaping the deal missed the action because he was assaulted by a homeless person. "This is like a Keystone Kops thing," U.S. District Judge Stanley Sporkin said to the witness, DEA special agent Sam Gaye.[23]

Because television is a visual medium, it deals well with issues that can be reduced to concrete, dramatic illustrations. Some important issues, such as the economy, are not easily reduced to tangible, dramatic 2-minute-and-35-second bites of information.

23. Tracey Thompson, "Buying Drugs for the President Was No Easy Task," report from the *Washington Post* carried in the *Philadelphia Inquirer*, 16 December 1989, p. 12 A.

The problems involved in news coverage of economic issues were exemplified by limited and delayed coverage of widespread failures of savings and loan associations. Ellen Hume, executive director of Harvard's Shorenstein Barone Center on the Press, Politics, and Public Policy, reports that when Michael Gartner, president of NBC News, was asked why television hadn't covered the crisis much even after it made headlines in 1988, he commented "that the story didn't lend itself to images, and without such images, 'television can't do facts.'"[24]

Finally, in 1990, the problem that had surfaced years earlier received wide coverage. There were several reasons for the increase in television attention: (1) it was estimated that the cost of a federal bailout might reach $500 billion; (2) respected members of Congress, including five prominent senators, were shown to have delayed measures to limit costs in response to lobbying and campaign contributions from the thrifts; and (3) President Bush's son Neil, a director of the Silverado Banking, Savings and Loan Association in Denver, was charged with a conflict of interest in its delayed closing and was sued by federal regulators who charged that "'gross negligence' had led to a collapse that could cost taxpayers more than $1 billion."[25] News coverage had been delayed by the lack of economic expertise among reporters and by the complexity and geographic spread of the story.

Specialized media outlets, whose reporters had the expertise to interpret what was occurring, broke the story earlier. In 1983, the *American Banker* linked a New York City deposit broker (later convicted of fraud) to a criminal investigation of several midwestern banks that were short of tens of millions of dollars. In 1985, the *National Mortgage News* began to detect that, in many cases, failing savings institutions had been defrauded. In 1989, two of its reporters, Stephen Pizzo and Paul Muolo, with Mary Fricker, a financial reporter at the Santa Rosa (Calif.) *Press Democrat*, published *Inside Job: The Looting of America's Savings and Loans*; the book won an award from the Investigative Reporters and Editorials Association at the University of Missouri, and in August 1990 appeared on the *New York Times* best-seller list.

Stan Strachan, editor and one of the founders of *National Mortgage News*, commented: "Had it [the savings crisis] reached the public consciousness a few years earlier, we could have saved a huge amount of money."[26]

Commenting on the difficulty in getting stories on this problem published, Tom Freedman, formerly legislative director to Representative Charles E. Schumer (D-N.Y.), asserts: "The nuts and bolts of banking and housing legislation were not 'sexy' issues," and adds: "In Washington, there is widespread acceptance of the idea that the public doesn't want complicated news."[27] In such cases, news norms

24. Ellen Hume, "Why the Press Blew the S & L Scandal," *New York Times*, 24 May 1990, p. A 19 Y.

25. Stephen Labaton, "F.D.I.C. Sues Neil Bush and Others at Silverado," *New York Times*, 22 September 1990, p. 17 Y.

26. Kathleen Quinn, "As S. & L.'s Sink, a Trade Weekly Is Soaring," *New York Times*, 27 August 1990, p. C 8.

27. Tom Freedman, "While Journalists Chase 'Sexy' Issues," *New York Times*, 16 September 1990, p. E 23.

affect political decision making. Only certain kinds of stories will attract coverage by journalists, which, in turn, creates the public concern that energizes law-makers. When complex issues don't attract news coverage, politicians are likely to ignore them to focus on simpler, more dramatic issues whose coverage has aroused public concern.

The economy is complex. Economists speak in a language not readily intel-ligible to the general population. No single economic indicator, of itself, gives a complete and accurate picture of the country's economic condition. Because it is a construct, the economy can't be televised in the same way a battle or a presi-dential inauguration can. Consequently, television seeks out the human interest angle in an economic story and focuses on the rate of inflation, translated into the increased cost of a basket of groceries in representative cities; on the FHA and VA mortgage rates, translated into how much more it will cost some average citizen this month to buy an FHA- or VA-financed home; and on the unemployment rate, translated into a story of the impact of continued unemployment on a specific worker in South Succotash. Because these facets of the economy lend themselves to bar graphs plotting change from month to month and to representative illustra-tions, coverage of these aspects is the mainstay of the economic news a viewer can expect to see on television, along with interviews of such national figures as Alan Greenspan, head of the Federal Reserve System.

Cover Newsworthy People An event is more likely to be covered and published if it involves certifiably newsworthy people or people who have been newsworthy in the past. Not only are such stories personal and about individuals, but also they satisfy a deep-seated curiosity of the mass audience about how the other half lives. Newsworthy people are leaders in their professions, celebrities of all kinds, and powerful people (world leaders, politicians, the very rich). It is axi-omatic, for example, that the president is news. So are past presidents—and their families—as news stories about the births of Caroline Kennedy's children and John Kennedy, Jr.'s struggle to pass the New York state law boards indicate. Their association with a past president and a current senator (Edward M. Kennedy, D-Mass.) make such events newsworthy.

Similarly, quite trivial happenings involving movie and television stars and well-known athletes receive coverage. When Zsa Zsa Gabor was arrested for slap-ping a police officer, the arrest and subsequent trial made news. Past celebrities like feminist Gloria Steinem continue to command sporadic treatment from newsgatherers, doubly illustrated when Steinem drew coverage after authoring a book on Marilyn Monroe, also a former celebrity. In short, an event involving people who have been newsworthy in the past is more likely to be reported.

Avoid Giving Offense An event is less likely to be covered and reported if it offends media owners, the government, advertisers, or the mass audience. For example, on November 30, 1989, NBC's "Today" aired a piece by investigative re-porter Peter Karl of NBC-owned WMAQ-TV in Chicago. The 3-minute piece sum-marized a five-part series that Karl had done for WMAQ on defective airplane bolts. The report omitted the fact that the defective bolts were produced by Gen-

---

The Interplay of Influence Between Stations and Advertisers

"Boston's WHDH-TV made a gutsy call in airing what it knew was dynamite: a tv spot urging a boycott of Folger's coffee because purchases contribute to 'misery, destruction and death' in El Salvador by indirectly aiding its coffee growers and right-wing government. Now it's dealing with the bang that followed, Procter and Gamble's yanking of all its ads from the station."[j]

[j]Editorial, *Advertising Age*, 21 May 1990, p. 28.

Self-Censorship

Failure of the news media to cover the United States's "news cartel" was the most under-reported story of 1987, according to Project Censored, which is directed by a Sonoma (Calif.) State University professor. The project's fifteen-member panel, heavily weighted toward academics, evaluated twenty-five subjects nominated by the public. The panel reported that twenty-nine corporations control half or more of the news-media business in the United States, and a half dozen companies will control most of the media by the 1990s. "The impact of this information cartel on a free society is ignored by the mass media," said a news release from project director Professor Carl Jensen.

Of the 149 daily newspapers in the United States with circulation of more than 100,000, only 11 percent are not part of multipaper ownership.[k]

[k]Lou Gelfand, "If You Ran the Paper," [Minneapolis] *Star Tribune*, 26 June 1988, p. 23 A.

---

eral Electric Company, the parent company of NBC. After a week of public criticism, "Today" broadcast a 4-minute follow-up that identified GE by name.[28]

The news media also avoid offending business. Lou Cannon accounts for the weakness of journalistic business reporting in part by the newspapers' desire to shield themselves against financial disclosure. He quotes Peter Silverman, business and financial news editor of the *Washington Post*, as saying "newspapers themselves are among the most secretive and the most protective about the facts and figures of their own business. They are not likely to ask others to do what they are unwilling to do themselves."[29]

When the audience is offended, the media usually listen. For example, under pressures from individuals and government, all three networks adopted guidelines for the coverage of riots. There are conventions for coverage of violence that

---

28. Diane Mermigas, "'Today' airs follow-up after GE controversy," *Electronic Media*, 11 December 1989, p. 2.

29. Lou Cannon, *Reporting: An Inside View* (Sacramento: California Journal Press, 1977), pp. 134–135.

exclude graphic presentations of blood and killing because it is assumed that dinner-hour audiences would be offended.

However, a dramatic, newsworthy event can disrupt the application of such norms. For example, on the morning of January 22, 1987, shortly after Pennsylvania State Treasurer R. Budd Dwyer committed suicide at a news conference, Harrisburg television station WHTM broadcast a videotape of the event. The station did not first warn its viewers, who included children home from school because of a snowstorm. The station repeated the film on its two evening newscasts, although it added warnings. Similarly, television stations in Philadelphia and Pittsburgh also showed complete footage of the tragedy immediately after it happened, although they did not rebroadcast it on evening newscasts. Viewers protested.

Newspapers that published only pictures of Dwyer waving or holding the revolver were praised. Newspapers that used a picture of Dwyer with the barrel of the gun in his mouth, such as the *Philadelphia Inquirer*, the *Kansas City Star*, the *Sacramento Bee*, and the *Washington Post*, received numerous complaints from readers.[30]

Don't Become the News Television is a more intrusive medium than print. In most cases, a print reporter will alter the observed environment less than a television reporter accompanied by a camera crew. Does television coverage change the nature of the story? The question was answered dramatically in June 1981 when ABC's crew for the newsmagazine "20/20" was filming a story about the emergency care of infants in Arizona. The filming focused on the Air Evac Rescue Program, a program that airlifts patients to physicians or physicians to patients. On June 2, "several Air Evac officials delayed for an hour the emergency departure of an emergency flight from Phoenix to Douglas, a mining town with a population of 12,000 near the Mexican border, so that a larger plane could be outfitted for the television producers and cameramen."[31] The infant waiting for the physician was suffering from "respiratory distress," but the child's life was not in danger.

The *Arizona Republic* covered the story on the front page. The director of the Air Evac service was suspended. ABC contended that it had not requested the delay; nonetheless, the delay would not have occurred if the film crew had not been covering the story. What if the infant had died as a result of the delay? Did the absence of a life-threatening situation justify delay in the name of televised coverage of the Air Evac unit? These are the sorts of troublesome questions posed by the intrusive nature of television.

In other words, news coverage and publication are influenced by the criteria of newsworthiness, the conventions of news coverage, and the characteristics of the medium itself. A story is more likely to be aired on television if there is footage available in the archive, if the event is visual, if the item concerns newsworthy people, if it is inoffensive to audience tastes, and if there is little chance that the sheer fact of coverage itself will become newsworthy.

30. Lou Gelfand, "If You Ran the Paper?" [Minneapolis] *Star Tribune*, 1 February 1987, p. 25 A.
31. *Washington Post*, 11 June 1981, p. A 38.

How the Story Is Presented

■

When an event is covered and a decision made to air or publish the story, the conventions governing news presentation come into play. These conventions are influenced by four factors: reporters' lack of specialized expertise; ideals of fairness and balance in publication of controversial material; story length and structure; and the norm of objectivity in news presentations.

Reporter Expertise

Although every effort is made to enhance reporters' on-air credibility, reporters cannot be experts on all the topics they cover. For the most part, journalists are generalists who rely on the expertise of others for information.[32] Most reporters begin on general assignment beats that require coverage of a number of varied topics; many are assigned to more than one beat. Whatever the beat, they are likely to cover stories related to a number of subjects. In addition, communication to a mass audience works against specialization, and reporters sometimes argue that their lack of expertise is an advantage—it puts them in the same position as their audience.

News organizations are also wary of acculturation. For example, the *New York Times* rotates its foreign correspondents every three years in the belief that greater familiarity with a country might slant reporters' stories. Finally, most reporters have limited research facilities and no research staff; library materials may be in some inconvenient centralized location or consist exclusively of materials drawn from the news outlet's archive or morgue. At best, reporters have access to a research department, such as that of ABC News with four full-time researchers and computerized information.

The research tool of most journalists is the interview rather than the library or other documents. The interview

> frees newsworkers from determining facts by using the sophisticated, expensive, or time consuming methods of other kinds of investigators. On the other hand, the principle [something is so because somebody says it] allows newsworkers to capitalize on the fruits of these more complex techniques by talking with those who have already used them . . . it must be somebody in a position to know what they say, somebody entitled to know what they say. . . . Typically, competent knowers for journalists are bureaucrats and agency officials.[33]

The interview not only is a research tool, but it also personalizes the story. When the interview format is used to present a story, it allows the reporter to

---

32. Stephen Hess, in *The Washington Reporters* (Washington, D.C.: Brookings Institution, 1981), documents this situation for journalists in the Washington press corps. According to his survey, most Washington journalists are generalists (p. 49). They use no documents in the presentation of nearly three-fourths of their stories; when used, documents are likely to be newspaper articles (p. 18). Although 93 percent of Washington reporters in 1978 were college graduates and 33 percent had graduate degrees (p. 83), a beat is considered more desirable if no documents research is required (p. 52), and, even on specialized beats such as economics or law, journalists tend to read popular rather than scholarly journals (p. 64).

33. Fishman, *Manufacturing the News*, pp. 92–93; Stephen Hess reports that Washington journalists in his survey conducted close to five interviews per story (*Washington Reporters*, p. 17).

C A S E   S T U D Y
Appearing on Television—Necessary to Be Credible in Print?

Chris Matthews, former speech writer and spokesman for House Speaker Tip O'Neill and author of *Hardball*, wanted to be a pundit, to be a regular on political television talk shows. Larry Kramer, executive editor of the *San Francisco Examiner*, agreed to make Matthews a columnist complete with the prestigious title of Washington bureau chief. "He needed to be a journalist," Kramer explained, "to have the kind of respectability to be on TV." Matthews had the sorts of talents that work on television; Kramer needed visibility for his afternoon newspaper, which Matthews could provide by appearing on these shows "with our name under his picture."

Matthews became such a familiar face on television talk shows that *Washingtonian* magazine named him "one of the top 50 journalists" in the city.

Matthews's story is not an isolated case. The *Chicago Tribune* employs a media consultant to coach and promote its Washington correspondents for television. Other print media have followed suit. Television commentator David Gergen became an editor at *U.S. News & World Report*; *Newsweek*, which gives reporters cash bonuses for television appearances, hired Morton Kondracke as its Washington bureau chief after he became a regular on television.

Some observers fear the impact of television opinion journalism on basic journalistic values of reporting, neutrality, and objectivity, as it reinforces the skills that get one and keep one on television—a knack for asserting opinions in concise, memorable sound bites. "I need someone who is glib, colorful, whose thoughts can be condensed into a conversational style," said "Face the Nation" executive producer Karen Sughrue.

Sue Ducat, producer of PBS's "Washington Week in Review," reports being inundated by requests from print reporters seeking to appear on the show. Although payment for an appearance on most talk shows is small, being on television is the surest way for print reporters to get rich—it leads to book contracts and, most lucrative of all, to the lecture circuit.

The journalist-as-Washington-insider, offering advice, is an essential part of these programs. Many of the shows, such as CNN's "Capital Gang," mix journalists, partisans, and government officials together as equals—a process likely to distance journalists from the public they are supposed to represent and to make criticism of the government policies supported by their "guests" less likely.[1]

[1]Thomas B. Rosenstiel (*Los Angeles Times*), "Some Say TV Show Culture May Change Values of Journalists," *Star Tribune*, 23 May 1989, pp. 1, 2 E.

---

remain a detached observer; and if conflicting views are presented, it is a natural way of dramatizing an issue and reporting material in a balanced format.

The lack of expertise can allow inaccuracies or bias to creep into a reporter's work. In order to compensate, reporters, particularly those writing for elite media, check their stories with informed sources. Problems can arise here too.

"Reporters are still uncomfortable about saying things on their own authority, so they turn to the experts," writes Stephen Hess, a speechwriter in the

Eisenhower White House, an urban affairs adviser to President Richard Nixon, now on the staff of the Brookings Institution and author of several books on the press; Hess received 1,294 calls from 183 news organizations in 17 countries in 1989.

Jack Nelson, head of the Washington bureau of the *Los Angeles Times*, agreed: "When you are going to make an opinionated kind of statement, particularly in the news columns, editors insist you attribute it to someone other than yourself—so you go shopping."[34]

Out of his experiences, Hess has come to surmise "that TV news is increasingly dishonest in that increasingly its stories gather quotes or other material to fit a hypothesis." Under the pressure of smaller budgets and staffs, reporters are under pressure to make every story usable and under pressure to do fewer interviews. "In other words, reporters tend to interview only those who fit a preconceived notion of what the story will be and a story's hypothesis becomes self-fulfilling," which he believes is beginning to erode a strength of journalism—its capacity to see for itself.[35]

Fairness and Balance

Presenting opposing viewpoints has become a staple of news presentation. One commentator writes: " 'Objectivity,' contrary to popular belief, does not refer to the truthfulness of media interpretation, but demands merely impartiality of coverage, which is stylistically supplied by quoting two opposing sources."[36] Given the importance of the interview as a journalistic technique, this is the natural way to extend it to provide balance.

However, many problems have more than two solutions, and many issues generate more than two opposing viewpoints. News stories almost never reflect such complexity; instead, they tend to present issues in terms of pros and cons, to look at social movements as made up of moderates and militants, to divide reaction into support for or resistance to administration policy. This reflects the emphasis on conflict and drama in hard news; the distortions it creates are often criticized for treating electoral campaigns as horse races or athletic contests.

The preoccupation with winning and losing was evident in coverage of the 1984 debates between Reagan and Mondale, in which news coverage focused on Mondale's use of "There you go again," the phrase Reagan had used so effectively in 1980 in responding to Jimmy Carter. What was forgotten in the process was the issue Reagan and Mondale were discussing—Social Security. We would argue that such treatment is a natural outgrowth of the criteria for hard news and the conventions governing news presentation. However, these do shape the resulting stories and influence the view of reality they present.

---

34. Barbara Gamarekian, "In Pursuit of the Clever Quotemaster," *New York Times*, 12 May 1989, p. 10 Y.

35. Stephen Hess, "New Phase Makes TV News Increasingly Dishonest," *Star Tribune*, 17 October 1989, p. 13 A.

36. Gertrude Joch Robinson, "Women, Media Access and Social Control," in Epstein, *Women in the News*, p. 89.

The emphasis on opposing points of view can create another kind of distortion. It is as if the media must find an opposition and, for purposes of balance, promote it as relatively equal in size and importance to its counterpart.

Story Length

The typical news story is short and simple. There are ordinarily fifteen to twenty stories on the evening network news, and each story averages slightly more than one minute in length. The "action news" approach to local newscasts, recommended by Frank N. Magid Associates of Marion, Iowa, largest of the news consulting firms, is thirty to forty short, fast-paced items in the twenty-two minutes of a typical half-hour newscast.

The nature of the television medium means that listeners cannot skip boring items, and bored listeners may switch channels or turn off the set. Broadcasters sometimes say that their stories would be longer if the nightly network newscasts were extended to forty-five minutes or an hour, but in 1963, when the networks moved from fifteen minutes to a half-hour of news, the length of the individual stories did not increase appreciably.

The constraints of time and space force reporters to simplify. Print reporters order their material into a pyramidal structure that opens with a lead (first paragraph) identifying who, what, where, when, how, and why; material is then developed in order of decreasing importance so it can be cut from the end if space runs short. The result is that a single, discrete event is reported, and such coverage tends to separate events from their context.

Special kinds of news stories have been developed to correct for this kind of distortion: feature articles that highlight human interest, interpretive and background stories that explain the more complex event or place events in a more meaningful frame of reference, news analysis and commentary, and editorials. These appear in all media, but they are most common in the elite media, although even here they are limited. Woodward and Bernstein, the *Washington Post* reporters who became famous for their investigative work on the events of Watergate, remarked that during their investigative reporting they had no time or opportunity to write a synthetic piece integrating their findings into a coherent whole.[37] For the most part, this kind of news coverage appears in specialized media or programming, in newsweeklies, in weekly commentary magazines, or in documentaries. The result is that such stories are more likely to reach smaller, more specialized audiences.

Walter Cronkite, the former anchor of "CBS Evening News" and a highly respected journalist, stated repeatedly that network news simply provides a headline service. In fact, a half-hour news program provides less verbal information than the front page of the *New York Times*. However, the success of such public television programs as the "MacNeil/Lehrer Newshour" attests to television's ability to discuss ideas in depth.

---

37. Cited in Timothy Crouse, *The Boys on the Bus: Riding with the Campaign Press Corps* (New York: Random House, 1972), p. 296.

But until the inception of ABC's "Nightline," a half-hour program devoted to one to three issues, no in-depth commercial news program had attracted an audience big enough to warrant regularly scheduled in-depth news. "Nightline," created to provide detailed coverage of the Iranian hostage crisis, defied conventional wisdom by drawing a high-income audience attractive to advertisers and, occasionally, reaching a larger audience than Johnny Carson on NBC.

"Nightline" succeeded by innovating. To help explain complex issues, "Nightline" dramatizes in unorthodox fashions. Kermit the Frog and Miss Piggy helped moderator Ted Koppel explain a complex economic issue. In a program dedicated to cocaine addiction, the Washington Ballet Company demonstrated what cocaine does to the human brain.

Koppel and "Nightline" have also broken news stories. As the PTL scandal began to unfold, Koppel was the first to interview Jim Bakker—the minister charged with misusing funds donated by his viewers. After the Donna Rice story broke, presidential hopeful Gary Hart did his first explanatory interview with Koppel. Koppel was also first to interview Ferdinand Marcos after he fled the Philippines.[38]

The different ways in which space and time are organized in newspapers and on television affect news coverage. Television has a limited number of available commercial minutes and cannot expand the hours of the day or the time available for advertising. By contrast, as the amount of advertising sold increases, the amount of news published in a newspaper (the "news hole") increases.

Story Structure

Stories are stories. News reports, particularly televised news reports, are likely to be shaped into a narrative-dramatic structure. This kind of structure not only gives coherence to various bits of data, but is the natural structure for emphasizing action, drama, and conflict. Even within the conventional structure of the print story—moving from more important to less important facts—a news item is likely to begin with an action identified as a problem, develop through a narrative of increasing tension or conflict (including the identification of opposing forces, often interviewed and quoted), and close with a suggested or predicted resolution. This structure dominates coverage in television news. It is ideally suited to reporting single, dramatic events, to presenting characters (spokespersons who are quoted), to focusing on action, and to covering novel, exciting events. Conversely, it is ill suited to coverage of an idea, concept, or process. Since journalists rely so heavily on the narrative-dramatic structure, this more abstract content is not only harder to report but more likely to be distorted. An example of this technique is presented in the news account shown in Figure 2.1.

Objectivity

Some of the roles that journalists play have already been mentioned, such as the "detached observer," the "investigator," or the "objective" reporter of events. Social historian Michael Schudson points out that objectivity became an ideal in

---

38. Ray Richmond, "A Pioneering Show's Anniversary," *Philadelphia Inquirer*, 8 November 1989, pp. 1, 8 E.

Write a Story

In 1963, Reuven Frank, then president of NBC News, wrote a memo to his staff that read as follows:

> Every news story should, without any sacrifice of probity or responsibility display the attributes of fiction, of drama. It should have structure and conflict, problem and denouement, rising action and falling action—a beginning, a middle, and an end.[m]

[m] Cited by John Corry, "TV: The News Movie, New Form of Program," *New York Times*, 26 January 1988, p. 24 Y.

---

journalism rather recently and that it became an ideal "precisely when the impossibility of overcoming subjectivity in presenting the news was widely accepted and . . . precisely because subjectivity had come to be regarded as inevitable."[39] One communications researcher notes that in the role of reporter, the journalist no longer uses mainly "an intellectual skill as critic, interpreter and contemporary historian but a technical skill at writing, a capacity to translate the specialized language and purpose of government, science, art, medicine, finance into an idiom that can be understood by broader, more amorphous, less educated audiences."[40] This detaches the journalist from the events reported and has a very important impact on the style of news coverage.

Reporters rarely speak in the first person, refer to their own actions in observing events and finding facts, or reveal their perceptions of the sources' motives; nor do they ordinarily indicate the validity of quoted statements.[41] Moreover, stories are written in the limited vocabulary of ordinary language accessible to the mass audience; the standard style for modern news writing removes all signs of

39. Michael Schudson, *Discovering the News: A Social History of American Newspapers* (New York: Basic Books, 1978), p. 157.

40. James W. Carey, "The Communications Revolution and the Professional Communicator," in *The Sociology of Mass Media Communicators: The Sociology Review Monograph*, No. 13, ed. Paul Halmos (University of Keele, January 1969), p. 32.

41. News coverage of Senator Joseph McCarthy's charges of subversion in high places illustrates the limitations of this conception of the journalistic role. Hillier Krieghbaum commented: "It was, in a way, a nose to nose confrontation with the realistic requirements of objectivity and fairness. [Now journalists] had to face up to the reality that a prominent individual, with senatorial privilege, could make virtually any statement that he wanted to. What did a reporter do if a senator's facts were in doubt—or obviously wrong?" (*Pressures on the Press* [New York: Thomas Y. Crowell, 1973], p. 11). Daniel Patrick Moynihan, now a senator from New York, wrote: "McCarthy went on . . . making such charges, and the national press, which detested and disbelieved him throughout, went on printing them. The American style of objective journalism made McCarthy" ("The President and the Press," in *The Presidency Reappraised*, eds. Rexford G. Tugwell and Thomas E. Cronin [New York: Praeger, 1974], p. 159). Reporter Lou Cannon points to still another dimension of the problem. "As McCarthy well knew, objective reporting gives the accuser a powerful advantage over the accused. This is because the accusation usually becomes the lead and the lead becomes the headline. The denial might be carried in a sub-lead in newspapers that used it; otherwise the reader had to plow through the story to find the denial even though all newspaper editors are aware that many readers do not get beyond the first few paragraphs (Cannon, *Reporting*, pp. 46–47).

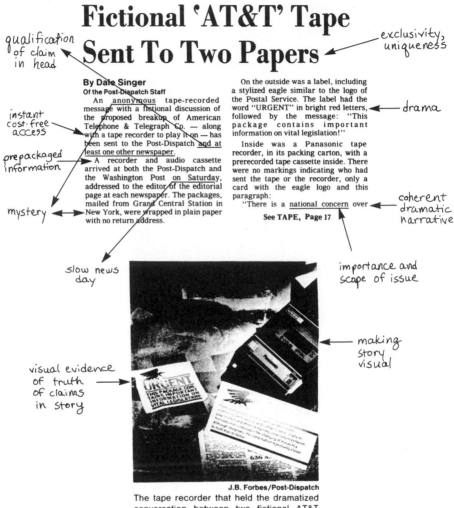

Fictional 'AT&T' Tape Sent To Two Papers

qualification of claim in head

exclusivity, uniqueness

By Dale Singer
Of the Post-Dispatch Staff

An <u>anonymous</u> tape-recorded message with a fictional discussion of the proposed breakup of American Telephone & Telegraph Co. — along with a tape recorder to play it on — has been sent to the Post-Dispatch and at least one other newspaper.

A recorder and audio cassette arrived at both the Post-Dispatch and the Washington Post on Saturday, addressed to the editor of the editorial page at each newspaper. The packages, mailed from Grand Central Station in New York, were wrapped in plain paper with no return address.

On the outside was a label, including a stylized eagle similar to the logo of the Postal Service. The label had the word "URGENT" in bright red letters, followed by the message: "This package contains important information on vital legislation!"

Inside was a Panasonic tape recorder, in its packing carton, with a prerecorded tape cassette inside. There were no markings indicating who had sent the tape or the recorder, only a card with the eagle logo and this paragraph:

"There is a <u>national concern</u> over

See TAPE, Page 17

instant cost-free access

prepackaged information

mystery

drama

coherent dramatic narrative

slow news day

importance and scope of issue

making story visual

visual evidence of truth of claims in story

J.B. Forbes/Post-Dispatch
The tape recorder that held the dramatized conversation between two fictional AT&T executives with its wrapping.

Figure 2.1   This article contains a fictional story within a nonfictional story within a news story. The story of Bill and Charlie is enveloped by the story containing its senders' purpose, which is contained within the news account. (Reprinted by permission of J. B. Forbes/Post-Dispatch.)

Tape

■ FROM PAGE ONE

tied to ongoing issue

our nation''s telecommunications' policy, and rightly so. Here, ready to play, is a fictional and entertaining conversation between two executives involved in the changing of this policy. Although imaginary, the conversation is probably closer to truth than to fiction.''

novel way of communicating information

The tape recording begins with a telephone call from a man identifying himself as ''Charlie Brown,'' asking to speak with the president of Illinois Bell Telephone Co., who is identified only as ''Bill.'' The chairman of AT&T is Charles L. Brown. The president of Illinois Bell is William L. Weiss.

personalized

Included on the professionally produced 10-minute tape is a discussion between Charlie and Bill about the proposed settlement worked out by AT&T and Assistant Attorney General William Baxter. The settlement was announced in January as an end to a longstanding antitrust suit against AT&T.

Under the agreement, AT&T would divest itself of its regional operating companies, which would become free-standing companies. AT&T would retain its Western Electric, Bell Laboratories and Long Lines, or long distance, operations.

As the taped discussion continues, the man portraying the president of Illinois Bell becomes increasingly disturbed as ''Charlie'' spells out the working details of the settlement. He makes it appear as if the parent company would be keeping all of the money-making activities, leaving the regional operating companies with unprofitable local service.

drama

''We'll really have some rate problems,'' Bill tells Charlie, in a voice that sounds close to tears. ''The state's going to get upset, the governor will get upset, the utility commission will get upset. Charlie, this is beginning to sound very difficult.''

Later, Bill moans, ''How in the world am I going to get and keep the best people?'' Charlie replies, ''With what we're leaving you, you won't need the best people.''

The tape ridicules Baxter, saying that the assistant attorney general was in such a rush to arrange the settlement that ''he called from the ski slope, then he hurried back here and we settled.''

At the end, Bill pleads with Charlie not to leave him hanging, and Charlie, before hanging up, assures him he will help out, but only on an ''arm's length'' basis. At the beginning and the end of the tape is the famous recording by the Coasters of the song ''Charlie Brown,'' including the refrain.

''He's gonna get caught, just you wait and see.
''Why's everybody always picking on me?''

balance

Officials with Southwestern Bell Telephone Co. in St. Louis and with AT&T in Washington said they had no idea who sent the recording. They criticized the tape as a poor way to try to influence editorial opinion.

Pickard Wagner, an AT&T spokesman in Washington, said, ''The fact that it is completely anonymous and disparages the head of AT&T and Illinois Bell illustrates the depths that whoever is behind this is sinking to.''

Dana Campbell, division staff manager for media relations for Southwestern Bell, added, ''It sounds like someone is trying to play games. It makes me a little angry. I get a little perturbed with anyone who sends out something in the mail without identifying himself.''

because readers might assume paper has been manipulated, editor assures readers ploy will have no impact on editorial positions

suggests that ploy is deviant

The package sent to the Post-Dispatch was addressed personally to William F. Woo, head of the newspaper's editorial page since 1974. He called the tape recorder ''some press agent's concept of a swell idea. I'm not at all amused by it. Inasmuch as it's anonymous, we will pay as much attention to it as we do to unsigned letters, which is to say none at all.''

uniqueness

Woo said he could not recall ever receiving an anonymous press release before. He noted that, like the tape-recorded message, the newspaper's editorials have raised serious questions about the proposed AT&T settlement.

we don't accept bribes!

''This sort of anonymous attack is really disgusting,'' he said. ''I wish I knew where it came from, and when we do find out where it came from, the tape recorder and message will be returned with a sharp note.''

tied to ongoing issue

Are There More Ads Now or Does It Just Seem That Way?

"Although the networks claim self-imposed guidelines limit their amount of commercial time, all three exceed the old National Association of Broadcasters nonprogram material standards of 10 minutes per hour in prime time and 16 minutes per hour in all other dayparts."

The 1989 survey[n] showed:

ABC in prime time	10 minutes 42 seconds
CBS	11 minutes 40 seconds
NBC	10 minutes 58 seconds
Fox	13 minutes 23 seconds

[n]*Advertising Age*, 2 July 1990, p. 19.

---

the reporter's identity or consciousness. This is the counterpart, in newswriting, of the impersonal, organizational, virtually anonymous source characteristic of mass communication (see Chapter 1).

Whereas the ordinary reporting role requires detachment, the investigative reporter's role moves from detachment to an adversarial position that uses skepticism to uncover hypocrisy, corruption, or misuse of power. This role is epitomized by Mike Wallace's stance on "60 Minutes." Wallace enacts the probing investigator determined to expose evil, to protect the underdog, to unearth the reality behind deceptive appearances.

Journalists who adopt this role tend to produce mildly skeptical stories, like the reporting done by CBS and ABC correspondents Bruce Morton and Sam Donaldson. Both Morton and Donaldson tend to cast doubt on motives, to debunk, to use the conventions of balance to raise objections or to suggest internal contradictions. This treatment, frustrating or infuriating to even the most powerful newsmakers, is a familiar journalistic perspective and a logical extension of the role of detached observer.

The roles of print and television reporters differ because the media themselves differ. However impersonal the style of the television reporter, "it is, above all, a personal voice that tells the day's news on the tube. One actually hears the voice; one sees the face, body, and manner of the person who speaks. This individual is constantly on view, intruding his person and personality almost continuously into the narrative."[42] This important difference between audience experience of print and television news may be one factor accounting for greater trust in television news.

42. Paul Weaver, "Newspaper News and Television News," *Television as a Social Force* 87 (1975): 89.

TO   SUM   UP

This chapter has explored how news organizations define what news is. We have set out five criteria defining hard news, we have explored the external and internal constraints affecting what will be covered and reported, and we have shown how conventions of news presentation influence the character of the story that emerges. The inescapable conclusion is that through their methods of news-gathering and reporting, the news media shape our views of reality.

Reporters influence us in many ways: by choosing what to write about, by deciding which sources to consult, by selecting a particular lead and structuring a story in a given way. All of the decisions made by newsgatherers combine to create stories that are rhetorical and persuasive.

In words that paraphrase rhetorical theorist Kenneth Burke, journalism professor James Carey expresses our point of view: "All journalism, including objective reporting, is a creative and imaginative work, a symbolic strategy; journalism sizes up situations, names their elements, structure, and outstanding ingredients, and names them in a way that contains an attitude toward them."[43] In short, all journalism is rhetorical.

Selected Readings

Hess, Stephen. *The Washington Reporters*. Washington, D.C.: Brookings Institute, 1981.

Levy, Mark R. "The Audience Experience with Television News," *Journalism Monographs* 55, April 1978.

Levy, Mark, and John P. Robinson. *The Main Source: Learning from Television News*. People and communication series, Volume 17. Beverly Hills: Sage, 1986.

Manoff, Robert Carl, and Michael Schudson, eds. *Reading the News*. New York: Pantheon, 1987.

Meyrowitz, Joshua. *No Sense of Place: The Impact of the Electronic Media on Social Behavior*. New York: Oxford, 1985.

Smith, Anthony. *Goodbye Gutenberg: The Newspaper Revolution of the 1980's*. New York: Oxford, 1980.

43. Carey, "Communications Revolution," p 36.

News as Persuasion

News functions as persuasion not simply in what it covers, a claim we made in Chapter 2, but also in how it is presented. In this chapter we analyze the presentation of news, including dramatizing and sensationalizing coverage, inaccurate and incomplete reporting, unbalanced interpretations of events, and direct intervention in the news event. Here we assume newspeople have decided something is newsworthy, and we examine how they present it.

In this chapter we consider the claim that media resources are used to influence our interpretations of events, to support certain perspectives and to reject others, and, in general, to function ideologically—that is, to promote "ideas which represent the interests of social groups and classes."[1] We examine this claim primarily in terms of television news, particularly network news, because it is now the most trusted news source in our society.

Dramatizing and Sensationalizing Content

The best-known statement about the mass media is probably Marshall McLuhan's "the medium is the message," later revised to "the medium is the massage." What these statements point to is the importance of technology in understanding how any medium can function persuasively. The impact of television news is, in part, a function of the screen, the camera, special effects, and the use of videotape.

The Screen

The television screen is small—very small indeed compared to a screen in a movie theater or to the size of people and objects in real life—and therefore it miniaturizes. Ballet dancers become tiny dolls; huge trucks are the size of toys.

1. Glasgow University Media Group, *More Bad News* (London: Routledge & Kegan Paul, 1980), p. 402.

Dramatic close-up

Medium close-up

Medium shot

Figure 3.1 Common television camera shots.

Within this frame, everything is tiny. Even cataclysms are shrunk to the size of small rectangles. In addition, the television screen reduces everyone and everything to the same size—an anchorperson is as large (or as small) as the Empire State Building. As a result, television alters our perceptions of space and proportion.

Some of what we now experience as television may no longer be true if high definition television becomes the norm. High definition television (HDTV) will provide a larger viewing screen able to carry a higher level of detail and quality. Whereas existing sets are one-quarter wider on their horizontal side than on their vertical, HDTV will be almost twice as long. From a distance, today's screens look square; HDTV will look rectangular. Among other things, this means that more horizontal eye movement will be required. Some scholars posit that "The combination of closer-viewing distance and wider screen will have the effect of putting the viewer 'in' the picture, because the screen will occupy a much greater proportion of the field of vision."[2] We now sit at some distance from the screen to dull the imperfections apparent at close viewing.

The language of the television screen is the language of close-ups. Close-up shots compensate for the poor quality of the television picture. The most common camera shots used on television are illustrated in Figure 3.1. These typical close up shots reflect the personal and social contact that is characteristic of television as a medium. The dramatic close-up reflects close personal distance or touching distance, the chest shot reflects far personal distance, and the medium shot reflects close social distance (just beyond touching distance), the distance at which we carry on impersonal business, as with salespeople.

Distance is related to intimacy. Television simulates intimate relationships between total strangers by bringing viewers close to actors and reporters; they enter our living rooms and bedrooms; they talk to us while we eat. The reliance on close-ups creates new rules for our sense of interpersonal space. For example, when viewers encounter newspeople face to face, they tend to treat them as friends despite the fact that they are total strangers. Because of the size of the screen and the use of close-ups, our experience of television, whether news or entertainment, involves personal and social contact and a sense of intimacy. As the last chapter noted, television news, unlike print, is personal in the sense that we

2. D. Lachrenbruch, "HDTV," *TV Guide*, 5 June 1989, p. 19.

see and hear a real person—an anchor or correspondent—presenting it. The television screen and the close-ups reinforce its personal character.

The Camera

The camera has a point of view; it becomes a viewer. Rules governing the shooting of news footage recognize the biases involved in camera angles and shots. For example, slow motion footage is considered tender, even romantic; jumpy images are considered dramatic; extreme close-ups are considered intense and dramatic.

Camera angles are also important. According to one study of journalistic practices, "For a news cameraworker, facticity is produced by meeting an event 'head on,' with camera placement fixed to simulate the angle of a person of average height confronting another person eye to eye. All else is condemned as 'distortion.'" If an interview is shot head-on, at eye level, that camera position suggests equality between the interviewer and the interviewee; if the camera looks up (worm's-eye view) at the person being interviewed, it suggests that the interviewee is more powerful and has a psychological advantage. Conversely, if the camera looks down (bird's-eye view) at the person being interviewed, it belittles the interviewee. That is why interviews and press conferences are shot head-on and from a fixed perspective.[3]

Camera shots and angles are important in television news. Reporters and anchors are shown in the medium close-up and medium shot, as are nearly all individuals in hard news stories. These distances are considered impartial and detached, the visual counterpart of journalistic objectivity. By contrast, more intimate shots are used for drama, to capture emotional reactions. Disaster victims, for example, may be shown in dramatic close-ups. But because this is an "emotional" and thus a nonobjective distance, reporters and anchorpersons will not be shown in this way. Similarly, news programs rarely show individuals full length in longer shots at what is public distance. Such distances depersonalize and decrease the emotional involvement of the viewer. They destroy the personal and social contact that is the hallmark of television news. Only crowds (such as audiences, rioters, or groups of soldiers) or persons in establishing shots (used to identify where the event is taking place), for example, will be shown full length in longer shots.

The camera has particular limitations and strengths. Photographic meaning is usually not self-evident; some explanation of context is required.[4] The camera eye is myopic; it cannot distinguish between trivial and important details. However, photographs are powerful and dramatic visualizations of emotion. Irving Kristol makes the claim this way: "What television *can* do, however—and do with extraordinary power—is to mobilize the audience's emotions around a vivid, sim-

3. Gaye Tuchman, *Making News: A Study in the Construction of Reality* (New York: Free Press, 1978), pp. 112, 114.

4. William C. Adams, "Visual Analysis of Newscasts: Issues in Social Science Research," in *Television Network News: Issues in Content Research*, eds. William C. Adams and Fay Schreibman (Washington, D.C.: Television and Politics Study Program, School of Public and International Affairs, George Washington University, 1978), p. 169.

Camera Angle as Point of View

Henry Hampton, producer of "Eyes on the Prize I" (1954–1965) and "Eyes on the Prize II" (1965–1980), documentaries on the history of the civil rights movement, advised those who reviewed thousands of feet of television news footage to look for those moments when the news cameras changed position, literally and figuratively, in reporting stories about the movement. These are the shifts he identifies:

In the beginning of the movement, in stories about the Supreme Court school desegregation decision, the cameras recorded basically a white point of view, showing the black characters sympathetically and the white racists as they were.

As the movement heated up, and it became increasingly clear where the violence lay, the cameras moved behind the march leaders and looked outward at the hostile sheriffs and their deputies.

Later, when "Black Power" became the cry of Stokely Carmichael and other activists, the cameras shifted away from the movement point of view and back toward the middle. By the time of the 1967 riots (for the record, he notes, many African-Americans still call them rebellions), the camera's point of view had shifted once again to look from behind the police lines aimed outward at the rioters.

"Millions of viewers have taken their racial lessons from the position of the lens, for the full impact of television is as much a result of by-product as it is of intent."[a]

[a]Adapted from Henry Hampton, "The Camera Lens as Two-Edged Sword," *New York Times*, 15 January 1989, p. 29 H.

Faraway Places and Tight Budgets

In the pursuit of pictures of events, the networks are increasingly buying and using videotape shot by stringers and by amateurs with portable videocameras.

These changes raise fundamental questions about the ethical standards of television news. They include:

1. Has increasing reliance on nonstaff personnel, because of budget cuts and the difficulties in reporting stories in remote parts of the world, had an effect on the coverage of network news divisions?

2. Does the dependence of network news departments on good pictures invite abuse of journalistic standards?

Questions such as these have been raised by a number of incidents. For example, in the fall of 1989, the *New York Post* charged that Mike Hoover, a freelance cameraman, faked and restaged battle sequences in film used in award-winning reports for CBS newscasts and in a 1987 documentary about the war in Afghanistan. CBS staff members had questioned him on details and edited out material if any aspect of the coverage had seemed vague. But film was extremely prized by the networks trying to cover Afghanistan. It rarely turned up on any newscast, and Hoover's film was of exceedingly high quality.[b]

[b]Bill Carter, "Questions of Method and Morality in the CBS News Case," *New York Times*, 4 October 1989, p. 13 Y.

plified, essentially melodramatic vision of the political world, in which praise and blame are the magnetic poles. What television can do, in other words, is what demagogic rhetoric used to do less efficaciously."[5] The emotional power of television is a by-product of its visual resources and the size and intimacy of the television screen.

Ordinary news footage takes advantage of the power of the camera. Correspondents reporting stories are framed against easily recognizable locations filled with symbolic significance: the White House, Big Ben, Red Square. A story about New York may be framed against its skyline; a strike is identified by a line of pickets or a silent factory; a murder is indicated by a pool of blood on a sidewalk or a drug bust by needles and a stack of plastic packets. In this way the topics of news stories are instantly identified for the viewer, and the authority of reporters is enhanced: they are there, on the spot.

Special Effects

Technology is changing the potential of the television camera and screen through Chyron machines, which superimpose text on pictures, Adda electronic graphics-storage units, and Quantel computers, which create visual excitement by manipulating television images. ABC News led in the use of such equipment. Mike Buddy, a director of ABC's "World News Tonight," is described as spending much of his day "packaging" news stories through technological equipment that gives editorial content a visual "shampoo."

To emphasize elements in a news story, news directors can use stop action, freeze frame, slow motion, or a zoom lens to focus on a postage-stamp sized image on the screen. With a Chyron 4 character generator, they can superimpose text in colors. The Quantel 5000 Plus, a computerized switcher, enables directors to mold electronic images. ABC director Buddy says, "This is where we add the bells and whistles."[6] He explains that ABC tries to make economic information visually interesting by using special visual effects: "We tell the story graphically: freeze a picture, shrink it, put a catchphrase underneath the picture that encapsulates a paragraph of what the correspondent is saying. We try to make our graphics move the story forward instead of being a reference mark."[7]

The 1980s produced major advances in the technological manipulation of images. Chyron's Scribe infinite character generator provides "full 3-D animation." With its Transform option, it "animates objects created by the character generator."[8]

Not all the technological advances have been visual. Now that 19 percent of U.S. households have stereo television, 3-D sound is emerging. Developed by Archer Communications Inc., Q-Sound "is a computerized sound-mixing process in which the voices, instruments, and other elements of a recording are separated

5. Irving Kristol, "Crisis for Journalists: The Missing Elite," in *Press, Politics and Popular Government*, ed. George Will (Washington, D.C.: American Enterprise Institute, 1972), p. 51.

6. Desmond Smith, "The Wide World of Roone Arledge," *New York Times Magazine*, 28 February 1980, p. 66.

7. Edward Tivnan, "The Cronkite Syndrome," *The Dial*, November 1980, p. 49.

8. *Electronic Media*, 12 February 1990, p. 18.

and then programmed to be heard from various locations. For example, the roar of a jet can be made to sound as if it is coming from above the listener and the babble of a brook as if it is at his [sic] feet."[9] A Coca-Cola commercial that made its debut in February 1990 used Q-Sound to create the sensation that birds were chirping as they flew overhead while wind seemed to whir through the living room.

The heavy use of special effects is designed to attract viewers and increase ratings. Its use by news producers is defended on the grounds that U.S. television viewers have been trained to absorb information via commercials, so news programs must apply the same techniques. The view is that, on television at least, action speaks louder than words, and that emotion-filled pictures speak loudest.

The persuasive impact of television news is directly related to the television screen, the use of close-ups, the power of the camera, and the resources of special effects. They are used not only to dramatize and sensationalize news content, but also to enhance the authority and credibility of correspondents and anchorpersons.

Editing

Both print and broadcast journalism compress time. Events that took days or hours to transpire are reduced to a few paragraphs or a few minutes of air time. In shortening an event it is difficult to maintain a sense of continuity. When continuous action is broken visually, by removing a section of tape or film, the image seems to jump; and this editing procedure is called a jump cut. When an editor wants the viewer to know that segments have been lifted from different parts of a speech, for example, a jump cut is deliberately used to tell the viewer that editing has occurred.

Ordinarily, producers do not want to draw attention to such breaks in continuity. To avoid breaks, "cut-aways"—shots that cut away from the main action—are used to show, for example, audience reaction. During a speech, the camera may cut away to the face of the candidate's spouse; during a football game, the camera may cut away to the scoreboard or the cheerleaders. Because the camera limits the visual field, viewers see what the camera sees and cut away from the action with it, even if they would prefer to keep watching the game.

Because of its editing capacity, television can distort by reordering events. For example, a 1984 Reagan commercial intercut Reagan on a whistle-stop train tour with clips of Reagan ads that had aired earlier. As a result, some of the people in the second ad who appeared to be watching Reagan's train were in fact nowhere in sight of it; they were actors who had filmed their segments of the ads long before the train had pulled from the station.

The ability to edit means that the character of an interview can be altered. Cut-away shots are often filmed at the beginning or end of a shooting session and later edited into the tape. At the end of a news segment, for instance, the camera will shift from the interviewee to the interviewer to shoot reaction shots that will

---

9. Kim Foltz, "Sound Becomes the New Frontier for TV Ads," *New York Times,* 5 February 1990, p. D 9.

be intercut into the interview. This is the procedure routinely followed on such newsmagazines as CBS's "60 Minutes," and it includes not only reaction shots but film of correspondents such as Mike Wallace re-asking the questions. When such procedures are used, interviews can be subtly altered.

In late October 1989, television minister Pat Robertson was interviewed by Rebecca Chase of ABC News about his reaction to the sentencing of fellow tele-vangelist Jim Bakker to forty-five years in prison for fraud. Chase asked Robert-son's reaction to "the rather stiff sentence received by Bakker." Robertson re-sponded that although the sentence was stiff, he had expected it. After all, the judge was termed "Maximum Bob" in the Carolinas. Then Chase asked whether Robertson felt that the sentence closed the era of church scandals. Robertson an-swered, "I am delighted to see it. I think that God really has done a job cleaning his church." When the interview aired, Robertson heard himself saying that he was delighted at the Bakker sentence. His answer to one question had been edited to follow a different question.

Since Robertson had taped the complete interview, he played it on his tele-vised "700 Club." The night after the "700 Club" broadcast aired, ABC admitted that editing had distorted Robertson's original statement.[10]

Related charges have been made against CBS's "60 Minutes," a Sunday night newsmagazine that has been described as "without question the most influential news program in the history of the medium."[11] "60 Minutes" is known for its hard-edged, often sensational investigative reporting, typified by those segments featuring correspondent Mike Wallace. Such dramatic stories have kept the pro-gram among the top ten in the Nielsen ratings, but both the confrontational or "ambush" interview (approaching the target of an investigation for an interview without warning or with a damning document or quotation) and program editing have raised journalistic and ethical questions. Bill Brown, one of the original producers of "60 Minutes," describes the confrontational device as intrinsically unfair because it is so heavily weighted in favor of the reporter.

Still, challenging the assumption that such coverage necessarily hurts its sub-jects is evidence three North Texas State University professors found that com-panies exposed on "60 Minutes" may have benefited from the publicity. After monitoring the stock prices of the thirteen companies featured on "60 Minutes" in the past five years, they concluded that, for fifteen days after the show aired, the shares of these companies did 12 percent better on average than the rest of the market.[12]

Many questions have been raised about editing that tends to sharpen the good versus evil, appearance versus reality themes described in Chapter 2. For example, when Daniel Schorr, a former CBS correspondent, was interviewed on "60 Minutes" about his unauthorized release ("leak") of the Pike Committee re-port, an interview that originally lasted over an hour and a quarter was reduced to thirteen minutes. "What had been deleted in the editing . . . was material that filled out his thought processes, lending the impression of a man under stress

10. "ABC Exposed by Pat Robertson," Accuracy in Media, *Electronic Media*, 4 December 1989, p. 6.
11. Harry Stein, "How '60 Minutes' Makes News," *New York Times Magazine*, 6 May 1979, p. 28.
12. *Time*, 28 April 1986, p. 55.

who had been trying to do the right thing. The elimination of that material also reinforced the impression of Wallace as the relentless interrogator."[13]

As viewers, we are aware of the subtle manipulation possible through editing, but our awareness is rarely conscious. However, we test the accuracy and reliability of some material based on our perceptions of editing. For example, reporters who wanted to demonstrate incoherence in Reagan's extemporaneous speeches and answers had to air longer than usual segments to confirm that the segments they were showing had not been edited into incoherence.

As our examples illustrate, disputes about editing arise most frequently about television newsmagazines and documentaries, although regular newscasts are also edited. The special effects we have described increase the possibilities for manipulation of filmed and taped material in order to make it more dramatic, more sensational, and hence more appealing to viewers.

Filmed and Taped Coverage

Since 1961, nearly all television programming has been taped or filmed. Although the electronic media, unlike print, are able to transmit news events as they occur, live coverage is rare and noteworthy: the space shots, the Kennedy funeral, the Kefauver, Army-McCarthy, and Watergate hearings, presidential debates and major speeches, political party conventions, royal weddings, and some coverage of breaking news—the happenings in Tiananmen Square, the aftermath of the 1989 San Francisco earthquake, and events in the war against Iraq.

The local anchorpersons delivering news are generally broadcast live. The first feed of the network news is live, although segments presented within the newscast have been taped; subsequent replays of the network news are taped. Thus "CBS Evening News" is fed live from New York at 6:30 P.M., but a tape of that feed is played on Channel 9 in Washington, D.C., at 7 P.M. The quality of the tape used to store and replay information is so good that viewers cannot distinguish taped from live coverage.

In the process of transforming live events into "taped, live, edited" events, verbal and visual errors are removed and, as a result, the spontaneity characterizing early television has been lost. Until viewers contrast live and taped coverage, they are unaware of the subtle distortion created when errors are suppressed. Occasional moments in the presidency of Ronald Reagan created such awareness as when he misread his note cards and, for example, announced in his second inaugural address that he wanted to fill the world with "sand" rather than the "sound" written on his cards. A similar awareness occurred when the nightly news carried candidate George Bush's ad-libbed comment during a speech that September 7 was the anniversary of the bombing of Pearl Harbor.

The San Francisco earthquake that occurred on October 18, 1989, demonstrated how accustomed we have become to the controlled, polished presentations of evening news. The earthquake struck at 5:04 P.M. Because ABC was prepared to carry the World Series game from Candlestick Park, Candlestick Park

13. Harry Stein, "How '60 Minutes' Makes News," *New York Times Magazine*, 6 May 1979, p. 80; see also Eric Barnouw, *The Sponsor: Notes on a Modern Potentate* (New York: Oxford, 1978), pp. 137–138. For a history and analysis of the series, see Stephen Zito, "Inside 'Sixty Minutes,'" *American Film* 2 (December 1976–January 1977): 31–36; 55–57.

appeared to be the epicenter of the quake. The Goodyear blimp, also at ABC's disposal, captured the first pictures of the damaged Oakland Bay Bridge. In the absence of fresh pictures, the networks violated the norm that news be new and repeatedly aired the same pictures: a fire burning out of control and the damaged bridge. Nonnewsworthy sources were interviewed simply because they were in San Francisco. Tom Brokaw of NBC interviewed an NBC reporter in a Bay Area traffic jam. Ted Koppel of ABC interviewed the pilot of the blimp. Neither interviewee had any information to add to the network coverage. Local reporters appeared with information about specific San Francisco locations. But the most important questions remained unanswered for hours. Where specifically had the epicenter been? How many had been killed and injured? What was being done to rescue those trapped by falling buildings and collapsing bridges? How many buildings had been destroyed?

"The communications wonders that we all take for granted were out of service," noted Walter Goodman of the *New York Times*. "There were pictures without sound and sound without pictures, jumpy pictures and ill-defined ones. The vulnerability of these men and the medium on which the nation depends was unsettling: matters must really be out of control when the controllers of the news are unable to deliver it." [14]

If the improvisation that characterized network coverage of the earthquake is at one end of the news continuum, the staging of events is at the other. For the past few years, re-enactments have been a staple of the so-called tabloid news programs such as Fox Broadcasting Company's "America's Most Wanted" and NBC's "Unsolved Mysteries."

The controversy over re-enactments in network news arose in July 1989 when ABC's "World News Tonight" hired actors to depict a supposed meeting between U.S. diplomat Felix Bloch, accused of being a spy, and a foreign agent. The camera angle, the shot through cross-hairs, the shadowy scene, the black-and-white footage all suggested that ABC had scooped its competitors by being on the scene to document the transfer of a briefcase presumably containing state secrets. As controversy swirled around the ABC re-creation, ABC formally reprimanded those who had aired the piece, instituted a policy on re-creations, and required that they only be used with the permission of ABC president Roone Arledge.

In November 1989, NBC News announced that it was banning dramatic re-enactments from all its programming.[15] CBS announced that it would not use re-creations on "CBS Evening News with Dan Rather" but would continue their use on "Saturday Night with Connie Chung." Chung's program used re-creations to show such things as a day in the life of a teenage drug dealer.

Editing allows television producers to exploit the potential of the screen, the camera, and special effects to dramatize and sensationalize coverage. Because nearly all television news is edited, even televised news that is not re-enacted differs from the actual event in important and predictable ways.

14. Walter Goodman, "How the Networks Coped with Scant Information," *New York Times*, 19 October 1989, p. B 16.
15. Adam Buckman, "NBC News Bans Using Re-Creations," *Electronic Media*, 27 November 1989, p. 3.

Anchorpersons and On-Air Reporters

Television legitimizes the carriers of news to a greater extent than print. Walter Cronkite, until March 1981 the anchor of "CBS Evening News," was the most trusted man in America. Cronkite's closing comment, "And that's the way it is," put him and his news team in the position of authenticators: if you saw it on the network news, it had to be important; it had to be true. In fact, some media analysts argue that the existence of a small group of individuals who regularly bring us word of happenings in the news is reassuring.

In the process of reporting, newspersons legitimize certain stories. Being on the news is evidence of being important. Newspeople rarely raise questions that remain unanswered on the news; instead, they tend to speak in declarative sentences and present stories that fit neatly into problem-solution formats. Network and local newscasts legitimize an evidence-giving process that relies on their credibility as reporters and on the credibility of television as a medium: you are legitimate only if we say so and only if viewers can actually see you on the tube. Within the newscast, individuals of higher credibility legitimize less credible reporters. Cronkite, for example, invested CBS reporters with some of his credibility when he said, "Here with the story from _____ is _____ ." The presence of a reporter in a location near the event being reported is used to bolster credibility.

There is fierce competition for ratings dominance among the nation's local television outlets, a competition fueled by the fact that stations earn a large share of their gross income (30 to 50 percent of it, usually) from their early- and late-evening local newscasts.[16]

Because anchorpersons seem to be an important factor in ratings and because they are relatively easy to change, there is widespread use of "skin-testing" by national rating services to measure audience response to anchors, a form of testing that may measure sexiness or empathy, but that cannot measure journalistic competence or ability. An anchor who attracts the most appealing audience for advertisers—viewers 18 to 54 years old—will generate premium rates for advertising even if the ratings of the news program are lower than the competition's. Equally important, a popular early-evening local news program supplies a crucial lead-in to the prime-time lineup. An appealing anchor is also a way to induce the audience to identify with a particular news program, one route to promoting loyal viewership.

Once again, producers and station owners are making news judgments that will dramatize and sensationalize coverage at the potential sacrifice of journalistic accuracy and competence. The pressure for ratings is also felt by the networks. Those who have functioned as anchorpersons on network newscasts have thus far been journalists with impressive credentials as reporters. But Roone Arledge, president of ABC News, believes the function of the anchor is the "excitement of a lead-in voice to mobilize the passion of the audience."[17]

---

16. Neil Hickey, "Have Hair Spray, Will Travel," *TV Guide*, 14 February 1981, p. 5.
17. Smith, "Wide World," p. 66.

Mass Media News: Women and Minorities

Women, 52 percent of the population, are quoted on the front pages of newspapers 11 percent of the time.

Only 6 percent of the top media bosses are female; 25 percent of middle-level management jobs are held by women.

Average female employees earn 64 percent of what male employees earn.

Fifty-four percent of newspapers have hired no minorities. Those that do, don't promote them; 95.5 percent of newsroom managers are white.

From 1975 to 1989 the percentage of female news correspondents on nightly network newscasts increased from 9.9 percent to 13.8 percent.

During February 1989, 13.7 percent of the stories on ABC, 10.2 percent of those on CBS, and 8.9 on NBC focused on women.[c]

According to the most recent American Society of Newspaper Editors' survey, although they constitute 20 percent of the total population, minority reporters and editors employed at daily newspapers make up only 7 percent of their editorial personnel.

Conditions at elite newspapers—which have higher salaries, greater resources, and more varied reporting environments—are somewhat better. Reporters and editors at the *Washington Post*, the *Baltimore Sun*, and the *New York Times*, for example, were 10 to 15 percent minorities; however, the *Post*, the *Times*, and the *Sun* publish in and around urban areas where 50 to 70 percent of the population is African-American or Hispanic. One study reports that 90 percent of minority journalists are concentrated at one-third of the newspapers, most of them in and around large urban areas.[d]

[c] Statistics released from the annual convention of the American Society of Newspaper Editors, whose members are 9 percent women and 2 percent minority, and from a special conference on Women, Men and Media, cited by Barbara Reynolds, "Media Leave Many Out of the Picture," *USA Today*, 14 April 1989, p. 13 A, and "Study Reports Sex Bias in News Jobs," *New York Times*, 11 April 1989, p. 13 Y.

[d] Adapted from David Hatchett, "Blacks and the Mass Media," *Crisis* 96 (June/July 1989): 20–21.

Like media technology, television anchorpersons are important elements in the processes by which television news is made credible as well as the ways in which it is dramatized and sensationalized.

Inaccurate and Incomplete Reporting

Deadlines and Competition

Newspapers, television programs, and radio shows are part of our scheduled lives. We expect our favorite programs to appear at their regular times; we expect the newspaper to be at the front door by a certain hour. If those in the news media are to meet our expectations, they must also meet the deadlines that make it pos-

According to the Mass Media Bureau of the Federal Communications Commission, between 1987 and 1989, of all full-time broadcast employees, females increased from 37.8 to 38.3 percent; minorities increased from 16.2 to 16.8 percent.

In the upper-four job categories (officials and managers, professionals, technicians, and sales workers), among full-time employees, 30.4 percent are women and 14.4 percent are minority.[e]

In the cable industry, at units with more than five employees, between 1987 and 1989, female employees increased from 40.4 to 40.7 percent and minorities increased from 19.5 to 21 percent.

Of all news director jobs in the country, 0.3 percent are held by African-American males, and to date, there have been only two African-American daily network anchors—Bernard Shaw and Max Robinson.

The absence of minority employees is reflected in the results of studies of coverage of minorities. One study analyzed the major newspapers and radio and television stations in Boston and found that 85 percent of the stories about the city's two predominantly African-American neighborhoods "reinforced negative stereotypes of blacks. Blacks were persistently shown as drug pushers and users, as thieves, as troublemakers and as victims or perpetrators of violence"; and "while only 7 percent of the crime news reported by the major news media involved black neighborhoods, two-thirds of the stories about black neighborhoods were about crime."[f]

----

[e]The overwhelming majority of minorities, specifically African-American females, swell the numbers in the fifth category, which includes office and clerical positions.

As a percentage of officials and managers, African-American females represent 2.4 percent, African-American males 2.8 percent. Listed as professionals, African-American women are 3.4 percent, men are 4.8 percent. As technicians, African-American females are 2.7 percent, males are 8.7 percent. This suggests that sexism as well as racism bars women from nontraditional roles.

[f]Noah W. Griffin, "Broadcasting," *Crisis* 96 (June/July 1989): 30–32. The study cited was by Kirk Johnson, editor of *East-West Magazine*, and was reported in the *Minority Trends Newsletter*, a publication of the Center for Third World Organizations.

----

sible for shows to air on time, for the newspaper to arrive on schedule. Events occurring too close to the deadline or after the deadline has passed tax the abilities of journalists, and may be omitted or treated superficially. Events that happen after today's deadline must be particularly novel, dramatic, and personal if they are to be tomorrow's news.

To make the morning edition of most daily newspapers, copy must be filed by early evening. Deadlines for large Sunday papers are even earlier, often early Saturday afternoon. If meetings are scheduled for the evening or if conferences are scheduled on weekends, as those of the early women's movement were, they are unlikely to receive coverage.

The fact of deadlines would not in itself cause journalists to scramble for the latest, freshest, most dramatic news, but in a competitive news environment deadlines create that kind of pressure. No producer or publisher wants to lose the audience to a competitor because the competitor has a scoop or a unique angle on an important story. The emphasis on being first with a story encourages superficial reporting and the publication and broadcast of inaccuracies. As *Washington Post* reporter Lou Cannon notes, speed "is a value which competes with the value of accuracy, and in competitive situations it is difficult for accuracy to gain the upper hand. We put half-baked stories that need further checking on the air on into the newspapers when the stories certainly could wait another day."[18] Competition also produces races among the networks to be the first to "call" the results of elections.

The desire to air material first sometimes causes complications. At 2 P.M. one afternoon in mid-summer 1990, for example, a federal judge presiding over the drug trial of Washington, D.C., Mayor Marion Barry, released a black-and-white surveillance tape showing the mayor smoking crack. The problem for broadcasters was deciding how to deal with the expletives on the tape and with the mayor's repeated attempts to seduce governmental informer "Rasheeda" Moore.

NBC-owned WRC-TV was on the air with the footage at 2:03 P.M. (EST). Because WRC had had the tape for over a month, it had had the time to edit out the potentially offensive language and scenes. For fear of influencing the trial, the station had opted to withhold the tape, an instance of self-censorship, until the judge officially released it. Starting at 2:22, CBS affiliate WUSA-TV pre-empted network programming with the video only. At 11:30 that evening WUSA-TV aired the complete tape with the expletives included. At 9 P.M. C-SPAN aired the entire tape.[19]

Breaking News

Breaking news is unscheduled news, a happening no one could have foreseen—an assassination attempt or a disaster. Such occurrences tax journalistic resources and pose problems for television news, despite its special ability to bring us events as they occur. First, it is very costly for television to pre-empt regular programming for news coverage because such pre-emption may affect ratings and, ordinarily, fewer commercials will be shown during breaking news. Imagine the alternative: news reports on assassination attempts against President Reagan and Pope John Paul II interrupted by commercials for soaps and soups! Roone Arledge explains the situation this way:

> Competitive factors militate against networks living up to their responsibilities. It's a major step for a network to pre-empt a prime-time entertainment program to do a news program, because the results are going to be that your ratings for the week or for that night are going to be lower. And huge things rise and fall on this.[20]

When the networks pre-empted their schedules to cover the aftermath of the San Francisco earthquake, the pre-emption cost between $1.5 and $2 million in lost advertising revenue per network.[21]

18. Lou Cannon, *Reporting: An Inside View* (Sacramento: California Journal Press, 1977), p. 31.
19. Doug Halonen, "Barry Tape Gets Wide TV Play," *Electronic Media*, 2 July 1990, p. 2.
20. "The Hottest TV News Controversies," *TV Guide*, 13 January 1979, p. 10.
21. Bill Carter, "ABC Expects No Loss from Series Suspension," *New York Times*, 19 October 1989, p. B 16.

Inaccurate reporting of breaking news events is attributable to the difficulties of on-air editing, to the desire to beat the competition to the story, and to new angles on that story. Both are illustrated by coverage of the assassination attempt on President Reagan in April 1981. *New York Times* television critic John J. O'Connor wrote that "ABC was the first to telephone my office about the attempt on Ronald Reagan's life, naturally anxious to announce that it had beat its network competitors to the air."[22] According to a report in *TV Guide*, they beat their competitors by four minutes![23]

The desire to be first with new information, combined with on-air editing, produced major errors in the coverage of the Reagan shooting. The first error was the report that the president was unhurt when instead he had been shot in the chest. The second was the report that press secretary Jim Brady had died of his wounds. CBS first made this false report, and the other networks followed. The third error was the report that Reagan was undergoing open-heart surgery, an on-air mistake made by NBC reporter Chris Wallace and picked up by the other networks. Because of competition, each network monitors the others closely; consequently, errors are spread within minutes. The fourth error was the report, at 7:15 P.M., that the president was still in surgery after four hours; in fact, he had been out of surgery for more than an hour.

Similarly, during the opening days of the war against Iraq in 1991, CNN mistakenly reported that a Scud missile that exploded in Tel Aviv had carried a warhead of nerve gas. Less than a half-hour later, they corrected their error.

These errors reflect the limitations of television news coverage. It is preeminent in fast transmission of videotape of recent events, as of the assassination attempt, but it is severely limited in covering stories that take place outside the range of the camera's eye, as inside a hospital. In such circumstances, television reporters are prone to make serious errors, such as substituting "open-heart" for "open-chest" surgery—errors that print reporters avoid because they usually have time to check such stories and do not face the pressure to put hearsay on the air immediately.

Coverage of breaking news illustrates the differences between broadcast and print reporting. Print reporting may allow time to check out a story and provide complete, accurate coverage. Television reporting permits the immediate transmission of tape, events, and rumors. Tom Wicker summarized the difference this way: "When information is speedily provided by impeccable sources, the advantage is all with TV." By contrast, a newspaper can sift out rumor, mistakes, and conflicting claims "to give its readers a reasonably accurate and comprehensive report—but well after the fact."[24]

The competition among the networks compounds the problems of coverage of breaking news. As these examples illustrate, such coverage is prone to be incomplete and inaccurate.

22. John J. O'Connor, "How the Three Networks Treat Breaking News," *New York Times*, 12 April 1981, p. D 29.

23. *TV Guide*, 17 April 1981, p. A 1.

24. Tom Wicker, "TV's Tough Problem," *New York Times*, 7 April 1981, p. A 19.

Story Structure

Inaccurate reporting also results from inflexible ideas about issues and about how a story should be written. For example, newspeople reject the notion that some things, like the consequences of enacting a piece of legislation, cannot be calculated. The press has a natural desire to know what the results of a newsworthy action will be on them and their audience. Consequently, because the audience wants to know what impact the legislation will have and what it will cost, and because the press knows that unforeseen effects often are significant and newsworthy, reporters are particularly interested in gathering information about the specific effects of proposed action.

But some data simply are not available. For example, during the debate over the bill banning mandatory retirement, reporters repeatedly pressed supporters of the bill for figures on the number of older workers who would be forcibly retired if the bill did not pass, but who would opt to stay in the labor force if it was passed. The staff of the House Select Committee on Aging rebuffed press requests for such a figure on the grounds that it could not be calculated accurately. This was the case for a number of reasons: workers will stay on the job if inflation has been or is projected to remain high, because inflation erodes their pensions, but these workers will not stay on for financial reasons if their pension plans contain an escalator to compensate for inflation.

Accurate data on how workers behave in periods of high inflation when given a choice about retirement did not exist, nor did data correlating types of pension plans to income and to workers facing mandatory retirement who would be protected by the bill. In addition, workers stay on the job longer if their health is good; it is difficult to predict the health of workers who face mandatory retirement or would face it in the next three to five years. In fact, data on precisely how many workers faced mandatory retirement were not exact.

Anonymous and Composite Sources, Misrepresented Tape

Early in the 1980s, four cases focused attention on journalistic practices that lead to inaccurate reporting and on the processes by which print journalism corrects for such practices. *Washington Post* reporter Janet Cooke won a 1981 Pulitzer Prize in the feature-writing category for a story, "Jimmy's World," that she later admitted was a fake. The story was a composite of fabricated quotations and events that never happened.

In a series of stories written by the *Washington Post* ombudsman Bill Green, some of the processes that produced the story were revealed. These include the pressure on reporters to write good stories in order to advance, the problem of anonymous sources, and the gaps in procedures for checking stories when reporters say that the identity of the main characters must be protected.[25]

The second case involved reporter Michael Daly of the *New York Daily News*. In a column reporting on violence in Northern Ireland, Daly told the story of a British army patrol through the eyes of gunner Christopher Spell, a name he later admitted was a pseudonym. A *News* editorial said that "a number of key facts in

25. Bill Green, *Washington Post*, 19 April 1981, pp. 12–15 A.

the account proved to be erroneous, and others could not be corroborated." Like Cooke, Daly resigned, but he said that the column that cost him his job was not very different from some 300 others he had written over the previous two years, in which he had often used reconstructions and pseudonyms.[26]

The third case involved Teresa Carpenter, the *Village Voice* reporter who received the Pulitzer Prize (the one Cooke had returned) for an article about Dennis Sweeney, the killer of Allard K. Lowenstein, published on May 12, 1980. By a 13-to-1 vote, the National News Council, a policing mechanism set up by journalists, decided that complaints about the story were warranted. The council wrote that it was "disturbed by a paragraph that reads as if Carpenter had interviewed Dennis Sweeney in his cell at Rikers Island, when in fact she had not," and said the article was "marred by the overuse of unattributed sources, by a writing style so colored and imaginative as to blur precise meanings and by . . . reckless and speculative construction." However, the *Voice* stood by the article and said that "Ms. Carpenter's principal sources corroborated to the National News Council's staff the material that was the subject of the complaint."[27]

The fourth case concerned a December 1981 *New York Times Magazine* article by Christopher Jones, who subsequently admitted that he had lifted quotations and an entire paragraph from *Time* magazine's dispatches and had plagiarized a passage from an André Malraux novel, *The Royal Way*, in order to fabricate a fictitious trip to southwestern Cambodia. The *Times*' executive editor, Abe Rosenthal, said: "The major mistake we made is in not following our customary procedures in showing an article in a specialized subject by any writer without outstanding credentials in the field to one of our own specialists."[28] Editorially, the *Times* commented:

> When a newspaper uses precious front-page space, as the *Times* did yesterday, to expose a lie in its own columns, it is trying to do much more than confess a procedural lapse. The point is to reaffirm a compact with the reader: that what is printed has been honestly gathered and labeled; that any credible challenge will be rigorously examined, and that serious error will get prompt and conspicuous notice.[29]

In all these cases, the pressure to write a good story led reporters to rearrange details to meet literary requirements, to use colorful language, and to create dramatic composite characters. The praise of editors and the awarding of prizes attest to such values in journalism. Bob Woodward, the former investigative reporter who was Cooke's editorial superior at the *Post*, said simply, "This story was so well-written and tied together so well that my alarm bells simply didn't go off."[30]

26. Michael Kramer, "Just the Facts, Please," *New York*, 25 May 1981, p. 19.

27. "News Watchdog Group Scores 'Voice' Pulitzer Prize Winner," *Washington Post*, 12 June 1981, p. A 2.

28. James M. Markham, "Writer Admits He Fabricated an Article in Times Magazine," *New York Times*, 22 February 1982, pp. 1, 4 Y.

29. "A Lie in the Times," *New York Times*, 23 February 1982, p. 26 Y.

30. Bill Green, "THE STORY: First the Idea, and Finally the Presses Rolled," *Washington Post*, 19 April 1981, p. 12 A.

More recently, Alastair Reid, a longtime staff writer at *The New Yorker*, described how in nonfiction articles over the years, he had invented characters, rearranged events, and composed conversations. Reid claimed that these techniques made his articles truthful in spirit, if not in detail.

Reid's views were sharply criticized by other journalists. Fred Friendly, former president of CBS News and senior program adviser at the Columbia University Graduate School of Journalism, said: "A composite is a euphemism for a lie. . . . It's dishonest, and it's not journalism." And Ken Auletta, a writer for *The New Yorker*, said:

> He's wrong. It is commonly agreed that we shouldn't take shortcuts without telling the reader we're taking shortcuts, and by that I mean labeling it as fiction. We cover public officials, and we expect them to tell the truth. Journalists must abide by the same standards.[31]

Newspaper readers' advocates are press efforts to prevent and expose such practices. (The *Columbia Journalism Review* and the *Washington Journalism Review* provide forums for peer review of journalistic practices.) In June 1967 the Louisville *Courier-Journal and Times* appointed an ombudsman to serve as readers' representative in adjudicating complaints about news coverage. Such major papers as the *Washington Post* and the *Los Angeles Times* added ombudsmen to their staffs in the following years.

The title of the person performing these functions varies from paper to paper. The *St. Louis Post-Dispatch*'s ombudsman is called the reader's advocate. Other titles are public affairs editor, Mr. Go-Between, editor of action-line, and reader-contact editor.[32] Readers' advocates have regular access to space and their unedited copy is printed in a prominent place, ranging from the op-ed (opinion editorial) page to the front page. To assure their independence, their contracts typically protect them from pressure and stipulate fixed terms of employment. A survey of eighteen ombudsmen revealed that ombudsmen have significant reportorial experience, are well-educated, professionally active, and did not apply but were sought out for the job by the newspapers' editors.[33] In the fall of 1990, the president of the organization of news ombudsmen placed the number of ombudsmen at U.S. newspapers at 31.[34] Since newspapers define the role differently, there may, in fact, be more than 31.[35]

Joseph Laitin, ombudsman for the *Washington Post*, reports that between March and June of 1986 he wrote "25,000 to 30,000 words, mostly of criticism, in the form of internal memos. These critiques covered about 300 separate items

---

31. Maureen Dowd, "A Writer for *The New Yorker* Says He Created Composites in Reports," *New York Times*, 19 June 1984, pp. 1, 5 Y.

32. Suraj Kapoor and Ralph Smith, "The Newspaper Ombudsman—A Progress Report," *Journalism Quarterly* 56 (Autumn 1979): 629.

33. Ibid., pp. 629–630.

34. *USA Today*, 6 September 1990, p. 2 B.

35. Mary J. Radford, "A Qualitative Study of the Ombudsman Position at *The Philadelphia Inquirer*," M.A. Thesis, Ohio University, places the number at 38.

Readers' Advocates

A survey of ombudsmen reveals that they instituted the following changes in their newspapers:

1. A regular location created for the corrections box
2. Ads for pornographic films eliminated
3. More headline room created to permit including important qualifiers
4. More local news placed out front in the edition appropriate to the territory
5. More attention paid to local group news and to local sports news
6. Addresses of witnesses to a crime no longer used
7. Continuing project adopted involving sending out clippings to principals in a story for them to check on articles' accuracy
8. Opinion polls checked more carefully for properly worded questions
9. Fairer coverage of racial controversies
10. Revision of tactics used in getting phone subscriptions to the paper.[8]

[8] Suraj Kapoor and Ralph Smith, "The Newspaper Ombudsman—A Progress Report," *Journalism Quarterly* 56 (Autumn 1979): 630.

---

and were distributed to the publisher and key editors." He added: "The protests I have dealt with in my internal memos range from matters of questionable taste, misleading headlines and alleged breaches of national security to charges of racism in, of all places, the Sunday comics."[36]

Inaccurate reporting has an impact on press credibility. According to a study, "Newspaper Credibility: Building Reader Trust," prepared by the polling company MORI Research Inc. of Minneapolis, people in the United States view newspapers with a mixture of faith and distrust. The study found that newspapers had high credibility with only 32 percent of the people polled, but in a somewhat contradictory finding, 84 percent said that they had some or great respect for newspapers, and 76 percent said they thought the "press helps keep public officials honest."[37]

News Analysis

Television reporting is less likely than print reporting to provide in-depth analysis, establish historical context, or probe for causes. And specialized print media are more likely than daily newspapers to deal in detail with complex stories. So, for example, the *National Thrift News* carried reports of the brewing savings and loan crisis long before that story surfaced in the large dailies.

Like print journalism, television news tries to present good stories. In these situations, television handled the breaking stories responsibly. However, the conventions of the medium make it difficult, if not impossible, for television news to

36. *Washington Post*, 26 June 1986, p. A 24.
37. Alex S. Jones, "Public Views Newspapers with Mixture of Faith and Mistrust, Poll Finds," *New York Times*, 13 April 1985, p. 8 Y.

analyze or probe the complex causes of events. When that kind of analysis appears, it is likely to be in print news.

Media Convergence

The impact of elite media outlets can also distort news coverage. For example, the sudden increase in media attention to drug use in the summer of 1986 was not merely a reflection of real world happenings. Although drug use steadily increased during the 1970s, among high school seniors and young adults it actually declined between 1981 and 1986. (Most of the decline was in usage of marijuana; cocaine use remained steady.)[38]

Using data from 43 Gallup polls reporting what Americans considered the "most important problem facing America today," Pamela Shoemaker, Wayne Wanta, and Dawn Leggett correlated public concern about drugs with fifteen years of drug coverage in three newspapers (*New York Times*, *Los Angeles Times*, and *Wall Street Journal*); on three networks (ABC, CBS, and NBC) and in three newsweeklies (*Time*, *Newsweek*, and *U.S. News & World Report*). Newspaper coverage, especially in the *New York Times* and the *Los Angeles Times*, turned out to be the best predictor of public opinion.[39]

In studying this issue, researchers developed the concept of intermedia "convergence" to describe "a process whereby the media discover issues and respond to each other in a cycle of peaking coverage." Convergence occurs most frequently when elite media discover the issue or when the story comes from the nation's capital, especially if an issue is stressed by national leaders such as the president.[40]

Unbalanced Interpretation

■

For years, media scholars have studied the discrepancies between events as experienced live and events as presented on television. In 1953, Gladys Engel Lang and Kurt Lang, for example, contrasted the Douglas MacArthur Day Parade as experienced by observers on the streets of Chicago with the parade as experienced via television.[41] Television dramatized the parade and exaggerated crowd responses, perhaps because television had created expectations for what the parade would be like.

The discrepancies persist. In July of 1986, seventy-four evening news segments on drugs were broadcast by the three major news networks. Half of these dealt with use of crack. In the fall of that year, CBS earned the highest Nielsen ratings of any comparable show in five years by reaching 15 million viewers—the

---

38. Peter Kerr, *New York Times*, 17 November 1986, pp. 1, 12.

39. "Drug Coverage and Public Opinion, 1972–1986," in *Communication Campaigns About Drugs: Government, Media, and the Public*, ed. Pamela J. Shoemaker (Hillsdale, N.J.: Lawrence Erlbaum, 1989), pp. 67–80.

40. Lucig H. Danielian and Stephen D. Reese, "A Closer Look at Intermedia Influences on Agenda Setting: The Cocaine Issue of 1986," in Shoemaker, pp. 57–58.

41. Gladys Engel Lang and Kurt Lang, "MacArthur Day in Chicago," in Lang and Lang, *Politics and Television* (Chicago: Quadrangle Books, 1968), pp. 36–77.

title of the documentary: "48 Hours on Crack Street." Yet, as sociologists Craig Reinarman and Henry Levine noted in 1989: "For every one cocaine-related death in the U.S. in 1987, there were approximately 300 tobacco-related deaths and 100 alcohol-related deaths."

How then does one account for the fact that in the seven months prior to the 1986 elections, over fifteen hours of airtime and over 1,000 print stories on crack flooded across the United States? Analysts concluded that "the issue conveniently served the interests of the media and politicians because it was dramatic, it afforded many opportunities for political posturing, and it reinforced stereotypes that minority groups (scapegoats) engage in deviant activities because they are fundamentally weak, uneducated, or immoral."[42]

Insinuation

On May 6, 1990, *Washington Post* ombudsman Richard Harwood wrote that his paper's "shabby" coverage of an April 28 pro-life rally in the nation's capitol "has left a blot on this paper's professional reputation." The paper had extensively covered a pro-choice rally of approximately 125,000 the previous year. The pro-life rally of 200,000 (the crowd numbers are police estimates) was given only two short articles. The dozens of stories on the pro-choice rally had featured charts and maps and appeared on page one. The pro-life rally received no comparable attention. How did the *Post* account for the lapse? Staffers were aware of one rally and not the other. Wrote Harwood of Managing Editor Leonard Downie, "Journalists here, he [Downie] thinks, not only are not part of the anti-abortion movement but don't know anyone who is." The conservative Center for Media and Public Affairs provided another possible explanation. Stories filed in the *New York Times* and the *Washington Post* by female reporters quoted nearly three times more pro-choice sources than pro-life ones.

Following the *Post*'s lead, David Shaw of the *Los Angeles Times* wrote a four-part series arguing that Harwood was correct. Shaw's series pointed out that protestors are frequently described as militant or asked by television producers to "look angry" to fit the stereotypes of sound bites.

The controversy also prompted an analysis of the biases of language. *U.S. News & World Report*'s John Leo wrote:

> About a year ago, I noticed that one of our major metropolitan newspapers had taken to using "abortion provider" as a neutral term in reporting the abortion debate. It is not neutral. "Abortion practitioner" and "doctor who performs abortions" are neutral terms. "Provider," with its overtones of nurturance and protection, is a one-word argument in favor of abortion, just as "abortionist" with its overtones of back-alley sleaze, is a polemic against it.[43]

(As noted in a later chapter, all language choices are selective.)

Unbalanced interpretations also result from quite subtle inequalities in press treatment. Coverage of the 1984 presidential campaign mentioned Democratic

42. Charles T. Salmon, "God Understands When the Cause Is Noble," *Gannett Center Journal* (Spring 1990): 26.

43. "Is the Press Straight on Abortion?" *U.S. News & World Report*, 16 July 1990, p. 17.

vice-presidential nominee Geraldine Ferraro's dress size but not nominee Walter Mondale's suit size; and in 1988 Barbara Bush was characterized as "grandmotherly," but George Bush was not described as grandfatherly and her white hair was noted, but his graying hair was not.

Senator Nancy Landon Kassebaum (R-Kan.), is also bothered by the way women politicians are described in the media. "Some day I'm going to hit someone over the head for calling me diminutive and soft-spoken."[44] Such insinuations may reflect prejudices in the society. Newsworthy women tend to be identified by their clothing, degree of attractiveness, size, and whether or not they are married and have children, whereas newsworthy men are not. Similarly, African-Americans are more likely than whites to be identified by race. Sensitive to charges by women's rights and civil rights groups, editors have changed these practices in recent years.

In these cases, unbalanced interpretations result from insinuations, from the choice of language, and from the ways in which stories are routinely covered. But a case can be made that news coverage is unbalanced precisely because it develops certain themes and perspectives and suppresses others.

Ideological Bias

The most controversial claims about distortions in news coverage are made by some contemporary sociologists and researchers who have studied the mass media intensively. They do not argue that there is a conspiracy or willful distortion in reporting and coverage. Instead, they argue that however unintentionally, press coverage is ideological, that it reflects the interests of some groups and classes and not others, that it conceals the interrelationship between the public and the private sector, and that, in the words of *New York Times* columnist Tom Wicker, "objective journalism always favors Establishment positions and exists not least to avoid offense of them."[45]

Without a laborious reconstruction of the social and political theory underlying these claims, one example may explain this. The author is the former British journalist Henry Fairlie:

> A few years ago I attended one of these pompous week-long seminars at the Aspen Institute to discuss "investigative reporting" with a number of celebrated American editors and newspapermen. I made my point that there was an economic system that needed inquiry, and at last burst out against the imperviousness of my American colleagues by saying that I would write without payment for them a series of articles to be entitled, "I Have an Enemy at Chase Manhattan." But there were no takers; and Walter Ridder, the owner of Ridder newspapers, made a very funny speech on the final morning of the seminar, saying that he had tossed and turned all night "wondering why we don't do what Henry asks, and attack the capitalists," and that as dawn had broken across the Rockies he had found the answer: "Because I am one of them."[46]

44. Bella Abzug, *Gender Gap* (Boston: Houghton Mifflin, 1984), p. 171.
45. Wicker, *On Press*, pp. 36–37.
46. Henry Fairlie, "Profit Without Honor," *The New Republic*, 7 May 1977, pp. 17–18.

The conclusions of researchers are remarkably similar. Erik Barnouw, a distinguished media historian, contends that commercial sponsors control all facets of television content from advertising itself to news and cultural programming on so-called public broadcasting.[47] Mark Fishman argues that the journalist's view of society is bureaucratically structured and, by definition, bureaucracies reflect the establishment—government and private corporations.[48] The Glasgow University Media Group documents a bias in favor of the powerful. Michael Schudson, a social historian, argues "that the process of news gathering itself constructs an image of reality which reinforces official viewpoints."[49] Gaye Tuchman not only contends that the news reflects the interests of those in power, but also that the news limits our knowledge of our own society.[50]

If these researchers and analysts are correct, news coverage will be informed by certain perspectives with ideological significance. First, and most important, we should expect the news to tell us repeatedly that "the system works," a major theme, for example, of Watergate coverage or of the Iran–Contra arms scandal. There is evidence of such a perspective in newsgathering. For instance, newscasts underscore the legitimacy of the three branches of government by treating each as an identifiable entity engaged in proposing and disposing, as in the phrase "the Congress today . . ."

In addition, television routinely covers the rituals of government, such as swearing-in ceremonies, inaugurals, welcoming addresses, and press conferences, that reinforce our sense of governmental process. One study quantifies the extent to which network news legitimizes existing governmental institutions in a finding that 50 percent of total network news coverage of domestic events from June 1973 to July 1975 pertained to Washington, D.C. Washington's domination of the news was enhanced by the tendency to seek Washington reactions to stories originating in other parts of the country.[51]

We are told not only that the system works, but that those who disrupt it in strikes or social protest are wrong or deviant—a bias that will always favor the status quo over change. Coverage of the problems of the homeless is illustrative. Studies have found that the homeless are consistently portrayed as psychotic, disordered, and not like us. This perspective carries the corollary that "we could not be like them." As one sociologist explains:

> The notion that the homeless are largely psychotics who belong in institutions, rather than victims of displacement at the hands of enterprising realtors, spares us from the need to offer realistic solutions to the fact of deep and widening

---

47. Erik Barnouw, *The Sponsor: Notes on a Modern Potentate* (New York: Oxford, 1978).

48. Mark Fishman, *Manufacturing the News* (Austin: University of Texas Press, 1980).

49. Michael Schudson, *Discovering the News: A Social History of American Newspapers* (New York: Basic Books, 1978), p. 185.

50. Tuchman, *Making News*, p. 210; elsewhere she writes of "television programming that reflects and reinforces the economic and socio-political structure of the United States" ["Introduction," *The TV Establishment: Programming for Power and Profit*, ed. Gaye Tuchman (Englewood Cliffs, N.J.: Prentice-Hall–Spectrum, 1974), p. 6].

51. Joseph Dominick, "Geographical Bias in National TV News," *Journal of Communication* 27 (Autumn 1977): 94–99.

Media Coverage Influences Foreign Policy

On August 21, 1983, opposition leader Benigno Aquino was assassinated as he arrived in Manila by plane from the United States. This dramatic, violent, public event focused media and public attention on political events in the Philippines, an important site for the United States because the Philippines had been a U.S. colony and because U.S. naval and air force bases are there.

As pressure grew on Ferdinand Marcos, the Philippine president, on November 3, 1985, he announced on U.S. television that an election would be held in mid-January 1986 and invited U.S. poll watchers to verify the fairness of the election. This second event, the announced election and campaign, a contest between Marcos and widow Corazon Aquino, to be refereed by Americans, heightened U.S. public and media interest.

Prior to these events, there had been little coverage of events there. The major U.S. networks' evening news programs had devoted fewer than three stories per year to the Philippines earlier, but one survey of the four weeks following Marcos's election announcement charted 180 minutes of coverage. "The Western media simply seized the Philippine election campaign and carried it for days at a time—with the full cooperation of both candidates."[h]

The election became headline news in newspapers, NBC and ABC anchored their evening news programs from the Philippines, and CBS sent its entire election polling team. Television cameras showed Marcos's thugs intimidating poll watchers, stealing ballots, and murdering opposition campaign workers. It was the sort of human story that viewers could appreciate: a story of unlikely heroes who formed human barricades against Marcos's soldiers and included nuns who knelt in front of tanks and recited the rosary and girls who offered flowers to soldiers—a kind of "fairy tale revolution" with a "fairy-tale heroine" [Corazon Aquino] and a happy ending.[i]

In a Gallup poll in March, 76 percent of Americans said they had followed the dramatic events of February 1986 in the Philippines very or fairly closely.[j]

Although the Reagan administration continued to support Marcos, Americans were so aware of what was occurring that, as one commentator concluded, "Reagan lost much of the latitude a President has to fashion foreign policy."[k]

[h] Bryan Johnson, *The Four Days of Courage: The Untold Story of the People Who Brought Marcos Down* (New York: Free Press, 1987), pp. 91, 92.
[i] Pico Iyer, "Woman of the Year: Cory," *Time*, 4 January 1987, p. 19.
[j] *The Gallup Report*, March 1986, 246 (Princeton, N.J.: Gallup Poll, 1986), p. 16.
[k] Stewart Powell, "Playing to the TV Cameras," *U.S. News & World Report*, 10 March 1986, p. 33.

---

extremes of wealth and poverty in the United States. It also enables us to tell ourselves that the despair of homeless people bears no intimate connection to the privileged existence we enjoy—when, for example, we rent or purchase one of those restored townhouses that once provided shelter for people now huddled in the street.[52]

52. J. Kozol, "Distancing the Homeless," *The Yale Review* 77 (1986): 154–155.

The difficulty with the view that the homeless are psychotic is that it doesn't comport with what surveys tell us about that population. "[M]ost current studies consider the mentally ill to account only for 20 to 25 percent of the total homeless population, with some estimates as low as 16 percent."[53]

Some researchers argue that news coverage systematically supports the powers that be. We have summarized their conclusions and some of the supporting evidence, but the argument also claims there is systematic self-censorship within the media, a form of internal regulation that denies the audience access to certain types of information and that mirrors the tastes of mass audiences and advertisers.

Self-Censorship

In the face of almost nightly reports of high oil company profits in 1980, Mobil sponsored an ad arguing that the profits of the networks exceeded the profits of the oil industry. All three networks refused to air it. This sort of censorship of material about media issues accompanies the self-censoring suppression of coverage of media issues on newscasts.[54] In fact, corporate struggles to air advocacy advertising on television confront the most pervasive form of self-censorship in the medium.[55]

The Fairness Doctrine   In 1987, the Federal Communications Commission repealed the forty-year-old Fairness Doctrine on the grounds that it was no longer needed. In an era in which there were numerous voices in broadcasting, the public interest no longer required the doctrine, argued the Reagan-appointed commissioners. A federal appeals court subsequently ruled that the FCC had the right to eliminate the doctrine. In 1988, the Congress wrote the doctrine back into law. Reagan vetoed it. President Bush has indicated that he will do the same.

The Fairness Doctrine required radio and television stations to air material on issues of public concern and to air opposing views. If opposing views were not broadcast, a person representing the ignored view could request response time.

Beats   Self-censorship also occurs as a result of the relationship between reporters and the sources who provide information on their beats. A symbiotic relationship develops between reporters and sources on a beat, with the result that stories having political implications may be suppressed. Reporters "can make news out of inside information that aids an agency in its competition with other agencies or helps it get its message into the White House, but they cannot so easily propose stories which can hurt the agency. Consequently, beat reporters must

53. Richard Campbell and Jimmie L. Reves, "Covering the Homeless: The Joyce Brown Story," *Critical Studies in Mass Communication* 6 (1989): 22.

54. Thomas R. Lindlof and William R. Canning, "Network News Coverage of the Broadcast Media," *Journalism Quarterly* 57 (Summer 1980): 333–338.

55. For information on issue or advocacy advertising by large corporations, see S. Prakash Sethi, *Up Against the Corporate Wall: Modern Corporations and Social Issues of the Seventies* (Englewood Cliffs, N.J.: Prentice-Hall, 1971) and *Advocacy Advertising and Large Corporations* (Lexington, Mass.: Lexington Books, 1977). In 1981, ABC accepted some issue advertising on "Nightline" on an experimental basis.

often practice self-censorship, keeping their most sensational stories to themselves in order to protect their beat." [56]

Reporter Seymour Hersh won a Pulitzer Prize in 1970 for his stories on the My Lai massacre. When he was asked to account for why editors missed one of the biggest stories of the year, he responded: "I honestly believe that a major problem in newspapers today is not censorship on the part of editors and publishers, but something more odious: self-censorship by the reporters." [57] Since Hersh was only able to write the story with the help of Army sources who leaked crucial information, it is possible that reporters who had to maintain good relations with Army sources felt unable to write this damaging story.

Government Support   Some self-censorship involves a predisposition to support the government line. For example, the press accepted the White House explanation that the U-2 shot down over Russia in 1959 was really a weather plane and later accepted the Johnson Administration's claim that a U.S. ship had been attacked in the Gulf of Tonkin. In both instances, administration officials were lying.

The press is particularly vulnerable to government claims that revealing certain information would not be in the national interest. As former White House correspondent David Wise explains, "When the flag is attacked, or reporters are told it has been attacked, their reaction is not likely to be very different from that of any other citizen. Besides, it is vaguely unpatriotic to dispute the official version of events." [58]

Even unusual opportunities for newsgathering may be rejected on such grounds. As media historian Michael Schudson reports, "In 1956 American newspapers refused a Chinese government invitation to send correspondents to China because, as *New York Times* editor Clifton Daniel recalled, 'We did not want to embarrass our government.'" [59] Stories from China at that time would have been highly newsworthy, but this was the height of the Cold War.

The 1986 trial of a government worker charged with spying illustrates the ways in which government encourages self-censorship by the media. Ronald Pelton worked on a computer job at the National Security Agency for fourteen years. His job gave him access to secret government information. After Pelton left NSA in 1979, he began selling secrets to the Russians. He was caught and brought to trial in 1986.

Then-CIA director William Casey was alarmed to hear on NBC's "Today" show that the spy had apparently given "away one of the NSA's most sensitive secrets—a project with the code name Ivy Bells, believed to be a top-secret underwater eavesdropping operation by American submarines inside Soviet harbors."

---

56. Herbert Gans, *Deciding What's News: A Study of CBS Evening News, NBC Evening News, Newsweek, and* Time (New York: Pantheon, 1979), p. 133.

57. Seymour Hersh, "The Story Everyone Ignored," *Columbia Journalism Review* 8 (Winter 1969–1970): 55.

58. David Wise, *The Politics of Lying* (New York: Random House, 1973), p. 311. See also David Halberstam, "A Letter to My Daughter," *Parade*, 2 May 1982, pp. 4–7.

59. Schudson, *Discovering the News*, p. 173.

Casey asked the Justice Department to consider prosecuting NBC under Section 798 of Title 18 of the U.S. Code, which forbids the revelation of classified information about secret codes and other communications intelligence. Meanwhile the *Washington Post* began its own coverage of the trial.

The *Post*'s coverage was the product of self-censorship. Casey had met with the editors of the *Post* to warn of possible prosecution. The meeting resulted in delaying a major article. President Ronald Reagan called Katherine Graham of the *Post* to stress the sensitive nature of the trial and to warn that he would back prosecution of the *Post* if the material Pelton had transmitted to the Soviets was revealed. The *Post* responded by withholding the controversial details. *Post* editor Benjamin Bradlee explained that the paper had been "unable fully to judge the validity of the national security objections of senior officials." He added "In my heart, I think the Russians already know what we kept out of the story. But I'm not absolutely sure."[60]

Support for government policies can emerge in more subtle forms. For example, during the crisis that followed Iraq's invasion of Kuwait and the deployment of U.S. troops in Saudi Arabia, some commentators pointed out that far more of those interviewed by journalists supported the government's policy than raised questions about its rationales or costs. For example, on August 21, 1990, Ted Koppel's primary guest on "Nightline" was Undersecretary of Defense Paul Wolfowitz, who was followed by John Lehman, secretary of the Navy in the Reagan administration, and Edward Luttwak, a military analyst. After describing the discussion that followed, which ignored Iraq's insistence that it has a historic claim to Kuwait—a nation created by the British as its protectorate—and which touted U.S. military strength and described Iraqi leader Saddam Hussein as insane, television analyst Noel Holston commented:

> What happened, or didn't happen, on "Nightline" is a perfect example of what watchdog groups such as Fairness and Accuracy in Reporting (FAIR) have complained about for years. On TV news and issue programs, debate and discussion too often begin at an official level where the range of options has already been decided. And they stay within narrow parameters because journalists such as Koppel allow it. They shouldn't, however, even if they run the risk of alienating their sources or some members of their audience by asking hard questions and appearing skeptical or unpatriotic (as if asking elected public officials to be forthright and accountable is unpatriotic).[61]

Holston was referring to a report released early in 1989 in which FAIR alleged a bias on ABC's "Nightline" based on who was and who was not invited as an expert participant on the central 20-minute discussion each night. As reported by its executive director Jeff Cohen, FAIR studied 865 programs with 2,498 guests and concluded that one's likelihood of appearing as a guest was enhanced by being a white male member of conservative government, military, or corporate elites. "Nightline" spokespersons responded that conservatives dominated the

60. *Time*, 2 June 1986, p. 67.
61. Noel Holston, "TV Ducking the Hard Questions on Mideast," *Star Tribune*, 24 August 1990, p. 7 E.

guest list because they have been in power lately, and that if a liberal administration were elected, the bias would shift in the other direction, a defense that FAIR saw as self-incriminating because it presented the news program as a forum for those currently in power.[62]

In some cases, journalists also are hampered by formal forms of governmental censorship. The examination reports of bank regulators, for example, are not available under the Freedom of Information Act because Congress fears that making such data available to the press and public could cause runs on banks. The inaccessibility of such data made it more difficult for reporters to document the existence of banks whose loans were undercapitalized. This made the early stages of the savings and loan crisis was more difficult to cover.

Journalistic self-censorship can reflect audience tastes as well as prevailing political views.

Audience Taste   The success of recent efforts by the Coalition for Better Television and the Moral Majority to pressure advertisers and the networks to eliminate sex and violence from television programming reflects the desire of television not to offend audience tastes. (See Chapter 9 for more extended treatment of how groups and individuals can influence the media.) The pressure of the audience is illustrated by coverage of racial matters. Paul Good argues that "television found it both spiritually rewarding and financially profitable to cover racism *so long as it was treated as a southern, not a national phenomenon.*"[63] His statement shows that the civil rights confrontations of the 1960s were dramatic and exciting news that, when confined to the South, were not perceived as an attack on the system.

However, some contend that current coverage of racism, or lack of it, reflects a desire to avoid offending the white-majority audience. Media analyst Edwin Diamond describes the conditions of African-Americans as "a story that many white Americans in the audience may not want to dwell upon too long, out of fear, or doubt, or guilt, or a combination of largely unexamined emotions."[64]

The same pattern occurred in network coverage of gay rights. Once the identified audience was demonstrated to be large enough to have economic clout, networks began to respond to its sensitivities. So, for example, on February 8, 1990, CBS News suspended "60 Minutes" commentator Andy Rooney for three months without pay. The action followed complaints by the 10,000-member Gay and Lesbian Alliance Against Defamation. The alliance charged that in his syndicated columns, on air, and in a letter to the *Advocate*, a gay rights publication, Rooney had made insensitive remarks about gays. But after suspending Rooney, counterpressures arose from viewers and columnists. Under the counterpressure, CBS reduced the suspension from three months to three weeks.[65]

62. Jeff Cohen, "ABC's 'Nightline' Serves as a Soapbox for Conservative Elite," *Star Tribune*, 28 February 1989, p. 11 A.

63. Good, "Network News," p. 5.

64. Edwin Diamond, "Miami Riots: Did TV Get the Real Story?" *TV Guide*, 30 August 1980, p. 20.

65. Jeremy Gerard, "Hurting Words, Fighting Words," *Columbia Journalism Review* (July/August 1990): 25.

It is, of course, very difficult to demonstrate the existence of self-censorship because much of the evidence involves the absence or omission of coverage. In addition, much of the evidence will be anecdotal reports of examples from which it is difficult to generalize. Nevertheless, as we indicate, there are powerful pressures for self-censorship and some evidence that news coverage is responsive to them.

Direct Intervention

In this final section, we detail the most extreme examples of persuasion by the news media, which involve direct intervention by journalists in news events. With few exceptions, they reflect audience acceptance of journalistic participation in the events that are covered.

Breaches of Neutrality

One of the more outrageous examples of direct journalistic intervention was reported in a series of articles in the *Toronto Globe*. As other news sources have verified, a 1981 invasion of the Caribbean island of Dominica was planned by American and Canadian mercenaries and members of the Ku Klux Klan and neo-Nazi groups. According to the *Globe*'s investigative reporter Peter Moon, "details of the operation had been known for months by the Toronto radio station CFTR, which had taped interviews with participants and planned to be on the island for the invasion. The articles quoted Robert Halliday, CFTR's news director, as saying, 'If we'd gone to the police, we'd have had to work alongside them, and then we wouldn't have had the story.'"[66]

The viewing public is not prepared to accept such breaches of journalistic neutrality in the effort to get a good story. However, viewers are prepared to tolerate considerable intervention when they approve of the goals the journalist is promoting.

Producing Social Change

In recent decades, we have witnessed instances in which reporters were instrumental in producing social change. Bob Woodward and Carl Bernstein of the *Washington Post* uncovered many of the abuses that ultimately led to the resignation of President Richard Nixon, for example.

But not all influential investigative reporting is done by major newspapers or the networks. Lea Thompson, a consumer reporter for the Washington, D.C., affiliate of NBC, WRC-TV, was responsible for legislation mandating standards for infant formulas. Two infant formulas, Mul-Soy and Cho-Free, were missing a necessary dietary supplement, so infants fed this formula became seriously ill. The Food and Drug Administration recalled these formulas, but Thompson discovered that they were still stocked in Washington area stores.

66. Andrew H. Malcolm, "Toronto Paper Recounts Intrigue to Invade Dominica," *New York Times*, 17 May 1981, p. A 4.

From October 1979 to March 1980, WRC pursued the story, which was eventually carried on "NBC Nightly News" (access was made easier by WRC's status as an NBC affiliate). Members of Congress and President Carter thanked Thompson for bringing the need for stricter standards for infant formula production to the attention of Congress, and Thompson was an invited guest at the ceremony at which Carter signed the standards bill into law.

In summer 1990, news coverage was responsible for action by law enforcement agencies against puppy farms. After the television shows "20/20" and "Geraldo" broadcast indictments of the pet-breeding industry, and the Humane Society of the United States called for a national boycott of puppies bred in six midwestern states, enforcement agents in those states began cracking down. The Kansas attorney general led a raid on a Topeka kennel, seized ninety dogs, and charged their breeders with cruelty to animals. Local newspapers took up the call. "Puppy breeding should be an ideal industry for Kansas," said the Wichita *Eagle*. "This state's image for Midwestern wholesomeness could be an invaluable marketing tool. Imagine the lines at pet stores in California and other states for puppies 'raised where Toto comes from.'"[67]

Journalists as Direct Participants

In some instances, journalists have become direct participants, not merely participant-observers, in news stories. It was Walter Cronkite, for example, not a State Department official, who made Premier Anwar Sadat's trip to Israel in 1977 possible.

On September 6, 1990, CBS News moved explicitly into an advocacy posture in a 2-hour prime-time documentary titled "America's Toughest Assignment," a report on U.S. education. The program was complemented that week by special segments on all of CBS's regular news broadcasts including "Sunday Morning," "60 Minutes," "CBS This Morning," and "The CBS Evening News with Dan Rather." On September 6, at 11:30 P.M. (EST), a live 1-hour national exchange among parents, teachers, and education experts was aired. Said CBS correspondent Charles Kuralt, the documentary's anchor, "We're actually going to be advocates for certain changes. We are going to tell America what needs to be done."[68] The proposed changes were rooted in the recommendations of Dr. Ernest Boyer, president of the Carnegie Foundation for the Advancement of Teaching and an adviser to CBS News's Project Education. The proposals included transforming kindergarten through fourth grade into a concentrated four-year program focused on basic reading, writing, and math skills.

Neither the CBS educational initiative nor Cronkite's efforts to mediate in the Middle East drew criticism because both were consistent with bipartisan national goals and with ends approved by the U.S. public. Who, after all, opposes peace or excellence in education?

---

67. "Dogs from 'Puppy Mills' Jam Midwestern Shelters," *Philadelphia Inquirer*, 31 July 1990, p. 6 A.

68. Diane Mermigas, "CBS News Takes on 'Project Education,'" *Electronic Media*, 16 July 1990, p. 16.

Terrorism and the Press

Terrorists almost always seek publicity, and to that end they try to use the press. Do they succeed?

All told, Gallup asked a national sample of Americans thirty-three questions about their views of press coverage of terrorism. Here's how they responded.

Ambivalence about Terrorist Coverage Generally

% National Sample Who Think:

Press coverage of terrorists:
serves public interest: 65%
harms it: 23%

Press coverage of terrorists is:
very/mostly satisfactory: 61%
very/mostly unsatisfactory: 37%

Press gives terrorists:
too much coverage: 51%
too little: 7%
right amount: 40%

Very likely terrorist acts would occur regardless:
agree: 28%
fairly likely: 39%
not too likely: 24%

Good or excellent coverage:
television: 75%
print: 74%

Press coverage effect on sympathy for terrorist cause:
increases: 29%
reduces: 14%
no effect: 48%

Press coverage effect on chances of future terrorist acts:
increases: 60%
reduces: 7%
no effect: 21%

Press coverage effect on hostages' time in captivity:
increases: 44%
reduces: 13%
no effect: 27%

Press coverage effect on hostages' safety:
more safe: 33%
less safe: 25%
no effect: 28%

When asked why the press sometimes doesn't cover terrorist incidents well, 52 percent said that terrorists' ability to manipulate the press was a major factor.[1]

[1]Adapted from *The People and the Press* (Los Angeles: Times Mirror, 1986).

When their actions are not in agreement with such broad public and political consensus, journalists are criticized for becoming advocates. During coverage of the TWA hostage crisis in Lebanon, Dan Rather's pointed on-air questioning of Nabih Berri, the Islamic leader ostensibly trying to negotiate release of the hostages, prompted criticism that Rather had crossed the dividing line between journalism and personal diplomacy.

Journalists also draw criticism when they appear to be channels of propaganda for those whose views are widely condemned by the public and the politicians in the United States. "Checkbook journalism," the practice of paying for an interview, is frowned on by most reputable news organizations. In the spring of 1986, a related practice generated controversy in the news community. On May 5, "NBC Nightly News" featured an interview with Mohammed Abul Abbas, the terrorist suspected of planning the hijacking of the cruise ship *Achille Lauro* in October 1985. During that hijacking, a wheelchair-ridden American, Leon Klinghoffer, was killed and his body dumped overboard. Abbas had offered NBC an exclusive interview with the condition that the correspondent and crew not identify the location of the interview. During the meeting, Abbas stated that the United States was now the target of his efforts because "America is now conducting the war against us on behalf of Israel."

Intervention by the media becomes even more controversial when the media intervention benefits one person but, in the process, harms another. When officials at the Loma Linda University Medical Center refused to consider an infant for a heart transplant on the grounds that his unwed parents could not provide adequate postoperative care, the couple took their case to the media. "Baby Jesse" appeared in stories on the three major networks and in the nation's newspapers. While the couple was being interviewed on "Donahue," a Michigan couple, whose son was brain dead at birth, agreed to donate their infant's heart to Jesse, whose story they had seen on television.

What the television coverage failed to reveal was that another infant had been waiting even longer for a heart transplant. But his parents had worked quietly through organ procurement channels instead of turning to the press for sympathy and help. After learning that Jesse had received the heart, the disappointed couple appealed through the media to Congress to "do everything possible to see that an improved system is set up to identify donors of organs." They added, "it almost seems like publicity is the only method that's working." *Time* magazine commented: "Another ethical issue was brought to light by the baby Jesse case: the growing role of the media in determining who gets organs."[69]

TO SUM UP

All news coverage shapes events. In this chapter we have examined elements of news presentation that not only shape but sensationalize, distort, modify, and create events.

69. *Time*, 23 June 1986, p. 68.

Media technology is used to dramatize and sensationalize news stories and to increase the authority and credibility of anchorpersons and correspondents. The pressures of deadlines, competition, and breaking news, along with the structure of news stories, all contribute to inaccurate and incomplete reporting. News coverage becomes persuasion when language is used to create insinuations, when news coverage supports or opposes governmental policies, and when self-censorship suppresses certain kinds of news stories. Finally, on occasion newspeople become participants in the events they are covering. Such direct intervention is accepted by viewers and readers when it supports widely approved goals but rejected when reporters' actions are controversial.

In all these instances, the news media influence us, not simply by selecting what events they will cover, but by deciding how these events should be treated and interpreted. In the next chapter, we examine countervailing forces that, in turn, influence the news media.

Analysis

Analyzing a News Item

Our analysis of news has illustrated principles with historical examples. Here we include questions that can be used to analyze a current news item.

Newsworthiness

Why was it considered newsworthy? To what event, if any, was it tied? Were drama, conflict, or violence incorporated into it? Was it personalized? Was it an extension of a continuing issue? Does it incorporate novelty, deviance?

How was its newsworthiness established in the report? Did it affect large numbers? A wide area? A celebrity? Did it have important consequences?

Was this a local, state, regional, or national story? What determined whether it would be reported in local, state, regional, or national media?

Did this story lend itself to coverage by one medium and not others, for example, a ballet on television but not on radio? If so, why?

Did the story appear in one newspaper or many? If it appeared in many, was the source of the story the same or different in different newspapers? (Did all carry AP? UPI? *New York Times* Syndicate? Or did some carry one and some another?) Did any of the accounts combine sources of information (a story based on AP and UPI accounts, for example)? If there were differences, were they significant, and, if so, how do you account for them? (Local angle on national story? Reaction to story event from prominent local person? Informed by different political points of view?) Did the story appear on any of the network newscasts? If it appeared on some but not others, how do you account for that? How did the reports on different networks differ from each other? If it appeared in some media and not others, how do you account for that? How did national coverage differ from local coverage?

What was the angle on the story? What other angles could have been chosen? How would the story have changed if it were framed by each of these other angles? Was the story pegged to some other event? If so, what, how, and why? How newsworthy was this other event? What other pegs could have been used (piggybacking)? If another peg had been used, how would the story have changed?

Reporter

Who reported the story? Was the person given a byline? If not, why not? Why did this reporter, not another, cover this story? (Regular beat? Special expertise? Special interest in this topic?) What are the stylistic, structural, evidentiary, and substantive predispositions of this reporter? If the story had been reported by some other specific reporter, say Lesley Stahl rather than Bruce Morton of CBS News, how would the story have differed, if at all? How did the reporter establish her/his credibility? What devices, if any, were used to suggest the reporter's "objectivity"?

The News Story

What sorts of claims were made in the story? What sort of evidence was marshaled to support the claims? Was the evidence accurate? Did the evidence warrant the claims? How was the evidence made credible? Was the source of the evidence identified? (A highly placed source?) If not, who do you think the source was? Were eye witnesses used? Were they interviewed willingly? Did the interviews seem to be an invasion of their privacy? Was expert testimony used? If so, was the authority quoted, paraphrased, or interviewed? What determined whether the authority was quoted, paraphrased, or interviewed? Why was this authority selected rather than some other? How was the credibility of the authority established? If the story was covered on television, did the authority look credible? Sound credible? Were other authorities cited? If so, what was the relationship among the authorities (pro–con; accusation–defense)?

Was a concrete example used? Were statistics used? Were governmental sources used? If so, how and why?

If the story involves an interview, what is the relationship between the reporter and the person interviewed (friendly, hostile, distant)? Were the questions asked by the reporter included in the story? If not, could you determine what the questions were from the answers? If the reporter paraphrased the questions, did the paraphrases seem consistent with the answers? Did the person interviewed seem to be facilitating coverage of the story or attempting to limit coverage? Was access to the person interviewed limited in any way? Were questions submitted in advance? Were some topics off limits? Did the reporter agree to print or air certain parts of the interview in exchange for it? Did anyone refuse to be interviewed for this story? If so, was that fact reported? How? Was the impression created that the person who refused was guilty of something? Hiding something?

Was the event reported a pseudo-event? If so, did it accomplish the purposes of the persons who staged it? If so, did the reporter note that it was a pseudo-event?

Was the story part of a series? If so, what was its function as part of the series?

Constraints

Did persons outside the media shape or try to shape the story? If so, why did they succeed or fail?

How did constraints in the media shape the story? Were media deadlines used strategically? Could the event be filmed or photographed? What were the costs of coverage? How did limitations of time and space affect coverage? How could these constraints have been overcome? (What would you have had to have argued to claim an exception?)

Did the elite media set the agenda for this story? If so, when and how? How was coverage by the elite media reflected in the story?

Framing

How was the news item introduced? (Headline? Prefatory statement by reporter or anchorperson?) What expectations did the introduction create about the story?

What other introduction could appropriately have been used? How would other introductions have reframed the report? Was there a summary statement at the end of the report? What interpretation, if any, did it impose on the report?

What values does the story support? (Problems can be solved? The system works? Legitimate authorities should solve problems? Hard work pays off? Our system of government is the best?)

Inclusion/Exclusion

What of importance about the story is not reported? Why? Were apparently trivial pieces of information included in the story? If so, why?

Setting

Where was the report situated? (Dateline London? On location in Newark?) Is the setting readily accessible to the news outlet? How costly is it to cover and, if television, send a camera crew? How did cost affect likelihood of coverage? Was the reporter actually at the scene of the event reported? If so, is that fact established in the story? If so, how? If not, is that fact evident in the report? If not, what is the reporter's source of firsthand information? Is the setting used to make the report more credible (televised report about politics from the steps of the Capitol)? How, if at all, did the setting serve to dramatize the story?

Timing

When (what time of day) did the reported event occur? Did the time of occurrence mean that it was reported by some media and not others? Was the event deliberately timed to maximize or minimize coverage? On what day of the week did the event occur? Did occurrence on that day increase the likelihood that the event would be covered (slow news day), decrease the likelihood that it would be covered, or not make much difference? Did the event occur at a time of year in which there is little competition for access to the news? (4th of July weekend? post-Christmas, pre-New Year's? Thanksgiving weekend?)

If the event was not reported in a brief span of time, would it have lost its news value (for example, a presidential press conference), or could the story be stored for another day if it couldn't be fit into today's broadcast or paper (for example, a report on some ongoing struggle)?

Placement

Was it treated as hard news or soft news? Could it have been transformed from hard to soft, or soft to hard? If so, how? Where was it placed in the news broadcast, newspaper, or newsmagazine? What items were placed in a more prominent space or time? What accounts for the placement of this item in relation to other items? How much space or time was this report allotted? Was that more or less than the other reports? Account for the differences. What sorts of news stories would bump this story from the lineup?

Patterns

Are authorities appearing on this broadcast familiar faces? Have they served as authorities on this channel before? Often? If so, why? What is the apparent bias of the authority, if any? Is the authority identified as being partisan? If so, is another point of view represented? What are the similarities among authorities used in this type of media outlet? How often and in what kinds of stories do women function as authorities? African-Americans? Hispanics? Older persons? How often are professors used as authorities? With what schools are they associated? Are the schools located near the media outlet? Are they Ivy League schools? Are authorities from regions of the country other than that in which the media outlet is located represented?

Who is likely to cover what kind of story? Are female reporters more likely to be assigned to cover the women's movement? Wives of candidates? Socially significant weddings (Prince Charles's or Caroline Kennedy's)? When do African-Americans, Hispanics, and older reporters appear? Are stories about some foreign countries more likely to appear than stories about other foreign countries?

Manipulation

Did those outside the media capitalize on any pre-existing patterns to manipulate media coverage? Did those outside the media capitalize on extrinsic or intrinsic constraints to manipulate the story? Did the effort succeed? Were the efforts reported in the story?

How much of the report, if any, was based on press reports, actualities, or news reports provided by outsiders? How, if at all, would the report have differed if it had been prepared in its entirety by the reporter, without press releases, and so forth?

How much, if any, of the story simply recycled information from some other news source? Which source, and how do you account for the recycling?

Impact

Who, if anyone, benefited from the coverage? Who, if anyone, was damaged by the coverage? How? If someone or some organization was likely to seek news coverage to counter an impression created by the story, who would it be? What would you expect them to do? What media outlets would you expect them to use? (Op-eds? Letters to the editor? Press conference? Ads?) Would they be entitled to equal time?

Selected Readings

Epstein, Edward J. *Between Fact and Fiction: The Problems of Journalism.* New York: Random House, 1975.

Epstein, Edward J. *News from Nowhere.* New York: Random House, 1973.

Gans, Herbert. *Deciding What's News: A Study of CBS Evening News, NBC Evening News,* Newsweek, *and* Time. New York: Pantheon, 1979.

Glasgow University Media Group. *Bad News.* London: Routledge & Kegan Paul, 1976.

Glasgow University Media Group. *More Bad News.* London: Routledge & Kegan Paul, 1980.

Herman, Edward S., and Noam Chomsky. *Manufacturing Consent.* New York: Pantheon, 1989.

Tuchman, Gaye. *Making News: A Study in the Construction of Reality.* New York: Free Press, 1978.

Wicker, Tom. *On Press.* New York: Viking, 1978.

4

Influencing the News Media

The power of the news media results from their capacity to select what is reported and to shape the content of news stories. The news media are pervasive and forceful persuaders with the ability to shape our perceptions and to influence our beliefs and attitudes. But there are limits to their power, countervailing forces that, in turn, manipulate the news media. These include persons, like ourselves, and groups, like those we belong to, who capitalize on journalistic norms and routines to create newsworthy events and to shape their coverage. The commercial pressures of profits and competition, and direct pressures from the political establishment, also limit the power of the media.

Influencing Journalistic Norms and Routines

"Manipulated journalism presupposes routine journalism."[1] The ability to influence news coverage is directly related to an understanding of the journalistic norms and routines described in the preceding chapter; hence, many successful public relations consultants are former newspeople. The news media are vulnerable precisely because reporters have deadlines and beats, because they are generalists who rely on sources, and because of demands for brevity and for dramatic, visual coverage. The media's criteria for what is newsworthy and the external and internal constraints and conventions influencing what is covered and published contribute to their susceptibility.

Manipulating Deadlines

Because the news media face deadlines and are induced by competition to favor the latest details and the freshest facts, information released shortly before a deadline by an important person about an important matter is likely to be re-

1. Mark Fishman, *Manufacturing the News* (Austin: University of Texas Press, 1980), p. 15.

ported uncritically. In such cases, the event is newsworthy and the source is known and familiar. If time is taken to investigate the legitimacy of the information, reporters risk having a competitor break the story first. As a result, press secretaries or news managers release controversial information as close to deadlines as possible to minimize critical scrutiny of it. This became the standard procedure of the Nixon Administration in the final months of the Watergate investigation.

And, once a medium has broadcast or published the story, a second constraint comes into play, which minimizes the chance that the released information will get the scrutiny it deserves. By tomorrow, the news is stale. Fresh information is competing for space. Rehashing yesterday's news is taboo.

The news media can also be manipulated by releasing potentially damaging information when deadlines have passed or when the audience is hard to reach. For instance, once the Sunday morning papers are on the newsstands and the breakfast tables of the American public, it is difficult to reach a mass audience until the regular Monday morning channels of news begin—Monday morning drive-time radio, talk shows such as "Good Morning America," and the Monday morning paper. Sunday evening network news is often pre-empted by special programming or not aired by affiliates. Consequently, President Ford's controver sial decision to pardon ex President Nixon was announced at 11 A.M. (EST) Sunday morning. The timing assured that even if the broadcast media, understaffed on weekends, turned their full attention to the pardon, few people would be reached by media news coverage.

David R. Gergen, former assistant to the president for communications, said: "If you've got some news that you don't want to be noticed, put it out Friday afternoon at 4 P.M."[2] The Reagan Administration announced the formal end of our participation in the international peacekeeping force in Lebanon on a Friday at 4 P.M. Other decisions announced at that hour included restoration of tax breaks to private schools that discriminate on the basis of race; a directive, later suspended, imposing lifetime secrecy agreements on more than 100,000 government officials; and the discovery of clinically benign polyps during a routine colonoscopy on President Reagan, conducted as part of a follow-up to his rectal colon cancer surgery.

Similarly, when President George Bush decided to break his campaign pledge of "No New Taxes," he did so in a memo released to coincide with Nelson Mandela's headline-stealing speech to a joint meeting of Congress. Whereas Bush spoke in first person in making the election pledge, his memo shifted to third person. Passive voice replaced active. The simple, straightforward word *taxes* became *tax revenue increases*. At the convention he had said: "The Congress will push me to raise taxes, and I'll say no, and they'll push, and I'll say no, and they'll push again, and I'll say to them, 'Read my lips, No new taxes.'"[3] By contrast, his memo stated: "It is clear to me that both the size of the deficit problem and the need for a package that can be enacted require all of the following: entitlement

2. Stephen Engelberg, "The Bad News Hour: 4 P.M. Friday," *New York Times*, 6 April 1984, p. 10 Y; *Washington Post*, 18 January 1986, p. A 6.
3. Acceptance speech to the Republican National Convention, August 18, 1988.

and mandatory program reform; tax revenue increases; growth incentives; discretionary spending reductions." But Bush's efforts to minimize media scrutiny did not stop with issuing a written statement on a news-filled day. Throughout the day, Bush avoided talking to reporters, noted the *New York Times*, and "when he was asked during one brief Rose Garden appearance to expand on his written words, he replied, 'I'll let the statement speak for itself.'"[4]

The media also can be manipulated by releasing good news when most of the audience is watching. For example, during prime time in the opening week of the fall 1978 television season, President Carter announced unexpectedly that he had just secured an agreement between Prime Minister Menachem Begin of Israel and President Anwar Sadat of Egypt on an Egyptian–Israeli peace accord. As a result, Carter reached an unprecedented number of viewers. The announcement found most audience members tuned to the first television showing of a remake of the movie *King Kong* or to a new program, "Battlestar Galactica" (mistakenly heralded as the hottest new show of the season).

Even an audience member uninterested in foreign affairs was likely to stay tuned through the peace accord announcement to see the rest of the prime-time program. And those more interested in public affairs could stay tuned for network news updates, read about it in the morning papers, hear about it on drive-time radio, or listen to it discussed on Monday morning's talk shows. Once again, manipulation required a highly newsworthy event and a reliable source, but timing was used to influence coverage to reach the largest possible audience.

Timing and speed affect the press's power to manipulate a public figure. The press manipulates the public figure if coverage of a gaffe or a problem is prolonged; the public figure manipulates the press if she or he can quash extended coverage with a quick explanation or confession. For example, President Gerald Ford made a significant error in a debate with Jimmy Carter during the 1976 campaign, asserting that Poland was free. After the debate, Ford did not admit immediately that he had made a mistake. The news media covered the process of his aides trying to persuade him to make such a statement, and played documentary footage showing the lack of freedom in Poland. The Carter campaign treated it as a major policy error, and Carter, speaking before a Polish group, assured them that *he* knew how terrible things were in Poland. Finally, Ford acknowledged his error and the topic quickly disappeared from the news, but the damage had been done. Ford's momentum in the polls leveled off and his ratings began to rise again only at the end of that week. Some Ford strategists credit that error and its handling with the loss of the election.[5]

Republican strategists learned their lesson. When in a fall 1988 debate with Democratic contender Michael Dukakis, Republican nominee George Bush stated that he favored criminalizing abortion, by the early hours of the next morning aides were on the air saying that after considering it carefully overnight, Bush

---

4. Andrew Rosenthal, "Bush Now Concedes a Need for 'Tax Revenue Increases' To Reduce Deficit in Budget," *New York Times*, 27 June 1990, p. 1.

5. Jules Witcover, *Marathon: The Pursuit of the Presidency 1972–1976* (New York: Viking, 1977), pp. 606, 608.

wanted to clarify his position: only the person performing the abortion, not the woman having the abortion, should be subject to criminal prosecution.

Deadlines can also be used to insert questionable material into news stories, such as surveys done by interested parties using questionable methodology. Michael R. Gordon, a staff correspondent for the *National Journal*, a Washington weekly on federal policy and politics, reports such successful manipulation. A public relations firm fighting trucking deregulation arranged simultaneous press conferences in five cities to publicize the results of a poll by the Group Attitudes Company, a subsidiary of the same public relations firm. The survey, said the press handout, showed "virtually no public support for the move in Congress to deregulate the nation's trucking industry" and was cited in a number of regional papers and wire service reports. None of these reports mentioned that the company that conducted the survey was owned by the public relations firm fighting deregulation, information not included in the press releases. Facing a deadline with limited knowledge of polling and statistics, the press did not bother to question how the poll was conducted or whether its findings really supported the claim in the press release.[6]

The pressure of deadlines also makes it possible to manipulate coverage by releasing information in advance to reporters. Reporters are eager to predigest the news. This enables them to write much or all of a story in advance. Consequently, news managers delay official public release of information while making it available to the news media generally or to selected outlets or reporters. For example, in advance of the committee hearing, the communication director for a Senate committee might release the text of the chairperson's introductory statement and the testimony witnesses will give before the committee. Reporters can then compose their stories in advance and attend the hearing to insert an update into the story or to report the unexpected. Those who provide such advance information to reporters influence the perspective reporters will take in their news stories.

Manipulating Access

There is constant tension between those assigned to ferret out the news and those assigned to control press access to news sources. Press secretaries, public information officers, and public relations firms are hired to encourage press access to favorable information and to minimize or block press access to unfavorable information. When negative information seeps out, it is the function of news managers to prevent or lessen its spread through the media and to cast it in the best possible light.

News managers control the press by controlling press access to those who have information—for example, by limiting the number of presidential press conferences or by communicating through press releases. Control can also be exerted by providing easy access to those likely to cover an issue or program

6. Michael R. Gordon, "The Profits and Perils of Progress in P.R.," *New York Times*, 3 August 1980, p. E 19.

favorably and limiting the access of those thought to be opposed to the interests of the news source.

Exclusive interviews with reporters function this way. It is also possible to manipulate coverage by leaking information favorable to one position or damaging to an opponent's position. Finally, government officials control access by refusing to respond to a specific question on the grounds that the requested information would breach national security, by asserting that the person being questioned is not empowered to reveal the information, or by answering that the matter is still under study or in litigation.

The press's desire for access is generally expressed as "the public's right to know." Problems emerge when this right conflicts with an individual's right to privacy (should a rape victim's name be included in a news story about a rape?), the right to a fair trial (does publicity minimize a defendant's ability to get a fair trial?), and national security (should the media voluntarily suppress information that may damage the nation's interests at home or abroad?).

Manipulation through control of access is best illustrated by relationships between reporters and government officials. The reporter wants information, and the official expects something in exchange—a friendly hearing, a neutral report, or muted criticism, for example. Concealing the actual source of information is often a condition of access.

Bill Green, former *Washington Post* ombudsman, explains the "rough categories of attribution" this way: When a source speaks or holds a briefing "on the record," reporters can and do "quote the source by name." When a reporter attends a "backgrounder," he or she "can use the material but not the source." A "deep backgrounder," according to Green, "calls on the reader for an act of faith, and it produces some familiar phrases: 'it is known that' or 'it is believed that.' In other words, the fact that it came from a source cannot be revealed." When a statement is given "off the record," the reporter knows he or she "can't use it after all." Green acknowledges that this system of code phrases is necessary to elicit information that would otherwise be inaccessible but also notes that "the code and its vocabulary call credibility into question."[7] (See Figure 4.1.)

Under such circumstances, readers and viewers are asked to trust reporters and to take their news judgments on faith, a situation that makes reporters extremely vulnerable not only to manipulation but also to backlash from the audience. UPI now has a policy of trying to help readers understand who the source is, or where his or her sympathies are, by the wording of the attribution: "sources opposed to the plan" or "Democratic sources in Congress."

Access also can be limited by denying reporters the ability to get to the scene of a news story. By expelling reporters from a country, its government ensures that internal unrest will not be transmitted, at least not by them, around the world. In 1983 during the U.S. government's invasion of Grenada, the press was kept out.

A blue-ribbon commission headed by a retired major general, Winant Sidle, concluded that this action had been improper. In the future, the report stated, military commanders should make provision for at least a pool of reporters to

7. Bill Green, "That 'Unnamed' Source," *Washington Post*, 29 May 1981, p. A 12.

Figure 4.1   Identifying the source.

witness such military operations. The Pentagon adopted the Sidle recommendations as its official policy.

In December 1989, the procedure was put to the test. Reporters selected to form the pool concluded that the policy was ignored during the invasion of Panama. Noted pool television correspondent Fred Francis, "The pool was repeatedly denied or ignored when it asked for access to front-line troops, wounded soldiers—simple interviews." When pool reporters asked to observe the securing of Panama strongman Noriega's headquarters, they were told that it was "too dangerous." The Army major general whose paratroops had taken the international airport informed journalists, "Sorry, my operational orders are that I cannot let you talk with any of my men. I can't speak with you."[8] By denying reporters access to the invasion itself and by permitting them in only after the territory was presumably secured, the Bush Administration minimized the likelihood that the stories would focus on bureaucratic inefficiency, needless civilian deaths, or confused soldiers who did not know for what they were fighting and dying. However, in

8. Arthur Lord, "Operation Just Cause—The Press in the Dark Again," *Nieman Reports* (Spring 1990): 7.

1991 only a select pool of reporters was allowed access to information about the Gulf war, and even those reports were censored.

Manipulating News Assignments

Although presidents have tried, it is difficult to manipulate reporters by attempts to change their beats; but it is possible to manipulate newspeople who are on general assignment. For example, the AP Calendar lists important events occurring in Washington. Virtually every news bureau in Washington uses them as a guide for what to cover on any given day. If an event is listed, it gets covered, whether it deserves it or not; if it's not listed, it probably won't get covered. When an event is listed, fears of competition prod the news outlets to cover it. This is also cost efficient in the case of television, as some pooling of crews is possible under such circumstances, thus lowering costs. Arranging to have an event listed in the Calendar is one way to manipulate media news coverage.

Reporters on beats are vulnerable to manipulation. An example can be drawn from coverage of the Reagan presidential campaign. Joel Swerdlow reports some clever manipulation by Reagan news managers:

> Raw footage of a typical Reagan campaign day, for example, revealed that the crowds always seemed much larger than they actually were. To a large degree, this resulted from clever advance work by the media-sophisticated Reagan staff. At almost every stop, it was the same: they positioned a raised camera platform close to the speaker's platform, and roped off a huge "press area," designated off-limits to the public. This forced the crowd to pack tightly into the space between the candidate and the camera, ensuring that Reagan always spoke to an impressive-looking mass of humanity.[9]

In the 1950s and 1960s, some reporters acted as informants for and as channels of information from the Central Intelligence Agency. Stories initiated by the CIA found their way into major newspapers and onto the wires. Newspeople considered the CIA a trusted source of information before the revelations about the Vietnam War and Watergate cast doubt on the truthfulness of such government agencies. The CIA was able to provide reporters with access to information that they could not otherwise secure, a situation that gave those reporters a competitive edge. This information came easily and inexpensively; reporters did not have to invest time in ferreting out information, following false leads, fighting for access to sources. The CIA also provided an angle by pegging their stories to local and international events and, most important, the CIA provided stories based on beliefs and attitudes consistent with the reporters' views of the world: "us" versus "them," patriotism, the dangers of communism, the threat of communist infiltration. A variety of factors contributed to the association of the CIA with the media, and access to information was an important one.[10]

---

9. Joel Swerdlow, "The Decline of the Boys on the Bus," *Washington Journalism Review* (January-February 1981): 16.

10. "The CIA's 3 Decade Effort to Mold the World's Views," *New York Times*, 12 December 1977, p. A 12; "CIA Established Many Links to Journalists in U.S. and Abroad," *New York Times*, 27 December 1977, pp. 1, 40 A.

Media Competition

Chapter 3 has indicated how competition and deadlines contribute to incomplete and inaccurate reporting. But competition also influences coverage, particularly competition to keep up with the elite media. Consequently, in many cases news managers focus their attention on manipulating the elite media. If a news manager gains access to an elite medium, coverage in other media follows.

Access to an elite medium works to the advantage of both the medium and the newsworthy person, in some instances. For example, in the 1988 presidential campaign as Democratic charges that the Republicans were running a dirty campaign began to take hold, campaign manager James Baker made himself available for interviews on the Sunday afternoon news shows. There he denied the charges. Coverage by one medium influences coverage in other media. This is particularly true of the elite media, and news managers make special efforts to influence elite media coverage.

Language and Symbols

The print and electronic news media can be manipulated through the effective use of language and visual symbols. Because of its preference for the visual, television news is particularly vulnerable to the strategic use of visual symbols. For example, both print and electronic media photographed Pope John Paul II receiving flowers from former prisoners wearing striped uniforms at Auschwitz.

No explanation is needed for the ideas represented in this scene expressing a personal, pastoral papacy (the pope as a servant, as a caring, compassionate leader). It is a visual denial of anti-Semitism in the Catholic Church, a nonverbal Vatican repudiation of the view that the Jews killed Christ. John Paul II is uniquely suited to this scene. He was a member of the Polish underground that acted to save Jews, so the scene is an extension of his personal commitment. In addition, Auschwitz is in Poland, and his presence is a reminder of Polish Catholics' suffering at the hands of the Nazis and, implicitly, at the hands of the Russians. Such events rivet photographic attention because little or no commentary is required—the picture is the story.

If such scenes were routine, they would not be newsworthy. It is both the freshness of the symbols and their ability to stand for more than themselves that make them attractive to news photographers. Nonverbal symbolic acts that require verbal commentary are less effective.

Similarly, in spring 1990, the wife of former Philippines' president Ferdinand Marcos, Imelda Marcos, shaped national network coverage of her acquittal on charges of misuse of state funds and at the same time secured front-page newspaper access. Mrs. Marcos accomplished this by inching her way up the aisle of a church on her knees in a black mourning dress to "thank God" for the trial's outcome. The black dress reminded viewers of her widowhood, kneeling suggested that she was religious, and movement up the aisle in the posture of a penitent suggested her humility and the injustice of seeking to convict her. How, after all, could one assume the guilt of a humble, religious widow, kneeling in church?

Nonverbal symbols are risky because sometimes they are open to more than one interpretation. At the close of the dedication ceremonies at the Nixon Library,

Imelda Marcos crawls on her knees to the altar at St. Patrick's Cathedral in spring, 1990, after her acquittal (UPI/Bettmann).

the former president raised his arms while shaping V's with the fingers of each hand. The gesture was one characteristic of Nixon-the-campaigner and Nixon-the-president. Parodists of the former president had used it to cue audiences that they were about to begin their impressions of Nixon. In the context of the library ceremony, the symbol could indicate a final victory over those who invited his resignation from office. Alternatively, it could suggest that this too was a campaign event, and as such a bid for a legitimacy not yet accorded him by history. In politics, a similar problem can arise when a campaign slogan is open to more than one interpretation or when it lends itself to easy parody (see Chapter 11).

The news media can also be manipulated by the language of a statement that is artfully constructed and skillfully delivered. Ideally, such a statement should be uneditable, dramatic, concise, and synoptic. It should be capable of being delivered in under 35 seconds by a skilled speaker. If it is delivered by a credible person, about an important topic, and on an occasion accessible to the news media, it is virtually irresistible to the press. An example of such a statement was Bush's promise: "Read my Lips. No New Taxes."

Language can be used to deter news coverage as well. For instance, the difficulties involved in covering highly technical, abstract material are exploited by those who want to minimize news coverage of their activities. *Politics and the Oval Office*, a report by the conservative Institute for Contemporary Studies, argues that the presidency has suffered from too much uncontrolled coverage by the media. To curb what it views as excessive coverage, the report urges the president to overwhelm media representatives with technical data: "This tactic should defuse complaints about total accessibility. It could reduce the total volume of reporting, since dry data are often defined as unnewsworthy."[11]

Adaptation to the style and perspective of specific news channels and to the interests, biases, and experiences of individual reporters is a means of manipulating the press. For example, news managers can tailor a story to the *Wall Street Journal* by filling it with technical, economic data or to *Time* magazine by providing anecdotal material and clever language.

Every reporter has special interests, biases, and experiences; for this reason, if news coverage is to be balanced, it is important to have newspeople from different ethnic backgrounds and with varied perspectives reporting stories.

In summary, language and symbols can be used to influence news coverage. Of particular force is the dramatic visual symbol, but dramatic or dull language can be used to attract or deter coverage as well. It is also possible to attract coverage by tailoring statements and events to the predispositions of the reporter or media outlet.

Manipulating Live Coverage

A special, limited opportunity to manipulate access arises with live coverage, where little or no editing occurs. The opportunities for manipulation are limited to persons who are newsworthy for some other reason—winners of awards or of major sports events, for example. In such circumstances, people can use live television coverage to make a statement they could not otherwise make; in the process they have access to an audience they could not reach if the statement were made under other circumstances and had to compete for regular news coverage. One example occurred in 1990 when profanities uttered by the heavy-metal band Guns 'N Roses were heard by millions of television viewers tuned in to Monday night's American Music Awards ceremony. The profanities brought a barrage of complaints and an apology from ABC. In fall 1989, comedian Andrew Dice Clay was banned for life from MTV after making sexist remarks and using profanity on a live nationwide September 6 broadcast, the MTV Video Music Awards.[12]

11. "Reagan Advised to Reduce 'Imperial Media' Access," *Washington Post*, 2 February 1981, p. A 2.

12. "ABC Apologizes for Rockers' Remarks," *Philadelphia Inquirer*, 24 January 1990, p. 4 D.

A Checklist for Creating Newsworthy Statements Likely to Be Covered and Published

To Be	Or . . . Not to Be
A single coherent statement clearly summarizing the issue in jargon-free English, written to be understood on first hearing or reading, which can be delivered clearly and dramatically in less than 14 seconds, requiring no additional information, available before deadline at a convenient place for newsgatherers, delivered in a symbolic setting	A rambling statement skirting the issue in gobbledygook, written to be figured out by a cryptographer, which could not be delivered effectively by Laurence Olivier in less than 35 minutes, requiring at least a paragraph of clarification, available at midnight at the North Pole, delivered in a setting with no apparent relationship to the statement
or by a person who dramatizes the issue in a manner not subject to parody.	or by a nondescript person who mumbles in a manner that brings joy to the hearts of Art Buchwald and Garry Trudeau, who hope the speaker will seek the presidency.

Other instances are more calculated. For example, a Native American woman was able to read a statement on Indian rights when she refused the Oscar won by Marlon Brando, and Vanessa Redgrave was able to make a controversial statement about Palestinian rights during her Oscar acceptance speech. Early in the 1988 primaries, presidential candidate George Bush agreed to an interview with CBS anchor Dan Rather on the condition that the interview be broadcast live. This move guaranteed that his remarks could not be edited. His success in controlling the agenda of the interview helped Bush dispel reporters' questions about his decisiveness, questions that had been summarized as "the wimp factor."

Admittedly, such opportunities are rare and special, but live coverage provides opportunities to air highly controversial messages and to reach exceptionally large and captive audiences.

Prepackaged News

Pseudo-events, news feeds, news conferences, and prepared or "canned" editorials are examples of news prepackaged for the convenience of reporters. News managers are well aware of reporters' weaknesses and endeavor to exploit

---

Ads Become News

In 1989, more than 70 million viewers, twice as many as typically watch top-rated entertainment series, saw portions of a video release in which Sears announced that it was temporarily closing its stores to switch to a new pricing policy. More than 15 million saw part of Maytag's video release announcing the retirement of its longtime commercial spokesperson, Jesse White, the "lonely repairman," according to Medialink, a New York company that distributed video news releases and, with Nielsen Media Research, monitors their use.[a]

[a]Randall Rothenberg, "Messages from Sponsors Become Harder to Detect," *New York Times*, 19 November 1989, p. E 5.

---

them through prepackaged news. As one public relations and political consultant wrote, "It is much easier for a reporter to be spoon-fed than to go on a scavenger hunt in government or industry to find his next story."[13]

Reliance on prepackaged news accounts in part for the fact that most reporters missed the emergence of the savings and loan crisis. "We usually depend on governmental institutions or groups like Common Cause or Ralph Nader or General Motors or somebody to make sense out of all this data for us," explained Brooks Jackson, an award-winning Cable News Network reporter.[14]

It is legal to buy news shows off the shelf. For example, a program called "Hard Copy" was aired on Channel 2 in New York in fall 1989. It was purchased from an outside vendor, Paramount, which produced it as a package for stations around the country affiliated or owned by the three largest networks. Nobody at CBS or at Channel 2 had anything to do with what the packagers put in the program, including the topics covered. Everything was decided and manufactured by the packager. Such packaged news programs are appealing because the station splits the ad revenue with the packager, making a lot more money than if they put the program together themselves. Due to the lack of a disclaimer, viewers are led to believe that reporters for the station put the story together and are responsible for its content, even though they are not.[15] But in such instances, the packager has a wide latitude for influence.

Pseudo-Events   An antiabortion group in Kansas City obtained several small white caskets, ordinarily used to bury very small children. After notifying the media, particularly local television stations, of their plans, they appeared with the caskets at a large local hospital requesting aborted fetuses that they hoped to bury. Shocked hospital administrators were angered at this unexpected request.

---

13. J. Kyle Goddard, "Let's Abolish News Conferences," *New York Times*, 2 December 1979, p. E 12.

14. Quoted by Ellen Hume, "Why the Press Blew the S & L Scandal," *New York Times*, 24 May 1990, p. A 25.

15. Anthony Lewis, "TV: Selling Off Credibility," *New York Times*, 13 October 1989, p. 23 Y.

Television cameras showed the heated confrontation and the poignant white caskets. As viewers watched the segment on the local news, they saw a pseudo-event, that is, an event created and arranged for coverage by the news media.

A pseudo-event is an arranged event, not an occurrence that happens of its own accord. Contrast this arranged event with the actual death of a baby and its removal to be buried. A pseudo-event, which takes account of newsgatherers' concepts of what is newsworthy, is arranged to exploit internal and external constraints on newsgathering and the conventions of news presentation. An ideal pseudo-event is therefore dramatic (here, the angry encounter between shocked hospital staff and the antiabortion group), personalized (abortion was reduced to individual fetuses symbolized by tiny white caskets), novel (this event got coverage because it was original; if many antiabortion groups imitate it, coverage will end), an event (there was a specific encounter between hospital staff and the antiabortion group), and it is part of an ongoing theme in the news (national efforts to have personhood defined as beginning at the moment of conception had been getting considerable news coverage).

In addition, the encounter took place at a convenient urban location, close to most local television stations, and at a convenient time (early afternoon) well before deadlines. The event was staged by a local group at a local setting (the hospital), making it attractive to local coverage. The event is visual (the encounter occurred just outside the hospital doors in good light and was easy to tape) and made use of highly charged, poignant symbols of sorrow and death. As taped with brief statements from both sides (the antiabortion group and the shocked, angry hospital administrators) and with a reporter's wrap-up, the event fit neatly into a 99-second news segment. As a result, its appearance on the local evening news could have been predicted.

Pseudo-events are designed to transform an issue, process, person, or the like into a newsworthy event that will be covered by the mass media. Many news events are staged to an extent to surmount the problems described in Chapter 2—scheduling, deadlines, access, and so forth. In a letter to the networks evaluating charges that coverage of the 1968 Democratic Convention in Chicago had involved "staged news," the Federal Communications Commission wrote:

> In a sense, every televised press conference may be said to be staged to some extent; depictions of scenes in a television documentary—on how the poor live on a typical day in the ghetto, for example—also necessarily involve camera directions, lights, action instructions, etc. The term "pseudo-event" describes a whole class of such activities that constitute much of what journalists treat as "news."[16]

In other words, a wide range of staged events are routinely treated as news. The news media can be manipulated into coverage of these pseudo-events because of what they define as news and because of the constraints under which they operate. Because cost and the need to meet deadlines with fresh stories are important to those who produce the news, there is pressure to cover events that

16. FCC letter to the networks (No. 69-19227767), 28 February 1969, p. 9, cited by Edward Epstein in *News from Nowhere* (New York: Random House-Vintage, 1973), p. 159.

have the dramatic, visual, concise characteristics the media crave. Congressional hearings, news conferences, and pseudo-events have these characteristics. In covering such events the reporter minimizes the amount of background information needed and the amount of time it takes to assemble a story, and has the news peg for the story—the event itself. The problem, of course, is that by covering such an event, the reporter often accepts the assumptions of those managing the event. The well-staged event invites coverage from a certain point of view.

An important adjunct to the press conference and to other staged events is the press release. The press release attempts to create a context for viewing a specific event. Written to include basic information (who, what, when, where, how, why) required by editors, it is filled with dramatic, synthetic statements related to the emerging news item.

Attracting media attention carries risks if the attention has been obtained under false pretenses. A candidate's opponents are eager to bring such discrepancies to the attention of the media. For example, when Marc Holtzman, a Republican congressional candidate in Pennsylvania, announced in a news release that he had facilitated the homecoming of a Vietnamese mother of a naturalized U.S. citizen in his district, the local press carried the heartwarming story. To Holtzman's embarrassment, the press reported days later that Holtzman's role had consisted of writing a letter to Vice President George Bush inquiring about the status of the case. Bush received Holtzman's letter a week after the State Department had issued the visa. The follow-up stories hurt Holtzman's chances for re-election in the 1986 campaign.[17]

News Feeds   News managers attempt to exercise even greater control by offering radio stations news feeds containing audio "bites" of a politician's speech complete with "wrapped around" context narrated by someone on the politician's staff. Statements recorded specifically for "feeding" are also distributed. Such news feeds are common on Capitol Hill, in political campaigns, in the executive branch, and, increasingly, are being used by business as well. A. Kent MacDougall of the *Los Angeles Times* reports:

> Business is supplying pre-recorded interviews with business advocates to television and radio stations which slip them into their newscasts, usually without reference to their source. And business is flooding small newspapers with ready-to-use canned editorials, columns, and cartoons that carry hidden corporate messages.[18]

By accepting such feeds, the broadcast producer or editor is spared the cost of gathering the material or sending a reporter to the event but sacrifices the ability to make editorial judgments. Small stations and small papers are more likely to accept such feeds than larger ones. With the exception of opinion-editorials and paid advocacy advertising, most large stations and newspapers refuse as a matter of policy to accept such prepared materials.

17. *Washington Post*, 27 May 1986, p. A 4.
18. "The Credibility Gap," *Washington Journalism Review* (July-August 1981): 21.

Cost prevents small radio and television stations from having their own correspondents in Washington or following the major campaigns, yet an interview with an important government official or candidate is a news coup. If they can make it appear that they have such desirable access, they may suppress details about how information was obtained. The FCC Code (Section 73.1212.d) requires that at both the beginning and end of a segment, broadcasters disclose the source of any such prepackaged news other than mimeographed or printed press releases. This restriction applies to feeds obtained when the station calls a predesignated number as well as materials sent or delivered to the station. This rule applies to political candidates and to anyone dealing with political subjects or controversial issues.

Video news releases (VNRs) were inefficient as long as they relied on videocassettes as their means of transport. Cassettes began to clutter newsrooms, unwatched and unaired. In the mid-1980s, public relations firms began switching to satellite transmission of news feeds. Medialink, a firm specializing in VNR transmission, reported that it distributed more than 1,500 VNRs by satellite in 1989. Estimates place the number of VNRs distributed each year at between 5,000 and 15,000. When Nielsen Media Research surveyed 200 stations in 1988, it found that 93 percent had the capacity to downlink VNRs from satellite and almost three-quarters said they were willing to use such releases.[19]

To increase the likelihood that they will be used, producers of VNRs include a 90-second B-roll of visuals accompanied only by natural sound. Local announcers can then "voice" the narration making it appear that the station itself produced the material.

Use of VNRs has enabled advertisers to circumvent bans on the advertisement of certain products. "In 1987, for example, the James B. Beam Distilling Company took to heart the admonition to hook an item to a news trend, and made a video news release that affirmed the patriotic preference of American distillers for domestic, instead of Canadian, grain. Television viewers in some 40 cities saw the report, illustrated with footage of workers packing crates with Jim Beam bourbon, on their local newscasts."[20]

Electronic press kits, the video equivalent of the written press release, now air routinely on hundreds of local television stations as coverage of entertainment news increases. Frequently this material is neither labeled nor described as film-studio publicity. No one knows how often local reporters inject themselves into these publicity kits, but the videotapes have been carefully created to allow local reporters to do so. For example, KABC-TV, the ABC station in Los Angeles, aired what appeared to be an interview with Al Pacino and KABC-TV reporter Nancy Gould. However, Gould never talked to Pacino. She had inserted herself into a taped interview with the actor made by Universal Pictures, the producer of the feature film *Scarface* in which Pacino starred. KABC-TV suspended and then de-

19. Randall Rothenberg, "The Journalist as Maytag Repairman," *Gannett Center Journal* (Spring 1990): 105.
20. Ibid., p. 107.

Editorials: Who Reads Them?

Age—not education, income, or sex—turns out to be the most reliable indicator distinguishing regular readers of editorial and opinion pages from nonreaders, according to a report by the 1980 National Conference of Editorial Writers. Regular readership increases from 39 percent of the 26-to-35 age group to 52 percent of those 36 to 45 and 63 percent of those over 65.[b]

[b]*Advertising Age*, 28 July 1986, p. S-3.

---

clined to renew Gould's contract over this incident. The issue is one of journalistic integrity, the responsibility to disclose to viewers that the material they are seeing is promotional and that the station's reporters have not participated in its filming.

Major studios have produced dozens of these kits. Producing the kits is expensive, but far less costly than comparable advertising. George Armstrong, who developed the electronic press kit at Universal Pictures as vice president in charge of advertising, noted that the kit for *E.T.* cost $125,000, but that it "brought in the equivalent of $700,000 worth of air time if we had [had] to buy it."[21]

Public relations firms attest to the fact that television and radio stations use materials prepared by public relations firms. For example, after a Food and Drug Administration ruling favorable to a client's product, one public relations firm made a videotape for the client in the form of a news report on the FDA ruling, which was distributed to hundreds of television stations—most of whom used it. Similarly, those advising clients on how to obtain news coverage suggest that if the news media do not cover the event, do it yourself—audio- or videotape the event, edit it into a 90-second package, attach a script for announcers, and ship it to radio or television stations in time for the evening news.

Prepared Editorials   Another kind of influence results from distributing prepared editorials and feature stories to newspapers, particularly to small, news-hungry weeklies. E. Hofer and Sons, a public relations firm, has been among the most successful in getting its prepared editorials printed in newspapers. Once again, newspapers cooperate in their own manipulation. As one commentator writes, "To publish editorials prepared by Hofer while crediting the editorial to *Industrial News Review* [the organ through which Hofer disseminates prepared editorials], of course, would not constitute publication of 'canned' editorials. It is when newspapers publish editorials from such sources as their own views [and hundreds do] that an ethical problem arises."[22] Editorial writing is difficult and

---

21. Sally Bedell Smith, "Electronic Press Kits Pervade TV Newscasts," *New York Times*, 30 January 1984, p. 18 Y.

22. Harry W. Stonecipher, *Editorial and Persuasive Writing: Opinion Functions of the News Media* (New York: Hastings House, 1979), p. 67.

time consuming. As a result, it is tempting to use prepared editorials, and to pretend that they were composed by the newspaper staff.

Success in attracting advertising can make newspapers more vulnerable to the manipulations of news managers and public relations consultants. This is the case because, as advertising linage increases, the size of the space to be filled by news (the "news hole") also increases. Because their news staffs are small, such newspapers tend to "rely on filler and fluff supplied by business publicists to supplement their own coverage."[23]

In other words, those who are knowledgeable about journalistic norms and routines have the ability to manipulate news coverage. By strategic use of the media's needs and constraints, public relations consultants and news managers, as well as individuals and groups, help determine what is covered and how news stories are presented.

Commercial Pressures

■

The news media are influenced not only by those who understand journalistic norms and routines but also by their desire for profit, their desire to beat the competition in the ratings, and by pressures created by advertisers. News programming has become one of the most lucrative sources of revenue for both the local stations and the networks. That is true, in part, because of its low production costs and because stations and networks own and produce the news, whereas in most cases they do not own and produce entertainment programming. For example, "World News Tonight" has become one of ABC's biggest revenue producers, bigger than many of its highly rated entertainment programs. The CBS news program "60 Minutes," among the top ten in the Nielsen ratings for thirteen consecutive years, has been the biggest moneymaker in network history, according to Don Hewitt, the program's creator: "My records tell me that we've had a net profit for CBS of over $1 billion."[24] Local news generates between 30 and 50 percent of the profits of individual television stations. As a result, there is intense pressure to achieve and maintain high ratings. Such pressures contribute to the tendencies to dramatize and sensationalize news content described in the last chapter.

What competitive pressures do not produce is an alternative news agenda. So similar is the content of most competing newspapers, for example, that one scholar dubbed them "rivals in conformity."[25] That conclusion has weathered the tests of four decades of research.[26]

23. A. Kent MacDougall, "Business Puffery Costs Press Credibility, Short Changes Readers," *Los Angeles Times*, 3 November 1980, sec. IV, p. 1.

24. Bill Carter, "Success of '60 Minutes' in Dollars and in Years," *New York Times*, 15 September 1990, p. 13 Y.

25. Stanley K. Bigman, "Rivals in Conformity: A Study of Two Competing Dailies," *Journalism Quarterly* 25 (Spring 1984): 127–31.

26. Stephen Lacy, "The Effects of Intracity Competition," *Journalism Quarterly* 64 (Summer-Autumn 1987): 281–290.

Costs of Pre-empting Programming

When the news division of a network pre-empts regular programming for special news—such as the funeral of Winston Churchill, the visit of Pope John Paul II, or a space shuttle launch—advertisers who have paid to sponsor the regular programming are not given what they paid for and either have their money refunded or are offered alternate times to air their ads. Networks are corporations governed by boards accountable to stockholders who expect to receive dividends. The decision to pre-empt regular programming is a costly one. If the news interrupts or pre-empts a program that attracts a small audience, the network loses less money than if a popular program is interrupted. Consequently, a network whose programs are unpopular risks less by interrupting them with breaking news.

The cost of pre-empting entertainment programming to cover government activities was documented by a government study, which concluded that there was one major reason for the "decline in network interest in matters of government—the enormous increase in network earnings and the huge loss of profits that would result from any pre-emption." [27]

Yet a network's prestige is, in part, a function of the quality of its news programming, and viewers are comforted by the assurance that if something important happens, the networks will interrupt regular programming to bring them that information. Therefore, whatever the cost, a network cannot afford to ignore important news. When John Kennedy was assassinated, for example, there was no question that the networks would pre-empt whatever was on the air to bring that word and ensuing developments to the audience. But most news is not as important as a presidential assassination. In such cases, profit and loss must be weighed against the gain in prestige that might result from the coverage, or the loss in prestige if the event is not covered. A network is particularly vulnerable when one of its competitors covers an event.

Television networks occasionally agree to rotate coverage of an important event to minimize loss of advertising revenue. Accordingly, the networks rotated coverage of the Iran–Contra hearings. This gave the audience a chance to choose between regular programming and coverage of the hearings. Audience members know what they have missed, or that television should have aired an event and didn't, because newspaper television critics tell them. Caught in this bind, television has sought ways to ensure audience awareness of the news without interrupting regularly scheduled programming except in extraordinary circumstances.

The "news break," sponsored by an advertiser, represents one such avenue. News breaks occur during commercial breaks in programming and are brief summaries of the day's headlines. This creates an association between news and advertising, which advertisers desire. With news breaks or news updates, advertisers, not the network, bear the cost of underwriting the time, and programming goes on as expected.

---

27. *The Second Report with Recommendations of the Temporary Select Committee to Study the Senate Committee System*, cited in Marvin Barrett, *Rich News, Poor News* (New York: Thomas Y. Crowell, 1978), p. 136.

Television also runs print information across the lower third of the screen during regular programming to bring important information to the viewer. This device is used more often to tell the viewer that the local news will follow a program that is running overtime than to convey important breaking news, but it is also used to keep audiences posted on the status of hurricanes or tornadoes and to indicate disaster warnings and watches.

Not everyone agrees that live news coverage is a blessing. In 1986, for example, the ABC and NBC television networks were flooded with calls from angry viewers who tuned in to watch their favorite soap operas only to find them preempted by live coverage of congressional hearings on the Iran arms sale. All three networks pre-empted regular daytime programming for coverage of the hearings. ABC News spokesperson Thomas Goodman said the network received 1,330 calls. "All objected to pre-emption of soap operas," he said. NBC reported receiving 1,100 complaints. CBS received fewer than three dozen calls.[28] Some coverage, such as network coverage of Nixon's trip to the Soviet Union, was criticized as political propaganda. This charge was given credence when two of Nixon's reelection campaign commercials in 1972 consisted of edited news footage of his trips to Russia and China.

Commercial pressures for high ratings and the revenues they assure affect judgments about what news will be covered, particularly if coverage involves the costly pre-emption of other lucrative programming. As a result, in 1988, all three major networks cut their coverage of the Republican and Democratic National Conventions.

Pressures from Advertisers

The price of subscriptions does not pay the total cost of producing a newspaper or magazine. Both are underwritten by advertising revenue, and commercial television and radio are almost completely financed by advertising. Their dependence on these external sources of funding renders them vulnerable to boycotts by advertisers. For example, in the spring of 1986, some Detroit car dealers cancelled their ads in the *Detroit Free Press* after the newspaper published an exposé detailing antitrust charges against local dealerships. The FTC had charged 105 dealers and 115 individuals with conspiracy for trying to limit showroom hours and for trying to limit competition by fixing prices.[29]

Television, too, is subject to pressure from advertisers. Prior to the accident at the Three Mile Island nuclear plant, Jane Fonda appeared on a Barbara Walters ABC special to discuss her film *The China Syndrome* and its antinuclear message. General Electric, one of the four biggest builders of nuclear reactors in the world, promptly withdrew its sponsorship of the program.[30]

28. *New York Times*, 11 December 1986, p. 10 Y.

29. *Washington Post*, 28 May 1986, p. G 1.

30. Marvin Barrett and Zachary Sklar, *The Eye of the Storm* (New York: Lippincott and Crowell, 1980), pp. 130–131.

In addition, corporations whose environmental practices are portrayed un-flatteringly on the news are striking back at the press with angry letters, point-by-point rebuttals, news releases, and paid ads. These include Hooker Chemicals and General Motors, among others.[31]

Still another example was action in early 1989 by the Washington State Fruit Commission, a growers' trade association, that withdrew $71,300 worth of tele-vision advertising for northwest cherries from CBS affiliates in St. Louis, Atlanta, and Tampa to protest a news report about Alar on CBS's "60 Minutes." "Our asso-ciation wanted to voice its displeasure over the way the CBS broadcast of the '60 Minutes' program sensationalized the Alar story," said Pat Dunlop, a spokesman for the commission. The money budgeted for advertising was diverted to other stations in those markets.

The account, televised February 26, 1989, on "60 Minutes," dealt with a study by the Natural Resources Defense Council on pesticides in foods that affect chil-dren and concluded that eating apples treated with Alar, a chemical used to con-trol ripening, increased cancer risks for children. The report was disputed by the apple industry, and federal regulators have declared apples safe to eat, but the report sent apple sales into a steep decline. Growers contend they lost millions of dollars as a result. Alar is not used on cherries, but many of the group's members grow both crops.[32]

As these examples demonstrate, advertisers actively attempt to affect news coverage.

Threat of Lawsuits

The costs of defending against a lawsuit are high. Coverage of controversial subjects, hard-hitting editorials, and investigative reporting are particularly likely to attract libel suits. Consequently local television stations, particularly those in small markets, tend to shy away from such reporting, according to a survey by the National Association of Broadcasters. Who threatens to sue? Businesspeople threaten to sue over consumer reporting on pollution, car defects, and the like. Politicians threaten to sue over politically damaging material.[33]

In recent years, the Supreme Court has let stand awards of more than $2 mil-lion each in punitive damages awarded to individuals who sued a daily newspaper and a network-owned television station. Punitive damages are now awarded in 60 percent of the cases won by plaintiffs against the media. Average awards exceed a million dollars. In early 1990, in *Sprague* v. *Walter*, a jury in Pennsylvania awarded $31.5 million in punitive damages against the *Philadelphia Inquirer* for a story written in the early 1970s questioning a local prosecutor's handling of a homicide case. In *CBS Inc.* v. *Brown and Williamson Tobacco Corp.*, the tobacco company

31. A. Kent MacDougall, "Reporting Environmental Hazards, Job Dangers Pose Risks for Media," *Los Angeles Times*, 23 November 1980, sec. V, pp. 1, 2.

32. "Fruit Growers Kill Ads in Protest to CBS," *New York Times*, 7 May 1989, p. 15 Y.

33. Steve Winberg, "New Coverage for TV News," *Panorama*, March 1981, p. 14.

sued a Chicago-owned CBS affiliate for libel arguing that its advertisements had been misrepresented. CBS countered that the piece in question was commentary and as such protected by the First Amendment. The court held that the station had falsely accused the tobacco firm of soliciting young smokers as customers.[34]

Private individuals and corporations are not the only ones able to bring legal pressure to bear on the media. As we mentioned in Chapter 3, in May 1986 then-CIA Director William J. Casey suggested that the Department of Justice consider prosecuting NBC News for violation of the 1950 law prohibiting disclosure of "communications intelligence." The NBC News report that Casey was objecting to concerned the trial of accused spy Ronald W. Pelton.

The limited amount of editorializing on radio and television stations reflects fears of legal reprisals. And when broadcasters do editorialize, they tend to take noncontroversial stands, such as "support your local blood bank" or "welcome the former hostages home." In many cases, the positions taken are vague and ambiguous. Threats of lawsuits, as well as the fear they will be obliged to provide free time for reply, contribute to such neutrality.

In June 1986 the Supreme Court made it easier for the news media to gain dismissal of libel suits without the high costs of trials. In a 6–3 ruling, the Court held for columnist Jack Anderson and against the conservative Liberty Lobby. A magazine edited by Anderson had called the group neo-Nazi, anti-Semitic, racist, and fascist. The Court held that judges should dismiss cases unless evidence of "actual malice" by the media was "clear and convincing." To establish actual malice, a complainant must show that the media knew the material was false or published with reckless disregard for whether it was false.

Political Pressure

■   Anthony Smith reports that "during the Carter Administration, government was spending $1 billion a year on its own information services (the Pentagon alone had 1,500 press officers, spending $25 million a year)."[35] That expenditure reflects the magnitude of the government effort to influence what and how information is disseminated. But the government has resources far more important than money.

The president is always news and has great power to influence press coverage through leaks, exclusive interviews, pseudo-events (like White House Rose Garden activities), and appeals to national security, among other means. Some of the ways campaigners manipulate the press are treated in Chapter 11. Here we consider the political pressure created by the federal government, particularly the executive branch.

34. Lee Levine and David L. Perry, "No Way to Celebrate the Bill of Rights," *Columbia Journalism Review* (July/August 1990): 38.

35. Anthony Smith, *Goodbye Gutenberg: The Newspaper Revolution of the 1980's* (New York: Oxford, 1980), p. 175.

Presidential Newsworthiness

The president is always able to make news. He can call a press conference, announce a forthcoming event (an agreement or a future summit meeting), or schedule a ritual (awarding a medal, for instance). As the *New York Times'* former White House correspondent, John Herbers, notes:

> No other institution can demand space and attention throughout the media when there is no news there. The White House does every day. The President can demand front-page coverage by holding a press conference in which he says nothing that has not been said before. He can command prime television time by granting an exclusive interview to one of the networks, and newspapers feel compelled to write about it at length because millions saw it on television.[36]

Facts that would not be newsworthy about anyone else become newsworthy when tied to the president. For example, network television as well as newspapers carried major stories on George Bush's declaration: "I do not like broccoli and I haven't liked it since I was a little kid and my mother made me eat it and I'm president of the United States and I'm not going to eat any more broccoli." By providing a moment of comic relief in an otherwise serious day, the comment humanized Bush. To laughter, he then added, "Wait a minute. For the broccoli vote out there, Barbara loves broccoli. She's tried to make me eat it; she eats it all the time herself. So she can go out and meet the caravan of [trucks bringing] broccoli . . ." With that as a tease, the story continued. On March 26, 1990, Barbara Bush's picture appeared in newspapers. In front of her was a table of broccoli.

A focus on "the human side" of the White House can displace other forms of coverage. Inviting such coverage is itself a form of manipulation of the news agenda. By early 1990, the Bushs' dog Millie had entered the annals of U.S. history along with Franklin Roosevelt's Fala and Richard Nixon's Checkers. When Millie delivered puppies, network stories followed. A survey for the Center for the Media and Public Affairs concluded that from Bush's first day as president until November 30, 1989, Millie had appeared more frequently on network news than Bush's Education Secretary, his Agricultural Secretary, or his Secretary for Veterans Affairs. "Let me give you a little serious, political, inside advice," Bush told a Republican fundraiser. "One single word. 'Puppies.' Worth ten points [in the polls], believe me."[37]

Such newsworthiness gives the executive enormous powers of manipulation. The Reagan Administration proved highly adept at managing presidential press contacts. As one reporter noted:

> The President delivers the good news, usually in situations that insulate him from questions, while aides deal with controversial matters. . . . Few White House teams have exhibited such expertise in associating an executive only with the popular decisions and dramatic moments of his Presidency.[38]

36. John Herbers, *No Thank You, Mr. President* (New York: Norton, 1976), p. 41.
37. David Hoffman, "The Frictionless Presidency," *Gannett Center Journal* (Spring 1990): 92.
38. Howell Raines, "Reporter's Notebook: Insulating a President," *New York Times*, 5 August 1981, p. A 12.

Such control maintains the president's personal popularity, protects him from situations in which gaffes might be made, and allows the anger generated by unpopular decisions to be deflected onto presidential assistants. Given such control of access, press coverage is inevitably limited and manipulated. More readily than any other politician or citizen, the president also can take to the air waves to speak directly to the American people.

When the networks judge the topic to be newsworthy, the president is granted what amounts to automatic access. After former House Democratic leader Tip O'Neill denied Ronald Reagan's June 1986 request to address the House on the issue of aid to the Contras in Nicaragua, Reagan asked for network time to speak directly to the American people. The three major networks declined on the grounds that the president's speech would not make news. Cable News Network, which carries news 24 hours a day, aired the speech.

National Security

Because information about foreign relations is more difficult to corroborate and because they are citizens as well as reporters, members of the press are susceptible to the administration's line on foreign policy. David Halberstam's *The Powers That Be* documents how the government sustained press support for Vietnam policy. Appeals to support presidential policies are made in the name of "national security" and "protection of vital interests." Such appeals usually prove irresistible.

Appeals to national security are complicated by competition among news outlets. In some cases, journalists keep a story off the air or out of the papers, only to see it broken by someone else. For example, for nearly a year the Carter and Reagan Administrations tried to prevent publication of the existence of two secret listening posts operating in China with American equipment and Chinese personnel.

The story was finally reported in June 1981 on "NBC Nightly News." Earlier, when they had learned of the posts' existence, two *New York Times* reporters were talked out of publishing the story—first by Carter's national security adviser, Zbigniew Brzezinski, and later by Reagan's CIA director, William J. Casey. NBC News, last in the ratings, had a strong incentive to break the story. However, the existence of the listening posts had been hinted at in the *Washington Post* several days earlier, and China's offer to replace posts lost in Iran after the revolution had been reported as early as April 1979. What gave the story such impact was the recent Reagan Administration decision to authorize the first sale of "lethal" U.S. military equipment to China.[39]

Government Manipulation

Strategic leaks of classified material are also used to manipulate the press. Just how common this practice is became clear during lawsuits over publication of the Pentagon Papers. In answer to claims by the Nixon Administration, the *New York Times* responded "with 15 affidavits which laid out some of the ways in

---

39. Murrey Marder, "Monitoring Not-So-Secret Secret," *Washington Post*, 19 June 1981, p. A 10.

which government officials had selectively leaked classified material to the *Times* in the past to achieve their ends. . . . The *Post* also argued . . . that government officials had for years leaked classified material for their own purposes and introduced affidavits from staff members including Ben Bradlee, the newspaper's editor, and its foreign affairs specialist Chalmers Roberts."[40]

Stephen Hess, an analyst at the Brookings Institution, has identified six types of leaks. Each is based in a different motive. The policy leak "is a straightforward pitch for or against a proposal using some document or insider's information." The trial balloon leak is an attempt to assess a proposal's strengths and weaknesses, assets and liabilities. Ego leaks satisfy the source's sense of self-importance. Goodwill leaks attempt to cultivate credit with a reporter. An animus leak is designed to embarrass someone else. A whistleblower leak is the last resort of a frustrated civil servant who feels that he or she has exhausted remedies within the government.[41]

The political use of strategic leaks illustrates the symbiotic relationship between the press and the government. The government needs the press to disseminate information and to support its policies. The press needs the government as a major source of information.

This close relationship was illustrated by the Reagan Administration's use of the press during trade talks held to persuade the Japanese voluntarily to limit automobile exports to the United States. The situation arose because the Reagan Administration did not want to make any overt effort to restrict Japanese exports. However, the press was used to put pressure on the Japanese through a news release from "sources close to U.S. trade officials" indicating that talks were going badly and that it was hoped that other proposals would be forthcoming from the Japanese. Reporters who were induced to print that story "later concluded that they had been gulled in a U.S. scheme to put overnight pressure on the Japanese." In effect, the Reagan Administration used the press as a conduit for its negotiations while maintaining the fiction that it was making no attempt to restrict Japanese exports.[42]

Cooperation between press and government is increased by movements from press jobs to government jobs and vice versa. For example, NBC reporter Ron Nessen, who had covered Ford as vice president, became President Ford's press secretary. Eileen Shanahan, economic reporter for the *New York Times*, took a position in the Department of Education during the Carter Administration and then became a reporter for the *Washington Star*. Leslie Gelb first worked in government for Secretary of Defense McNamara, then became a reporter at the *New York Times* after a breather at the Brookings Institution. After four years at the *Times*, he moved to the State Department as Cyrus Vance's assistant secretary for politico-military affairs. Two-and-a-half years later he left the State Department,

---

40. William E. Porter, *Assault on the Media: The Nixon Years* (Ann Arbor: University of Michigan Press, 1976), pp. 97–98.
41. Stephen Hess, *The Government/Press Connection: Press Officers and Their Offices* (Washington, D.C.: Brookings Institution, 1984), pp. 75–94.
42. William Chapmen, "Reporters Gulled into Being a Channel for Auto-Imports Haggling," *Washington Post*, 7 May 1981, p. A 31.

paused at the Brookings Institution, and returned to the *Times*. Meanwhile, Richard Burt, who had taken Gelb's job at the *Times*, left his position to take Gelb's former job in the State Department under Alexander Haig. Such musical chairs between government and press raise questions of journalistic integrity. Can a reporter write objectively about a person now doing her or his former job or about policies or programs that she or he once defended? Can a reporter write without bias about those who have the power to advance his or her prospects for a government job?[43]

There is considerable evidence of the power of government to manipulate press coverage. Government agencies spend huge sums of money to disseminate their messages through the mass media. The power of the presidency is also used manipulatively. By managing the president's ability to make news, to control access to information, to plead national security, to schedule staged news events, and to leak material strategically, the executive branch can gain implicit news media endorsement for administration policies. For example, when asked how the administration would respond to Soviet leader Mikhail Gorbachev's televised speech on the Chernobyl nuclear accident, former White House spokesperson Larry Speakes responded, "If it's something really big, the President would say it. . . . If it was semi-big, I'd come out and say something. If it was teeny-tiny, we'd give out a piece of paper. And if it was teeny-tinier than that, we'd let the State Department do it."[44]

The resignation of Bernard Kalb as chief spokesperson for the State Department climaxed allegations of blatant press manipulation by the Reagan Administration. Kalb described his resignation as a protest against the deception and disinformation campaign launched in August against Libyan leader Muammar Qaddafi. "You face a choice—as an American, as a spokesman, as a journalist— whether to allow oneself to be absorbed in the ranks of silence, whether to vanish into unopposed acquiescence or to enter a modest dissent." He added: "Faith in the word of America is the pulse beat of our democracy. Anything that hurts America's credibility hurts America."[45] Before accepting the post of assistant secretary of state for public affairs, Kalb had been a correspondent for the *New York Times*, CBS, and NBC for almost forty years.

Charges that the Reagan Administration had engaged in a disinformation campaign about Libya and its leader arose after a story by Bob Woodward appeared in the *Washington Post*. The story disclosed details of a memorandum by Vice Admiral John M. Poindexter, then White House national security adviser, reportedly urging a campaign against Qaddafi involving "real and illusory events— through a disinformation program."

The White House denied that the administration had planted false reports with news organizations in the United States, but former presidential spokesperson Larry Speakes had no comment on whether the administration had tried to conduct such a disinformation campaign against Libya in foreign news organizations.

43. Philip Nobile, "Covering Yourself: From Bureaucrat to Beat," *New York*, 30 March 1981, pp. 8–9.
44. *Washington Post*, 15 May 1986, p. A 19.
45. *Minneapolis Star and Tribune*, 9 October 1986, p. 1 A.

According to the *Post* story, major newspapers had carried erroneous news reports generated by this plan. A front-page article appeared on August 25 in the *Wall Street Journal* saying Libya was planning new terrorist attacks. Citing unidentified "U.S. and West European intelligence officials," the story said that the United States was on a "collision course" with Libya, that "growing evidence suggests" new Libyan terrorist attacks were being planned, and that "the Pentagon is completing plans for a new and larger bombing of Libya in case the President orders it." All three network television evening news programs repeated the substance of the *Journal*'s report the night after it appeared, and on August 26 many major newspapers quoted identified and unidentified officials who seemed to confirm the *Journal* article. Some newspapers, including the conservative *Washington Times*, began to question the reports and to suggest that a disinformation campaign was underway.

In a news conference, Secretary of State George Shultz refused to comment on whether or not such a campaign of disinformation had been undertaken, but seemed to confirm the report through his answers, which praised the use of deception if it would cause problems for the Libyan leader. An unidentified White House official was quoted making similar statements.

> We think for domestic consumption there will be no problems. It's Qaddafi. After all, whatever it takes to get rid of him is all right with us—that's the feeling, we think, in the country. On the foreign scene it will cause problems, though. We're constantly talking about the Soviets doing disinformation. It's going to cause difficulties for us. We don't think it's a major, lasting firestorm, but there will be some ripples.[46]

As these comments suggest, public attitudes about the proper roles of the press and the government are an important factor in setting the parameters of government manipulation of the press and press interference in political events.

It may seem peculiar that this chapter contains no discussion of influence exerted by the Federal Communications Commission. In our judgment, that influence ranges from minuscule to nonexistent. Network executives frequently express fears of licensing nonrenewal, but no such fears are warranted by past FCC action, at least in regard to news programming. "A renewal application has never been denied solely because of a failure to meet community needs and problems, an excess of commercials, a lack of public service announcements, or an inadequate amount of news, public affairs, or other nonentertainment material."[47]

TO SUM UP

The news media influence and are, in turn, influenced. The most effective manipulators of media news are those who understand journalistic norms and routines and use them to gain media access and to influence the nature of coverage. The news media are influenced by highly paid news managers and their

46. Bernard Weinraub, "White House and Its News," *New York Times*, 3 October 1986, p. 4 Y.
47. Barry Cole and Mal Oettinger, *Reluctant Regulators: The FCC and the Broadcast Audience* (Reading, Mass.: Addison-Wesley, 1978), p. 134.

clients and by other individuals and groups. The news media are also affected by commercial pressures for ratings and revenues and by the protests of those offended by news coverage. Finally, they respond to pressures from those in position of political power.

The next chapter explores the roles of ratings and revenues in mass media social systems.

Selected Readings

Cole, Barry, and Mal Oettinger. *Reluctant Regulators: The FCC and the Broadcast Audience*. Reading, Mass.: Addison-Wesley, 1978.

Gitlin, Todd. *The Whole World Is Watching: Mass Media in the Making and Unmaking of the New Left*. Berkeley: University of California Press, 1980.

Goldenberg, Edie N. *Making the Papers*. Lexington, Mass.: Lexington Books, 1975.

Hess, Stephen. *The Government/Press Connection: Press Officers and Their Offices*. Washington, D.C.: Brookings Institution, 1984.

Hess, Stephen. *The Rise of the Professional Specialist in Washington Journalism*. Washington, D.C.: Brookings Institution, 1986.

Porter, William E. *Assault on the Media: The Nixon Years*. Ann Arbor: University of Michigan Press, 1976.

Ranney, Austin. *Channels of Power*. New York: Basic Books, 1983.

Schmidt, Benno C., Jr. *Freedom of the Press vs. Public Access*. New York: Praeger, 1976.

Ratings and Revenues:
The Audience in Mass Media
Social Systems

This chapter is about money. More specifically, it is about how sellers (the mass media) and buyers (advertisers) determine the price to be paid for advertising in the print or broadcast media. This chapter is also about how mass media systems function. As we discussed in Chapter 1, *the primary function of the mass media is to attract and hold a large audience for advertisers*.

Here we examine how audiences are measured and how advertising rates are set. Because the price of an ad is determined by the size and makeup of the audience, this chapter is also about ratings. Ratings services measure and describe the audiences of radio and television programming and the readership of magazines; circulation size and intensity serve a similar function for newspapers.

The Mass Media: Social Systems

Wherever they exist, the mass media are complex systems composed of interrelated elements or parts.[1] Because mass media in the United States are wholly or partially commercial, measures of audience behavior (what audiences watch, hear, or read and what they buy) and revenues (the results of audience behaviors) are central to the system.

Audiences, as measured by ratings, determine the success or failure of *programming* or *content*. Content reaches the audience through *distributors*—outlets such as the networks, individual stations, wire services, theaters, magazines, and newspapers. *Producers* of content (including subsystems of reporters, actors, camera crews, labor unions, and publishers) are financed by *advertisers* or backers who, in turn, depend on advertisers for their money.

1. The ideas in this section are drawn from the work of Melvin L. De Fleur. (See Melvin L. De Fleur and Sandra Ball-Rokeach, *Theories of Mass Communication*, 3d ed. [New York: Longman, 1975], pp. 156–172.)

Advertising agencies connect advertisers with distributors (outlets), with content producers, and with *audience- and market-research organizations* such as Nielsen and Arbitron, which gather data on audience behavior (ratings and purchasing patterns).

Government regulators include the Federal Communication Commission (FCC), which licenses distributors, and the Federal Trade Commission (FTC) and the courts, which set limits on advertising, news, and program content.

Citizen regulators, which generate political pressure, include watchdog groups such as Action for Children's Television, the Gray Panthers Media Watch, and the Coalition for Better Television. *Self-regulatory mechanisms* arise to forestall government or legal regulation, or to defuse political pressure; some of these are newspaper ombudsmen and women, the National Association of Broadcasters, the Electronic Media Ratings Council, the National Advertising Division of the Better Business Bureau, and the National Advertising Review Board.

As social systems, the mass media are part of the larger social system of our society. U.S. social norms are expressed in laws, moral codes, conventions (what we find entertaining, appropriate, or offensive), and values (what we believe in, such as the efficacy of free enterprise, the legitimacy of the profit motive, and the importance of freedom of speech). These norms influence audience behavior and underlie all forms of regulation.

All social systems seek to survive, to maintain their stability and equilibrium. In the United States, the chief requirement is commercial: in order to survive, mass media must generate profits or adequate financing, which requires attracting mass audiences. Ratings measure how well the mass media do this, and revenues depend on such ratings. Audience behavior (what is listened to, watched, read, and bought) and audience norms (what entertains, what offends) are fundamental to mass media systems. These, in turn, reflect how the mass media have developed in the history of this society.

A Brief History of the Mass Media

Many older Americans remember a time when there were no radios; many more of us remember a time before television. The brevity of film history was underlined when Lillian Gish, a star of the earliest silent films, made a presentation at the 1981 Academy Award ceremonies. Only the print media date back beyond living memory, and even their current forms are quite recent. Today's newspaper was born in the nineteenth century with the advent of the "penny press"; the pocket-sized paperback book, making all kinds of books accessible to nearly everyone, is a twentieth-century creation.

The development of the mass media coincides with U.S. growth into an industrial, mass, affluent society. This societal transformation means that nearly all of us now depend on a system called "the market" for producing, distributing, and selling goods to satisfy our needs. We do not produce what we consume; instead we sell our labor for wages and buy goods produced by others.

If such a marketing system is to work well, we need to get information about available goods and services, their location, price, and comparative advantages. Making that information known is advertising's central function.

Even this brief description shows that an industrial society is a highly organized society. In addition to market dependence, such a society fosters and depends on a division of labor so that goods can be produced more cheaply and efficiently. Carried to its obvious conclusion, this division of labor created the assembly lines that transformed cars from rare, luxury items for the wealthy into Model T Fords most Americans could afford.

Such a society also depends on technology. As the cost of both labor and raw materials rises, items like ready-to-wear clothes can be kept within the price ranges of most Americans only when machines speed up and simplify the processes of production, enabling industries to mass produce the items. The elements of mass media systems reflect this division of labor and this reliance on technology.

Industrial societies are mass societies. If an industrial system is to work, there must be a large market for goods because the savings that come from machines and assembly lines can only be realized if many cars or dresses can be produced and sold to many people. Industrial societies also tend to be affluent societies. Industries require large amounts of capital, and successful industries must sell their goods to many individuals who must have the money to buy them. Like other industries, the media reach large audiences who must be able to afford newspapers, magazines, radios, and television sets, and the products they advertise.

The Role of Mass Media Advertising

Mass media are central to such industrial, mass, affluent societies. We depend on them to know what jobs are available, what goods we can buy, where, and for how much. The essential role of mass media advertising under such conditions is described by David Potter:

> It is when potential supply outstrips demand—that is, when abundance prevails—that advertising begins to fulfill a really essential economic function. In this situation the producer knows that the limitation upon his [sic] growth no longer lies, as it lay historically, in his productive capacity, for he can always produce as much as the market will absorb; the limitation has shifted to the market, and its selling capacity which controls his growth.[2]

The advertising Potter describes is done through the mass media—their primary function is to attract and hold a large audience for advertisers. Mass media in the United States are commercial media; their job is to gather an audience for persuaders. They also inform and entertain, of course, but informing and entertaining are only means to the end of delivering a mass audience to advertisers.

2. David Potter, *People of Plenty: Economic Abundance and the American Character* (Chicago: University of Chicago Press, 1954), pp. 172–173.

The Audience

As central elements in mass media systems and the mass society, advertisers have two related purposes: to reach the largest possible audience, and to reach the ideal (target) audience for their products. An "efficient advertising buy" (reaching the largest number of the ideal or target audience at the lowest price) is measured in terms of cost per thousand (CPT) persons reached and in terms of audience desirability—the age, sex, income, education, occupation, region, location (urban, suburban, rural), and ethnic background of audience members reached.

For example, in 1990, CBS Evening News had two financial problems. First, it had been displaced by ABC as the most watched evening news show. This meant that whereas ABC could command up to $85,000 for 30 seconds of ad time, in the second quarter of 1990, CBS could only sell that amount of time for around $45,000. The drop in audience also meant that CBS had to offer more "make-goods" (additional ad slots at no extra charge) to compensate for not delivering the promised audience.

The second problem for CBS was that its audience had been and continued to be older overall than the audience of its two prime competitors. And as *Electronic Media* commented, "older viewer demographics . . . are less marketable."[3]

In the 1970s there was a shift away from "shotgun" advertising, aimed at the largest possible audience, to advertising targeted at specific audiences, such as homeowners, children, teenagers, Hispanics, or working women. For large national advertisers, the most desirable audience is women between the ages of 18 and 49 who make the largest number of consumption decisions, followed closely by men of the same ages, who are believed to make more of the decisions about such durable goods as automobiles.[4]

Advertisers speak of "upscale" and "downscale" audiences. An audience is upscale if its members are above average in education and disposable income and in the prime age group. An audience is downscale if it is older, less affluent, less well-educated, rural, and in blue-collar occupations. In 1990, the publication that attracted the largest number of readers with incomes over $60,000 was *National Geographic*, followed by *Better Homes and Gardens*, and *Reader's Digest*. The newspaper that reached the largest number of wealthy readers was the *Wall Street Journal*, followed by *USA Today*, and the Sunday *New York Times*. The news-magazine with the largest number of wealthy readers was *Time*, followed by *Newsweek*.[5]

The averages for 1989–90 reveal how the viewing preferences of the audience differ by age. Among adults 18–24, the most popular prime-time program was Fox's "Simpsons." Among adults 25–54, it was "Roseanne." But those 55 and

3. "Network News Cost-Cutting Spreads," *Electronic Media*, 9 April 1990, p. 46.
4. The accuracy of this perception may be open to question. In "Sex, Lies & Advertising," *Ms.*, July/August 1990, Gloria Steinem indicates that "long after figures showed a third, even a half, of many car models being bought by women, U.S. carmakers continue to be uncomfortable addressing women" (p. 20).
5. Mendelsohn Media Research reported in *Advertising Age*, 19 July 1990, p. S-1.

VALS—State of the Art Advertising

The newest marketing techniques hone in on a consumer's lifestyle (marital status, education, region, sex) and attitudes (religion, ambition, optimism, and so on), which are considered better bases for appeal than income.

VALS, short for "values and lifestyles," generates a series of categories: survivors (poor, old), sustainers (struggling, young), belongers (traditional conformists), emulators (macho yuppies), achievers (familial workaholics), and "I-am-Me's" (young 80s individualists), experientials (menopausal new-agers), and the societally conscious (60s nostalgics). The most prestigious are the "integrated": mature, intelligent, sensitive, successful—and 2 percent of the population.

The categories sell: they're used by *Time*, AT&T, Procter & Gamble, Tupperware, as well as the British Conservative Party—institutions not known for romantic delusion.

They assume a certain self-consciousness on the part of the consumer, an increasing awareness of personal as well as socioeconomic identity. They succeed by flattering individuals' fantasies about themselves, not by expressly relating identity to a class. They work because they play more on our fantasies about the future than on any reality about our past.[a]

[a]Andrew Sullivan, "Buying and Nothingness," *The New Republic*, 8 May 1989, p. 37.

Targeting Virile Females

On February 16, 1990, the *Washington Post* revealed R.J. Reynolds' plans for Project V.F. for "Virile Female." "The marketing plan's chief goal is to capture the market among 18-to-24-year-old women, the only group of Americans whose rate of smoking continues to increase. . . . The advertising campaign focuses on women whose favorite pastimes include cruising, partying, and attending hot-rod shows and tractor pulls with their boyfriends. . . ." The marketing recommendations dated September 21, 1989, describe the preferred Dakota (the brand name) smoker as a woman with no education beyond high school, whose chief aspiration is "to get married in her early twenties" and spend her free time "with her boyfriend doing whatever he is doing."[b]

[b]Michael Spector, "Reynolds Plan Taps 'Virile' Female Smokers," *Philadelphia Inquirer*, 18 February 1990, p. 3 A.

older preferred "60 Minutes," which didn't make the top ten shows viewed in either of the two younger age categories.[6]

Psychodemographics, the study of the interests, attitudes, and activities of specific population groups, is becoming increasingly important, although such ratings are only in their infancy. For instance, Ronald Frank and Marshall Greenberg have done an extensive study of television viewers; they divide them into

6. "TV Favorites Affected by Audience Age," *Advertising Age*, 21 May 1990, p. 46.

fourteen different audiences based on interests and activities. As they demonstrate, there is little relationship between traditional demographic analysis of television viewers and the fourteen interest groups that they identify.[7] Advertisers and programmers are very interested in such studies because activities and interests may be better predictors of viewing habits and consumption patterns than age, sex, income, or location.

Many advertisers advertise in more than one medium; they buy a "mix," which may be composed of billboards, direct mail, newspapers, magazines, radio, or television. Because ratings are subject to error, advertisers frequently shift their mix to discover, for example, if advertising in newspapers and regional magazines is more effective than in national newsmagazines. Some advertisers, though, are limited to certain media; for instance, cigarettes may not be advertised on television.

Media cross-advertise themselves and their products, as well. In 1988, newspapers spent $4.5 million heralding their accomplishments on billboards.[8] Radio stations promoted themselves to television viewers.[9] They also use advertising to promote their prime-time and daytime programming to viewers of news and vice versa. For example, when CBS fell from first place in news viewership, the network responded by creating and airing a half dozen promotional spots on news anchor Dan Rather. The spots showed Rather addressing high school audiences across the country and bore the tag, "More than Just an Anchorman."

Cable television and videocassettes expanded the number of options for advertisers. The advent of these outlets and the decline in network audience levels translated roughly into a 5 percent decline in network ad revenues in 1989 over 1988.[10]

Each medium differs in terms of its system of ratings and revenues. In this chapter we examine the ratings and revenues of television (commercial and public), radio, newspapers, and magazines. Once again, we focus on the dominant media and on those media most directly involved in news and political communication.

Technology

The nature of the media and their relationship with their audiences can be profoundly influenced by changes in technology. In 1975 SATCOM I, the first domestic communications satellite, was launched. Up to that time most broadcast messages were transmitted through land lines. By the mid-1980s, most radio, broadcast, and cable signals were delivered by satellite. Satellites multiply the quantity of programming to which the typical viewer has access and make pos-

---

7. Ronald E. Frank and Marshall G. Greenberg, *The Public's Use of Television* (Beverly Hills: Sage, 1980), pp. 215–216.

8. Pamela M. Terrell, "Newspaper Advertising in the Great Outdoors," *Presstime*, August 1989, p. 608.

9. "Using TV to Build Radio Station Identity," *Broadcasting*, 18 June 1990, p. 42.

10. "Media Firms Facing Turbulent Economy," *Electronic Media*, 13 August 1990, p. 38.

sible direct and almost immediate transmission of broadcast information from one point on the globe to another.

The advent of home video recorders also altered the media environment. VCRs increased the viewer's control over what was watched and when it was watched. The concept of "daypart" (a segment of a broadcast day), once a mainstay of media planners, is potentially rendered obsolete by VCRs. Viewers who are not even home when the program originally aired can now view it at their leisure. VCR tracking by Nielsen in November 1989 revealed that VCR owners spent approximately 2 hours, 11 minutes recording. The households spent 3 hours, 45 minutes a week in playback.[11]

VCRs also made it possible for viewers to eliminate commercials from programming by fast-forwarding through them. Such "zipping" (fast-forwarding through commercials) is a major concern of advertisers who are eager to learn the extent to which VCRs are whittling down the size of their audiences. Barry Kaplan, chairperson of the Advertising Research Foundation Video Electronics Media Council, believes that up to a quarter of the programming recorded is never played back and that as many as two-thirds of the commercials are "zipped" when playback does occur.[12]

Computers have altered newsgathering techniques as well. Reporters now use computers to scan archives and to reduce large amounts of data to manageable form. Inequities are found and reported. In 1984, reporters at *Newsday* used a computer to search every state-awarded highway contract and county-awarded sewer contract for an eleven-year period. The computer parsed out a pattern that would otherwise have been difficult to see. As it turned out, five firms had collected a disproportionate amount of government business.[13] In April 1990, *Los Angeles Times'* reporters Sara Fritz and Dwight Morris used computers to search the disclosure files of candidates to track political contributions by more than 100 wealthy individuals. Donald Trump was among those found to have contributed more than the legal $25,000 limit.[14]

The increased use of computer data by political reporters is a function of reporters' increased comfort with computers and the existence of purchasable magnetic tapes containing all of the federal election data for a political cycle. Additionally, Federal Election Commission data are now accessible through computer-tied phone lines at a low charge of $25 an hour.

Commercial Television

■

When television networks solicit the attention of advertisers, they do so in terms that make plain the fact that what they are selling is their audience. For example, in *Advertising Age*, "CNN Headline News" is touted this way: "There are

11. *Nielsen Media News*, April 1990, p. 3.

12. "Industry Pushing for Accurate Measure of Commercial Zipping," *Television/Radio Age*, 28 April 1986, p. 96.

13. *Time*, 7 July 1986, p. 56.

14. "At FEC, Reporters Are Finally Getting Their PCs On-Line," *Roll Call*, 25 June 1990, p. 11.

Crisis News-Watching

During the first week of August 1990, NBC, CBS, and ABC evening newscasts had an overall rating of 28.8 and a 60 percent share of the audience. Prime-time programs had a 28.1 rating and 53 share.

Each rating point represents 921,000 homes. The audience share is the estimated percent of households tuned to a program in a given time period.[c]

At 6:35 P.M. (EST) on January 16, 1991, ABC News reported the beginning of the U.S. air attack on Baghdad. Nielsen numbers for the first hour after the attack showed CNN with a 20.7 rating among U.S. cable households, against first-hour total television households for ABC (17.2 rating with a 27 share), NBC (15.2 rating with a 22 share), and CBS (12.6 rating with a 19 share).

During the week of January 15–21, CNN showed an average 7.5 rating with a 19.4 share, meaning 4.3 million homes were watching the network during any given minute. In that same period ABC showed a 5.7 rating with a 14.7 share, CBS garnered a 5.5 rating with a 14.3 share, and NBC had a 5.5 rating with a 14.1 share.[d]

[c]Nielsen Media Research.
[d]*Broadcasting*, 21 January 1991, pp. 23, 26.

Advertising on Cable

Thirty seconds of ad time sold for an average of $1,500 to $2,500 in 1989. A 30-second spot on "high ticket sporting events" sold for $75,000.[e]

[e]*Electronic Media*, 13 August 1990, p. 4.

many CNN viewers who watch virtually no other television. And 43 percent are elusive light viewers of primetime network. They may not have much time for TV, but they have the means. With a median income 21 percent higher than the U.S. average, they're as prosperous a group as you can reach through television."[15]

Audiences are drawn to news in times of perceived crisis. The result is a revenue windfall for news networks. For example, when in summer 1990 Iraq moved into Kuwait, coverage of the resulting Middle East crisis pushed network news ratings up by 19 percent. This meant that in early August 1990, the network news programs had a larger average audience than did prime-time entertainment.

Commercial television is almost entirely financed by advertising. Network and station profits are the difference between programming costs (including salaries, equipment, and facilities) and the prices advertisers are charged to air commercials. For example, if the price of producing the network evening news is $100,000, but $400,000 worth of advertising can be sold, the network's profit is $300,000.

15. 28 May 1990, p. 39.

The prices charged for advertising on individual programs are determined by Nielsen and Arbitron ratings. Nielsen dominates network television ratings, whereas Arbitron competes actively in local market ratings.

Audience Ratings

Nielsen Ratings   The A.C. Nielsen Company is the biggest marketing research firm in the world, and it operates in twenty-two countries. Most of its income comes from research checking supermarket and drugstore shelves to find out how well certain products, brands, and sizes are selling. The Media Research Division, which computes the ratings, is only a small part of the Nielsen Company.

The Nielsen Company developed and patented a device called an audimeter that could be attached to television sets to record set-on, set-off information and the channel to which the set was tuned. In 1974, Nielsen began nationwide use of the Storage Instantaneous Audimeter (SIA), capable of reading up to four sets in a household, including battery-operated portables.

Field representatives, offering a small fee, tried to persuade families to join the ratings panel for five-year periods. During any biweekly rating period, not all Nielsen homes were counted. Some had not yet been hooked up; others were lost because of malfunctions in audimeters or telephone lines. Sets that burned out or went dark because of power failures and families out for the evening or away on vacation were all counted as "no viewing for that day." Thus, on a typical ratings day in 1977, Nielsen reported viewing information from about 993 homes.

In 1986, there were approximately 1,700 SIA households in the national Nielsen sample, each connected to a special telephone line. At least twice a day a central computer dialed the audimeters and retrieved the stored viewing information. Network Nielsen ratings, reported in the Nielsen Television Index (NTI), were based on this secret sample of homes across the country picked randomly from a Census Bureau list but with a geographic spread. Major markets, including New York, Los Angeles, and Chicago, were metered with SIAs for overnight ratings. In actuality, ratings could be delivered to customers two days after programming was aired, allowing networks to make rapid programming decisions.

The Nielsen meters recorded only what was being watched—not who, if anyone, was doing the watching. For all the meters knew, the family dog may have been tuned attentively to reruns of "Lassie." Ratings based on meters were supplemented by ratings from diaries, which were the basis for demographic breakdowns, showing how many men, women, and children in different age groups, by area, watched each program on the air, and they provided the data for local market reports. The Nielsen Company reported that about half the people they asked to keep a diary refused.[16] Keeping a diary indicating program, channel, station, number of persons watching by age and sex for each quarter hour is tedious work, as one of the authors knows from personal experience!

The national Nielsen ratings, collected in the Nielsen National TV Ratings Report, statistically estimate the number of homes viewing a program projected

16. David Chagall, "The Viewers Who Go Uncounted," *TV Guide*, 1 July 1978, p. 21.

Television Ratings and Shares

TV set off   Channel A   Channel B

Both ratings and shares measure how many people watch a given program. Ratings measure the percentage of people viewing a program out of all U.S. households *with television sets*, whether turned on or not. Shares measure the percentage of people viewing a program out of those U.S. households *watching television at any given time.*

Rating = % of U.S. households *with television* tuned to channel *x.*

Share = % of U.S. households *watching television* tuned to channel *x.*

	Rating	Share
Channel A	40	66.6
Channel B	20	33.3

from the viewing patterns of the homes with audimeters, combined with data from viewer diaries. There is an acknowledged 3 percent margin of error in the Nielsen ratings with the present sample size.[17] To halve the margin of error, thus doubling the precision of the ratings, would require a sample four times as large as the one Nielsen now uses. The networks, the ad agencies, the advertisers, and the program suppliers have not been willing to pay the price for greater accuracy.

17. For an indication of what this can mean for programming decisions, see David Chagall, "Can You Believe the Ratings?" *TV Guide*, 24 June 1978, especially p. 13.

In Defense of Network Television Advertising

Citing A.C. Nielsen Company figures, Richard Kostyra, executive vice president and director of media services for J. Walter Thompson, USA, points out that during the prime-time hours in the first quarter of 1989, the three major networks reached 94 percent of U.S. homes with television sets. Audiences for the five most highly rated series exceeded 30 million people, with the top-rated "Cosby Show" watched by 36.6 million people on average each week during the 1988–89 season. "You read article after article saying that network TV is going down the tubes because of all the new media coming up," Mr. Kostyra said in an interview. "It's not completely untrue. But network TV is still the biggest and most popular form of communications to product users."[f]

[f]Randall Rothenberg, "A Ringing Defense of Mass Media," *New York Times*, 25 August 1989, p. 27 Y.

A national rating represents the percentage of sample homes tuned in to the same show. For instance, if a program scores a 20 rating for the week, that means that 20 percent of the sample homes had that show turned in for at least six minutes (about 199 sets out of the average 993 reporting). A rating is the estimated percentage of television homes (households with television sets) that watched a program.

Nielsen also reports what percentage of households actually watching television is tuned in to a particular program. This number is called "share of audience."[18] In August 1990, HBO's presentation of the Madonna concert "Madonna—Live! Blonde Ambition World Tour 90" became the highest rated program, excluding sports, in the history of cable. The show drew a 21.5 Nielsen Media Research rating, and a 31 share—numbers that translated into an audience of 4.3 million households.[19]

Several hundred companies (advertising agencies, advertisers, program suppliers, and the networks) subscribe to the Nielsen ratings, but the networks are the largest customers in terms of the prices they pay for the service. Networks rely on Nielsen for about 90 percent of their information, and each pays Nielsen roughly $10 million a year for its services.

One weakness in the ratings is that they measure viewing demographically—by age, income, education, and family size—which has little to do with interests, tastes, attitudes, or activities. The ratings are distorted to an extent because they do not reflect viewing in hotels, hospitals, bars, prisons, clubs, summer camps, military bases, college dormitories, or homes for the elderly.

---

18. The required share for a program to survive has been declining as the total share of viewers watching network television has declined; it will continue to decline as public and cable television, videogames, and videotaped programs attract larger shares of the total audience.

19. *Electronic Media*, 13 August 1990, p. 32.

Audience measurement changed dramatically with the introduction of a device known as the people meter. Originally marketed in Europe by the London-based AGB Research, this device instantly analyzes the age, sex, and income of viewers. These are the demographics of greatest interest to advertisers. The people meter resembles the hand-held remote control devices that many people now own. The meter has buttons assigned to individual members of a family. A watcher punches in when starting to view a program and punches out when leaving. A central computer monitors who is watching what and when. The people meter not only indicates more accurately who is watching but also provides better data than diaries on what is being watched. With the proliferation of cable channels and other independent stations, it had become increasingly difficult for diary keepers to record their own viewing. The meter eliminates that problem. Moreover, because it gives a minute-by-minute account of viewing, rather than the diary report every fifteen minutes, the people meter is better able to tell specific advertisers who is watching their ads. Nielsen began using such meters in the fall of 1987.[20]

The Nielsen meters are push-button, hand-held devices on which viewers record viewing in the 4,000 homes that have agreed for participate in each two-year cycle. When Nielsen replaced other forms of monitoring with meters, reported network viewership dropped by 6 percent in the first year. By 1990 the falloff had reached 10 percent. Nielsen argued that the meters were more accurate than previous measures.

By the summer of 1990, the audience shares of the three major networks (NBC, ABC, CBS) had fallen to 53 percent. This meant that Fox, whose rise we noted in Chapter 1, independent stations, and cable commanded 47 percent of the viewers watching in July 1990.[21]

Facing the resulting decline in advertising revenues in early 1988, the networks commissioned a 22-month study through the Committee on Nationwide Television Audience Measurement, a group created by the networks in 1963. The study, completed by Statistical Research Inc., cost a million dollars and was reported in seven volumes. Just before the winter holidays in 1989, the report was released, with several recommendations:

> Nielsen should appoint an ombudsman to monitor measurement.
> Small sets and sets in unusual places such as garages and hotel rooms should be monitored.
> People away from home should be monitored as well.
> Households should be replaced more than once every two years (the report found that fatigue reduces the reliability of the reports after the first year).

---

20. For a brief time, AGB, a British company, and Nielsen faced off in the U.S. market. But after losing $67 million and failing to sign up two of the three networks, AGB withdrew from the U.S. market.

21. "Networks Face Higher Risk of Being Shot Down in Fall," *New York Times*, 30 July 1990, p. D 10.

The meters should be simplified to encourage use by children.

Techniques for encouraging participation should be found (only 55 percent of those asked agree).

Multiple sets in the same home should be followed.[22]

ABC, NBC, and ESPN commissioned the A.C. Nielsen Company to study viewing outside homes, and a survey was conducted from November 2 to November 29, 1989. More than 4,000 people 12 years of age and older participated, filling out diaries that logged all their viewing over the period, inside and outside the home. The results indicated than an average of 500,000 to 1.3 million people were watching television somewhere other than in their homes during some part of the day. Thirty-five percent reported viewing at work. Twenty-one percent took place in college dorms, 16 percent in hotel rooms, 9 percent in bars and restaurants, and 4 percent in second homes; 15 percent fell into other categories. The overall increase in viewing averaged 2 to 3 percent, equivalent to three-tenths to seven-tenths of a rating point, as much as the average rating for most cable channels, and an increase in audience that would be worth almost $225 million to network television.[23]

The very rich, the well-educated, the poor, and minority groups—particularly poorer African-American and Hispanic families—have been underrepresented in the Nielsen samples. Minorities and poorer Americans have been underrepresented because Nielsen field representatives tended to be whites who encounter hostility when they knock on doors in ghettos or barrios. It was difficult to find African-American and Hispanic families who would agree to fill out diaries, and Nielsen only began distributing Spanish-language diaries in 1978. The high level of literacy required and the tediousness of the task limited all diary participation to the better-educated and middle class; thus African-Americans and Hispanics who agreed to fill out diaries tended to be those whose viewing patterns resembled the viewing of white middle-class audiences. The dissemination of people meters faced similar problems.

The underrepresentation of African-Americans and other minorities created significant problems for television stations that appealed to such audiences. Because their primary viewership was underrepresented in the ratings sample, such outlets got lower ratings and therefore found it difficult to attract advertisers. This, in turn, made it harder for minority programming or minority outlets to survive.[24]

By November 1989, Nielsen was able to show that 11 percent of its respondents were African-American.[25] Census figures indicate that 11.3 percent of the U.S. population is African-American. In early June 1990, Nielsen announced that it

22. Jeremy Gerard, "TV Networks Want Nielsen to Change Ratings Methods," *New York Times*, 14 December 1989, p. D 1.

23. Bill Carter, "TV Viewing Cited Outside of Homes," *New York Times*, 10 May 1990, p. C 15 Y.

24. Chagall, "The Viewers," pp. 20–22, 24, 26. See also Edwin Diamond, *The Tin Kazoo: Television, Politics and the News* (Cambridge, Mass.: MIT Press, 1975), pp. 152–153, for evidence gathered by the A.C. Nielsen Company that African-American households watch television "significantly more" than households generally.

25. Michael Couzens, "Berating the Raters," *Channels*, 7 May 1990, p. 17.

The Nielsen Sample

According to a study by the Committee on Nationwide Television Audience Measurement, in June 1989 only 47 percent of the households Nielsen had chosen for its sample agreed to take its "people meter," forcing the company to go to alternative homes. Eleven years earlier, 68 percent of Nielsen's first-choice homes took its meters.

The study attributed the steady decline to "an increasing societal tendency to refuse participation in surveys."[g]

[g]Randall Rothenberg, "Surveys Proliferate, But Answers Dwindle," *New York Times,* 5 October 1990, p. A 6 Y.

The Hispanic Audience

"Hispanics number at least ten percent of the population nationally, and much more than that in key markets such as Los Angeles, New York, and Miami. Yet advertisers spend only $300 million plus annually on network Spanish language TV. The two national Spanish networks, Univision and Telemundo, struggle to sell 60 percent of their inventory. And the rate of advertiser spending growth on Spanish TV is plummeting. . . . The new Nielsen numbers could change all that fast."[h]

[h]*Channels/Field Guide 1990,* p. 83.

was "enhancing" the methods it uses to collect and report on African-American and Hispanic audiences.

> Starting in 1991, Nielsen will expand its monthly National Audience Demographic Report to include Black households and about 20 Black demographic categories. Nielsen will also add marketing information, including penetration estimates to determine what percent of a local market is Black or Hispanic. Nielsen will also introduce a National Black "Pocketpiece," similar to the ones produced for the broadcast-cable networks and the syndicators. The Pocketpiece would provide ratings, shares, households and demographic information based on television viewing among Blacks.[26]

At the same time, a number of organizations, including Tribune Entertainment and Burrell Uniworld, pledged to launch educational campaigns designed to increase the cooperation rate among African-American and Hispanic households.

In summer 1990, the three major networks agreed on a new uniform policy for providing guarantees that the advertisers reach the size of audience for which they have paid. Fluctuations in the people-using-television (PUT) numbers and what the networks view as "inexplicable falloff" in audience viewing have

26. "Nielsen Expanding Minority Measuring," *Broadcasting,* 18 June 1990, p. 66.

prompted the networks to base the guarantees on trends since the 1982–83 viewing season. A PUT number is the combined ratings of all stations and channels available for viewers at a specified time. Since the people meters showed a falloff in audience, the networks have viewed the Nielsen PUT numbers with suspicion; 1982–83 was set as the starting point because that was the first year in which viewing stopped increasing. In the fourth quarter of 1989–90, Nielsen set the PUT level for one prime-time minute for women 18–49 at 39.3 percent. The new network methodology set the number at 39.9 percent.[27]

Arbitron Nielsen has competed in television ratings with Arbitron, the rating service of the American Research Bureau, a subsidiary of Control Data Corporation.

ScanAmerica, a Denver-based research service developed with help from Arbitron, is one example of efforts to tie viewing to the purchase of products. Viewers are not only being given people meters but electronic scanners that function as do supermarket decoders by reading the information on the bar codes of products. Viewers then run the scanning wands over the products they purchase. By correlating the information from the people meters (telling which advertisements the viewers have seen) with the scanners' information (specifying which products are purchased, in what quantity, and so on), advertisers can determine how their television ads are influencing buying habits.

Arbitron also produces Broadcast Advertising Reports (BAR) that detail the number of minutes devoted to advertising in each day part. The figures we cited earlier that indicated an increase in the number of commercial minutes on the major networks were BAR figures.

Arbitron's specialty is local media. In 1990, Arbitron began promoting its Local Media Report. The report indicates which advertisers are concentrating space buys on newspapers, the dollar amount of space purchased and when they advertise. Such knowledge can aid local television stations in luring advertisers from print to television.

Utilizing the Ratings

Arbitron and Nielsen ratings, which are actually percentage figures for the number of television households that have tuned in a program, are used to estimate the size of the total audience. As a result, they determine how much an advertiser will pay to air a commercial at various times and, thus, determine how large a network's or station's profits will be. Networks and stations base their charges for commercial time on ratings. Advertisers buy time in terms of ratings, total cost, and the number of target-audience members among viewers. Ratings are the only bases for all of these.

From the data gathered by the ratings services, the networks have learned that although 98 percent of U.S. households have television sets, only one-third of that potential audience does two-thirds of the daily viewing. These are the habitual watchers.

27. "Three TV Networks Line Up Behind PUT Plan," *Broadcasting*, 18 June 1990, p. 22.

Income Levels for Prime-Time Viewing

	Under $30,000	$30–40,000	$40–50,000	$50–60,000	$60,000+
NBC	53.7	14.6	11.3	7.8	12.6
ABC	46.9	15.6	13.0	8.5	15.8
CBS	52.7	15.2	11.3	7.8	13.0
CNN	45	15	13	8	19

Source: Broadcasting, 18 June 1990, p. 53.

In 1989, one prime-time rating point (1 percent of the nation's 90 million households) was worth as much as $140 million a year.[28] One percentage point in prime-time audience share means more than $30 million to a network in a year.[29]

Mini-Series   Mini-series are an attempt to gain an audience with a compelling story and hold it through subsequent prime-time evenings as the story winds to a conclusion. CBS's 8-hour "Lonesome Dove" was the highest rated mini-series not only of 1988–89 but of any mini-series in the five previous years. "Lonesome Dove" generated over $30 million in ad revenue for CBS. By contrast, "War and Remembrance," another widely promoted mini-series, lost nearly $40 million for its network.

Competition for Time Periods   Networks not only compete for overall ratings, they compete for ratings and revenues in various time periods.

In spring 1990, "ABC World News Tonight" was the number-one-rated evening news broadcast with a rating of 11. Whereas 30 seconds on ABC's news cost $58,100, the same amount of time on CBS sold for $46,700.[30]

There is also competition over "late fringe time," the period from 11 P.M. to 1 A.M. In 1989, the number one late-night show was NBC's "The Tonight Show," which had a rating of 5.6, sold advertising at $38,700 for a 30-second spot, and had a CPT of $7.31. ABC's "Nightline" followed with a rating of 4.6, but since its demographics were those upscale ones prized by advertisers, "Nightline" was able to sell 30 seconds of ad time at $39,500 for a CPT of $9.68.[31]

The demographic shifts in the audience are mirrored in the advertising. The company spending the most on network news ads in 1989 was Kellogg's, followed by American Home Products. The company spending the most on ads in late-night time was Anheuser-Busch.[32]

28. Jay Sharbutt, "Network-Backed Study Urges Changes in Nielsen Rating System," *Philadelphia Inquirer*, 16 December 1989, p. 8 D.

29. Ben H. Bagdikian, "Global Media Corporations Control What We Watch (and Read)," *Utne Reader*, June/August 1990, p. 88.

30. *Advertising Age*, 28 May 1990, p. 39.

31. Ibid., p. 40.

32. Ibid., pp. 39–40.

The Complexities of Television Economics

Turner Broadcasting System promised "advertisers an average 5 Nielsen Television Index rating over the [1990 Goodwill] games' span ending August 5, yet in ratings from the first six days of telecasts through July 25, TBS was 50 percent behind that place with a 2.5 rating. . . . Usually, the superstation penetrates 53 million homes, yet cable operators serving 10 million viewers refused to sign up subscribers at a cost of $1.10 each for the Goodwill Games telecast. Should TBS fail to improve on its initial ratings, it will again have to offer advertisers make-goods as it had with the first games in 1986."[1]

[1]*Electronic Media*, 30 July 1990, p. 3.

The Super Bowl

Five of the ten most popular television shows have been Super Bowls. In Nielsen history, the only shows to outscore Super Bowls were the final episode of "M*A*S*H" in 1983, the 1980 "Who Shot JR?" episode of "Dallas," and the final segment of "Roots" in 1977. In 1990, a 30-second spot on the Super Bowl cost $700,000. During the 1990 Super Bowl, 27 minutes of commercials appeared.[1]

[1]Nielsen Media Research.

Network Affiliation

Network affiliation is very profitable for television stations and for the networks. Advertisers pay the network to air commercials according to the number of viewers. The network pays a set station rate per ad, regardless of the price paid by the advertisers. If a program increases in popularity, advertisers must pay more to the network, but the network has no obligation to pay more to the stations. However, network compensation is negotiated, and more desirable affiliates are paid more.

The schedule for broadcasting is divided between network time, in which network programming is aired, and affiliate time. Affiliate time is divided between locally originated programming, including news, and syndicated programming. Profits from these go directly to affiliates. The evening news broadcasts on all three networks are scheduled during affiliate time, which is one reason affiliates resist network efforts to extend these newscasts to 45 minutes or an hour. One commentator explains:

> When the networks scheduled their 15-minute news broadcasts and later the 30-minute broadcasts in the affiliates' time slots, each network gained 2 minutes and 30 seconds of advertising time per 15-minute block. These extra 5 minutes of

commercials bring in $30 million to $40 million a year in added revenues to each network. But they [affiliates] aren't likely to give up any more time; when they do their own local news programming, they can keep 100 percent of the revenues.[33]

Affiliates have resisted such encroachments energetically, arguing that the networks should program news in the evening hours they already control.[34]

The same problem occurs at other times in the day. In spring 1990, Phil Beuth, senior vice president, ABC Network Group, noted that affiliate resistance was the largest barrier to expanding the number-one-rated "Good Morning America" to weekends. "It's hard to get the stations to give up that time," noted Beuth, "which is profitable and also used as [community] service time. Some of our [network-] owned stations are even reluctant to give up the time."[35]

The relationships between networks and affiliates is complex. No network can compel an affiliate to air or clear any network program, but there are strong inducements to do so. For all three networks, compensation to affiliates is relatively low for the weekly program base of 21 to 24 hours. Program time taken over that base brings a higher rate of compensation. This encourages higher levels of program clearance by affiliates. Most affiliates clear 95 percent of the network programs they are offered, and this programming makes up about 65 percent of their total programming time.[36]

Network ownership of twelve stations ("owned and operated" by the networks, thus known as "O&Os") in major markets, and their relationship to affiliates, made the development of new networks difficult. Network O&Os usually clear network programming, and they control over 20 percent of the total television market. Similarly, affiliate patterns of clearing such large amounts of network programming work against the development of ad hoc networks formed to present special programs. Until the advent of CNN and Fox, there were few exceptions. David Frost's interviews with former President Richard Nixon were one such exception.

The success of CNN changed the network-affiliate equation. By summer 1990, CNN had created profitable relationships with 122 network affiliates. These affiliates pay CNN to receive its 24-hour-a-day newsfeed and provide CNN with material they have produced for their own programs.

The competition from CNN and from such independent services as CONUS prompted the major networks to consider increasing their news programming. In spring 1990, CBS was producing 41 hours of news programming a week, almost twice the amount of NBC and ABC. By January 1, 1991, NBC was providing its 209 affiliates with a 24-hour enhanced newsfeed.[37]

33. Diamond, *Tin Kazoo*, p. 77.

34. Marvin Barrett, *Rich News, Poor News* (New York: Thomas Y. Crowell, 1978), p. 33; cited from a 55-page petition filed with the FCC by Donald McGannon, president of Group W, requesting an inquiry into network practices in response to the threat of expanded network news.

35. "Resistance to Weekend 'GMA,'" *Broadcasting*, 4 June 1990, p. 56.

36. Christopher H. Sterling, "Television and Radio Broadcasting," in *Who Owns the Media?* ed. Benjamin M. Compaine (New York: Harmony Books, 1979), pp. 108, 112.

37. J. Max Robins, "Network News Explodes in Off Hours," *Variety*, 1 August 1990, p. 1.

Public Television

▪

Ratings and revenues are also important to public (educational, nonprofit) television, which is heavily dependent for support on the same U.S. corporations that advertise on commercial television. The funding for public television comes from three sources: government appropriations, contributions from viewers, and corporate sponsors of programming.

Corporations often transform sponsorship of public television programming into image ads with the goal of demonstrating that the corporation is a good citizen. Such promotion not only ensures that large audiences in the commercial media are aware of corporate good deeds, it also increases the size of the upscale audience reached by the program itself.

Reaching this audience is a second reason for corporate largess. One of public television's main selling points is the quality of its audience, "made up largely of well-educated, affluent adults who are often in a position to influence your business," writes KCET-TV's director of development to prospective corporate clients. Thus, although the cost per thousand viewers is very high, it is a good investment.

When advertising agencies and corporations argued successfully that corporate funding could only be maintained or increased if the FCC were persuaded to change its rule prohibiting institutional advertising and corporate logos on public television, new regulations were adopted permitting the use of corporate logos and the identification of the products that underwriters produce.[38] In other words, public television has become more commercial. Some limitations exist, because two-thirds of all public television stations are licensed to educational institutions prohibited from running advertisements, but some stations currently sell advertising in their program guides—an action that has aroused controversy.[39]

Despite the important role of corporate underwriting, the need for the Public Broadcasting Service (PBS) programming to appear untainted by commercial control was evident in the controversy surrounding the firing of "This Old House" host Bob Vila. Commercial suppliers of the materials used in rebuilding houses had become so prominent that one might have mistaken the PBS program for an extended advertisement. The conflict that led to Vila's ouster occurred when the underwriter of seventeen local stations' broadcast of the show complained that Vila was a paid promoter of a home supply chain that competed head to head with the underwriter. When the underwriter pulled its $750,000 funding from the program, WGBH, the producing station, fired Vila.[40] Within months Vila reappeared in ads for Sears.

As noted in Chapter 1, competition from cable, among other factors, caused a decline in viewership of public television in the last half of the 1980s; member donations leveled off simultaneously.

38. John Weisman, "How Creeping Commercialism Is Sneaking Up on Public Television," *TV Guide*, 27 June 1981, p. 44.

39. Tony Schwartz, "Four Possible Ways out of Public TV's Crisis," *New York Times*, 17 May 1981, p. D 39.

40. "A Rude Education in Competition," *Channels/Field Guide 1990*, p. 84.

Cable Television Advertising

The Cable Television Advertising Bureau reported that advertisers spent about $2 billion on cable in 1989. The figure pales against the $23 billion spent on total broadcast television for the same year, but it was still 30 percent more than what was spent on cable for 1988.

Turner Broadcasting System is still the biggest. WTBS-TV had gross ad billings of $278 million in 1989. ESPN followed, with $176 million; USA Network's total was $160 million. CNN billed $180 million, MTV $106 million; Nickelodeon had about $51 million.

Advertisers increasingly view cable as they do regular television, and demographics are in cable's favor. Jerry Hogan, head of sales for Turner Broadcasting System, said: "The lowest economic and educational categories don't have cable, so the demographics just go up."[k]

[k]Geraldine Fabrikant, "Cable TV Is No Longer a Stepchild," *New York Times*, 10 January 1990, p. 45 Y.

Since 1984, viewing of public TV in cable households has declined, particularly in homes that subscribe to pay TV, according to the Public Broadcasting Service. In the 1984–85 season the average monthly average-minute prime-time ratings in pay TV households averaged 2.2; in the 1988–89 season the average monthly rating had plummeted to 1.6. Overall monthly prime-time ratings dropped 8 percent—from 2.7 to 2.5, according to PBS.[41]

PBS has responded by exploring the introduction of a new cable channel. Under the proposal, PBS and its New York and Boston stations, WNET-TV and WGBH-TV, would run a noncommercial cable channel in conjunction with Discovery, an existing cable channel. The new channel would operate with Discovery during the day. Discovery alone would program for prime time and night. Neil Mahrer, PBS executive vice president, explained that the advantages include subscriber fees for PBS.

From PBS's affiliates' standpoint, the problem, of course, is competition. PBS supplies one-third of each of its affiliate's broadcast slate. The rest is programmed locally or obtained elsewhere. Mahrer acknowledged the concern but argued that "the cable channel's content would be designed to augment that of PBS's broadcast affiliates and wouldn't compete directly for either viewers or possible funding sources." And even if the two did experience some crossover, "at least they wouldn't surrender any ground to other alternatives. 'If we don't take one or two or three of those cable channels, someone else will, and we'd be better off competing with ourselves rather than having others compete with us.'"[42]

In spring 1990, the Television Ratings Analysis Consortium (TRAC) reported the results of a study of public television use. The study confirmed the traditional

---

41. Ibid.
42. Thomas Tyrer, "PBS to Centralize Programming," *Electronic Media*, 30 July 1990, p. 4.

profile of public broadcasting. Homes whose household head graduated from college watch more public television than homes headed by those with lower educational levels. Approximately one-third of the public television audience reported being attracted to public television by children's programming. Interestingly, however, homes with older children watch less public television than do homes with younger children. In the past decade, the amount that young children have viewed public television has declined.[43]

The educated audience is attracted to high quality programming, illustrated by the high viewership for the documentary series, "The Civil War," aired in 1991. In the last half of the 1980s, PBS-produced programming took more news and documentary Emmys than its competitors. Emmy-award winners included "National Geographic Specials," "Nova," "Frontline," and "The American Experience."

Radio

■

Radio receives less advertising revenue than its audience would appear to warrant. Industry figures indicate that radio accounts for 40 percent of the public's consumption of media but receives only 7 percent of the available ad revenue.[44]

To a greater extent than television, radio reaches its largest audiences outside the home. The times during which we drive to work (morning drive time), drive from work (afternoon drive time) and listen in the office while working are what attract advertisers.

Radio divides into AM and FM. FM offers superior fidelity and is preferred by those who have grown up on FM stereo. Twenty years ago, 75 percent of the radio stations in the country were AM. By 1990, the percents had reversed with 75 percent now FM. Moreover, FM stations received 77 percent of advertising revenues.[45] Some radio manufacturers are now producing radios without an AM band.

Because FM sound quality is generally superior to that on AM, most AM stations deliver news and talk; a few, such as the news station WINS-AM in New York, are very profitable. Many surviving AM stations are institutions in their communities. WGN-AM, which airs Chicago Cubs baseball games, is one such station. In 1989, it generated $37.4 million in advertising revenue, leading all other radio stations in the United States.

The ratings system for radio is very similar to the local market and demographics ratings systems for television. However, radio ratings measure individual, not household, listenership, and they include out-of-home listening.

Arbitron ratings dominate radio in the same way that Nielsen ratings dominate television. Radio stations charge advertisers on the basis of how many listeners Arbitron determines they have (measured in terms of listening five minutes out of a quarter hour). Drive time (6 to 10 A.M. and 3 to 7 P.M.) is radio's

43. *CPB Report*, vol. 9, no. 7 (26 March 1990), p. 3.
44. "Counting Radio's Assets," *Broadcasting*, 4 June 1990, p. 70.
45. Geraldine Fabrikant, "Struggling Stations in Search of a Niche," *New York Times*, 20 May 1990, p. 10 F.

equivalent of prime time for advertising, and delivers an audience that cannot readily switch to television.

ABC, CBS, National Black, Sheridan, Satellite Music, Unistar, Westwood One Radio Networks, advertisers, and agencies jointly sponsor what are known as RADAR studies. These studies report radio usage. The RADAR report for spring 1990 found that more than 96 percent of those 12 or older listened to the radio during the course of a week. In an average quarter hour, nearly 24 million individuals are listening to radio. The FM share of this audience is 77 percent. Between 1985 and 1990, the FM share grew by about 1 percent a year.[46]

Just as prophets speak of HDTV as the future of television, so, too, they speak of digital audio broadcasting (DAB) as the future of radio. DAB promises "to deliver noise-free, interference-immune, compact-disk quality audio with a vastly more spectrum-efficient scheme than is possible with the current analog (AM and FM) systems."[47]

Arbitron Ratings

Until March 1980, Arbitron made its surveys four times a year, with each survey lasting four weeks. In 1986, Arbitron expanded its radio audience measurements in seventy-five markets to year-round reporting by conducting four 12-week-long surveys per year. This change prevents stations from altering their programming during rating periods. Formerly, during rating periods, radio stations came alive with special programming, contests, and giveaways of all kinds, and disc jockeys were told to announce the station's call letters as often as possible.

Restricted Formats

Like the content in other media, radio programming has been influenced by the desire to maximize profits. One illustration of this is the Drake format (named for its originator), used in top-40 radio. The Drake format or variations on it are designed for maximum efficiency in holding listeners and for standardizing music selection.

It is also ideally suited to Arbitron ratings because it is planned in terms of quarter-hour periods. Each quarter hour is organized into specific categories of record popularity, such as a current hit, an "up-and-comer," a "golden oldie," and so on. "With this format a station could use as few as thirty records for an entire broadcast day. . . . Program directors now had absolute control over what records were played and when they were scheduled."[48]

The Drake format maximizes profits because it is a proven means of attracting and holding audiences. The format functions rhetorically; listeners are introduced to new selections in the context of music that is familiar. Such a format creates and exploits audience identification.

46. "Radar Readings," *Broadcasting*, 18 June 1990, p. 43.
47. "DAB: The Next Generation of Radio Broadcasting?" *Broadcasting*, 4 June 1990, p. 62.
48. David L. Altheide and Robert P. Snow, *Media Logic* (Beverly Hills: Sage, 1979), p. 27.

Except for all-news and public radio, as noted previously in Chapter 1, radio is a headline news service in a form even more abbreviated than that of television. Most newscasts range from 3 to 5 minutes in length. However, because it is a relatively inexpensive advertising medium, ideally suited to reaching specific target audiences, radio is an important medium for political mass communication.

Just as it is difficult for most cities to sustain two major newspapers, it is difficult to sustain two all-news radio stations.

Newspapers

The circulation of most newspapers is small, with the median circulation under 25,000. In this pool are a few very large circulation papers—the *Wall Street Journal*, with a 1989 circulation of 1,931,410—among them. More than 60 percent of the daily newspapers in the United States are owned by chains. Over 97 percent of the cities that have a daily newspaper have only one, making most newspapers monopolies.[49]

The demise of the *Washington Star*, the *Philadelphia Bulletin*, and the *Los Angeles Herald Examiner* and the mergers of the *Minneapolis Star* and *Minneapolis Tribune* and the evening *Kansas City Star* with the morning *Times* are dramatic examples of changes occurring in U.S. newspapers. There is less competition in general and fewer afternoon or evening papers in particular. There are now only about fifty cities in the United States with two or more separately owned, competing newspapers. Only one city, New York, has four—the *Daily News*, *Post*, *Times*, and *Newsday*. Independently owned afternoon newspapers that compete with a morning newspaper are particularly vulnerable, as they must also compete with more up-to-date network and local television news and the problems of rush-hour delivery to suburban readers. In most cases, this has been fatal. Surviving afternoon papers tend to be in smaller markets.

Economic forces have created a situation in which 97 percent of the nation's daily newspapers enjoy a local newspaper monopoly, and nearly half are owned by some group or national chain.[50] Competition among alternative media has taken the place of competition among newspapers.

In 1970, Congress passed the Newspaper Preservation Act, which permitted newspapers threatened with bankruptcy to share manufacturing plants and commercial operations that would otherwise violate the antitrust laws. The *Washington Post* estimates that from 1970, when the law was enacted, until 1986, newspapers in at least twenty-one cities were spared extinction by being able to share facilities with other papers.[51] Although two papers may share printing, advertising,

49. John Sokoski, "Sources and Channels of Local News," *Journalism Quarterly* (Winter 1989): 864–865.

50. Raymond B. Nixon, "Trends in U.S. Newspaper Ownership: Concentration with Competition," in *Mass Media and Society,* 3d ed., Alan Wells, ed. (Palo Alto: Mayfield Publishing, 1979), p. 35.

51. *Washington Post*, 13 July 1986, p. 1.

Los Angeles Herald Examiner
Ceases Publication

The demise of the *Herald Examiner* is the latest in a long pattern of failures among number two papers in large cities. Hurt by a general decline in newspaper readership and intense competition from other newspapers and from television, twenty-three newspapers in the nation's major cities and scores of papers in small cities have closed since 1950, said John Morton, a newspaper analyst for Lynch, Jones & Ryan in Washington. Adding to the pressure on the *Herald Examiner* were the gains of two large suburban papers in the region, the *Daily News* in the San Fernando Valley to the north, and the *Orange County Register* to the south.

With a circulation of more than 700,000 in the mid-1960s, the *Herald Examiner*, founded by William Randolph Hearst as the *Los Angeles Examiner* in 1903, was the largest afternoon paper in the nation. In 1982, the paper switched to morning publication, and circulation stabilized at its 1989 level of 238,000.[1]

[1] Richard W. Stevenson, "Hearst to Cease Publication of the *Los Angeles Herald*," *New York Times*, 2 November 1989, p. 41 Y.

Newspaper Companies' Revenue, 1989[m]

1.	Gannett Co.	$2,852,000
2.	Times-Mirror Co.	$2,065,900
3.	Knight-Ridder	$1,988,400

[m] *Advertising Age*, 25 June 1990, p. S-6.

and circulation functions, the act stipulates that the papers' newsrooms and editorial pages must remain separate and independent. In winter 1989, Joint Operating Agreements (JOAs) were in place in nineteen cities with three other cities pending.[52]

The results of this act are controversial. Its critics charge that such mergers hike advertising rates. Advertisers who must use the newspapers to reach readers, such as supermarkets, for example, must pay the price. Such costs are passed on to the consumer.

Defenders of the act note that it has preserved two editorial voices in some major cities. These include Albuquerque, Honolulu, Madison (Wisconsin), Miami, Pittsburgh, Salt Lake City, San Francisco, and Tucson, among others. In 1983, for example, Seattle's two major papers—the morning *Post-Intelligencer* and the evening *Times*—combined. The *Post-Intelligencer*, which appeared to be failing before the venture, is now prospering.

52. Stephen Lacy, "Impact of Repealing the Newspaper Preservation Act," *Newspaper Research Journal* (Winter 1990): 2.

The African-American Press

The total circulation of all African-American newspapers is perhaps more than 5 million, but no reliable numbers exist because the papers do not all count their circulation the same way.

African-American newspapers arose in the South and in many cities of the North after the adoption of Jim Crow laws and the rise in racial violence in the 1890s. The newspapers often were the only medium available for the dissemination of news about such subjects as lynchings and education and health care for African-Americans.

After the victories of the civil rights movement in the 1960s, many older newspapers suffered sharp declines in circulation. In the meantime, younger African-American publishers introduced newspapers like the *City Sun* in Brooklyn that were more aggressive in demanding equal rights and economic change than many established publications.

"We have never managed to capture a share of advertising revenue proportionate to what black consumers spend," said Steve G. Davis, the executive director of the National Newspaper Publishing Association, a trade group representing the African-American press. "Thanks to some of our work, appealing directly to corporate chairmen and other executives, we are beginning to attract some national advertising for our members, but many major corporations do not even know that a black press exists."

But editors and publishers say the African-American press still has an important role to play. "Black people are largely not accepted as a part of the American family, and until we are, we have to be able to communicate with each other in our own way."[a]

[a]Albert Scardino, "Black Papers Retain a Local Niche," *New York Times*, 24 July 1989, p. 21 Y.

The ongoing existence of the Newspaper Preservation Act is uncertain. In 1989, the Supreme Court voted 4–4 to let a JOA agreement go forward between two Detroit papers. In the same year the House Committee on the Judiciary's Economic and Commercial Law Subcommittee held hearings to determine, among other things, whether the act should be repealed. Although the act withstood both of these encounters with opponents, the existence of a narrow court win and of increased congressional scrutiny means that its continuing existence is no longer assured.

Newspaper publishers report that in 1990, approximately 40 percent of their ad revenue came from classifieds, 10 percent from national advertising, and 50 percent from retail advertising. In the first quarter of 1990, ad revenue in newspapers declined because classified advertising dropped 6.4 percent. The drop was attributed to a weakening economy and competition from other sources including direct mail.[53]

53. Janet Meyers, "Classified Ads Slip With Economy," *Advertising Age*, 2 July 1990, p. 13.

The relationship between readership and advertising is complex. When a paper begins to lose circulation, a downward cycle begins. Readers purchase the paper for its news content and its advertising information. The newspaper with the larger circulation gets the greater share of advertising. Increased advertising increases the news hole, which in turn attracts more readers and with them more advertisers. A newspaper trailing another in a market may find itself with 40 percent of the readership but, because of this cycle, only 25 percent of the advertising. Because advertising accounts for up to 80 percent of a newspaper's revenue, decreases in advertising can spell a paper's demise.[54]

Impact of Television

Although there are some disconfirming studies, in general scholars have found that those who rely on newspapers for their political information are better informed than those who rely on television. The two audiences start with different dispositions. The better educated are more likely to rely on newspapers for information.[55]

From 1962 to 1977, total newspaper circulation increased from 55 to 56 million, while the number of households increased from 54 to 74 million.[56] So, although circulation increased slightly, it did not keep pace with the rapid increase in households. Nonetheless, there are still many more newspaper readers than nonreaders. In general, those who do not read newspapers fall at "the lower end of the socio-economic ladder; [they] lack resources and cognitive skills due to low education, and lack of social contacts and lack of leisure time."[57] Those more involved in their community tend to be regular newspaper readers.

Television has replaced newspapers as the prime source of information for the U.S. public. Researchers account for this decline by noting the increased mobility of the population, a mobility that works against the community involvement and familiarity with coverage and layout that characterize newspaper subscribers.

Classified advertising provides about 25 percent of total newspaper revenues; retail advertising provides another 60 percent. Retail advertising comes primarily from food and drugs, entertainment and hobbies, housing and decoration, and clothing and general merchandise. Clothing and general merchandise represent nearly half of all retail advertising in newspapers, which makes newspapers vulnerable to any new medium able to provide a large audience for advertising from department and clothing stores.[58]

---

54. For a lucid discussion of this downward cycle, see James N. Rosse, "The Evolution of One Newspaper Cities," in the FTC's *Proceedings of the Symposium on Media Concentration*, December 14–15, 1978 (Washington: Government Printing Office, 1978), pp. 429–471.

55. Jack M. McLeod and Daniel G. McDonald, "Beyond Simple Exposure: Media Orientations and Their Impact on Political Processes," *Communication Research* 12 (1985): 3–33.

56. William A. Tillinghast, "Declining Newspaper Readership: Impact of Region and Urbanization," *Journalism Quarterly* 58 (Spring 1981): 23.

57. Steven H. Chaffee and Sun Yuel Choe, "Newspaper Reading in Longitudinal Perspective: Beyond Structural Constraints," *Journalism Quarterly* 58 (Summer 1981): 201.

58. Anthony Smith, *Goodbye Gutenberg: The Newspaper Revolution of the 1980's* (New York: Oxford, 1980), pp. 65–66.

Cable television may pose such a threat because it can carry advertising to selected audiences, and when it is interactive, consumers can order products without leaving their living rooms.

Many national advertisers have chosen television over newspapers as their commercial outlets. Such choices, plus regulation of cigarette advertising, are reflected in the fact that only six industries provide two-thirds of all national advertising in newspapers: transportation, automobiles, tobacco, publishing, foods, and hotels. Because the newsstand price provides only about one-quarter, and advertising three-quarters, of a newspaper's revenues, newspapers are vulnerable to pressures from major advertisers.[59]

Separation of News and Advertising

Newspaper advertisers feel their messages are more believable and persuasive when they are printed next to news reports; hence, advertising charges are higher for such positioning. On the other hand, journalists wish to protect the credibility of the news by separating it clearly from advertising.

Advertisers have made ingenious proposals to circumvent this journalistic concern. For example, R.J. Reynolds Industries, the nation's largest cigarette manufacturer and the country's largest newspaper advertiser, in 1981 offered to sponsor the sports results most papers publish on Mondays.

The proposal was analogous to television's news updates that are sponsored by product advertisers. The new format has "Camel Scoreboard" in three-inch letters across the top of the sports page. Below it appear the usual box scores and sports statistics. Pillars similar to those on the Camel package are drawn down each side of the page, and a picture of the Camel cigarette package, the Camel slogan, and the mandatory health warning appear at the bottom of the page.[60] The "Marlboro Sports Calendar," a variant of this, appeared in the sports section of the (Minneapolis) *Star Tribune* of Monday, August 22, 1988, listing September events, including the Summer Games in Seoul, with dates, location, and the schedule of television coverage.[61]

Some newspapers rejected this proposal on the grounds that it would look as if a tobacco company, rather than the newspaper, were providing the news. Others, including the *New York Post* and most newspapers in the Newhouse chain, have accepted it primarily out of a need for revenues. The format raises serious questions about journalistic ethics and the ability of newspapers to withstand pressures from advertisers who spend hundreds of thousands, even millions, of dollars on newspaper advertising. This blurring of the distinctions between news and advertising is sometimes tried by politicians, as discussed in Chapter 11.

The rise of "advertorials" poses similar questions. Advertorials are "advertiser paid blocks that combine clearly identifiable advertising with simulated edi-

59. Ibid., p. 65.

60. Jonathan Friendly, "R. J. Reynolds Ad Format to Sponsor Newspaper Sports Data," *New York Times*, 7 August 1981, p. A 13.

61. *Star Tribune*, 22 August 1988, p. 3 C.

torial text." Travel, food/cooking, sports, and health are among the recurring themes of advertorials. Since the early 80s, use of advertorials has steadily increased, in part because print media have become increasingly specialized, in part because magazines have offered such blocked space at a discount.[62]

Local Advertising

Advertisers are not attracted by total circulation but by the density of penetration in a locality: once a newspaper reaches 50 percent of the households in an area, it becomes indispensable to most kinds of advertisers. "Analysts say the crucial factor in newspaper competition is 'dominance' of the market. 'When you get 51 percent of the circulation, you get 70 percent of the advertising,' said one financier who specializes in newspaper operations."[63] In other words, patterns of local advertising are directly related to the high percentage of localities with only a single newspaper. Thus, despite the impact of television, newspapers are by and large profitable.[64]

One analyst contrasts newspapers and television this way: "The typical newspaper audience of today has been constructed on the opposite, but in a sense complementary, principle from that of the television networks. The newspaper is local, uncompetitive, reliant on small advertisers; the television network is widespread, highly competitive, dependent upon large national advertisers."[65]

Magazines

On August 6, 1990, the Media Business section of the *New York Times* illustrated one of its purposes for existence. Page D-13 contained ads for *Newsweek* and *Time* touting their coverage of the crisis in the Middle East. The goal of the ads plainly was to entice readers of the *New York Times* to buy those issues and to persuade advertisers to advertise in these two newsweeklies.

The same page contained an ad for *Ebony*. In this ad, a publisher is appealing to would-be advertisers:

> This November the *Ebony* Magazine 45th Anniversary Issue is the biggest in our history offering a chance for your ad message to reach 9,519,000 consumers with a 43 percent penetration of the Black consumer market. The closing date is August 24th. The November *Ebony* 45th Anniversary Issue offers the single largest concentration of the estimated $260 billion Black consumer market ever available. Be a part of it by calling . . .

The ad then provided telephone numbers in New York, Chicago, and Los Angeles.

Like television and radio, but unlike newspapers, magazine advertising prices are determined by ratings. Magazines are rated by Simmons Market Re-

---

62. Patricia Stout, Gary B. Wilcox, and Lorrie Greer, "Trends in Magazine Advertorial Use," *Journalism Quarterly* (Winter 1989): 960–964.

63. Jonathan Friendly, "Requiem for a View," *New York Times*, 24 July 1981, p. A 12.

64. Arnold H. Ismach, "The Economic Connection: Mass Media Profits, Ownership, and Performance," in *Enduring Issues in Mass Communication,* eds. E. E. Dennis, D. M. Gillmor, and A. Ismach (St. Paul, Minn.: West Publishing, 1978), pp. 243–259.

65. Anthony Smith, *Goodbye Gutenberg*, p. 302.

search Bureau, the Media Research Institute, and the Magazine Publishers' Association. Surveys by Simmons determine the number of readers per magazine copy. A very high rating is 6, and 1.8 is a very low rating, meaning that, on the average, six persons read the first magazine but fewer than two read the second. Simmons gathers data through interviews and questionnaires. Such surveys provide advertisers with information about how long readers look at the ads in a particular magazine, as well as how much it costs to reach a target audience. In the spring of 1986, for example, the cost of reaching a thousand (CPT) 18-to-34-year-old males was $8.76 through *Playboy*, but $10.14 through *Sports Illustrated*.

Advertising is what makes most magazines financially viable. The exceptions are noteworthy. *Consumer Reports*, whose assessment of products would be questioned if it accepted ads, does not. It has a readership of 3.8 million. In late July 1990, *Ms.* re-appeared, this time ad-free. Founded as a feminist mass medium in 1973, *Ms.* lost money for most of its 17-year existence. When it suspended publication in 1989, its circulation was 543,000 with $5 million in advertising revenue.

In the lead article of the first ad-free issue, Gloria Steinem, one of the magazine's founders, detailed the frustrations of publishing an ad-reliant magazine. For example, a cover story on Afghanistan cost *Ms.* a long-term contract with Revlon, notes Steinem; the women on the cover had worn no make-up. Steinem's lead article, "Sex, Lies & Advertising," indicated that she could not previously have published the article in *Ms.* for fear of alienating advertisers.

The ad-free move is risky. Whereas its competitors sell for $1.75 or $2.00, *Ms.* will now cost $4.50 an issue. The first issue contains ninety-six pages. In 1988, *Ms.'* twelve issues carried 382 pages of advertising.[66]

Casualties of Competition

Like newspapers, magazine profits are a combination of advertising and circulation revenues, and like newspapers, magazines are dependent on certain kinds of advertising—chiefly from the tobacco, liquor, and automobile industries.[67] A magazine's health is measured by the number of its advertising pages. Compared with the first half of 1989, the number of magazine ad pages had dropped 3.3 percent in 1990.[68] "Automotive, the largest category, dropped 12.6 percent in the first half (of 1990) to $415 million. Cigarette and tobacco advertising showed the steepest first-half decline, 27.2 percent to $154.6 million."[69] Two explanations were given: "tighter ad budgets resulting from the skittish economy" and "increasing competition from other media." Highly specialized magazines are more attractive to advertisers when they seek to reach specific markets. The same advertising director said, "We're not crazy about broad-based publications [like the women's service magazines]. We would rather take a rifle shot in *Parents*, *Self*, or *Working Woman*."[70] The competition among media is acute, and television is generally more attractive for major national advertising.

66. Deirdre Carmody, "Ms. Magazine Returns with New Spirit, but Without Ads," *New York Times*, 30 July 1990, p. D 10.
67. N. R. Kleinfield, "Recharging Saturday Review," *New York Times*, 8 August 1979, p. D 1.
68. "Ad Industry Fears Falloff," *Advertising Age*, 23 July 1990, p. 1.
69. Wayne Walley, "Magazine Declines Mount," *Advertising Age*, 23 July 1990, p. 32.
70. Philip Nobile, "Worry Lines at the Women's Magazines," *New York*, 18 May 1981, pp. 19–20.

It is difficult for magazines to compete with television for national advertising. In fact, by the end of the 1950s, national magazines had discovered it was too expensive for their advertisers to buy pages in all copies of the magazine; therefore, different editions were created to reach different regions, occupational groups, and income levels.[71]

However, a form of network has been created in magazine advertising in order to overcome some of these problems. Advertisers are offered a discount for placing ads in several specialized magazines. For instance, it is difficult to convince a cigarette manufacturer to promote its brand in *Stereo Review* with a possible CPT (cost per thousand readers) of $22.84 on a circulation base of 525,000. However, by selling a package with *Boating and Skiing*, Ziff-Davis offers over 1 million circulation and a CPT of $14.49. A black-and-white page in *Boating, Car and Driver, Cycle, Flying*, and *Skiing* offering the equivalent of a 2.2 million circulation, yields a CPT that begins to be competitive with *Playboy*.[72] Such networks combine the best of national advertising (low rates and large audiences) with the best of demographic pinpointing to attract large advertisers.

At the same time, a growing number of magazines, including *U.S. News & World Report*, are beginning "selective binding" programs for advertisers. In 1989, as publishers were searching for new ways to attract advertisers, Time-Warner, publisher of *Time, Sports Illustrated*, and *People*, among others, introduced its TargetSelect program. The program enables the magazine to tailor ads to a specific group of subscribers while not paying to reach the rest. Ink jet printing processes make it possible to include the name of the reader in the ad. The service enabled Isuzu to run ads in *Time, Sports Illustrated*, and *People* in January 1990. The ads not only addressed the consumer by name but after inviting the reader to take a test drive, listed the address of the nearest Isuzu dealer.

In February 1991, Meredith Corporation began selectively binding *Ultimate*, a special section for 100,000 subscribers whose median net worth exceeds $300,000, into *Metropolitan Home*. A color page ad in *Ultimate*, which reaches only this economically elite audience, costs $15,000; a page in *Metropolitan Home*, which reaches 600,000 more subscribers than *Ultimate*, costs $33,450. "It's an opportunity for [marketers of affluent products] to buy minimal circulation in *Met Home* with no waste," explained publisher Steve Burzon.[73]

Newsweeklies

Before the advent of the national television networks and of such national newspapers as the *Wall Street Journal* and *USA Today*, the newsweeklies were the only mass circulation publications bringing news to the whole country. Although their impact has diminished, it is still great.

The covers and cover stories of *Time* and *Newsweek* are important to the magazines and to newsmakers. "A good cover can significantly increase the normal total of 300,000 copies a week each sells at the newsstands. Even though street

---

71. Anthony Smith, *Goodbye Gutenberg*, p. 137. See also Chapter 1.
72. Benjamin M. Compaine, "Magazines," in Compaine, *Who Owns the Media?* (New York: Harmony Books, 1979), p. 158.
73. Scott Donaton, "Personalized Ads, Editorial Growing," *Advertising Age*, 16 July 1990, p. 15.

sales are less than 10 percent of the magazines' total circulations, advertisers tend to look at the figures as a measure of which is the 'hot book' that lures a nonsubscriber."[74]

A cover story can also be influential. President Lyndon Johnson was allegedly influenced not to run for a second full term by the appearance of Bobby Kennedy on the covers of *Time* and *Newsweek,* and David Halberstam reports that President Richard Nixon agreed to grant an interview to Hugh Sidey in exchange for his appearance on *Time*'s cover.[75] *Time*'s selection of a man or woman of the year has become a news event in its own right, attesting to the continued influence of newsweeklies.

The national newsweeklies are important because their weekly publication forces them to emphasize analysis and features. Their leading stories, which interpret major news events, can influence public opinion about administrative policies because they are written for a mass popular audience (despite advertising targeted to specific audiences). They provide the news background and analyses that are precluded by the brevity of television network news and that are more difficult for newspapers with daily deadline pressure.

Like the networks, newsweeklies follow political campaigns closely; their coverage of campaigns influences public opinion about the political fortunes of aspiring presidential and vice-presidential candidates.

Time and *Newsweek* are both owned by large corporations or conglomerates. By contrast, *U.S. News & World Report* is employee-owned. *Newsweek* is owned by the Washington Post Company, which also owns several television stations and ranks among the Fortune 500 with sales of nearly a half-billion dollars a year. Time Inc. has revenues of over $1 billion a year, but only a small part of its revenues come from sales of *Time*. Robert Sherrill indicates some of the implications of *Time*'s conglomerate ownership: "A majority of its income is from the sale of corrugated containers and lumber; its forest products company, Temple Eastex, is the biggest private landowner in Texas, with a million acres of timberland—which readers might want to bear in mind when they judge *Time*'s position on environmental legislation and housing prices."[76]

Media Consolidation

∎

The 1980s produced a new trend: media consolidation. Time Inc. and Warner Communications merged to form the world's largest media organization worth $18 billion. Gulf & Western, owners of Simon & Schuster books and Paramount Pictures, divested itself of its nonmedia industries and changed its name to Paramount Communications, Inc. The world's largest agency is Saatchi and Saatchi of London which buys 20 percent of the world's broadcast ads for clients such as

74. Jonathan Friendly, "When News Magazine Covers Match, Is It a Coincidence?" *New York Times,* 22 March 1981, p. A 56.

75. David Halberstam, *The Powers That Be* (New York: Alfred A. Knopf, 1979), p. 666.

76. Robert Sherrill, *Why They Call It Politics* (New York: Harcourt Brace Jovanovich, 1979), pp. 273–274.

Procter & Gamble. Saatchi and Saatchi has offices in eighty countries. Analyst Ben Bagdikian observes that: "A handful of mammoth private organizations have begun to dominate the world's mass media. Most of them confidently announce that by the mid-1990s they—five to ten corporate giants—will control most of the world's important newspapers, magazines, books, broadcast stations, movies, recordings, and videocassettes." [77]

T O   S U M   U P

These facts about ratings and revenues in television, radio, newspapers, and magazines demonstrate the importance of commercial considerations in the operation of the mass media. These processes are reflected directly in advertising—discussed in the next three chapters—and indirectly in mass political communication—the subject of the last two chapters.

Selected Readings

Beville, Hugh M., Jr. *Audience Ratings: Radio, Television, and Cable.* Rev. ed. Hillsdale, N.J.: Lawrence Erlbaum, 1988.

Compaine, Benjamin M., ed. *Who Owns the Media? Concentration of Ownership in the Mass Communication Industry.* New York: Harmony Books, 1979.

Greenfield, Thomas. *Radio: A Reference Guide.* Westport, Conn.: Greenwood Press, 1989.

Montgomery, Kathryn C. *Target Prime Time.* New York: Oxford University Press, 1989.

Reel, A. Frank. *The Networks: How They Stole the Show.* New York: Charles Scribner's, 1979.

77. Bagdikian, p. 84.

What Is Advertising?

In the first half of 1990, 6,476 new products were introduced in the United States; 13,300 would be introduced by the year's end. Of these, 74 percent will be food products.[1] What we'll know about them by New Year's Eve will have been the by-product of some form of advertising.

When the woman who edits this book for Wadsworth sits down at her nationally advertised computer, she wears clothes advertised both by local retailers and through national ad campaigns. We have never seen her office, but we would bet that the paint on the walls, the desk on which the computer rests, the lamp on the desk, and the pens in the drawer are as familiar to us as they are to you, although we may live thousands of miles apart. All have probably been nationally advertised.

In a sense advertising through the mass media has given us a world in common—you are familiar with the products we purchase, we are familiar with the products you purchase, and that familiarity transcends large geographical distances. In other words, we live in a world filled with advertised products; often the presence of one of these products rather than another in our lives is determined by the effect of the ad campaigns for competing products.

In this chapter we examine what advertising is and what advertising through the mass media does.

Defining Advertising

The Romans identified three goals of rhetoric—to teach, to delight, and to move. Of course these goals rarely occur in complete isolation from one another. As we argued in our discussion of news, the process of choosing a topic, narrow-

1. *Advertising Age*, 16 July 1990, p. 39.

ing it, and selecting evidence in its support gives all messages a persuasive component.

Taken at face value, news professes to inform or teach, and ads profess to move—to advocate one purchasing decision rather than another. By contrast, most prime-time programming (sit-coms, crime shows) professes to delight.

In contrast to news or other types of programming, the end of advertising is more likely to be explicit action. Here ads are more akin to editorials, which urge action, than to the other sorts of content surrounding them. An ad asks us to go somewhere, do something, try something, buy something, accept some single idea, add a new word—generally a product's trade name—to our vocabulary, and to associate positive images with that name. In order to accomplish any of these objectives the ad will contain a simple, highly repetitious message. So, in general terms, we can sort the ad from its surrounding content by its simplicity, its redundancy, and by the clarity with which it urges adoption, choice, or action.

A broadcast commercial is to some extent that unit of content that appears in 10-, 15-, 20-, 30-, 60-, or 120-second time units and breaks unapologetically into the narrative line of some content. Televised programming usually consists of larger units of 30, 60, or 120 minutes, interrupted by commercials. The smaller, 10- to 120-second units of information appear at regular and predictable intervals within the 30- to 120-minute units of content.

Because, unlike the early days of radio and television, television programs today are rarely sponsored by just one advertiser, the subjects discussed in the 30–120 minute units may differ drastically from those discussed in the adjacent 10–120-second blocks. For example, the evening news may report on the president's trip to Kennebunkport and cut to commercials for a shampoo, a laxative, an automobile, and to a promotional ad for a prime-time program on the same network that evening—and then cut back to the news, where the anchor introduces a report about a hearing on organized crime.

This segmentation and aggregation of discrete, often incompatible thematic units violate all of the rules by which we normally judge communicated content. Suppose you heard a speech discussing the president's trip, an upcoming prime-time program, a hearing on organized crime, as well as the merits of a shampoo, a laxative, and a car. Such a potpourri of topics could not be blended into a coherent speech. As an audience member you would doubt the speaker's grasp of the rules governing public communication, and possibly question the speaker's sanity as well. After all, the ability to address a subject coherently is one sign of a person's command of the environment.

Yet we do not react negatively when television and radio break our train of thought, disrupt the story line, and introduce a series of unrelated messages. Indeed, we expect it. Consequently, "Sesame Street" built "commercials" ("This part of 'Sesame Street' is brought to you by the letter A") into the program.

In the United States $222.9 billion was spent on advertising and promotion in 1989. That figure represents a 5.8 percent increase from 1988. By 1994 network advertising alone should total $12.8 billion. Cable advertising should grow to $3 billion by that date, magazine advertising to $9.4 billion.[2]

2. Gary Levin and Wayne Walley, "Ad Boom Seen for Brands, Europe," *Advertising Age*, 23 July 1990, p. 13.

Table 6-1   How the Advertising Pie Divided, 1989*

Magazines	16.7%
Cable television	18.7%
Network television	21.6%
Radio	1.5%
Newspapers	36.0%

*Advertising Age, 25 June 1990, p. S-1.

Unless we plan to spend our lives in a darkened room, wearing ear muffs to block the sound of radio and shunning television, magazines, and newspapers, we will be exposed to advertisers' efforts to persuade us. Even those who do not subscribe to a newspaper pass newsstands as they move from place to place and see discarded newspapers and magazines on buses, subways, planes, in cabs, or on coffee tables in homes they are visiting. In order of their occurrence, what they will see and hear are ads for passenger cars, nonfood retail products, restaurants, cereals, beer, airlines, movies, trucks and vans, cigarettes, and telephone companies.[3] The brand name they will hear most often is McDonald's, which in 1989 spent $424.8 million to persuade us to eat Big Macs, Quarter Pounders with Cheese, and such new products as yogurt sundaes.

People who want to avoid radio commercials have to ignore the ads being played over the portable radios carried down the street or at the beach, over car radios when they are carpooling, or over the P.A. system in the supermarket or shopping mall.

The mass media pervade our environment. And with the mass media come the advertisements that underwrite them. A message tailored to persuade an audience to accept a product is not, of itself, advertising. But when the people selling the product *pay* for time or space to enable them to *bring the message in a specific unalterable form to that audience*, we call the message advertising. An advertiser, within the bounds of taste and the law, controls what the message says, how it says it, where, and how frequently it appears.

The mass media have rules of conduct guaranteeing that the advertisers are able to communicate what they want at the time or in the space purchased. For example, when a television ad is cut short due to technical malfunction, or the programming in which the ad is embedded fails to reach an audience of the size guaranteed by the network, the advertiser is entitled to a "make-good," a rebroadcast of the commercial at a comparable time at no additional charge. Similarly, when a newspaper transposes two prices in an ad, the newspaper will, at no cost to the advertiser, run a correction in the next edition or in the next day's paper.

Some forms of advertising do not fit neatly into this definition because they reach their audiences without the purchase of time or space. The dividing bar that separates your groceries from the next customer's at the checkout counter of the supermarket, for example, may carry a message from a cigarette manufacturer: "For a light smoke—try X." The cigarette manufacturer has given the dividers to

---

3. LNA/Arbitron Multi-Media Service in *Advertising Age*, 21 May 1990, p. 25.

the store free, in the hope or with the agreement that they will be used. Their use functions as advertising. When your groceries are bagged, you may notice a message about the store on the bag. When you carry the groceries from the store or use the bag as a garbage bag in your home, you have become the carrier of an ad for the store, just as you have become a walking ad for Calvin Klein when you wear jeans with his name stitched onto the hip pocket.

A movie hero may drink a certain soft drink—a form of advertising purchased by the soft drink manufacturer in exchange for supplying cast and crew with the product, or in exchange for what is called a "promotional consideration." You may have noticed, for example, that the characters in *Moonstruck* always celebrated with the same brand of champagne.

Video rentals too have become carriers of advertising, often for other movies by the same company. For example, the introduction to the video of *The Fabulous Baker Boys* urges viewers not to rewind when the movie ends. Following the credits, they will see a video of the star singing one of the movie's songs. The promoters obviously hope that this extra plug will entice us into purchasing that compact disc.

Realizing that movie cassettes reach a predictable local audience—those living within a specifiable distance of the rental store—an inventive local marketer began placing local ads on video rentals. Those in Wichita, Kansas, renting *She's Having a Baby* saw ads for a local tire service. Since Paramount had released the film, it sued, charging copyright infringement. A Kansas circuit court judge dismissed the suit saying, "This court is frankly skeptical that viewers actually care whether Paramount is the source or sponsor of the advertisements." But the local firm lost anyway. Fearful that they would be taken to court by Paramount, his customers returned to more traditional advertising channels.[4]

Marketers also are giving away videocassettes containing their messages. In November 1990, major toy companies gave away 1.5 million copies of *The Video Toy Chest*, a 35-minute videocassette that includes 28 minutes of ads for toys. The remaining 7 minutes contain trivia contests and games. Companies whose toys were advertised on the videocassette include Milton Bradley, Playskool, and Fisher-Price. The promotion was an attempt to increase the companies' share of the $13.5 billion toy market. The target audience: boys from 4 to 14. The motivation: competition from videogames and products tied to the Teenage Mutant Ninja Turtles.[5]

Kids aren't the only market for free home video ads. In October 1989, R.J. Reynolds, the nation's second largest cigarette maker, announced that it was mailing 78-second video ads to thousands of U.S. smokers. At a cost of less than $3.00 apiece, the mailing compared favorably to a national time buy. The difference, of course, is that cigarettes can't be advertised on the nation's air waves.[6]

Ads are also included in faxed newspapers, which usually are two- or three-page summaries of the day's top stories sent to businesses that can't get same day

4. Joanne Lipman, "Local Video-Ad Business Goes on Blink," *Wall Street Journal*, 23 August 1990, p. B 6.

5. Kate Fitzgerald, "'Video Toy Chest' Brimming with Ads," *Advertising Age*, 23 July 1990, p. 49.

6. John Cleghorn, "Cigarette Makers Bypass TV Ban," *Philadelphia Inquirer*, 31 October 1989, p. E 1.

delivery. The *Hartford Courant*'s faxpaper sells ads for $100. That fee gives the advertiser a 1.5-inch area at the bottom of a legal-sized sheet.[7]

Some advertising is faxed directly and without invitation to the fax machines of those owning them. But unlike junk mail, whose cost is borne by the sender, the cost of junk faxes is absorbed involuntarily by the receiver who actually winds up paying in paper and toner costs for the printing of often unwanted messages. In summer 1990, Congress considered legislation that would permit those who do not wish to receive junk faxes to enter their name on a list. Advertisers who transmit to the fax machines on that list would be violating the law.

Telephones too are becoming the conduits of unwanted advertising. We assume that most of our readers have at one time or another rushed to their phone expecting a call from a friend only to hear a recorded voice telling them that they had won a trip or a prize or were eligible to receive a deep discount on magazines. Such intrusive use of the telephone can be life endangering when the numbers reached are those of the fire station, the police department, or a hospital's emergency line. By tying up the line, the advertiser blocks the access of those who need quickly to reach the hospital or the fire or police station.

Some also contend that such calls are an invasion of personal privacy particularly when, through random digit dialing, they reach individuals who have paid to have their phone numbers unlisted. A U.S. Congress Energy and Commerce Committee report reveals that "more than 180,000 solicitors call more than 7 million Americans every day with recorded messages sent by automatic dialers and more than 2 million businesses send more than 30 billion pages of information by fax each year."[8] Pending congressional legislation would curb such distribution by phone as well.

In other words, television, radio, and newspapers are not the only conduits of advertising, and many forms of advertising do not appear in purchased time or space. However, this chapter focuses on advertising found in the mass media because without this advertising the mass media as we know them in the United States would not exist.

Mediated Advertising

Before the advent of the mass media, salespersons would often be the carriers of their own advertising, repeating the same message and carrying the same products from door to door. With the rise of mass media, such door-to-door advertising has become prohibitively expensive for most nationally sold products. Even with products like Avon cosmetics that are still sold door to door and person to person, television ads are used to predispose residents to open their doors and purchase the product.

When the door-to-door salesperson was replaced by a mediated salesperson, the ability of the salesperson to tailor the message to each individual receiver or

7. Janet Meyers, "It's Sink or Swim for New Revenue-Pullers," *Advertising Age*, 20 August 1990, p. S-6.

8. "House Considers Restriction on Advertising by Telephone and Fax," *New York Times*, 31 July 1990, p. A 13.

adapt the message in response to audience reaction was reduced. The producer of an ad carried by the mass media, rather than in person, must create a message that speaks to what a mass audience shares rather than to the individual differences of the millions who will hear or see the message.

A second major shift occurred when television, radio, and print became the conduits of advertising. None of these media could bring a real product into your home. Instead, each carried a representation of the product. So, although the traveling salesperson could show you that the product worked and could actually sell you the product, the mass-mediated ad was forced to add an additional step in the persuasive process. The ad needed to persuade you to go where the product could be found and buy the product. But first the ad would often attempt to give you a vicarious experience of using the product satisfactorily, so the next time you had the option to buy the product it would already seem comfortable and familiar. Thus, the seller who would throw dirt onto a cloth stretched out on your carpet in order to demonstrate that the vacuum cleaner would efficiently pick it up was replaced with a mediated salesperson in an ad who showed you what the producer hoped would be something comparable. But in your home you could see the dirt, see the vacuum, and testify that there were no tricks. The door-to-door salesperson offered firsthand experience of the performance of the product. In the ad, all sorts of tricks could be employed to make it appear that the vacuum was more effective than it really was. Consequently, a need arose for rules governing what an advertiser could and could not do in ads.

Kinds of Mass Media Advertising

As we argue in the next chapter, all advertising identifies a product, service, or idea, differentiates it from related products, services, or ideas, associates it with things we value, induces us to participate in the creation of its claims, and repeats its key concepts. Most ads also are part of a campaign, and all employ slogans in some form. Yet despite these similarities, ads can be divided by type.

The regulations governing some ads (for example, political) differ from others (commercial and p.s.a.'s—public service announcements); the space or time to air some ads must be purchased (commercial, political, and advocacy or issue ads), but others (p.s.a.'s) are aired at no cost to the producer; and the objectives of different types of ads range from marketing a corporate image to electing a candidate. Therefore, here we differentiate in general terms the different kinds of advertising.

Obviously, some of these types overlap. Some ads sell both a product and a service, for example, and some p.s.a.'s urge us to vote, an appeal that may benefit one candidate or party more than another. Distinctions are also complicated by advertisers' deliberate blurring of image-building ads and p.s.a.'s.

Similarly, product ads occasionally incorporate politicians whose re-election is ensured by judicious use of a certain brand of toothpaste or mouthwash. But, in general, these distinctions are a useful way of understanding the special forms an ad can take.

Ads can be classified by the product they sell (service, goodwill, or special product ads); whether the time or space in which they run are purchased (commercials) or provided by the outlet as a community service (public service announcements); or the type of information they provide, the types of appeals they make, and the types of regulations that govern them (advocacy and political ads).

Product Ads

Some ads market a product or a product line. Ads for Dairy Queen, for example, create a world filled with Dairy Queen products and their ingredients. Mountains of chocolate, fields of fresh strawberries, pineapple, and bananas are all part of this world. Some of the ads argue that we ought to participate in this world without identifying specific products. Others tell us about a special kind of sundae or a banana split.

The televised ads for Dairy Queen illustrate well the purpose of an ad for a product or product line. By showing us the texture of the fresh fruit, the vibrant colors of the strawberries, the rich "rivers" of chocolate, the ads preview the product, familiarize us with the product's name, and induce us to experience the sensations of eating the product. Although the actual world is a miniature one, the close-up shots create the illusion that there is actually a tropical retreat with larger-than-life fruit and mountains of chocolate. The world in close-up is the size of our television screen.

A food is a consumable commodity with which we've all had experience. The function of food is clear. Consequently, the strategy of an ad for food is generally to make the food appear as delectable as possible. But what is the function of a camera or of a specific type of film? Ads for Kodak cameras and Kodak film define and clarify the function of photography and at the same time personalize it. Kodak's ads tell us that Kodak is a means of preserving the best of the past by making it possible to save and treasure memories. Ads for Kodak show us symbolically important events in the lives of believable people and demonstrate the way in which film makes it possible to preserve those events. In the ads for Dairy Queen, the product is an end in itself. We see the product. We want the product. We buy and consume the product. Kodak could, of course, show us an unexposed roll of Kodak film, but such a strategy would be impersonal and would provide no rationale for purchasing the product. So, instead, Kodak shows us what the film and the camera make possible.

Service Ads

The ads for Kodak make the product personal by showing the intimate important moments Kodak film can capture for us. But how does an advertiser personify a service? An ad for First Bank positions a bank official on camera looking at us, the banking customers. As the bank officer entangles himself in the esoteric jargon of his profession, his image is blurred on the screen and his voice muted. Everyone in the audience who has experienced institutional doubletalk has a frame of reference for this type of institutional officer. The camera is reacting for us; we make little sense of such presentations. The audio track becomes our ears as we tune the message out. The ad has induced us to re-create a familiar experience. The announcer now can tell us that First Bank has simplified the banking process; the simplification brings the bank official back into focus. The ad has told us that this bank provides a service. Our past experience is used to help us make that service seem desirable.

Ads for a service often show us what it is like without, and then with, the service. An ad for an airline, for example, shows a large person crammed into a small seat being elbowed by the passengers on either side. The service? Wider seats, fewer persons per row. In the second scene the same person is in an uncrowded seat with ample room.

Goodwill Ads

The ads we have described are clearly intent on selling something—a product, a product line, or a service. One type of ad is noteworthy for the absence of a specific sales pitch for a tangible profit-making item.

In the late 1970s it was difficult to find an ad for a gas company that was selling gasoline or the services a gas station provides. Instead, oil companies were selling their concern for the environment, their conviction that we ought to conserve energy, or their safe driving tips. These ads were an attempt to alter the public image of the oil companies in the wake of rising gasoline prices, the long lines at the pumps, the oil spills that had endangered wildlife here and abroad, and accusations of influence peddling that had pervaded the political climate during the Watergate investigations.

This type of ad falls under the general heading of "image advertising." Related forms are more specific in relating their appeals to a product. IBM, for example, does not want to be associated with the notion that computers are dehumanizing and threatening. Consequently, ads for IBM show the humane uses of computers. IBM computers are instrumental in saving lives, argues one ad. Weyerhauser, "the tree-growing people," shows planned planting that, the ads argue, will make it possible for today's children to build houses tomorrow.

Such image advertising can produce substantial results. After sponsoring the 1984 coast-to-coast Olympic torch relay, AT&T conducted a survey to assess the relay's results. Every potential long distance customer in this crucial time of divestiture was aware of the relay. Half were aware of AT&T's sponsorship. More important for the phone company, those who recognized that AT&T had sponsored the event were, by a statistically significant margin, more disposed to choose AT&T as their long distance phone company.[9]

In 1986, the growing awareness of such potential rewards prompted major companies, from Eastman Kodak to American Express, to tie their corporate identities to the reconstruction of the Statue of Liberty.

In 1990, the images with which products tended to identify were environmental. Crest toothpaste's print ad reads: "Turn this page back into a tree. Simply send in this certificate with proofs-of-purchase from two Crest cartons. And, together with The National Arbor Day Foundation, we'll plant a seedling in a Yellowstone-area National Forest on your behalf." An IBM spot shows the corporation

9. *New York Times*, 6 July 1986, p. 6 E.

working with the United Nations to solve environmental problems. The spot contrasts a grid-locked traffic jam with a swarm of beetles. Pictures of nature are intercut with topographical maps on computer screens. We see nature, then nature through the computer. IBM and nature conjoin.

The causes to which goodwill advertising are tied are noncontroversial. No one opposes use of a designated driver to reduce traffic fatalities. Accordingly, Coca-Cola distributes free products to those identified as designated drivers who attend the home games of the Milwaukee Brewers. And because beer companies don't want to be associated with traffic fatalities, it is not surprising that one of the corporate sponsors of the baseball team's Designated Driver Program is the Miller Brewing Company of Milwaukee.

Image advertising is designed to identify a company and its products with a positive image and to dissociate them from any negative images that may have been created in news channels.

Companies that sponsor programming on Public Broadcasting Service stations are also engaging in image advertising. Instead of linking their name with some socially approved idea (conservation, for example), sponsorship links the company with bringing culture or quality programming at no direct cost to American homes. Such sponsorship argues that the company is a good citizen of the community. We are less likely to believe evil of a good citizen. Consequently, such sponsorship insulates the company from criticism and creates positive associations for the company's products.

Advocacy Ads

When the company as good citizen takes a position on a public policy in an ad, the ad becomes an advocacy ad. Many stations refuse advocacy ads out of fear that they will then be bound to air the other side as well. Determining what is and is not an advocacy ad is difficult. In 1981, ABC became the first of the networks to agree to air advocacy ads, but stipulated that the ads could only run on late-night television, a less-than-desirable time for most advertisers and a time when advertising space is more difficult to sell. By October 1990, NBC, CBS, and ABC's owned and operated stations were all being permitted the latitude to determine whether or not to accept such ads. The change in policy was prompted by the willingness of the stations' cable competitors to accept advocacy ads and by the demise of the Fairness Doctrine. Airing such an ad no longer carries an obligation to provide free air time for opposing points of view.

In summer 1990, Anheuser-Busch aired a 30-second advocacy ad that opened by showing workers at lunch and farmers in their fields. The announcer notes that America was built by individuals willing to give their fair share. The ad then says that Congress now wants Americans (note, not Anheuser-Busch), who already pay about $3 billion in excise taxes on beer, to pay more than their fair share. As a foaming stein of beer appears on the screen, the tag says "Can the Beer Tax. 1-800-33-Taxes." When viewers call, they are asked if they would like to have a letter of protest over a proposed hike in the excise tax sent for them to their congressional representative. In the campaign's first month, 110,000 callers asked to have the letters sent.

To magnify the power of the campaign, beer industry officials hinted that if the tax were increased, their companies might reduce sponsorship of sporting events and decrease advertising spending on television. Increasing the economic impact should increase the number of groups supporting the beer industry's position. However, critics noted that reduction of advertising was unlikely because that is the industry's major means of sustaining sales and introducing such new products as dry beer.[10]

Still, controversies over advocacy ads persist. In spring 1986, J. Peter Grace, chairman of W.R. Grace and Co., protested to the press and public that one of his ads had been rejected by the networks. Set in the year 2017, the ad showed an elderly man in a witness cage. The man is being cross-examined by a child who wants to know how the man could have let federal deficits reach $2 trillion. The networks refused to show the ad. In so doing, they were within their rights. In *Democratic National Committee* v. *CBS*, the Supreme Court held that the editorial judgment about what to air and what not to air belongs to the broadcaster.

Infomercials

The informercial is a 30-minute ad that looks like a program but is instead selling a product. Throughout the program, a toll-free number appears. By calling it, viewers can order the product. On January 1, 1990, when the Federal Communication Commission's regulation called "Syndex" went into effect, use of infomercials by cable stations rose. Syndex, an abbreviation of "syndication exclusivity," means that cable stations cannot show syndicated programs if the same programs are being shown on local television in the market. During the time that is now blocked out by Syndex, cable can, if it chooses, pick up infomercials beamed to them 24 hours a day at no charge via satellite.

One infomercial has the look of a rock 'n roll special. For that infomercial, one producer gathered the rights to 150 past hits and packaged them on twenty cassettes. He then paid disc jockey Wolfman Jack to endorse the product as "Wolfman Jack's favorite all time hits"; $200,000 of production costs later, the infomercial offering the cassettes was ready to air. Another infomercial featuring chef Arnold Morris resembles a Julia Child cooking show. Its title: "Arnold's Gourmet Kitchen."[11]

By producing programming to go with its commercials, companies create a kin to the infomercial and also ensure that their ads will not be lost in the clutter of other messages. Valvoline oil, for example, had its advertising agency, Bozell, create both the Second Annual Valvoline National Driving Test and the ads for it. Since the program bore the sponsor's name, it too was a form of advertising. The Valvoline Driving Test, which aired in late August 1990, harkens back to an earlier age in broadcasting. The "Dinah Shore Show" was sponsored by Chevrolet and featured the tune "See the USA in your Chevrolet." During the 40s and 50s, radio shows routinely carried the names of their sponsors.

---

10. "Busch Spots Fight Rise in Beer Tax," *New York Times*, 30 July 1990, p. D 11.

11. Anthony Gnoffo, Jr., "The Ad That Looks Like a Show," *Philadelphia Inquirer*, 27 November 1989, p. E 1.

Public Service Announcements

Unlike the advertising we have discussed so far, public service announcements (p.s.a.'s) are not aired in purchased time or space. Television stations meet part of their FCC-stipulated obligation to be responsive to the needs of the community by airing public service ads. A public service ad is generally created and sponsored by a nonprofit organization to convey noncontroversial information to the public.

Ads for charities such as United Way and the Children's Hospital of Washington are p.s.a.'s. The National Institutes of Health sponsors p.s.a.'s to remind hypertensives to take their medicine, to warn us to watch for cancer's early warning signals, and to discourage us from smoking. During election years, the League of Women Voters, the networks themselves, and specially created committees will use p.s.a.'s to urge us to register and vote.

The p.s.a.'s most likely to be aired are sponsored either by an agency of the government or by the Advertising Council. The Advertising Council, which accepts a limited number of campaign assignments each year, is sponsored by ad agencies. It costs a nonprofit agency from $100,000 to $300,000 to pay the production costs for an Ad Council campaign. Ad Council campaigns have been criticized for their pro-industry bias. In one often-run ad, for example, a Native American is shown paddling his canoe down a polluted stream. As he steps to the shore someone throws a bag of garbage from a passing car and a tear runs down his cheek. Critics of this ad argue that littering is a minor form of pollution. Significant air and water pollution is industry caused. Littering could be reduced by banning nonreturnable bottles—a proposal industries have fought bitterly.

Critics raised similar objections to an Ad Council campaign showing an older person in a rocker that said, "Get Off Your Rocker." The appeal urged the audience to examine its stereotypes about aging. Of course, the elderly person was the victim of many social policies over which she had no control. Getting off her rocker would not end age-based mandatory retirement, eliminate government policies that encourage institutionalization of the elderly, or end age discrimination in employment. Those problems were the fault of industry and government; changing the attitudes of older people about them would not produce institutional change. Under fire for embodying stereotypical assumptions, the ad campaign was changed to show an empty rocker, and an appeal urged all of us to examine our attitudes about aging. These two Ad Council campaigns provide some support for the contention that the Ad Council deflects criticism from industry and shifts blame and responsibility to individuals who are often powerless to correct the problems isolated in the ads.

The major advantage of an Ad Council campaign is the ability of ad industry to place its p.s.a.'s in desirable free time. In 1990, the president of the Media-Advertising Partnership for a Drug-Free America, a partnership that includes the Ad Council, reported that: "The donated media time and space have included a large percentage of prime-time, drive-time and full page, high-visibility levels that compare favorably to paid advertising campaigns."[12] In 1989 the Ad Council

---

12. Thomas A. Hedrick, Jr., "Pro Bono Anti-Drug Ad Campaign Is Working," *Advertising Age*, 25 June 1990, p. 22.

produced thirty-eight campaigns. The media donated slightly more than a billion dollars' worth of time and space to these ads.[13]

Many effective p.s.a.'s are not sponsored by the Ad Council. A Clio-award-winning ad for the Humane Society shows the violence that occurs at rodeos in slow motion, while a Strauss waltz plays in the background. The ad focuses our attention on an often-ignored facet of the rodeo. The ad argues persuasively that rodeos are inhumane. Similarly, Mothers Against Drunk Driving (MADD) sponsored a series of p.s.a.'s encouraging youths and the public at large to consider the cost in human life that is exacted by those who drive while intoxicated.

One $2 million p.s.a. radio campaign is privately funded. Martin Himmel, former president of Jeffrey Martin Inc., commissioned media guru Tony Schwartz to produce an antismoking campaign. In one of Schwartz's spots, Patrick Reynolds, grandson of the founder of the R.J. Reynolds Tobacco Co., reveals that his grandfather, a tobacco chewer, died of cancer as did his heavy-smoking father. His mother and three brothers all have emphysema, says Reynolds. "Now tell me," the ad concludes, "do you think the cigarette companies are truthful when they tell you that smoking isn't harmful? What do you think?"

Because its producers do not pay for the time in which the p.s.a. is aired, they cannot control its placement. Stations tend to place p.s.a.'s in times no one has purchased. Consequently, p.s.a.'s often air early in the morning or late at night, when few viewers are watching, or in documentaries for which the network could not find enough sponsors.

Political Ads

Some ads argue that we should elect one person rather than another or urge us to vote a specific way on a resolution or referendum. These ads, which differ in some important ways from other types of ads, will be discussed in Chapter 10.

How to Determine Whether It's an Ad

Advertising can also be defined by distinguishing it from the content that surrounds it. In the mass media, advertisers pay for access to the audiences attracted by programming. How does the ad itself differ from that programming?

How Ads Reveal the Advertiser

What distinguishes a televised soft news story about Jamaica, presented from a human interest angle, from a televised commercial brought to you by the Tourist Bureau of Jamaica? The commercial will identify itself as a commercial by disclosing its source. This disclosure, called a tag, generally takes a visual form and usually is placed at the end of the commercial.

What distinguishes a televised view of a candidate's day, broadcast as a news segment on the evening news, from a slice-of-life commercial paid for by the candidate's campaign committee? The commercial is required to contain a tag identifying the committee paying for the ad. Again, the tag generally occurs at the end.

13. *Advertising Age*, 16 July 1990, p. 39.

Because we are less likely to be manipulated by a message that warns us that it is manipulating us, as a commercial warns us by identifying itself as a commercial, producers of commercials try to incorporate the identifying tag in an inconspicuous way. Political committees, for example, are often legally incorporated under such titles as "Friends of Reuben Spellman," precisely because the commercial can then legally be tagged ". . . and that's why this message was paid for by Friends of Reuben Spellman." Such a tag is called a no-tag tag.

How Ads Reveal the Intended Audience

The biblical injunction "seek and you shall find" takes on a new meaning when we are in the market for a product or have a problem that potentially could be remedied by a product. Have you ever noticed that when you have a cold, television and radio are filled with ads for cold remedies? And when you are trying to determine which car to buy, the number of automobile ads seems to increase? When we are troubled by a problem or an unmet need, we become information seekers about that problem or need. Communication that was always in our environment suddenly becomes relevant, and we recognize it and attend to it. We seek information to help us make a decision. At the same time the presence of the information assures us that our problem is not an imaginary one and that the problem is important. Ads about our problem tell us that it is a real one, that it is significant, and that we are justified in being concerned about it.

We also seek information once the decision to purchase has been made. But after the decision, the reasons for seeking the information change. Before the decision we seek information comparing products, arguing the unique benefits of one over the other. After we have purchased the product, we seek information to assure ourselves that the decision was a wise one. In these two instances, we function as active communication participants: we seek information.

Often, however, we are passive receivers of information. We are frequently receptive to information and willing to become involved in the creation of messages about products when we are not deliberately seeking certain types of information. How do advertisers alert the passive receivers that a product is designed for them?

Often ads tell us verbally that we are the intended audience. In summer 1990, Campbell-Taggart introduced a soft white bread labeled "IronKids." Ads for Iron-Kids claim that it's "as wholesome as whole wheat but has the look, taste and feel of white bread." Other products that identify children as the intended market include Kids Deli, Kid Cuisine, and Kidstuff pizza. (The focus on this market is a byproduct of the realization that children 6 to 14 have approximately $6 billion in discretionary income.[14])

Other ads telegraph their audience both visually and verbally. If an ad says, "Trabo, the fun game for the whole family," and shows a mother, a father, a boy, and a girl playing a board game, that ad is not soliciting the attention of single adults. Although single adults might buy the product, the ad is picturing youngsters and their parents as its prime audience. The tone of the ad—the laughter,

14. Trish Hall, "Younger Consumers: More to Spend, More to Want," *New York Times*, 23 August 1990, p. C 1.

the upbeat music, the good-natured comments among participants—may also be speaking to those in the audience who view recreation as a social rather than solitary activity, whether they identify themselves with the family in the ad or not. But the ad is clearly not speaking to the single adult whose idea of an enjoyable evening is dancing into the wee hours of the morning at the hottest nightspot.

By showing the game being played by children with adults, the advertiser is also establishing that this is a game better suited for both children and adults than for adults alone. It is not a game too difficult for children; moreover it is not rated X. Yet it can be played satisfyingly by adults and children. Many products from toothpaste to breakfast cereal can be used both by children and adults.

When Pepsi-Cola signed Grammy-winner M. C. Hammer to promote its "cool cans" in rap's rhythmic chants, it was targeting the younger market. Similarly Coca-Cola hired Heavy D & the Boyz to turn Sprite's "I like the Sprite in you" into rap ads for radio and TV. In addition to its clear attraction to younger viewers and listeners, rap has a number of persuasive advantages. Rhyme is memorable. Moreover, as the senior vice president-group creative director of J. Walter Thompson, USA, notes, "You can, without being untrue to the form of rap, get more lyrics per 30 seconds than any other form of music." [15] In summer 1990, four of the country's top albums were by rap groups. And one of MTV's top-rated shows was "Yo! MTV Raps."

Comparatively few products dictate use exclusively by either adults or children, as diapers and after-shave do. Yet many products are marketed to the whole family with the argument that the product is good for the children. One toothpaste, for example, is advertised with the appeal that if this product is used, the children will brush longer because they will like the taste of the toothpaste. The assumption, of course, is that mom or dad will buy the same brand for the whole family. Another toothpaste promises that it gives your mouth sex appeal—a claim that reveals that its target audience is very different from the ad featuring 6-year-old Johnny who brushes longer with the better-tasting toothpaste.

Indeed, if the advertiser used children as spokespersons to claim that the toothpaste gives your mouth sex appeal, the ad would be offensive. Both of these ads identify an intended audience implicitly. An explicit identification of intended audience is made in ads for Gleem toothpaste that say, "If you're an adult you have an adult set of dental problems." Gleem, according to the ad, is for the "care of your adult mouth." Ads not only reveal the likely age of those targeted by the advertiser but also reveal whether the ad is designed to reach men or women or both. Again, some ads do this explicitly. One deodorant ad, for example, tells us that the product was specially formulated for women.

In another ad for a deodorant soap, a male character tells us that the product is strong enough for a man. Then an attractive woman adds that she likes it too.

The ways in which ads signal the gender of the intended purchaser can be seen by turning off the sound on the television set and comparing the visual texts of ads for after-shaves and for perfumes. Without hearing the verbal pitch we can tell whether the product is being sold to men or women by determining whether

15. Patricia Winters, "A Trend, Friend: Is Rap 4 U, 2?" *Advertising Age*, 25 June 1990, p. 3.

a man or a woman is the visual focus of the ad. Is she turning to look at him or is he turning to look at her? Are a number of men in pursuit of one woman or a number of women in pursuit of one man?

An ad can also solicit the attention of the intended audience by re-creating the lifestyle that the audience member either has or desires. Why do ads for beer show groups of people rather than individuals? Why are men rather than women shown in most beer ads? In what sorts of environments are the people in beer ads shown? How are the people in ads for beer dressed—formally or casually? Are the people in beer ads middle class or upper class?

Now consider the same questions about an expensive scotch (Chivas Regal) or gin. The lifestyle created in beer ads is different from the lifestyle portrayed in ads for more expensive hard liquor. The ads tell us that beer is an out-of-doors as well as an indoor drink, that beer drinkers are active, often in sports, that beer is a drink for people who are comfortable in casual clothes with groups of friends; it is not a drink for the solitary drinker or for the man in the tux. Within these general lifestyles the advertisers single out their market by preference for certain sorts of activities. One beer urges us to grab all the gusto you can get; the appeal is assertive, rugged. Another beer tells us that it is the beer for "when it's time to relax."

The mood of the two ads will be different because the basic appeal is different. One is more active than the other and one is more individualistic than the other. Beer ads also single out their audience by the types of environments in which the ad situates the product. Some ads place the beer drinkers in a bar; others place their beer drinkers outdoors. One beer's advertising tactic has been to show appropriate and inappropriate times for enjoying a beer, with the slogan "It's the right beer now."

Many beer ads appeal to sports enthusiasts by including famous hockey, base-ball, or football professionals in the ads. Some beers set themselves apart by appealing to an upper-class market. They do this by adopting an exotic name (Michelob rather than Pabst, Schlitz, Budweiser), by packaging in a bottle with foil wrap, by implying that they're made by more expensive processes, by charging more for the product, by labeling themselves "premium" beer, and by stressing that they are imported or that the recipe is imported. So, ads themselves provide some of the clues about the identity of the intended audience.

The place in which we find the ad also provides clues. Ads targeted to children appear during certain types of television programming, such as children's specials or cartoons, and at the hours at which children's programming occurs—early morning, especially Saturday. They also appear in magazines such as *Boy's Life*. Ads designed for homemakers are seen at all hours, particularly during soap operas in the afternoon and during morning talk shows; they appear in so-called women's magazines such as *McCall's*. Ads for older persons appear more often during news and public affairs programming, the types of programming older adults are most likely to watch. Ads for men appear during sports events or in so-called men's magazines; ads for adults appear during prime time.

An image-building ad for a corporation will appear adjacent to a prestigious public affairs program such as "Meet the Press" because highly educated persons, opinion leaders, and those who control the other media are more likely to attend to such programs.

Some targeting is controversial. When R.J. Reynolds Tobacco Company announced that it was introducing a new cigarette called "Uptown" intended primarily for African-Americans, protests from the African-American community and from U.S. Health and Human Services Secretary Louis Sullivan followed. The cigarette, which was to have been market-tested in Philadelphia in December 1989, was withdrawn by the company.

In some cases, the actual audience for a product is different from the audience one would posit. One might guess, for example, that the *Wall Street Journal* is read primarily by those who work in finance, those who are older and employed by large corporations. To ensure that those who might otherwise advertise on its pages are not misled by the stereotype of the *Journal* reader, the newspaper takes out ads in trade publications telling advertisers:

> Some surprising facts about *Wall Street Journal* subscribers. 83% work in fields outside of financial services. 42% are younger than 45. 44% work for companies with fewer than 100 employees.

Advertising and Reality

Ads do not necessarily accurately mirror the audience they attempt to influence. An analysis of the ways ads portray age and aging shows the ways they underrepresent some sectors of the population and also the ways in which ads perpetuate stereotypes.

Demographic Distortion

If you knew nothing of the demographic makeup of the population of the United States and gained your only information from broadcast and print ads, you would draw the following mistaken conclusions:

The United States is a country dominated by attractive younger women. Younger women appear more often than persons of any other age group in ads. In 1978, 32.7 percent of the persons appearing in television ads were younger women.

There are fewer women than men. An analysis of the gender of those appearing in ads aired during Saturday children's programming in 1987 found that only 39 percent were women. By contrast, 51 percent of the actual U.S. population is female.[16]

Americans disappear as they age. A content analysis of *Ebony* and *Life* from 1978–1987 revealed that less than 2 percent of the ads showed elderly people. The researchers concluded: "Advertising in the two magazines is geared toward younger people and largely treats the elderly as if nonexis-

---

16. Daniel Riffe, Helene Goldson, Kelly Saxton, and Yang-Chou Yu, "Females and Minorities in TV Ads in 1987 Saturday Children's Programs," *Journalism Quarterly* (Spring 1989): 136.

tent."[17] Walter Gantz and colleagues analyzed the ads in seven popular national magazines with large circulations and found that only 5.9 percent of the 6,785 ads contained at least one elderly character.[18] Of the over 17,000 characters who appeared in these ads, only 3.1 percent were older adults. Yet older persons currently make up over 10 percent of the population. In print ads older men were more likely to appear than older women; 74 percent of the older persons appearing in them were men.

The people who inhabit commercial advertising are disproportionately male and young because ads mirror not the actual population of the United States but its consuming population. But as the population has aged and the baby boomers approached middle age, advertisers have adjusted their messages to this concentration of consumers. The average age of the characters in ads has risen accordingly.

Stereotypes

Stereotypes are simplified, inaccurate conceptions or images that have become standardized and are widely held. A stereotype may either idealize or demean the group it types. If a depiction of a group reflects reality, we do not consider that depiction a stereotype.

Stereotypes make it possible for us to form generalizations about a person or advertised character without requiring a great deal of information or evidence. The less time we have to process information, the more likely we are to rely on stereotypes in drawing conclusions. The less time a television producer has to communicate a message, the more likely he or she is to rely on stereotypes.

For example, in a 30-second commercial, a writer cannot create three-dimensional characters but must instead deal in the shorthand of stereotypes. The Harried Housewife, the Bumbling Husband in the Kitchen, the Archetypal Grandmother, the Nosy Neighbor are stock characters in commercials whose type we recognize immediately. Consequently, the writer can introduce a limited number of cues about them in a few seconds and proceed to deliver the message through them because we fill in the appropriate characteristics for this type of character.

Often the stereotypes found in commercials are so ridiculous or so harmless that they provoke no protest. "Mr. Whipple," the storekeeper who lurks behind the display cases waiting to ensnare shoppers for squeezing the Charmin, and Aunt Bluebell, who arrives at the homes of relatives with toilet paper hidden in her purse, are two such eccentrics. These characters are so implausible that if we identify with them at all, it is as comic foils.

By contrast, when a lazy, greasy, conniving thief in a sombrero and gunbelt speaking in a parody of a Mexican dialect was chosen as the trade character for Frito's corn chips, Hispanic groups protested. The Frito Bandito embodied and consequently reinforced negative stereotypes about Latin Americans in general

---

17. Sharon Bramlett-Solomon and Vanessa Wilson, "Images of the Elderly in *Life* and *Ebony*, 1978–1987," *Journalism Quarterly* (Spring 1989): 188.

18. Walter Gantz, Howard M. Gartenberg, and Cindy Rainbow, "Approaching Invisibility: The Portrayal of the Elderly in Magazine Advertisements," *Journal of Communication* 30 (1980): 56–60.

and Mexicans in particular. By drawing public attention to the stereotypes on which the Frito Bandito was based, the protest made it more difficult for the ads to use the stereotype to convey a commercial message. The protests also demonstrated that the Bandito offended a large, vocal group of potential customers, a result no advertiser desires. Consequently, the Frito Bandito disappeared from the ads.

Stereotypes that are universally held do not draw protests because we are unable to see them as stereotypes. For decades the public tolerated ads predicated on the senility of older characters. Then gerontological research established that senility among older persons is rare, and the gray rights movement focused attention on ads that embodied the myth of pervasive senility. As a result, the number of ads decreased in which older characters' seeming inability to hear, understand, or recall the product's name provided an excuse for repetition of that name.

Stereotypes are powerful means of reinforcing societal attitudes about groups of people because the process of stereotyping involves the receiver in creating the message. When the negative attitude that is reinforced is about a large, politically and economically important group such as Hispanics, African-Americans, women, or elders, and is recognized by spokespersons for that group as destructive (such as, a woman's life is fulfilled if her floors shine, older persons are senile, Hispanics are lazy and dishonest), protest will follow because representatives of the stereotyped group fear that the stereotype will reinforce undesirable role models and will perpetuate discrimination against the group. Some groups have used the media to change the way in which they are portrayed by the media, as we will show in Chapter 9.

Advertising Values

Often we are unaware that advertising embeds assumptions not directly related to the products being advertised. These assumptions are diagrammed in Figure 6.1.

Television transports people to a middle-, upper-middle, and upper-class world. In the process television creates expectations in us all, expectations based on the assumption that the norm or standard in this country is a middle-class existence—or better. People in ads have spacious kitchens, large lawns, expensive appliances, cars; they travel worldwide. Ads take for granted that the audience routinely buys soaps, deodorants, makeup, and cologne, and that the audience is not making a decision about *whether* to buy the product but rather is deciding *which* brand to buy.

The World According to Commercials

In the process of being urged to purchase the multitude of products that ads advocate, we are also being persuaded to a certain style of living. Contrast, for example, our standards of personal hygiene with those of our great-grandparents at the turn of the century. Underarm deodorants, in the forms we know them, did

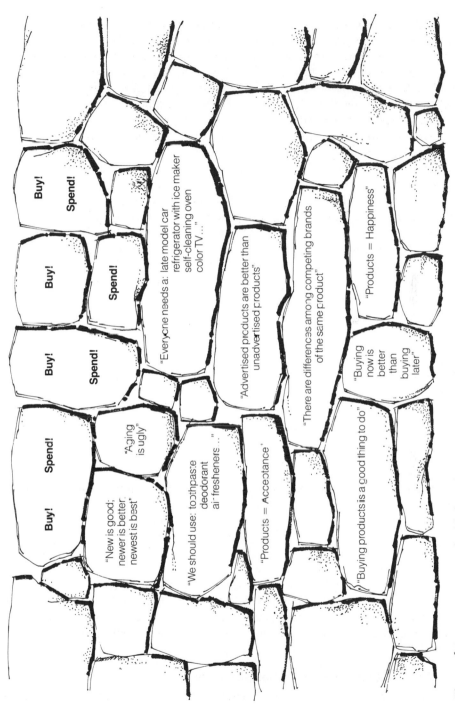

Figure 6.1 Assumptions embedded in advertising.

not exist and no one seemed to mind. Advertising has persuaded us that certain types of body odors are offensive and ought to be camouflaged or altered. Embedded in the argument that we ought to use a specific mouthwash is the assumption that we ought to use a mouthwash.

Similarly, the argument that we ought to use a specific floor wax assumes that we ought to wax our floors. Embedded in the argument that we ought to use a specific room deodorant is the assumption that we ought to use one.

Reliance on packaged products has contributed to the growing problem of waste disposal in the United States. If we didn't use so many packaged products and such heavily packaged products, the problem would be smaller. But since advertisers want us to continue to use their products, they reassure us that doing so is environmentally responsible, a responsibility new-found in a climate in which the public is expressing concerns about the vulnerabilities of the planet.

Accordingly, in 1990, a number of companies began using and touting their use of recycled materials in their packaging. Lever Brothers announced in July 1990 that the plastic bottles containing Wisk, All, and Snuggle would contain "up to" (note the careful use of language) 35 percent recycled resins. Procter & Gamble announced that it would include at least 25 percent recycled high-density polyethylene in bottles of Tide, Cheer, Era, Dash, and Downy. Spic 'n Span liquid cleaner bottles will be made entirely of materials that have been recycled. The scope of the industry's contribution to the land fill problem is evident in its claim that "In the first year of P & G's bottle recycling program, the company will produce 110 million containers that use the recycled plastics, keeping about 80 million bottles out of the nation's waste stream." [19]

In the process of embedding these assumptions, advertising has created norms governing our sense of the acceptable home: a home in which the faucets, floors, furniture, mirrors, dishes—but not the faces of the women—shine; a home that is odor-free—no smell of cat, fish, cigars, feet—and filled with artificial, chemically created outdoor scents—lilac, rose, herbs, evergreen.

The home is filled with subtle deceptions. Spouses marvel at the cleanliness, unaware of how little effort it took with the new product to achieve that effect; and they assume that foods created from chemically enhanced mixes are homemade.

In the world of commercials, avenging guardians of the social order exist to ferret out those who fail to use the sanctioned products. Nosy neighbors and socially superior guests are ever alert to spot the smell of cat or cigar, or to comment snidely about spots on glasses, dull dishes, or dust on the furniture.

The characters who live out their lives in the 30- to 60-second world of the broadcast ads and in the pages of print ads seek and obtain almost instant gratification. Problems arise and are met. Promises of product performance are made and kept. All of this occurs in a very brief time span. The answer to all of the problems, needs, and expectations in the ads is ultimately found in the purchase of some product. The link between problem and solution is clear and unequivocal. Not only is the gratification instant, but it occurs as a result of the product

---

19. Laurie Freeman, "Lever, P & G Green Plans Differ," *Advertising Age*, 23 July 1990, p. 46.

advertised. In contrast, our lives are more complicated and more ambiguous than the lives of advertising's population.

Characters in ads are also what psychologists would define as "other-directed." Characters seek the approval of others in ads. When that approval is withheld, it provokes crises. Neighbors detect odors in the house and crisis ensues; an air freshener is the answer. Parents detect spots on drinking glasses and a crisis occurs; a new dishwashing product eases the tension. Acquaintances spot "ring around the collar" and the family is thrown into turmoil. A clothes washing product resolves the crisis. In each of these instances, the others disapprove not only of the condition (the ring, the odor, the spots) but also implicitly, if not explicitly, disapprove of the ad's protagonist *because of* the condition. It is not only the product that ultimately wins approval in the ad but also the person who uses the product.

The need for social approval is strongly felt by all of us. It is a need that advertising exploits. In the process of exploiting the need, advertising reinforces it, legitimizes it, and enhances it.

In one sense, advertising is powerfully conservative—it is loath to offend; it reinforces institutional values. In another sense, advertising is radical because it holds out a world full of products and promises the good life to those who buy them. Yet the mass media reach many who lack the money to buy the products. Ads are materialistic. Purchase and consumption of material goods are glorified in commercial ads. Our assumptions that ads are merchandising products are so deeply ingrained that we distrust ads created to enhance the image of a corporation, which claim "this corporation is a good citizen of the community." The notion that a manufacturer might pay to bring us a noncommercial message is suspect because until recently we had seen few such ads. In fact, the manufacturer is still merchandising a product. The product here is the company's good name, and when we respect it, the advertiser can link it to the product line and urge us to buy.

The acquisition of material goods brings happiness in the ads; material goods are satisfying. Because the ads simplify, we do not see other factors that make a happy ending possible; we do not see those factors that make the happy ending impossible even with the product or see the unhappiness that may be caused by the product.

Seeing the Other Side

Although it is generally true that ads reinforce the assumption that consumption of products is good, there is at least one major exception. In the name of fairness, the FCC required stations that broadcast cigarette ads also to run free of charge a certain number of antismoking ads. During the period in which both pro- and anticigarette ads were aired, audiences were exposed to messages that argued that consumption of a product (cigarettes) was not only not good (as the procigarette ads claimed) but harmful and should be avoided or stopped. The antismoking campaign challenged an unspoken premise in commercial advertising—the premise that consumption of products is a good. By challenging the premise, the antismoking ads made us aware of it. In a sense, the counter-ads were not merely countering smoking but also countering advertising.

The Interplay of News and Advertising

■

We live in a complex world in which messages interact with each other to form impressions. Because people pay attention to information on topics of importance to them, public recall of news about health is high. When scientific studies seemed to confirm that oat bran had the potential to lower cholesterol, advertisers hurried to capitalize with new products such as Ralston Purina's Oat Bran Option, and with new claims for old products, such as General Mills's Cheerios and Quaker Oats. Kellogg's brought Common Sense onto the market achieving national distribution in late 1988. By mid-1989, Common Sense had attracted a 2.5 percent market share in the ready-to-eat cereal market.

But the legitimacy that news can endow, news also can take away. In mid-January 1990, the prestigious *New England Journal of Medicine* published a major study downplaying the ability of oat bran to reduce cholesterol. The study was carried in print and broadcast media reports. In March, Arbitron/SAMI scanner reports showed that oat bran cereals, which had peaked at a 4.9 percent of the cereals market in January, had plunged to a 3.18 market share. Common Sense had dropped from attracting 2.5 percent of the cereal eaters to occupying a place on the breakfast tables of only 1 percent.

T O   S U M   U P

It is more common to see the premises underlying a given ad campaign challenged in news and public affairs programming. News programs carry word of recalls, of FTC investigations, of court cases in which advertisers' claims are challenged; consumer advocates in newspapers and on television investigate harmful effects of products. These exposés constitute a form of counter-advertising. They make us aware that ads do not tell the "whole truth" about a product and that ads ought to be evaluated critically. In the next chapter we focus on the critical evaluation of advertising's claims and evidence.

Persuasion Through Advertising

The Advertiser's Aims

If we are to be persuaded to buy a product or service, we must be able to recognize it, distinguish it from its competitors, conclude that we want it or need it, and remember our desire for that product when the opportunity to obtain it arises or when we create that opportunity. To accomplish these goals, advertisers create product *recognition* through use of trademarks, packaging, and slogans; *differentiate* the product from others by creating a unique selling proposition; encourage us to want the product by enveloping it in a set of favorable *associations*; commit us to the product and its associated promises by inducing our *participation* in the creation of the ad's meaning; and ensure that we recall the product and our need for it by capsulizing these means of identification and differentiation and these associations and acts of participation in *redundant* messages, messages that are repeated again and again. In this chapter we examine the function served by advertisers' messages and expose some of the ways in which ads can entice the unwary consumer into false conclusions about products.

Creating Product Recognition

Trademarks

A trademark identifies a company's product. A trademark is a symbol—sometimes verbal, sometimes visual, sometimes both—that tells the consumer who makes the product. Trademarks do not have to be words found in the language, although once a trademark has been widely advertised, it may find its way into the dictionary. *Exxon* and *Xerox* are words created specifically to serve as trademarks.

Sometimes advertisers are so successful in identifying the trademark with the product that the trademark becomes a common equivalent for the product.

Generic Murphy Bed

The United States Court of Appeals for the Second Circuit in Manhattan declared that anyone who might wish to manufacture a bed of the type that stumped the likes of Charlie Chaplin and Jackie Gleason can call it, if they want to, a Murphy bed. The judges, reversing a lower-court decision, said that many people had come to use the term "Murphy bed" "to designate generally a type of bed." The dictionary says a Murphy is "a bed that may be folded or swung into a closet." Thus, the judges said, "Murphy bed" has become a generic part of the language that cannot be owned by anyone.[a]

[a]William Glaverson, "Open and Shut Case? Generic Murphy Bed," *New York Times*, 2 May 1989, p. 13 Y.

Cellophane, aspirin, escalator, trampoline, nylon, linoleum, and thermos were once trademarks held by individual companies. Because the manufacturers of these products and their advertisers did not protect these names adequately, the trademarks slipped into the public vocabulary and the public domain. To protect a trademark, manufacturers insist that it be used with the term for the generic product. So, for example, ads do not promote Kleenex but Kleenex *tissues*. In addition, the trademark is always capitalized.

A product may also be identified by a trade character who personifies the product's important characteristics. Often the trade character speaks for the product and functions visually as a substitute for the product, as, for example, the Pillsbury Doughboy personifies and speaks for Pillsbury Biscuits. The Doughboy resembles the biscuits—he's white in color, responds to touch by bouncing back (as freshly baked biscuits do), is immaculately clean (he wears a white baker's hat), and he's called Poppin' Fresh, suggesting that the biscuits rise, bake quickly, and taste fresh.

Some trade characters are a clear and simple extension of the name of the company. The greyhound of Greyhound buses symbolizes the company's name and at the same time suggests the buses are fast, sleek, and efficient.

Packaging

Packaging is another potent means of providing product identification. For example, we associate Quaker Oats with the smiling Quaker on a cylindrical box, and L'eggs pantyhose with their plastic egg-shaped container. Ideally, the name of the product and the package will reinforce each other the way the picture of the Quaker underscores Quaker Oats and the egglike container is a reminder of the name L'eggs.

Selecting an appropriate name and appropriate packaging generally precedes selection of the slogan. The slogan describes either the product or the reasons people will want or need the product; like the name and the package, it is usually repeated in all major forms of advertising for the product.

Packaging

"Changes in packaging can increase an ad's effectiveness by more than 45 percent," Elliot Young, president, Perception Research Services, told a Cosmo/Expo packaging session. . . . "The new Diet Rite package . . . contributed to sales gains of more than 35 percent."[b]

[b]"Packaging Linked to Ad's Effect," *Advertising Age*, 3 May 1982, p. 63.

A Cracker in Another Box

"When RJR Nabisco introduced a bite-size version of graham crackers last fall, the company was abuzz. . . . But to the company's dismay, sales were sluggish. As it turns out, looks—at least the looks of the box—were the problem. So, in a crash program, Nabisco's marketing people changed the logo and changed the name to Graham Bites from Honeycomb Graham Snacks. And perhaps most important, in their eyes, from a subdued blue to a bright yellow. As a result, sales of the six-sided snack . . . are strong and getting stronger."[c]

[c]Anthony Ramirez, "Lessons in the Cracker Market," *New York Times*, 5 July 1990, p. D 1.

Not Wanting to Offend . . .

Darkie toothpaste will start disappearing from Hong Kong bathrooms next month as its manufacturer attempts to end charges of racism. Bowing to international criticism, Hawley and Hazel Chemical Co., Ltd., said yesterday that its popular product would be marketed as Darlie in Hong Kong.

"We want the name of our toothpaste to be internationally acceptable. However, some people consider the word *Darkie* racially offensive, particularly in America," said Alvin Au, regional commercial director for Hawley and Hazel.[d]

[d]Reuters, 20 February 1990.

Slogans

An effective slogan summarizes the ad and provides a memory peg on which the name of the product is hung. If someone says "when you care enough to send the very best," we think "Hallmark cards" because the trademark and the slogan are now fused in our minds.

While identifying a product and helping to differentiate one from another, a slogan may transcend the ad and enter the vocabulary through which we think about and discuss our lives. For example, one college student surprised his parents by arriving home unexpectedly. When his mother opened the door, he said "I cared enough to send the very best," a meaning Hallmark had not intended when it created that slogan.

Similarly, at your last birthday party, someone probably said "you're not getting older, you're getting better." That statement formed the core of an extended ad campaign for Clairol hair coloring. As a slogan it capitalized on our fears of aging to reassure us implicitly that if we used the product we would look younger and better. But the slogan also underscores age stereotypes. It is, after all, possible both to get older and better. In addition the slogan promises the impossible; unless we've died we are getting older. Aging is an inexorable biological process. Moreover, there is no reason to assume that we should not want to get older. The ad plays on common fears that are unfounded. Most people, for example, report that youth was a more troublesome and traumatic time than older age. When the statement "you're not getting older, you're getting better" is made, it is no longer a statement about a hair coloring. It is a linguistic convention—an expression both parties know is only partially true. You may indeed be getting better.

Some slogans are more susceptible to parody than others. In 1964, for example, Republican presidential candidate Barry Goldwater erred in selecting the slogan, "In your heart, you know he's right." Billboards bearing the slogan were quickly defaced to read "extremely right," "but in your head you know he's wrong," or "but in your guts you know he's nuts." The parallel construction invited reconstruction.

Long after a product has abandoned a slogan, the slogan retains currency because we tend to store highly redundant messages in our memories for later retrieval. Consequently, chicken producer Frank Perdue says in one of his ads that "golden yellow is the natural color of a chicken. . . . So don't wonder why my chickens are so yellow, wonder why some chickens are so white [lifting up a competitor's white chicken]. I wonder where the yellow went?" . . . That last sentence becomes a barometer of the age of the auditor. Those of us old enough to remember the Pepsodent toothpaste slogan, "You'll wonder where the yellow went when you brush your teeth with Pepsodent," hear the line as a clever reconstruction of an old claim and also as a literal statement. Those unexposed to the campaign hear only the literal statement.

As our discussion so far indicates, any trademark, package, or slogan that identifies a product also distinguishes that product from those employing a different trademark, package, and slogan. Indeed, the package may be all that distinguishes one product from another.

Differentiation

Rosser Reeves, one of the pioneers of advertising, coined the phrase "unique selling proposition." The unique selling proposition is a claim that differentiates one ad from another. In an era when advertising floods the environment, the unique selling proposition is even more important than it was when there were fewer products of the same kind and less advertising.

Crest toothpaste, for example, contains fluoride. When it was introduced, Crest was distinguished from other toothpastes by the claim, certified by a major dental association, that it would reduce the number of new cavities. Once the

---

Differentiation

"'All the cosmetics companies use basically the same chemicals. It is all the same quality stuff,' says Heinz J. Eiermann, a former cosmetics chemist and industry executive who directs the Food and Drug Administration's division of cosmetics technology. 'The art of cosmetics is as much in marketing as in chemistry. Much of what you pay for is make-believe.'"[e]

"'I've never worked on a product that was better than another. They hardly . . . exist. So what I have to do is create an imagery about that product,' said George Lois, chairman of Lois Pitts Gershon Pon/GGK on '60 Minutes' in 1981."[f]

[e]Blaine Harden, "Vanity Fare," *Washington Post Magazine,* 30 May 1982, p. 10.
[f]Quoted by Roger Draper, "The Faithless Shepherd," *New York Review of Books,* 26 June 1986, p. 16.

---

other products were able to make the claim that they too could reduce the number of new cavities, Crest lost its unique selling proposition. Other competitors then entered the market claiming that they whitened teeth; some claimed to freshen breath. Once the unique selling propositions of a product such as toothpaste are well known and accepted, a competitor can combine the unique selling propositions of all the others. So, a toothpaste was marketed that promised fluoride *and* fresher breath: "Double Protection Aqua Fresh."

It is also possible to adopt and extend a competitor's claim. A long distance phone company, for example, urges you to use the phone to keep in touch. An airline extends the claim, arguing that flying there is the best way to keep in touch—which assumes that you have granted that keeping in touch is a good thing.

A competitor can counter a unique selling proposition by co-opting it, as Aqua Fresh did in co-opting the claims of its rivals. Alternatively, it can undercut the selling proposition by granting that it is unique but implying that that uniqueness is a disadvantage. Dove soap claimed as its unique advantage that it is one-quarter cleansing cream. A competitor responded by claiming that its product doesn't contain any greasy cream. The unique selling proposition had been re-contextualized by a competitor, and in the new context it was a negative, rather than a positive, attribute of the product.

The package may be the product's major selling point. When a deodorant is advertised as "a convenient roll-on," when a frozen dinner is advertised as "oven-to-table service," it is the package, not the product being packaged, that we are being sold. *Once a mode of packaging has been widely adopted, it loses its utility as a unique selling point for any single product.* We now take for granted, for example, that rolls of waxed paper, foil, or plastic wrap will come in a box with a serrated edge so we can cleanly cut off the amount needed. By contrast, the use of plastic containers for products once bottled in glass is sufficiently new that the "unbreakable" or "squeezable" bottle is still advertised.

Association

■

Advertisers attempt to associate their products with a slogan, a trademark or trade character, and a package; then they try to associate the product, slogan, package, trademark, and trade character with positive experiences. Ads create wants and transform wants into needs by associating products with desirable experiences. If the ad is to succeed, it must create a strong associative link between the experience portrayed in the ad and the product. That experience must be one we would like to share, and the experience portrayed must be different from and better than that promised by competitors.

Participation

■

By involving us in the creation of the meaning of the ad, an advertiser can increase the likelihood that we will identify with the experience portrayed in the ad. At the same time, this involvement ensures that our experience of this product as portrayed through the experience in the ad will be different from and better than that portrayed in other ads.

Identification with Ad Characters

Ads establish commonality with us by creating characters and situations with which we identify. Some of the characters represent the sorts of people advertisers think we would like to be (rich, famous, glamorous); some represent the persons advertisers think we think we are (unappreciated, overworked). Some ads represent persons advertisers think we do not want to be. The purpose of such ads is to tell us that if we use the product, we will not become like that person (old, ugly, irritable, pain-ridden, covered with dandruff, disfigured by acne).

Significant Experiences

Some experiences, such as birth, are universal. Others—such as weddings, graduations, or anniversaries—are more culture-bound. But in this culture all of these moments of change function as important elements in our lives. Memorable, culturally significant moments are awaited expectantly—as a boy waits eagerly for the opportunity to shave (an activity greeted with less enthusiasm after years of confronting the need for it daily). Retirement is another such moment, although it is one more dreaded than embraced by many.

When advertisers re-create such important moments for us, they invite us to identify with their creation, to invest it with our own experience or the experience we hope to have. If an advertiser can induce us to invest the ad and, by implication, the product with our own positive feelings and experiences, we ought to emerge with a positive feeling about the product. It will not have the desired effect, of course, if we feel manipulated by the ad and feel that it cheapens our memories or projections for the future.

Some moments in our lives are almost off limits for advertisers because the associations we bring to those events are not happy but sad. Death is one such moment. Consequently, life insurance ads seek to minimize the trauma. Indeed, one life insurance ad features an escalator to the sky. The man being escorted up

---

Brand Recall

The Newspaper Advertising Bureau, in its most recent study of the recall of television commercials, has found that the average percentage of respondents who could recall the brand advertised in the last commercial seen had not changed since 1981 when that statistic was 7 percent.[g]

[g]William F. Gloede, "TV Ad Recall Still Low: NAB Study," *Advertising Age*, 4 August 1986, p. 50.

---

the escalator (presumably to heaven) is protesting that he's not ready to go yet. The ad reassures us that he is indeed ready because his life insurance is in order; he need not worry about the well-being of his survivors. Another ad for life insurance shows a man with his family, and then simply removes him from the picture as the narrative tells what their lives will be like if he's not there.

Because we fear our own death and grieve when a person we love dies, death is almost taboo as a basis for ads. The indirect treatment of death in the ads for life insurance testifies to this. Yet an ad for the Catholic Church of Maryland fractures that taboo deliberately by showing a baptism and then making a transition to a funeral, with the narrator saying "You only live once, shouldn't you go to church more than twice?" The ad is jarring, in part because it has capsulized two moments, birth and death, which we all confront. In part it is jarring also because such bold, direct treatment of death in an ad shatters expectations about ads that we are not even aware that we have until they are violated.

Making the Audience an Accomplice

Verbal and visual commonality forms the base from which the advertiser builds the ad's claims. If the advertiser then can lure us into the role of accomplice in endorsing the product, the ad will succeed. To do this, the advertiser determines what content we are willing to invest in the ad and then creates a structure that links that invested content to the product.

The ad may do this with a rhetorical question, as a 1968 presidential campaign ad for Democratic candidate Hubert Humphrey did when it asked, "Who is your choice to be a heartbeat away from the president?" The Humphrey-Muskie campaign knew from polling data that when the choice was reduced to Edmund Muskie (Humphrey's running mate) and Spiro Agnew (Nixon's running mate), the audience would be more likely to answer "Muskie" than "Agnew." So the rhetorical question was designed to elicit a response favorable to Humphrey. When the audience answered "Muskie," that answer made it more difficult to vote for Nixon, because in the process of accepting the question as legitimate, the auditor had accepted the assumption of the importance of the vice president. If the vice-presidential candidate could be made a salient element in the determination of voting behavior, then Humphrey would gain an advantage because Muskie was viewed as the better vice-presidential candidate—even by a proportion of Nixon supporters. The ad itself did not tell us that Muskie was the right answer. The advertisers knew that we would fill in Muskie's name. In the process of answering

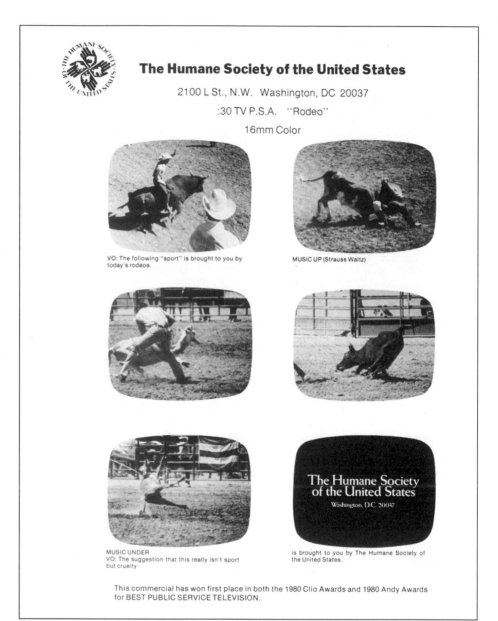

The Humane Society of the United States

2100 L St., N.W. Washington, DC 20037

:30 TV P.S.A. "Rodeo"

16mm Color

VO: The following "sport" is brought to you by today's rodeos.

MUSIC UP (Strauss Waltz)

MUSIC UNDER
VO: The suggestion that this really isn't sport but cruelty

The Humane Society
of the United States
Washington, D.C. 20037

is brought to you by The Humane Society of the United States.

This commercial has won first place in both the 1980 Clio Awards and 1980 Andy Awards for BEST PUBLIC SERVICE TELEVISION.

Figure 7.1 This award-winning p.s.a., created for The Humane Society of the United States by the Earle Palmer Brown Advertising Agency, attracts attention by its use of slow-motion scenes of a calf-roping at a rodeo. Because we are unaccustomed to slow-motion footage in television ads, this technique focuses our attention on the content of the shots. The ad also grabs attention by violating our expectations because it substitutes a Strauss waltz for the shouting crowds we expect to hear. But as the ad progresses, we sense that a tension is building between the grace and gentleness of the waltz and the wrenching, agonized animals we see on the screen. The visual message is not aesthetically pleasing, although the music tells us it ought to be. If we are accustomed to view rodeos as sport, as a the question by saying to ourselves "Muskie," we participated in creating a pro-Humphrey-Muskie message, and the strategy underlying the ad succeeded.

In addition to the use of resonant symbols such as weddings and the construction of rhetorical questions for which the audience has a ready answer, advertisers also induce participation by:

1. Juxtaposing images that have no necessary relation to one another but that, when associatively linked, lead the audience to infer a relationship ("Have a Coke and a smile").

2. Employing double entendres that prompt the audience to fill in a second meaning ("My men wear English Leather or they wear nothing at all").

3. Employing a phrase outside its normal context to induce the audience to ask how, if at all, that phrase can be applied to the product. For example, automobile dealers appropriate a phrase from the film *The Godfather* to assert, "We'll make you an offer you can't refuse."

4. Creating a questionable grammatical construction such that, in the process of untangling the statement's meaning, the audience draws a new meaning from the words. For example, an automobile ad claims that "we" not only make the car "*well, we make it good.*"

5. Using explicit content that triggers unarticulated audience predispositions. In summer 1990, a black glossy insert in *Advertising Age* declared "*Playboy* has put me in the hearts of 10 million men." The fold-in was designed to look like the *Playboy* centerfold fold-out. Anticipating a nude female centerfold, readers opened the page to find a three-page pull-out, similar to *Playboy*'s in form, but of a fully clothed businessman. The data sheet, also a carryover from *Playboy*, revealed that this was David Warren, president of Jordache. In the data sheet, Warren plugs *Playboy*. "Our previous print campaign didn't consist of major menswear publications. A big mistake. To correct it, we chose *Playboy* because it's got the largest readership among the men's magazines. And their reader is our customer: affluent, younger, contemporary with a disposable income. A perfect fit— pardon the pun."

By luring us into participating in the creation of the ad's meaning, the advertiser increases the persuasive power of the ad. But unless the message is repeated often, it is unlikely that we will either be exposed to it or persuaded by it. The ad in Figure 7.1 is highly creative in its selection of means to induce participation.

---

spectacle to be appreciated and enjoyed, or as a form of relaxation and entertainment, the ad is forcing us to re-evaluate our attitude. The jarring contrast between the music and the visual message is forcing that re-evaluation. The ad induces participation by placing the viewer in the position of a judge who must determine whether the activities shown are "sport" or "cruelty." The claim that this is sport is offered by the announcer on behalf of "today's rodeos" in the opening frame. The alternative claim is offered on behalf of The Humane Society of the United States in the fifth and sixth frames. The visual and audio content of the ad biases the viewer in favor of the second interpretation. (Reprinted by permission of The Humane Society of the United States.)

Redundancy

■
Repetition

We are more likely to remember a message we have heard often. Consequently most ads are highly redundant; they repeat the same claim visually and verbally, underscoring the claim in the slogan and whenever possible in the packaging and in the name of the product as well. Note the number of times the name of the product and its chief selling point, capsulized in the slogan, are repeated in this ad:

> *MERIT* ANNOUNCES NEW *MERIT* ULTRA LIGHTS. NOW THE *MERIT* IDEA HAS BEEN INTRODUCED AT ONLY 4 MG. TAR—NEW *MERIT* ULTRA LIGHTS. A MILDER *MERIT* FOR THOSE WHO PREFER AN ULTRA LOW TAR CIGARETTE. NEW *MERIT* ULTRA LIGHTS. IT'S GOING TO SET A WHOLE NEW TASTE STANDARD FOR ULTRA LOW TAR SMOKING.

Once the product's name and its slogan have been deeply embedded in the audience, the advertiser can enlist the audience as an accomplice in filling one or the other into the ad—thus heightening audience participation and the persuasive impact of the message. In one ad for Coke, for example, the announcer did not utter the word *Coke*. Instead the chorus sang "It's the real thing," and where the ad would ordinarily have said "Coke" we heard instead the sound of the bottle being opened and the soda fizzing. Meanwhile, bottles of Coke were shown to encourage us to fill in our part of the slogan.

Repeated Exposure

Ads also are aired repeatedly, or printed again and again, in the hope that sooner or later we will be reading, listening, or watching when they occur and will pay attention. The likelihood that we will remember a part of the ad increases as exposure to the ad increases. For this reason, advertisers often create radio ads from their televised ads' audio tracks and use pictures from television ads in magazine ads. If the advertiser is successful, repetition ensures that the ad reaches the consumer with a message that creates product *recognition, differentiates* the product from its competitors, *associates* the product with favorable experiences, and *repeatedly involves* the audience in creating the ad's meaning. In this way ads create or underscore wants and transform them into needs to be satisfied by purchase of the advertised product.

Often, as a result of this process, we purchase products with which we are satisfied. Our experience with the product and the experience promised in the ad are comparable. But sometimes, after purchase of the product, we realize that the ad led us astray. On examination, we realize that the deception did not reside explicitly in the ad but in our eagerness to make faulty inferences, an eagerness abetted by the advertiser.

To recap the functions served by name recognition, differentiation, association, participation, and redundancy, we will analyze in the following case study an award-winning ad (Figure 7.2), created to market the *Washington Post*.

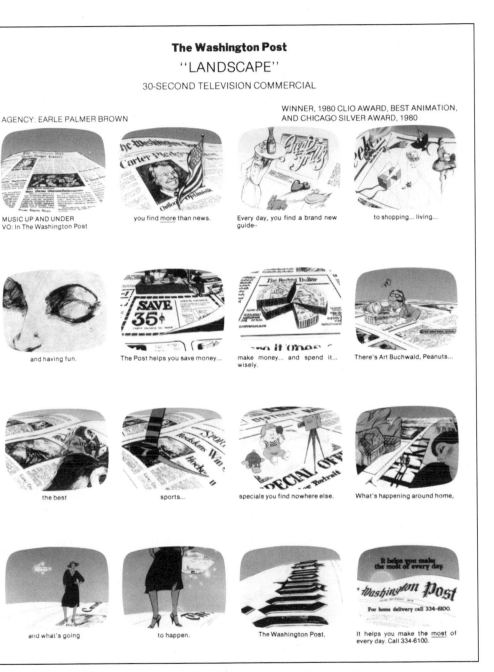

Figure 7.2 This commercial for the *Washington Post* is analyzed in the case study. The commercial was created by Dan Rosenthal for the Earle Palmer Brown Agency of Washington, D.C. (Reprinted by permission of the *Washington Post*.)

C A S E   S T U D Y
Analysis of "Landscape"

Identification

Throughout the commercial, the reader familiar with the *Washington Post* is exposed to sights that identify the newspaper. The style of print is familiar; the headline type and captions are familiar; columnist Art Buchwald is familiar. The name of the newspaper also appears clearly in frames one, two, and sixteen. In frame fifteen the end of the word *Washington* and the beginning of the word *Post* appear as the announcer says "The Washington Post." This mix of aural and print cues encourages the reader to participate in creation of the full name of the newspaper, the name that will appear in the next frame to reinforce this act of participation. The announcer also adds the name of the paper to the visual image in frames one and six as well as frame fifteen.

Differentiation

The ad is a series of claims about how the *Washington Post* differs from its unnamed competitor, the now-defunct *Washington Star*. The ad argues that the *Post*, presumably unlike its competitor, has "*more* than news" (frame two); every day it has "a brand new guide" (an implied claim of improvement over the old *Washington Post* and an inducement to *Post* subscribers to remain loyal to their ever-improving, always useful paper); it "helps you save money (frame six) . . . make money . . . and spend it . . . wisely (frame seven). Presumably the *Star* will also help you save, make, and spend money, but by noting that advantage the *Post* reminds the viewer that this advantage is not unique to either paper. But uncritical viewers may hear this too as a claim to uniqueness. Then the ad notes two popular features its competitors cannot claim: the *Post* has Art Buchwald and "Peanuts." The viewer is willing to grant that claim to uniqueness. The ad capitalizes on this act of acquiescence by asserting that the *Post* also has "the best sports" (frames nine and ten). The ad then moves to another claim that the viewer is willing to grant: because the *Post* attracts more advertisers, it does indeed include "specials you find nowhere else" (frame eleven). The ad closes with a reminder that the *Post* tells its readers what is happening and what is going to happen. Again this is a claim that the competitor can make, but here it is couched in a series of admittedly unique claims—Buchwald, "Peanuts," unique specials—so the viewer is likely to infer that because it has "more than news," the "best" sports, unique features, and unique specials, it is also better able to keep the reader up to date on current and future events "around home." The ad closes with an implied comparison: unlike its competitor, "it helps you make the *most* of every day."

Association

The basic strategy underlying this ad is association of information we want, such as news, guides to shopping, sports, specials, and information about our community, with the advertised source of this information, the *Washington Post*. The ad also associates things we want to do with reading the *Washington Post*. Do you want to have fun (frame five), save, make, and spend money wisely (frames six and seven)? Then read the *Washington Post*. The ad also associates the paper with the Washington area by showing then-President Carter in frame two, Buchwald raising the dome of the Capitol in frame eight, headlines about the home-team Redskins in frames nine and ten, and by visually highlighting the word *Washington* in the paper's title in frames two, fifteen, and sixteen.

The stream-of-consciousness narrative that gives the ad its internal coherence functions by juxtaposing important sections of the newspaper. This process of visual association creates the sense that we are reading the newspaper. The ad takes us from the front to the back of the paper with stops at popular sections. This process of association creates audience participation in the act of reading the newspaper through the ad.

The most subtle of the associations in the ad occurs in the last frame. The sun is rising as the ad invites the viewer to call for home delivery. This frame reminds the viewer that the *Post* is a morning newspaper, thus implying that you don't have to wait for its evening competitor to bring you news, savings, sports, and so on. Yet, as the lamp in the thirteenth and fourteenth frames suggests, the *Post*, although a morning paper, contains information that is current and relevant about evening activities in the Washington area, thus muting what might otherwise be a unique selling proposition of the *Star*.

Participation

We have already noted the ways in which the ad induces us to participate in the creation of the paper's name and draws us into the process of creating the ad itself by duplicating our sense of what it is like to read a newspaper. The structure of the ad moves from long shots to close-ups in frames one and two, four and five, thirteen and fourteen, creating expectations satisfied by participation in the ad. In frame one we cannot determine what is actually present on the page; frame two satisfies our curiosity: the top story is about Carter. Frames three and four show some of the kinds of fun the *Post* makes accessible, but it is not until the close-up in frame five that we are visually assured that the viewer would enjoy these activities. Frame five has personalized the offer made in frames three and four.

The ad offers inducements to both men and women to identify with its claims. The promise of the best in sports is a clear appeal to male readers; the child in frame eleven is an appeal to parents and grandparents; the high-fashion female in frames thirteen and fourteen implies that women can obtain confidence, fashion advice, and power by reading the *Washington Post*. The confident, fashionable woman knows what is going to happen (see announcer's copy) because she is literally on top of the *Washington Post*. By showing animated figures raised from the printed page, the ad also implies that the act of reading the *Post*, an act simulated in the ad, brings Washington alive. The *Post* gives its readers special access to what is important internationally (frames one and two), nationally (frames seven and eight), and locally (frames nine through fourteen).

Redundancy

As we have noted, the name of the paper and the claim that it gives its readers the best of everything pervade the ad. The ad is also visually repetitive. The visual images are underscored by each other and by the announcer's copy. Because the ad creates

(continued)

a sense of what it is like to read the paper, in a sense each time we read the paper after seeing the ad we are repeating the ad's claims. Furthermore, the ad was aired repeatedly.

Assumptions Embedded in the Ad

We have already discussed many of the assumptions embedded in the ad. To these should be added the assumption that reading a newspaper is necessary. In addition to positioning itself against its print competitors, the *Post* must position itself against televised news. The ad assumes the viewer's willingness to grant that the newspaper is a good place to find news. What differentiates it from televised news is every frame after the second. The *Post*, unlike television news, provides "*more* than news."

The ad also assumes that consuming a newspaper is important for both men and women. In addition, the ad legitimizes or assumes the legitimacy of shopping and of saving, making, and spending money. If we do not grant these assumptions and fail to buy products advertised in the paper, the paper would lose its advertisers—and would be forced to charge exorbitant subscription rates or to go out of business. So reinforcing the value of consuming and purchasing is important if the newspaper is to survive.

The ad also assumes that having fun is a legitimate and desirable activity, an assumption that might make our Puritan ancestors shudder. But note that having fun is contextualized by shopping in frame four and saving, making, and spending money in frames six and seven. Advertisers offer ways of having fun that cost money. Legitimizing having fun is, in this sense, of value to the paper's advertisers.

This focus on assumptions of value to advertisers suggests that the ad is also designed to reinforce the commitment of advertisers to stay with the *Post* despite the competing *Star*'s special ad rates. The ad implies to advertisers that the *Post* is receptive to their philosophy and able to reach those who can afford the frills advertised in frame three, the homes shown in frame twelve, and the expensive clothes found in frames thirteen and fourteen.

Advertisers' Strategies for Persuasion

We are culturally conditioned to recognize and respect certain argumentative forms and to accept certain forms of evidence. Advertisers can exploit this training by couching their claims in forms of argument and evidence we are inclined to trust. So, for example, instead of simply urging you to use our product, we might adopt the language of social science research and claim that "four out of five professors surveyed recommended that you read this book." We are hoping, of course, that our use of social scientific language will lull you into uncritical acceptance of the claim. The four professors in question are close friends who recommended it after we bought them an expensive dinner. Because you might be sus-

Advertisers' Influence on Women's Magazines

"Advertisers' control over the editorial content of women's magazines has become so institutionalized that it is . . . dictated to ad salespeople as official policy," writes Gloria Steinem, and gives these examples:

Dow's Cleaning Products stipulates that ads for its Vivid and Spray 'n Wash products should be adjacent to "children or fashion editorial"; ads for Bathroom Cleaner should be next to "home furnishing/family" features.

The De Beers diamond company, a big seller of engagement rings, prohibits magazines from placing its ads with "adjacencies to hard news or anti-love/romance theme editorial."

Procter & Gamble products were not to be placed in any issue that included *any* material on gun control, abortion, the occult, cults, or the disparagement of religion.

Steinem picked random issues of women's magazines and counted the number of pages, including letters to the editors and the like, that were not ads and/or copy complementary to ads. Some examples were:

Magazine and Issue	Total Pages	Non-ad or Ad-related
Glamour, April 1990	339	65
Vogue, May 1990	319	38
Redbook, April 1990	173	44
Family Circle, 13 March 1990	180	33
Elle, May 1990	326	39
Lear's, November 1989	173	65

Steinem quotes Sey Chassler, former editor-in-chief of *Redbook*, as saying: "I also think advertisers do this to women's magazines especially because of the general disrespect they have for women."[b]

[b]Gloria Steinem, "Sex, Lies and Advertising," *Ms.*, July/August 1990, pp. 20, 21, 25, 27.

picious if we said that 100 percent of those surveyed supported one side, we didn't pressure the fifth professor. If she'd endorsed the book, we would have found a hostile sixth professor, ensuring that the claim would be phrased in a familiar manner. We used exactly five, but implied that "four out of *every* five" professors in a large-scale survey recommended our book. Similarly, in visual ads we might show glamorous, wise media moguls holding the book, in the hope that potential consumers would assume a necessary connection between the juxtaposed images.

Content analysis of 2,000 print ads from ten major magazines from 1900 to 1980 found that the informational content of ads has been decreasing. Ads have become more focused and present a more limited amount of information more dramatically than they did in the past.[1]

1. Cited by Michael Schudson in *Advertising: The Uneasy Persuasion* (New York: Basic Books, 1984), p. 60.

Television Ad Strategies

Most of the ads you see on television are terribly, terribly phony. They have to be, because you're trying to cram into 30 seconds something that people would never say in their lives, and if they did, it would take half an hour. I think good advertising today doesn't try to tell people exactly what they're supposed to think. It lets them make up their own minds. Which takes realism, . . .

So said Hal Riney, of Hal Riney & Partners, an advertising agency with branches in San Francisco, Chicago, and New York; this agency created the series of ads for Bartles & Jaymes Premium Wine Coolers.

Riney also produced three ads for President Reagan's 1984 campaign. In one of them viewers saw images of a grizzly bear in the forest as Riney narrated: "Some people say the bear is tame. Others say it's vicious and dangerous. Since no one can really be sure who's right, isn't it smart to be as strong as the bear—if there is a bear?" At the end, a silhouetted rifleman stood facing the bear.

The commercial was in response to an ad for Democratic presidential candidate Walter Mondale that suggested that Reagan was trigger-happy. The shrewdness of the ad was that it sidestepped Mondale's argument.

Riney explained: "I was . . . trying to figure out how to show the Republican views on armament in a 30-second spot, without having to get into a lot of laborious details. So this parable form occurred to me. And it seemed to work very well for a controversial theme, because it didn't force you into committing to any particular point of view."[1]

[1]Art Kleiner, "Master of the Sentimental Sell," *New York Times Magazine*, 14 December 1986, pp. 58, 72.

In this section we will examine some of the ways in which advertisers use claims and evidence to prompt us to make the desired inferences about the product, its competitors, and its promises.

Naming the Product

The name of a product may be misleading. Butterball turkeys, for example, contain no butter. Similarly, McDonald's Quarter Pounder, as served, does not weigh a quarter of a pound. McDonald's ads now reveal that the meat weighed a quarter of a pound before it was cooked. This disclosure appeared only after consumer groups protested that the name was misleading.

Best Western is the name of a motel chain. By what criterion or standard are these motels the best? Who says so? Easy-Off is an oven cleaner. The name implies that the product makes cleaning your oven easy. The ads carry through this theme: "Don't put it off, use Easy-Off. Easy-Off makes oven cleaning easier." Easier than what? Some other product? If so, which one? Who found that Easy-Off made the job easier? When? Where? Or is it easier than using no oven cleaner at all? The ad has not disclosed the criteria for assessing its claim. If the claim means that it is easier to clean your oven using this cleaner than using no cleaner at all, then it is a

---

The Enthymeme

Enthymeme is a Greek word for the special kinds of arguments found in rhetoric. Enthymemes are arguments that rely on the knowledge, values, attitudes, and experiences of the audience. An enthymeme is a partial or incomplete argument that prompts the audience to complete it with whatever the audience already knows, believes, or values. An argument that invites you to fill in your own experience or to draw a conclusion when no claim is made explicitly is an enthymeme.

Enthymemes are described in Aristotle's *Rhetoric*, translator W. Rhys Roberts (New York: Modern Library, 1954). Although he doesn't use the word, Tony Schwartz describes the enthymematic process in *The Responsive Chord* (New York: Doubleday, 1974).

---

weak claim. But if it means easier than with other products, then the claim is considerably stronger, and the burden of proof on the advertiser is correspondingly heavier. Without specifics, we must assume only the weaker claim. Of course that is not what the advertisers hope we will do. They hope we will interpret this ad as a statement from some unseen authority about the comparative efficiency of Easy-Off.

Differentiating Products

In his book *Confessions of an Advertising Man*, David Ogilvy, founder of one of America's most successful advertising agencies, admits that he is "continuously guilty of *suppressio veri* [suppression of truth]." "Surely," he notes, "it is asking too much to expect the advertiser to describe the shortcomings of his product? One must be forgiven for putting one's best foot forward."[2] But advertisers are often guilty not only of suppressing a product's shortcomings but of concealing the criteria and the evidence on which their claims are based. Such suppression makes it difficult to use advertising as a basis for comparing one product with another.

Pseudo-Claims   The problems involved in interpreting misleading slogans often involve meaning. What does it mean, for example, to say that product X "fights" bad breath or product Y "fights" dandruff? A promise to control is stronger than a promise to fight, but neither claim promises to eliminate the problem. What is a consumer supposed to hear when an advertiser says that a certain shampoo "controls" dandruff with regular use?

Helps is another word used to weaken claims subtly. What does it mean to say, "Vaseline Intensive Care *helps* heal roughness, dryness"? Take *helps* out and the statement claims that this lotion, acting alone, heals. Its action is direct, not indirect. The claim to "control" or "help" suggests that using the product will produce positive results. The promise to "fight" is a promise that the product will

---

2. David Ogilvy, *Confessions of an Advertising Man* (New York: Ballantine Books, 1963), p. 140.

try to produce results, that it will oppose the negative condition (the dryness, the dandruff) but may not overcome it.

"And Texaco's coal gasification process could mean you won't have to worry about how it affects the environment." But what *does* that mean? "Could" suggests possibility without making a specific promise that any given outcome will occur.

Comparison with an Unidentified Other Ads often promise "more" cleaning power, "better" cleaning action, "stronger" whitening power, or that a product has more or better ingredients. But more, better, whiter, stronger than what? No product at all? Some specific product? When an advertiser says that product X is better than product Y, a comparative claim has been made. Of course, advertisers often do not tell us what product this product exceeds and on what grounds the performance of one is superior to another. Nonetheless, "better" implies comparison. The rules of grammar would suggest that a product that is the "best" has no superiors. But what if all of the products in a class are essentially equal? Then all are both "the best" and "the worst" because there is no basis for distinguishing one from another. (Such essentially identical products are called parity products.) However, we incorrectly interpret a claim that a product is the "best" to mean that it is better than all others. Similarly, we hear the claim that "Crest is unsurpassed in reducing new cavities" to mean that Crest is the best when instead the claim literally means that there are no products that are better at reducing new cavities. Others are *as good as* Crest, but none is better.

Ads often compare their product to an unnamed other product. "This trash bag is stronger than the cheap bargain bag." It probably is stronger than some cheaper bargain bag, but which one, and is the comparison a fair one? One ad claims that wine experts (which experts, and by what standards are they experts?) prefer one brand of wine over another, but the ad does not reveal that the price of the advertised brand is higher than that of its competitor. In effect, a top-of-the-line product has been compared to a middle-of-the-line product and the middle product has been found wanting. But what if similar products had been compared?

In 1971 the FTC began encouraging comparative advertising. In 1972, the networks lifted their bans on mentioning a competitive product by name.

Comparison of the Product to its Earlier Form "Lysol deodorizing cleanser has a great new fresh scent." New improved product X has 50 percent more cleaning power. In order to maintain their share of the market against competitors who are continually introducing new products with new additives, advertisers adjust the familiar image of a comfortable product to include something new or improved. In the process, they hope that they will not undercut our reasons for buying the product in the first place. The promise that a familiar product is now new or better—a claim that must be backed by an actual change in the product—aims to reinforce the buying habits of those who already use the product and to insulate them from the claims of more recent market entries. At the same time, it aims to attract new customers.

Irrelevant Comparisons   We tend to assume that the best seller is the best product. Instead, the best seller may be inferior to another product but have better distribution, a big early lead in the market, or better advertising than its competitors. Yet advertisers capitalize on our best-seller-is-best assumption by telling us when a product is outselling others of its type. Claims of this sort invite the audience to infer that the product's high quality accounts for its status as best seller.

Irrelevant criteria are often applied to establish uniqueness. Because we have been taught that you get what you pay for, advertisers can persuade us that costlier is better. Of course, cost may reflect factors other than quality, including inefficient production techniques, high tariffs, high profit-taking, or even a large advertising budget. Nonetheless, a product can be made to seem unique by having a higher price than its competitors. So, for example, Boodles gin is advertised as "the ultra-refined British gin that only the world's costliest methods could produce. Boodles. The world's costliest British gin." Note the qualifier. It is not the *world's* costliest gin but the costliest *British* gin. If we accept the assumption that costliness is next to godliness, perhaps we should scan the liquor store shelves to see if there is a more expensive gin, British or not.

The Pseudo-Survey   We live in a society impressed by the natural and social sciences and accustomed to trust their authoritative, quantitative claims. Surveys appear regularly in the news media telling us how we plan to vote, what we think about specific issues, and whom we trust. By wrapping their claims in scientific language, by expressing claims in the style of valid surveys, by placing actors in the settings we associate with the medical and scientific professions, advertisers increase the chance that we will mistakenly attach scientific validity to the claims they make.

When an ad claims that "four out of five dentists surveyed recommend sugarless gum for their patients who chew gum," it is using the familiar language of the survey report. A legitimate survey will disclose the population sampled (from what group were the dentists drawn—all dentists in the United States, dentists in a single state, dentists in a certain association or at a certain meeting?), how the survey population was chosen (random sample?), the total number of dentists asked, and the error we can expect in generalizing from this sample to the whole population. But the ad tells us *only* that four out of five dentists surveyed recommended a certain product for patients likely to engage in a certain activity. Conceivably only five dentists were asked the question. Alternatively, the question may have been asked only of dentists already predisposed to the product. From the evidence offered in the ad, we simply don't know.

In addition, there is an important qualifier in the ad. Do the dentists who recommend sugarless gum for their gum-chewing patients recommend gum chewing? Perhaps the dentists would say, if asked, that gum chewing is foolish. Because the claim carries the qualifier "for their patients who chew gum," the dentists may not have recommended gum chewing at all. So we don't know how representative these dentists' views are, and we don't know whether they endorse gum chewing.

Creating Associations

In this section we examine the promises implied by the associations created in ads and the sources upon which ads draw to build associations.

Associations with Celebrities and Authorities

Use It. Be Like Me.   When celebrities appear in commercials, they are often there to testify to the worth of a product. Sometimes they function as pseudo-authorities. What qualifies Ed McMahon as an expert on mayonnaise, motorcycles, or sunglasses? At best, celebrities speaking outside their field of achievement give testimony about their ordinary experience, experience no more authoritative than yours and mine, about how coffee tastes, or how well a detergent works. Often, the celebrity not only tells us why he or she uses the product but also hints that if we want to be like him or her, we ought to use this product.

Actors also attempt to transfer the trust we have in their characters to products. John Houseman, who played a curmudgeonly law professor in the series "Paper Chase," carried that role with him in his endorsement of a brokerage firm that makes its "money the old-fashioned way. They earn it." After pleading guilty to 2,000 counts of wire and mail fraud, another brokerage firm, E.F. Hutton, hired Bill Cosby, the star of NBC's top-rated show of the 1985–86 season, to appear in ads designed to mend its image.

Use It. I'm Doctorlike.   Advertisers associate their products with persons we are likely to trust. We are culturally conditioned to trust older white males, for example, a cultural predisposition reinforced by the leadership positions held by older white males in government and in the major religions. Consequently, it is not surprising that older white males appear more often as authority figures in ads than older women. We are also conditioned to respect the advice and information provided by certain types of professionals such as doctors, nurses, and pharmacists.

Cannibalizing the Past for Associations

The pervasive presence of claims that this or that product is "new" or, in the advertising cliché, "new and improved," tells us that advertisers regard *new* as a positive term. Indeed, they must. If we repaired small appliances rather than replacing them, if we faithfully repaired our cars instead of changing models, if we wore clothes until they became unpatchable, sales of new appliances, cars, and clothes would drop precipitously—and so would the advertising budgets of their manufacturers. Advertisers must persuade us that new is better if they are to survive in the manner to which they have become accustomed.

In order to wed us to the new, advertisers adopt the commercial equivalent of Social Darwinism: change is improvement. Because we hold the distant past in nostalgic reverence, advertisers often argue for change in the name of recapturing something we have never experienced firsthand. This reverence for the mythic past is consistent with the cult of the new insofar as what is old-fashioned is identified not with our experienced past (if the new product isn't better we stay with the old) but with a past that predates us. For example, Country Time, which is not lemonade, claims that it tastes just like good old-fashioned lemonade. The key characters in the Country Time ad are old and speak of real lemonade—the kind made by squeezing lemons—as a memory from their youth, a time clearly beyond the recall of anyone under 80. The ad implies that Country Time is better than anything else available now. Of course, we can still buy and squeeze fresh lemons, but in the world created by the ad that activity ceased at about the time the first Model T approached a highway.

In an ad for Xerox copiers, a monk miraculously makes multiple copies of a rare manuscript faster than his superior imagines possible. The contrast between the ancient manuscript and the modern copies underlines our contentions that advertisers venerate newness and change, and that advertisers are committed to the sale of large quantities of mass-produced, identical products.

Before the advent of the printing press and its cousin, the photocopying machine, monks and others copied books by hand. Treasured texts were beautifully written and ornamented by gold or illuminated letters, borders, and delicate illustrations. The process took years, but the result was often a magnificent work of art. Each manuscript was unique. Because the manuscripts were usually sacred texts, the monk's work was a labor of love and service to God. The painstaking labor of such monks made possible the transmission of learning during the Dark Ages; many classic texts survived because they had been copied and hidden in cloisters. The monk, laboring by candlelight, quill in hand, evokes images of the quality and artistic value of the hand-lettered manuscript.

The ad for Xerox copiers would have us believe that the copier increased the speed with which the monk could produce manuscripts but did not diminish their quality. In place of a unique product, we now have a standardized product in as many units as we want. But the copier cannot produce the gold leaf of the original, the colors of the illuminated letters, or the intricate patterns drawn into the margins.

The copier can produce a readable copy of the text itself. Is this better? The ad implies that it is. At the end of the ad, the monk is no longer hand-copying manuscripts. Xerox copiers have made the monk who could produce a beautiful manuscript obsolete. The subtext of this ad tells us that new is better than old, change brings improvement, uniqueness is neither necessary nor desirable, faster and more are better. Here, as in the ad for Country Time, the commercial identifies the product with the kind of quality that you and I have not experienced directly. Such quality presumably existed only in the distant past.

Because our memory of the distant past is based on historical reconstruction, we have no primary experience with which to test claims about it. Yet the distant past is the source of powerful and evocative symbols. Advertisers cannibalize the past in order to link their products with those symbols. In the process advertisers desacralize the sacred and trivialize the historically significant.

Appropriating Historical Persons and Events   The only widely accepted ritual employed to commemorate Presidents' Day, honoring the birthdays

---

Philip Morris Sponsors the Bill of Rights

The Philip Morris Company paid $600,000 for the right to link itself in televised and printed promotions with the National Archives, the official custodian of the United States' historic documents. The ads read: "Join Philip Morris and the National Archives in celebrating the 200th anniversary of the Bill of Rights. For a free copy of this historic document, call [an 800 number] or write Bill of Rights, Philip Morris Companies Inc. [followed by a Washington, D.C., address]."

The law forbids Philip Morris to sell cigarettes on television. The company insists that it is selling its diversified corporate image, not cigarettes.

The association with the archives lends the company great prestige, but spokespersons for the archives insist that the deal is a good way "to stretch the taxpayers' dollars."

Congress made the National Archives an independent agency in 1984, and authorized the agency to solicit and receive gifts to enhance its role as "keeper of the nation's history."[1]

[1] "The Bill of Rights, For Rent," *New York Times*, 19 November 1989, p. 22 E.

---

of Washington and Lincoln, is the Presidents' Day Sale. In order to draw us into stores, advertisers reduce George and Martha Washington to cartoonlike hucksters. Actors in white "Washington" wigs hector us about unbelievable bargains and swear that, like George Washington, they would never tell a lie. Similarly, ads for Fourth of July sales urge us to "declare our independence" from everything— from an old car to a malfunctioning air conditioner—and Thanksgiving Day sales imply that what we have to be thankful for are the "fantastic buys."

Another version of this tactic is employed in televised ads for Calvin Klein's Obsession. In the ads the fragrance is associated with passages from the world's great love stories including Hemingway's *The Sun Also Rises*, D.H. Lawrence's *Women in Love*, and Gustave Flaubert's *Madame Bovary*. In one of the spots, a young woman is shown running her fingers over a man's face as the announcer reads from D.H. Lawrence, "How perfect and foreign he was, how dangerous. . . . This was the glistening forbidden apple . . . "

Trading on Someone's Good Name   Companies appropriate the names of respected historical figures, such as Lincoln and Jefferson, to trade on the truth associated with those names. Service companies are more likely to adopt such names than manufacturers of more tangible products. Life insurance companies and banks are called Lincoln Life or Jefferson Trust, not because they were founded by Lincoln or Jefferson, but because the names themselves have residual credibility. Customers take the name, whether consciously or not, as a promise of the honesty and reliability associated with the historical person. Although the company may be only twenty or thirty years old, a name from the past suggests that the company has been providing that reliable, trustworthy service for a long time.

Bush and Gorbachev for Drixoral

CBS and ABC announced that they would not broadcast a cold remedy commercial using pictures of President Bush and Soviet President Mikhail S. Gorbachev unless the drug company got permission from the two heads of state.

Schering-Plough Corporation is promoting Drixoral, its own weapon against the cold war, which includes shipping boxes of Drixoral to the heads of state of East Germany, Poland, Hungary, Czechoslovakia, Romania, and Bulgaria "to ease the effects of their treacherous winter," the pharmaceutical company said in its news release.

NBC plans to run the ads, and Schering is considering placing them on cable television channels.

In the past, the White House has sent stiff cease-and-desist warnings to companies using the president's picture to endorse a product. Schering said it had not asked Bush's permission before making the ads. Matthew Margo, a vice president for program practices at CBS, said that it is "not appropriate" to use the presidency to sell products.[k]

[k] Marcy Gordon (AP), "Two Networks Bar Cold-Medicine Ads with Bush, Gorbachev," *Star Tribune*, 28 December 1989, p. 8 D.

Appropriating a Famous Phrase   We carry about with us a repertoire of phrases identified with important persons or occasions from the past. For example, when someone says "of the people, by the people, for the people," we call up an image of Abe Lincoln. Such phrases gain our attention by drawing from that common repertoire and proceed to make us accomplices in creating the ad's meaning.

However, each of the strategies we have identified will backfire if the audience is offended by the linking of the product and the phrase, person, or event. The two instances we are about to analyze, in our opinion, overstep the bounds of acceptable use of the past and become tasteless. An ad for a light beer included a photograph identified as that of Goethe—the German poet, scientist, and novelist—on his deathbed. In the ad, Goethe is calling—as he actually did just before he died—for "more light!" By twisting the last words of a great man into an appeal for a beer, the advertisers have trivialized his death and reduced an important historical figure to a huckster.

The strategy in a print ad for a motel is similar. That ad rephrased the invitation on the Statue of Liberty ("Give me your tired, your poor, your huddled masses yearning to breathe free. . . . Send these the homeless, tempest-tossed to me") to a come-on for the motel: "Give us your tired, your homeless, your weary, your thirsty." The motel did not invite "your poor." By reducing Emma Lazarus's stirring words to an invitation to choose one motel over another, the ad misappropriated a phrase we respect, a phrase that forms part of our cultural heritage.

Exploiting Social Movements   We learn the meaning of words from their use. Many words and phrases have gained especially rich meanings for some segments of the audience because they have been identified with an important social movement.

Because advertisements face severe time and space constraints, they tend to use symbols rich with cultural meaning. Using symbols drawn from social movements with which members of the audience still identify, however, is risky. A cookware manufacturer created the message, "Black is Beautiful; White is Beautiful," to accompany a print ad showing a black and a white pot. Remove the pots from the ad and the statement "Black is beautiful" reflects the ideology of the civil rights movement. Add the pots to the ad and the ideological statement is trivialized. People who hear the statement "Black is beautiful" as a commitment to civil rights are likely to respond to this ad with anger. The statement used to express an ideological position can no longer express that position if it gains currency as a slogan to sell kettles.

Feminist reaction to the slogan for Virginia Slims cigarettes is similar. "You've come a long way, baby" combines affirmation of progress for women with a complete denial of that progress. If those of us in the audience who are women have come such a long way, then why can you still call us "baby"? By using "you" rather than "we" in the slogan, the advertiser dissociates *him*self from the woman in the ad and assumes a superior position to her. At the same time, the photographs occupying the upper third of the print ads reduce women's struggle for equality to a fight with some man over the right to smoke. This trivializes women's demands for the vote, for equal pay, for equal access to job opportunity, for equal access to housing and credit. If equal access to lung cancer is all the women's movement has accomplished, then the "you" in the ad hasn't come very far. However, by identifying itself with independent women and by implying that smoking this product controls weight (Virginia *Slims*), this brand has captured a sizable share of the women's market. This suggests that the campaign has not alienated its target audience.

In the 1990s, the social cause most exploited by advertising is environmental. The advertising was capitalizing on powerful public sentiment. As concerns about pollution of the water and air spread around the globe, they took political form. The Green movement was launched in Europe. Environmental summits of world leaders were held. Within an environment saturated with claims that this package was environmentally better than that, this detergent more biodegradable, *National Geographic* set itself apart with an ad campaign claiming "Only one magazine covered the environment before it was an issue."

No sector of marketing has been left untouched by environmental claims. In summer 1990, Estée Lauder announced, for example, that it would "become the first major U.S. beauty company to bring natural, non-animal-tested products packaged in recyclable containers into department stores."[3]

Nationalistic Associations   Some nations are associated with certain products, often as the product's place of birth or most notable manufacturer. So when I say "whiskey" and ask for a high-quality nationality, you might say "Irish,"

---

3. Pat Sloan, "Cosmetics: Color it Green," *Advertising Age*, 23 July 1990, p. 1.

What Is Degradable?

"Packaging that claims to be made of biodegradable plastic material may in fact be a technically true claim, because the plastic may break up due to biological action," said Procter & Gamble associate ad manager Robert Viney. "But if placed side by side with a non-degradable plastic material in a landfill, there is no real difference in how quickly the landfill fills up. Then we believe such a claim would be misleading."[1]

[1]Testimony at a Senate Commerce Subcommittee Hearing, cited in *Advertising Age*, May 21, 1990, p. 2.

"Scotch," or "Canadian," but probably not "French." An advertiser can capitalize on these associations by creating an image consistent with them. In order to capitalize on the national identification of some products, advertisers give a name evoking the original country to a product of that type made elsewhere. Consequently, perfumes are often given French or French-sounding names, and beers are often given German or German-sounding names.

Exploiting Argumentative Forms to Create Associations and Participation

Implying Causality   Many ads imply a cause-and-effect relationship: use this product, get that desirable effect. Critics of advertising ask if the effect occurs at all, if the effect is a result of using this product, if the effect is a *necessary* result of using the product, and if the effect is a result of using the product in conjunction with other factors or of the other factors alone. When a toothpaste claims, for example, that brushing with it regularly will give you brighter teeth, fresher breath, and fewer cavities, are these good things the result of the brushing or of the toothpaste? If you substitute baking soda for the toothpaste, for example, would you achieve the same result? When a breakfast cereal, bar, or drink claims that when served with milk, toast, and juice it gives you a completely balanced and nutritionally sound breakfast, would the milk, toast, and juice alone have the same result? What does the advertised product contribute to the total nutrition of the breakfast?

Juxtaposition   Ads commonly juxtapose products and smiling people. Are the people smiling because they are using the product? (They're probably smiling because they are being paid to smile and will earn a lot of money in residuals when the ad is repeatedly aired.) Juxtaposed images encourage us to infer a relationship between the images, in this case between the smile and the product. Often we assume a causal relationship. Scenes that would not otherwise be juxtaposed can be edited together for television, and we accept such editing as part of the grammar of television and are comparatively uncritical of it. Televised ads can therefore create arguments by association more readily than print ads or speeches. The relationships between the juxtaposed images imply arguments. When an ad says, "Gimme sunshine . . . gimme a Dew" (Mountain Dew, a soft drink), as scenes of young people are intercut with pictures of the soft drink, we need to ask what the relationship is between the product and the other scene. The relationship is not inherent; the ad has simply juxtaposed two images. The audience fills in the relationship. If we assume a causal relationship, then the ad comes to mean either that drinking Mountain Dew gives the drinker sunshine, friends, and fun—or that having sunshine, friends, and fun gives us Mountain Dew. Since the last relationship makes no sense, we will probably conclude that those who drink Mountain Dew are more likely to have the fun shown in the ad than those who do not.

We may also see the relationship as one of identity. In this case sunshine and Mountain Dew would function as synonyms, and the relationship we read into the ad is described with the simile "drinking Mountain Dew is like experiencing sunshine." The ad may also be expressing a list of things important to us: give us friends, sunshine, fun, Mountain Dew.

Exploiting Coincidental Relationships   There is no necessary relationship between use of a product and status, taste, or love. If these characteristics are related to the product at all, the relationship is coincidental. Advertisers would like us to believe the relationship is a necessary one and to infer causality where none exists.

Did Mom make the Skippy peanut butter sandwich "because she knew peanut butter is more nutritious than salami or ham or liverwurst and has no cholesterol?" "No," responds the child in the ad, "she made it because she loves me." For years Pillsbury's ads claimed that "nothin' says lovin' like somethin' from the oven and Pillsbury says it best." Some ads are indirect in their claim that purchase or use of a product is a sign of love. If we accept the Hallmark slogan, "when you care enough to send the very best," sending the card becomes a sign of caring.

Because ads have allied products with status and taste, and because we are aware that this is a manipulative ploy, other advertisers capitalize on our awareness of the ploy by inverting it: "this product is for people who don't need to establish that they have taste or for people who don't need to demonstrate to the world that they have high status." One manufacturer of small cars, for example, employed the stock background (an estate with a mansion and circular drive) and the stock foreground (an elegantly dressed couple) for an ad making a claim of status or taste, but claimed instead that theirs was the car for those who don't need to prove that they have status. Of course, the claim is the same as the claims in the other ads; that the car is a sign of status. But here the car is more—it is also a sign that the buyer does not have to prove that he or she has status. By implication, then, the other cars making the status claim are for insecure people, but this car is for the truly secure (in itself, a kind of status claim).

Implying "If . . . Then"   Ads make promises visually as well as verbally. This is possible because we invest juxtaposed visuals with an "if . . . then" link. A beautiful woman uses a certain brand of lipstick in the ad, and men follow her everywhere. Without making the argument explicit, the ad implies that if you use this product you will be beautiful, and if you are beautiful (or if you use this product), you will be more attractive to men. One could as readily take the visuals to mean that if you are already beautiful, why bother?

The "before and after" ad is the advertiser's way of countering this interpretation. In its classic form, a person or place is shown before using the product and then after: eyelashes before application of mascara, eyelashes after application of mascara. Argument: if you use this mascara then you will obtain this difference. But look carefully at the before and after pictures. Is the mascara the only thing about the model that has changed? Has other makeup, a new hairstyle or clothing, a more pleasant expression, more dynamic action, different lighting, been added to the after segment? In other words, the critic asks, is the "if" necessary and sufficient to produce the promised "then"?

Implying "If Not . . . Then Not"   Ads often imply that if you buy and use the product, you will be happier, more likable, and so forth. The converse of this strategy is used in ads designed to make us feel guilty if we don't buy the product. For example, the Hallmark slogan "when you care enough to send the very best," uses "when" to imply there are times when you don't care enough. Sometimes you don't. Sometimes you care but not *enough*—a very personal indictment when the person you care about is someone you ought to care about a great deal. In case you are having trouble envisioning someone you care enough about, the visual portion of the ad will fill in a son or daughter, mother or father, grandparent, or best friend in an environment or on an occasion (Christmas, birthday, graduation) at which remembering is expected social behavior.

Now that the ad has encouraged you to conclude that this is one of those times *when* you do care *enough*, it needs to legitimize *sending* as the appropriate expression of caring. By contrast, AT&T wants you to believe that phoning is the best expression of caring; the FTD floral delivery company wants you to think that sending flowers is the best expression of caring. So "sending" is slipped into the Hallmark slogan, and the joy the recipient experiences in the ad at "receiving" provides reinforcement for the claim that sending was the correct choice. But in case AT&T and FTD have made equally plausible claims, the ad will probably show the loved person enjoying the card again and again (its unique selling point): unlike phone calls, which are brief and fleeting, and flowers, which wilt and die, a card, if you believe the ad, will be saved and cherished forever. Indeed, one ad shows an older person going through a trunk filled with loving cards.

Now that the slogan has us sending, it must differentiate its card from its competitors. It does this with the claim that you are sending, not just the best, but the very best.

Why not send a letter instead? It would be more personal, equally permanent, and more thoughtful. To counter this option, the ads also show people whose exact feelings are better expressed by the card than by their own words, persons too shy or too inarticulate about their feelings to be willing or able to write a letter. So, the slogan has positioned the product against its competitors, one of which is the personal letter, and has done so memorably.

What It Costs to Advertise

Listed below are the approximate costs of one television rating point for a 30-second spot in sample media markets for fall 1990. Most political media planners recommend that candidates air at least 500 points per commercial to penetrate the market effectively. We calculated the cost of an average 30-second political spot based on a 500-point penetration.[m]

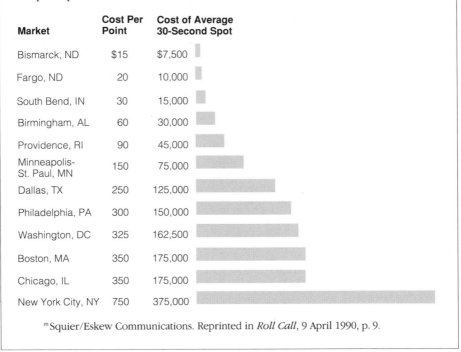

Market	Cost Per Point	Cost of Average 30-Second Spot	
Bismarck, ND	$15	$7,500	
Fargo, ND	20	10,000	
South Bend, IN	30	15,000	
Birmingham, AL	60	30,000	
Providence, RI	90	45,000	
Minneapolis-St. Paul, MN	150	75,000	
Dallas, TX	250	125,000	
Philadelphia, PA	300	150,000	
Washington, DC	325	162,500	
Boston, MA	350	175,000	
Chicago, IL	350	175,000	
New York City, NY	750	375,000	

[m] Squier/Eskew Communications. Reprinted in *Roll Call*, 9 April 1990, p. 9.

But the real genius of the slogan is its implied "if not . . . then not." If you don't send Hallmark, and you accept the assumptions inherent in the slogan, then you don't care enough to send the very best. Within the terms of this slogan, not sending Hallmark cards is a sign of not caring.

But Does Advertising Work?

By the time the class of 1990 college students had finished their senior finals, the typical student had seen an average of half a million commercials. What this generation finds persuasive differs from that which moves its parents. The 18-to-25-year-old market differs from the older markets, advertisers argue. Psycho-demographic research reveals that the old hard sell doesn't work with those reared on television. Accordingly, in an ad for Pepsi featuring performer Michael Jackson, the word *Pepsi* is never spoken by the star.

The 15-Second Ad

Karl Gensheimer, general sales manager of KSTP-TV (St. Paul, Minn.), told an American Marketing Association meeting in May of 1989 that the proportion of 15-second ads has risen from 21 percent of all network spots in 1986 to 37 percent in 1988, while the proportion of 30-second spots has dropped from 74 to 60 percent.

He also said that 15s generated 24 percent of the three major networks' total daytime ad revenue ($1.4 billion) in 1987–88 and 19 percent of the much larger pool of prime-time revenue ($3.7 billion), excluding 1988's Olympic coverage.

Despite the revenue they generate, however, Gensheimer said that neither he nor his parent network, ABC, encourages the use of 15s. They set a maximum of five 15s within a pod; they do not guarantee, as they do with 30s, to keep a competing product's spot out of the same pod; they charge premium rates for stand-alone 15s during certain highly rated programs such as the Academy Awards; they also charge extra to integrate the 15s with longer commercials because of the special handling required.

Lee Lynch, co-founder of Carmichael-Lynch Inc., a Minneapolis ad agency, said that the 15-second spot "ain't working, and we discourage our clients from using it," adding that there's a built in inability to tell a story in 15 seconds.

James Gould, professor of marketing at Pace University (White Plains, N.Y.), conducted a limited study that seemed to support Lynch's reservations. He gathered three groups totaling eighty people ostensibly to preview the pilot of a new television program. Interspersed in the show were three 1-minute commercials. One group saw only 30-second spots, another only 15s, and the third a mixture. They were asked later to recall spots without help and, later, with prompts.

Recall rates for the 15s were significantly lower than for 30s. Gould suggested that "recall is dependent on a commercial's creative content rather than frequency of exposure."[n]

[n]Dan Wescoe, "TV Ad(dition): Two 15s Don't Necessarily Equal a 30," *Star Tribune*, 15 May 1990, p. 3 D.

The appeals that do work are discernibly different as well. Because surveys show this group to be more preoccupied with making money, more willing to take risks, and more eager to venture into its own businesses, a Pepsi ad shows a young person establishing his own vending operation on a beach.

The generation raised on television and attuned to the fast-paced visuals and music of MTV expects rapid cuts and edits in ads. Peter Kim of J. Walter Thompson believes that this younger generation's attention span is decreasing while its ability simultaneously to grasp many bits of information is increasing.[4]

Still, in this generation as in others, ads seldom create needs. Instead, they guide our selection from among competing products. And, as Michael Schudson argues in *Advertising: The Uneasy Persuasion*, those selections often are not based on legitimate differences among products. From this essential comparability of competing products and from advertisers' need to differentiate one from the

4. *Washington Post*, 29 May 1986, p. A 12.

Print Ad Comprehension

At a cost of more than $250,000, Jacob Jacoby, professor of consumer behavior and retail management at New York University, conducted a study sponsored by the Advertising Educational Foundation that found that 37 percent of the people exposed to magazine ads and articles don't comprehend them. The study involved 1,347 respondents over the age of 18 living in forty-eight states who were questioned on 108 advertising and editorial communications taken from eighteen magazines. Ads were understood better than editorial material, and facts were understood better than inferences, although the differences were slight. Miscomprehension rises as age increases and decreases as income increases.

This study followed an earlier study of television viewers with similar results.

The results of Jacoby's study have been presented to the FTC, which is intensely interested in misleading advertising, and its results are important for advertising educators and government regulators alike.°

°Philip H. Dougherty, "Cold Water at Florida Gathering," *New York Times*, 27 March 1987, p. 42 Y.

---

other come a marketplace full of claims that are less than fully informative. Nonetheless, advertising not only cannot save a bad product, it can hurry its demise. When a product fails to deliver on its promises, customers do not purchase it a second time.

T O   S U M   U P

In this chapter we have examined some of the ways advertisers use claims and evidence to persuade us to purchase one product rather than another. This persuasive end is particularly difficult when, as is often the case, the advertisers' product differs little if at all from several others on the market. In addition, advertisers operate in extremely limited time and space. Many of the complaints registered against advertising arise from these limitations. Unless checked by regulation, advertisers tend to tell us what is good but not what is bad about their products, relying on our willingness to invest messages with meaning to induce us to hear stronger claims than those actually being made.

Selected Readings

Arlen, Michael J. *Thirty Seconds*. New York: Farrar, Straus & Giroux, 1980.

Barnouw, Erik. *The Sponsor: Notes on a Modern Potentate*. London: Oxford University Press, 1978.

Clark, Eric. *The Want Makers: The World Advertising Industry—How They Make You Buy*. New York: Viking, 1989.

Ewen, Stuart. *All Consuming Images: The Politics of Style in Contemporary Culture*. New York: Basic Books, 1989.

Ewen, Stuart. *Captains of Consciousness: Advertising and the Social Roots of the Consumer Culture*. New York: McGraw-Hill, 1976.

Ogilvy, David. *Confessions of an Advertising Man*. New York: Atheneum, 1980.

Schudson, Michael. *Advertising: The Uneasy Persuasion*. New York: Basic Books, 1984.

Schwartz, Tony. *The Responsive Chord*. New York: Doubleday, 1974.

Sethi, S. Prakash. *Advocacy Advertising and Large Corporations*. Lexington, Mass.: Lexington Books, 1977.

8

Influencing Advertisers

Listerine was compelled to confess in its ads that it will not help prevent colds or sore throats.

Producers of a diet product were told that they could not show a thin Santa Claus who stated that he lost his job because he lost weight.

The appearance of an elderly schoolteacher was changed in an ad before it was permitted to air.

In this chapter we examine the regulatory and self-regulatory mechanisms that produced these changes. Chapter 9 shows how consumers can use these channels to influence news and advertising practices.

Regulation and Self-Regulation

Advertisers are influenced by formal regulation from government agencies and by agencies created by industry to pre-empt and forestall government regulation.

The Federal Trade Commission

The Federal Trade Commission (FTC) regulates "unfair methods of competition" (Section 5), "unfair or deceptive acts or practices" (Section 5), and "false advertising" (Section 12). The FTC's Bureau of Consumer Protection has issued a handful of guides to aid advertisers and the public in determining how certain types of products should be advertised and what techniques may be used. One guide discusses use of testimonials, for example. These guides are advisory, as are the FTC's opinions about the applicability of federal laws to specific cases.

The Trade Regulation Rules issued by the Bureau of Consumer Protection are, by contrast, legally binding. These rules govern what is and is not considered

---

The Costs of False Advertising

Being charged with false advertising can cost a company millions of dollars, even if no fine is ever levied.

In an analysis of the effects of advertising regulation, the FTC said that when charges of false advertising have been brought against a company, its stock price has usually declined, often significantly.

The FTC study focused on 122 false-advertising cases between 1962 and 1985. In the cases settled by consent order, the companies' stock value lost an average of 2.5 percent in the five days after the announcement, the study found. In cases in which companies contested the FTC charges in court, but eventually lost, stock-price losses average 1.3 percent at the time of the complaint, 1.8 percent when the administrative law judge ruled, and 1.9 percent on final commission action.[a]

[a] "False-Ad Cases Can Be Costly," *New York Times*, 7 June 1988, p. 46 Y.

---

an illegal practice. The Advertising Evaluation Section of the Bureau of Consumer Protection was set up in 1973 to oversee advertising and to review the substantiation of advertising claims. The staff of the Advertising Evaluation Section draws samples of televised and print ads for evaluation and also reviews complaints filed by the public.

When the FTC concludes that a complaint is worth pursuing, staff members will determine whether, in their judgment, the ad has violated the law. If so, they may seek voluntary assurance that the practice will be discontinued. Such an agreement is not legally binding, but if the advertiser violates it the FTC may reopen the case against the advertiser. When the case is serious or the advertiser stubborn, the FTC institutes formal proceedings. To halt these proceedings, the advertiser may sign a consent order stipulating the facts in the case, the findings of the commission, and the conditions accepted by the advertiser, and indicating that the practice will not be repeated. This order is legally binding.

If, instead, the advertiser wishes to contest the findings, a hearing is held before an administrative law judge who may dismiss all or some of the charges, issue a legally binding cease-and-desist order, or order corrective advertising. Either the FTC staff or the advertiser may appeal this decision to the five FTC commissioners. An advertiser who loses at this level may appeal to the Federal Court of Appeals and, losing there, may appeal to the U.S. Supreme Court.

The appeal process may go on for years, during which the contested advertising practice may continue. For example, in 1965 the FTC told the producers of Geritol to eliminate the claim that Geritol combatted "tired blood." Being tired is not a reliable indicator of iron deficiency. Nonetheless, Geritol reintroduced the claim in subsequent ads. The FTC sued and finally won in 1976. Geritol's maker, which had since switched advertising strategies, was fined $125,000 for noncompliance.

The use of corrective advertising to counter false impressions is a relatively new phenomenon. In 1971, the FTC demanded that the producers of Profile

Bread devote one-quarter of one year's media budget to countering the impression that eating their product would produce weight loss. The corrective ad asked, in part, "Does Profile have fewer calories than other breads? No. Profile has about the same calories per ounce as other breads. To be exact, Profile has seven fewer calories per slice. That's because it's sliced thinner. But eating Profile will not cause you to lose weight."[1] Similarly, the producers of Domino Sugar were required to spend one-quarter of a year's budget to correct the impression that their sugar was a better source of energy than other brands.

In the first court test of the FTC's right to require corrective advertising, the Supreme Court let stand the Second Federal Court's order that the makers of Listerine mouthwash state in their next 10 million dollars' worth of advertising that "Listerine will not help prevent colds or sore throats or lessen their severity."

In the corrective advertising agreements, the FTC indicates the type of corrective language that is necessary, the dollar amount or percentage of the advertising budget to be spent on correcting the false impressions, and even the size of the ads and the outlets in which they will appear. This development has taxed the ingenuity of copywriters to incorporate the required disclosure without undercutting the ability of the ad to sell the product.

Appointees of the Reagan Administration made three changes in FTC operations. Rather than focusing on abuses in an entire industry (such as funeral operations and used car sales), the FTC worked on a case-by-case basis. Second, the conditions required to establish deception were circumscribed. Whereas formerly the potential to mislead was considered deceptive, now a consumer acting reasonably in the circumstances must prove that an ad's representation, omission, or practice affected the actual buying decision. The FTC policy articulated in 1984 stated that "any representation, omission, or other practice that is likely to mislead the consumer acting reasonably under the circumstances to the consumer's detriment" was deceptive. Under the earlier definition, "any representation, omission, or other practice that has the capacity to mislead the consumer who is not sophisticated, wary, or cautious" constituted deception. Finally, the ground rules for substantiation of advertising claims were reframed. Inquiries are no longer conducted in public. Substantiation investigations are now revealed only upon completion. These changes shift the burden of proof from the advertiser to the consumer.

This shift indicates the power of regulatory agencies to set their own course. Reagan's FTC Chair James Miller tried unsuccessfully to get Congress to redefine "deceptive acts or practices." Miller then offered the FTC Commission, controlled by like-minded appointees, a statement of policy that supposedly analyzed the law of deception but actually narrowed FTC jurisdiction in ways consistent with his failed congressional initiative.

The Powers of Other State and Federal Agencies

The Food and Drug Administration (FDA) has the authority to recall products that it determines pose hazards to public health. The United States Postal Service can also obtain court injunctions barring companies from receiving mail orders.

---

1. "Profile Bread's Well-Buttered Correction," *Consumer Reports*, February 1972, p. 64.

Additionally, states can sue corporations for consumer fraud. Outcomes of such suits include agreements not to market some products in some states. The case of Cal-Ban 3000, a so-called miracle diet product, is illustrative.

In ads in the pages of beauty magazines and tabloids, Cal-Ban 3000 was touted as a means of losing "up to 30 pounds in 30 days or your money back!" In July 1990, after documenting one death and numerous injuries, the FDA asked the company to recall it. But the FDA was not the first agency to act. In 1987, the U.S. Postal Service had obtained a court injunction barring the company from receiving mail orders for the diet product. The manufacturers responded by substituting an 800 telephone number. In 1989, the state of Iowa went to court against the product. The result was the company's agreement not to sell Cal-Ban 3000 in Iowa. Florida also moved to ban the sale. The company that produced the product, Health Care Products Incorporated of Tampa, settled the civil suit against it in Florida by agreeing that it would never again sell the product in the United States The company also paid a $1.3 million fine. In early July 1990, federal officials obtained a court order of their own barring both mail and phone sales of the product. This last action effectively ended the company.

Cal-Ban used guar gum, a commercial thickening agent found in some beverages and diet products. When combined with moisture, guar gum swells. The swelling inside the stomach was supposed to make the dieter feel full. While still marketed in an uncoated form, Cal-Ban could swell while in the throat, causing life-threatening obstructions. One Florida user died of complications from surgery to remove the swollen gum from his throat. A postal inspector estimated that before its demise, between $20 and $30 million of Cal-Ban had been sold.[2]

The National Advertising Division

The National Advertising Division (NAD) of the Better Business Bureau is industry's main mechanism for policing its own advertising. The NAD reviews all charges of deception in advertising brought by consumers and manufacturers, or submitted by local Better Business Bureaus. The NAD also monitors advertising on its own.

The NAD's own monitoring is the greatest source of complaints. Information released by the NAD indicates that 96 of the 100 leading advertisers have participated voluntarily in the NAD review process—either as advertisers or complainants.

The NAD evaluates all complaints received. If the NAD concludes that the ad violates good advertising practices or contains falsehoods or inaccuracies, the NAD tries to persuade the advertiser to change or drop the ad. If the advertiser and the NAD cannot reach agreement at this level, either may appeal the case to the National Advertising Review Board (NARB). A panel drawn from the fifty-member NARB serves as a court of appeal at this stage, and a public member sits on each review panel.

The NARB members employed by a company that manufactures or sells the product being evaluated or a competing product may not serve on a review panel.

---

2. Barry Meier, "Diet-Pill Death Raises Questions on F.D.A. Role," *New York Times*, 4 August 1990, p. 48.

AT&T v. *Sprint*

In summer 1990, the NAD found for AT&T and against Sprint. Sprint challenged an AT&T ad that read: "On average, MCI and US Sprint take over 50 percent longer than AT&T to set up a long distance call . . . and when you multiply that by the number of calls a large company makes a year, it comes out to hundreds of wasted work hours. . . ." NAD ruled that AT&T had supported the claim.

Examples of NAD/NARB Decisions

Advertising Modified or Discontinued

Tonka Corporation, Minnetonka, Minn. (Jordan, Case, Taylor & McGrath—N.Y.), and Hanna-Barbera, Hollywood, jointly advertised the *GoBots: Battle of the Rock Lords* movie in the children's magazine *GoBots*, a practice the NAD's Children's Advertising Review Unit (CARU) found questionable because it could lead to "confusion between advertising and editorial content." Tonka agreed and said it would discontinue the practice.

Advertising Claims Substantiated

Ragold, Chicago (Tatham-Laird & Kudner), in television spots for sugar-free Velamints claimed, "You see, most Tic Tac and Life Savers are over 90 percent sugar." A visual depicted sugar being poured into containers. New York-based Ferrero USA, marketer of Tic Tac mints, challenged the ad on the basis that it implied that the Tic Tac container is filled to 90 percent of its capacity with sugar and that Velamints contain fewer calories. Ferrero provided tests indicating that Tic Tacs are only 65 percent sugar by volume and actually contain far fewer calories than Velamints. Ragold countered with tests indicating that Tic Tac contains 93 percent sugar by weight and that its sugar-free claim is distinct from a low-calorie claim. The NAD agreed that the Ragold claims were substantiated.[b]

[b]These examples of NAD Decisions reprinted with permission of the NAD.

Similarly, advertisers who represent a competing product are disqualified from serving on such review panels.

The NAD claims that "of the more than 1,800 investigations completed by the NAD, only 2 percent" required an appeal to the NARB, and of that 2 percent, no advertiser "who has gone through the procedure has ever refused to follow the NARB recommendation."[3] Advertising professor Eric Zanot concludes that the "NARB decisions and guidelines are generally consistent with those of both the FTC and the courts."[4]

3. *News from NAD* (press release), 15 July 1981.
4. Eric Zanot, "A Review of Eight Years of NARB Casework: Guidelines and Parameters of Deceptive Advertising," *Journal of Advertising* 9 (1980): 26.

Figure 8.1 Steps in the NAD/NARB process (chart provided by the NAD/NARB and used with permission).

Figure 8.1 details the review and appeals process. Note that if the matter cannot be resolved by the NARB panel and the advertiser, the case can be referred to the Federal Trade Commission for further action. The industry would clearly prefer to resolve its own differences and respond to consumer dissatisfaction without government intervention. Indeed, the NAD and NARB were created to forestall restrictive legislation.

Critics of this self-regulatory procedure point out that it is a post hoc mechanism—no action can be taken until a violation has occurred. Industry defenders respond that the outcomes of previous cases clearly show advertisers what sorts of tactics to avoid. One side argues that asking the industry to police itself is like asking the fox to guard the chicken coop; the other side responds that a member of the public now sits on all the NARB review panels and that the number of findings against advertisers attests that this procedure is not a sham. Critics charge that the NAD/NARB procedure has no mechanism for meting out punishment or for correcting false impressions already created. Defenders concede this point, but argue that U.S. antitrust laws make it difficult for the board or the panels to levy punishments.

The National Association of Broadcasters

The National Association of Broadcasters (NAB) adopted a radio code in 1929 and a television code in the early 1950s. A code authority director and a limited staff were established in 1952. In the early 1960s, when the payola and quiz-game scandals like the rigged "$64,000 Question" triggered fears of stringent new regulations, the staff was enlarged and the function of overseeing the two codes was combined under a single code authority director.

In March 1982, U.S. District Court Judge Harold Greene ruled that the section of the NAB Code barring a sponsor from advertising more than one product in an ad shorter than 60 seconds violated the antitrust laws. The NAB responded by suspending enforcement of the advertising standards of the code. The code has not been reinstated. However, under pressure to clean up the broadcast air waves, in June 1990, the NAB's board adopted voluntary guidelines. The guidelines urged that depictions of "physical or psychological" violence be responsible, that the details of violence not be "excessive, gratuitous, or instructional," and that violence for its own sake be avoided. The guidelines also recommended that "the use of illegal drugs or other substances abuse should not be encouraged or shown as socially desirable." The NAB statement reiterated that the guidelines were purely advisory and carried no enforcement mechanism.[5]

The fact that in 1983 stations and networks did not rush to air ads for contraceptives and hard liquor, did not solicit ads for palm readers and phrenologists, revealed the extent to which the NAB norms had been adopted by the industry. Indeed, in many instances the networks, whose screening of ads remains, impose more stringent criteria than the NAB. Also the restraining power of public sentiment continues to operate.

The print media also have policies governing acceptance of advertised material, although these policies are less uniform than those governing broadcast ads.

Network Standards

Public sentiment acts as a powerful constraint on broadcast advertising. As a *TV Guide* editorial noted: "It doesn't take a fortuneteller to predict the result if broadcasters opted for making an easy buck: viewers would be up in arms."[6]

---

5. Doug Halonen, "NAB Sets Standards for Cleaning Up Airwaves," *Electronic Media*, 25 June 1990, p. 3.
6. "As We See It," *TV Guide*, 17 April 1982, p. A 2.

The extent to which broadcasters fear offending the viewing community was evident when in February 1987 all three national commercial networks refused a request by the surgeon general to air ads for condoms. Use of condoms could protect sexually active persons from transmitting the AIDS virus, argued the Surgeon General; accordingly, broadcasters should air them. Arguing that such ads are offensive to a significant part of the viewing audience, the networks initially refused.[7]

Each network is responsible for determining that its commercials meet its own standards. ABC, CBS, and NBC estimate that each receives 18,000–25,000 tapes a year. Only 1–2 percent are rejected outright.[8]

Because FCC regulations apply to the air waves, which are publicly owned, but not to cable networks, some ads that have been rejected by the networks air instead on cable. USA Network estimates that it refuses about half as many commercials as do ABC, CBS, and NBC. So, for example, when the major networks rejected or required disclaimers on a Yoplait ad depicting supposed "news reporters" reporting on the heist of frozen yogurt, Vroman Foods simply took the ad and its $5 to $6 million account to cable television.[9]

The competition from cable is a factor in network standards. "In the past, it was easier to say no [to such ads]," notes Matthew Margo, vice president for program standards at CBS in New York. "But in a more complex media world today, it's critical that people come up with solutions to get [the commercials] on the air. There is a lot at stake to turn down an ad today. That's millions of dollars in revenue down the drain."[10]

To insulate the reviewers from economic pressures, each network has separated its broadcast standards division from its sales and programming divisions. If the staff in the broadcast standards division reported to the sales division, for example, it might conceivably be subject to pressures from major sponsors. Instead, the broadcast standards division reports directly to top management.

Typically an advertiser will submit the storyboards or shooting scripts for a set of commercials to all three television networks at the same time. If the commercial involves a demonstration, many advertisers will not wait for the network to ask for an affidavit from the producer testifying to the authenticity of the action in the commercial; they will supply this documentation and substantiation for any questionable claims when the storyboard is submitted.

The internal standards set by the three networks differ. Occasionally, a commercial will be accepted by one network, rejected by a second, and sent back for changes by a third. The type of changes broadcasters demand was revealed in testimony before the House Select Committee on Aging. A representative of NBC reported that "one editor recalls requesting a change in the portrayal of an elderly school teacher in a commercial message. The editor objected to the characterization of an excessively prim and unfashionable woman."[11]

7. "Surgeon General Urges Ads on TV for Condoms in Combatting AIDS," *New York Times*, 11 February 1987, p. 1.

8. Wayne Walley, "Network Ad Rejections: At What Cost?" *Advertising Age*, 9 April 1990, p. 22.

9. Ibid.

10. Ibid.

11. Congress, *Age Stereotyping*, p. 58.

Obstacles to Regulation

Problems Faced by Regulators

By acknowledging that audiences cooperate in acts of influence, we raise an important and troublesome problem for regulators. Once regulators admit that an ad may induce the audience to draw a false conclusion even though the ad itself is explicitly truthful, the regulators must examine the ad's implied content. Because that content resides not in the ad but in audience interaction with it, a regulator concerned with monitoring implied deception is forced to study the audience.

The audience of concern to regulators is the general public. The courts have characterized the general public as

> that vast multitude which includes the ignorant, and the unthinking, and the credulous, who, in making purchases, do not stop to analyze but too often are governed by appearances and general impressions. . . . The ordinary purchaser . . . is not an "expert in grammatical construction" or an "educated analytical reader" and, therefore, he [*sic*] does not normally subject every word in the advertisement to careful study.[12]

Because the law was established to protect "the trusting as well as the suspicious,"[13] an ad can be deceptive if it deceives persons who are naive, uncritical, or even careless. Consequently, when a claim has two possible interpretations—one truthful, the other misleading—the advertiser can be found guilty of deceptive advertising.

In order to determine what an ad promises, the FTC and the courts must rely on the testimony of experts such as scholars who have studied certain types of advertising, consult surveys of consumers to determine whether or not they were deceived, and trust their own common sense.

In its review of a claim against the makers of Anacin, the court dismissed the testimony of two experts in marketing research and relied instead on tests of consumer reactions that the court called "the best evidence of what meaning consumers take from advertising." Customers had concluded from a television commercial for Anacin that Anacin was a superior analgesic. The ad claimed that "for pain other than headache, Anacin reduces the inflammation that comes with pain. These [Tylenol and Datril] do not. Specifically, inflammation of tooth extraction, muscle strain, backache, or if your doctor diagnoses tendonitis, neuritis." The court concluded that the makers of Anacin had misrepresented its properties by claiming that Anacin was a superior analgesic to Tylenol. A permanent injunction was issued restraining the makers of Anacin from making such claims in other ads.[14]

---

12. FTC v. Sterling Drug, Inc. 317 F. 2d 669, 674 (2d Cir. 1963).
13. FTC v. Standard Education Society, 302 U.S. 112, 116 (1937).
14. American Home Products v. Johnson and Johnson, 3 *Med. L. Rptr.* 1097 (1977).

A Claim by Any Other Name . . .

David Minton, Washington counsel for the Magazine Publishers Association, told the Senate Commerce Committee that "the cigarette firms, unlike producers of some foods and other products, do not claim that their brands are good for health. 'Cigarette advertising pictures things, cowboys, pretty girls [sic], and so on, but there is no claim,' he said."[c]

   [c]Lawrence M. O'Rourke, "Tobacco Industry Flexes Its Muscles," *St. Louis Post-Dispatch*, 16 May 1982, p. 6 F.

Determining Deception

The FTC's own sense of what constitutes deception is sometimes so strong that it relies on its own judgment to determine that an ad is deceptive, rather than on expert testimony or survey data.[15] And the courts have acknowledged that the FTC is often better able than the courts to determine what is and is not deceptive.[16]

When a claim is implied but not explicitly stated, the FTC and the courts try to determine what is implied and whether that implication deceives. An interesting situation arises when a deceptive claim is implied not by the ads currently on the air but by advertising that the audience remembers. Here the audience invests new ads with an old claim, and if the old claim was a powerful one, its residual power gives the maker of the product an unfair advantage in the marketplace.

For example, for almost 100 years, ads for the popular mouthwash Listerine claimed that the product prevented colds and sore throats. It does not, and its new ads do not claim that it does. But in 1977 the court upheld the FTC requirement that the next $10 million of Listerine's regular advertising include the corrective statement: "Listerine will not prevent colds or sore throats or lessen their severity." To justify its decision, the court cited evidence that six months after the challenged claim had been removed from the ads, 64 percent of those responding to a survey cited as the main theme of Listerine ads the claim that Listerine was "effective for colds and sore throats." Sixty percent concluded that Listerine was one of the best mouthwashes because of its effectiveness against colds and sore throats.[17] Some claims, then, are not in the ad; they reside wholly in the audience.

Effects of Stricter Regulation

Our discussion to this point may have created the impression that advertisers make any claims they think the audience will find persuasive, and continue to make these claims until challenged. Indeed, before 1971, the government regulatory system was reactive, not proactive, and corrective, not preventative. In 1971,

---

15. Ira M. Millstein, *The Federal Trade Commission and False Advertising*, 64 *Col. L. Rev.* 439, 469 (1964).
16. FTC v. Colgate Palmolive Co., 380 U.S. 375, 385 (1965).
17. Warner-Lambert Co. v. FTC, 562 F. 2d 762 (1977).

however, the FTC began requiring that advertisers be able to prove claims about a product's performance, characteristics, quality, safety, effectiveness, or comparative cost. If the FTC challenges a claim, the advertiser has thirty days in which to provide proof.

Two unfortunate by-products of this stricter regulation of advertising have been claims that are more meaningless and information that is less specific. Fewer than half of the commercials sampled in one study were found to contain useful consumer information.[18] Although no one need bemoan the loss of misleading claims, the new ads are not exceptional either. Excedrin's makers used to contend that Excedrin was an "anti-depressant." Now they claim it is more effective for pain "other than headache." Anacin's makers used to claim that it relieved pain faster than any other analgesic available; instead, the ads now claim that it is "better" and "stronger." Profile Bread used to claim that it promoted weight loss. Now it isn't advertised on television anymore. Ivan Preston identified the logic underlying this shift when he wrote:

> The effort to get information of greater quality and quantity has spurred tighter laws against false advertising, but the ad industry's response to them has brought something other than hoped-for improvements. . . . Why not discontinue using information, they asked themselves, and substitute a type of content not subject to being called deceptive. . . . The law may have achieved its goal of making more information nondeceptive, but only in conjunction with the sad yet perfectly legal fact that a lesser proportion of message content now is informative.[19]

What Advertisers May Not Say and Do

The mass media can be used to invest products with characteristics they do not in fact possess, and the potential consumer has no immediate way to test many of the claims in ads. Therefore, in the United States a number of rules and laws have been developed to combat deceptive advertising.

Limitations on Distortion

In 1914 Congress passed the Federal Trade Commission Act. Section 5 declares "unfair or deceptive acts or practices in or affecting commerce" to be unlawful. In Section 12 the act forbids false advertisements for "food, drugs, devices or cosmetics." False advertisements are defined in Section 15 not only as those containing "material" misrepresentations but also as those failing to reveal material facts about the consequences that may result from use of the advertised product.

In June of 1986, the Federal Trade Commission charged the R. J. Reynolds Tobacco Company with violating the law banning false and deceptive advertising.

18. Alan Resnick and Bruce L. Stein, "An Analysis of Information Content of Television Advertising," *Journal of Marketing* 41 (January 1977): 50–53.

19. Ivan L. Preston, *The Great American Blow-Up* (Madison: University of Wisconsin Press, 1975), p. 276.

At issue was a print ad titled "Of Cigarettes and Science" that ran in twenty-five newspapers and magazines from February through June of 1985. The ad, cast as an editorial, alleged that the results of a major, federally funded, national health study (the Multiple Risk Factor Intervention Trial or MRFIT) called into question the link between smoking and heart disease. The ad argued: "The controversy over smoking and health remains an open one."

But administrative law judge Montgomery K. Hyun ruled against the FTC, noting that the advertisement did not name any of the Reynolds's brands or discuss their attributes. Rather, Hyun said, it expressed the company's view on smoking and health. The ad did not lose its status as constitutionally protected speech, he went on, merely because it coincided with the company's economic interest.

The FTC indicated it would appeal the ruling. Matthew L. Myers, director of the Coalition on Smoking or Health (a private organization that had asked the commission to file the complaint), said the ruling "amounts to a license to lie to the American public."[20]

In June 1990, the issue was resolved. Under the settlement, R. J. Reynolds agreed in future ads not to misrepresent the results of the government study. During the four years of the controversy, however, the distorting information had stood. The tobacco company had, in effect, gained a four-year reprieve.

Determining whether an ad distorts is not as simple as it may at first seem. An examination of a number of advertising claims will illustrate when an ad is materially deceptive and when it is not.

Product Characteristics   The product seen in the ad must look and act like the real product that the consumer buys. The color of the product as shown in the ad must approximate the actual color; the advertiser cannot recolor the grape juice to make it look a deeper purple than it actually is, retouch the milk to make it look whiter, retouch the lipstick to make it look rosier. Color can be enhanced in products other than the one being sold, however. So, if the display in the ad shows chicken, the product being sold, on a plate with green beans, the advertiser can add color to the beans but not to the chicken.

The size of the product also must be represented accurately in the ad. An advertiser may not use a small soup bowl to make the amount of soup in the can seem more than it actually is. When the product is enlarged or visually distorted by camera angle, that fact must be disclosed. Often a product must be enlarged visually if the consumer is to appreciate its fine points, as with small articles of jewelry.

In such ads, the product's actual size will be noted, the fact that the picture is an enlargement will be made clear, and a picture of the jewelry in its actual size will probably be included somewhere in the ad.

Advertisers are not permitted to construct a special instance of the product for the sake of the commercial. The product shown in the ad must be comparable to the typical product being produced, and it must be sold under the same name advertised.

20. *New York Times*, 10 August 1986, p. 7 E.

Product Performance   In a classic case of the deceptive use of a mock-up, the Colgate Palmolive Company showed its Rapid Shave shaving cream softening sandpaper to the extent that the sandpaper could actually be shaved. The FTC received complaints from consumers who had tried to shave sandpaper with the product and had failed.

An investigation established that it was not actually sandpaper that was being shaved in the ad but glass lightly covered with bits of sand. The FTC challenged the ad. Colgate countered by arguing that sandpaper covered with Rapid Shave could indeed be shaved, but that the sandpaper was of such a fine quality that the television viewer would not be able to see that it could be. Hence, Colgate argued, shaving glass was a simulation of what the product could actually do.

Could the product enable a razor to shave coarse sandpaper, the kind of sandpaper suggested by the demonstration? No, Colgate conceded. Colgate said, however, that it had tested its claim on fine sandpaper, but had to use a mock-up suggesting coarse sandpaper because the fine sandpaper would simply look like flat paper on television.

In the course of the investigation, the FTC also learned that even fine sandpaper could not be shaved as quickly as the mock-up implied, but only after being soaked for a long time. In the commercial, Rapid Shave was applied and almost immediately the razor shaved the glass clean. The commercial did not indicate that it was taking place in a time span longer than that actually shown. Had it indicated that the elapsed time was 10 or 15 minutes, the FTC probably would not have challenged the ease and speed with which the shaving took place. The contest between the FTC and Colgate ultimately reached the Supreme Court, which ruled that when the point of the ad is to establish the reality of what is being demonstrated, the audience must be informed that a mock-up is being used.

This does not mean that viewers always see actual demonstrations on television. But when more time has elapsed in the course of a demonstration than that shown, that fact will be indicated in the ad. When a demonstration is a re-creation of what happened, the commercial is likely to disclose that fact. And when substitutions are made for products—when, for example, whipped potatoes are substituted for ice cream because ice cream would melt under the lights—the ad will not draw attention to any characteristic of the ice cream that might be misrepresented by the potatoes.

The nature of television makes it difficult to represent some products such as ice cream accurately. When captured by the television camera, for example, coffee looks muddy. Because coffee advertisers have legitimate reasons for wanting to show coffee in their commercials, advertisers are permitted to substitute something that looks more like coffee than coffee does. Ironically, use of the actual product instead of a substitute would in this instance distort and be deceptive. But the FTC banned the substitution of oil for coffee because it looked both darker and richer than actual coffee.

In order to differentiate their product from others, advertisers often offer demonstrations supposedly showing their product's comparative superiority. As a general rule both the FTC and the NAD require that such comparisons employ comparable products. So, for example, the NAD concluded that an advertiser could not compare its bias-belted tire with a competitor's lower-grade tire. Bias-belted tires must be compared to other bias-belteds, not to the lesser-grade bias-ply tires.

Similarly the NAD ruled that an extra-thick spaghetti sauce must be compared to the extra-thick sauce manufactured by the competitor, not to the competitor's regular sauce. In the ad in question, the advertiser's extra-thick sauce and the regular sauce of the competitor were poured through kitchen strainers creating an obvious but irrelevant demonstration of superiority for the advertised product.

Puffery   Advertising copy creates a world in which superlatives are commonplace. Products are "the very best," "the finest"; they produce "the cleanest, freshest washes," the "most beautiful," "softest" faces and hands. The systematic, habitual use of hyperbole has diluted the power of the advertiser's vocabulary. If everything is "the best," how is a genuinely superior product to be described?

In keeping with this penchant for exaggeration, advertisers tend to place adjectives before nouns and adverbs before adjectives. For example, a wine isn't simply "fine," it is "really fine wine." The tar in a cigarette is not "low" but "ultra low," and Hallmark and Nestlé make not the "best" but "the very best." This tendency conflicts with the need to make short, memorable claims. When adjectives and adverbs are pared from ad copy, it is often because the need for brevity has overcome the tendency toward hyperbole.

Most hyperbole is legally acceptable because it consists of subjective, nondocumentable, nonfactual opinions. Although I may taste a product touted for its fine taste and find the taste disagreeable, my opinion does not invalidate the claim in the ad. Taste is a matter of . . . taste. For legal purposes, esthetic and value judgments generally fall under the label "puffery." So I can claim that a paper napkin is "beautiful," that the soft drink on which you are gagging "tastes great," that cookies as hard as cement are as good as mother used to make; although you may disagree on all counts, I have made legally acceptable claims.

But a hyperbolic claim is not protected as mere puffery when it claims an attribute the product does not have. An ad cannot claim that a candy bar is the finest chocolate if it contains no chocolate. An ad cannot claim that oleomargarine is a dairy product. A puffed statement in an ad is in effect a nonfalsifiable claim. But if falsity cannot be proven, then neither can truth.

So what value does puffery have for the advertiser? The advertiser benefits when we take the subjective claim to have objective validity, when we assume that there are criteria governing the determination of the quality claimed and that someone is assuring us that the quality as claimed exists. Rather, puffed statements should be treated as bald assertions of superiority with no evidence to back them up.

For example, the NAD concluded that the claim "Europeans . . . love Kronenbourg" was an expression of the opinion of the manufacturer and "not subject to substantiation by objective research data," but that the claim "Europeans drink more Kronenbourg than any other bottled beer" was a factual claim requiring proof. When the advertiser provided sales figures from the European brewers' association confirming that Kronenbourg was the best-selling bottled beer in Europe, the NAD concluded that the claim had been substantiated and closed the case.[21]

An ad may not promise something a product cannot do, however, and the FTC now has the power to force advertisers to include statements remedying past deceptions in current advertising. That is why Hawaiian Punch told us in one series of ads what percentage of its product is fruit juice, and Listerine conceded in its ads that it does not prevent colds.

Fantasy   No reasonable person believes that a cleaning product comes with a giant who will clean your sink, or that its competitor releases a white tornado. The rationale for permitting such claims is the same as that permitting puffery: reasonable people do not believe such claims. The difficulty arises when some consumer believes the claims. If you believe that a support shoe will really enable you to walk on air, and buy the product expecting to be transported above the crowd, the ad has deceived you. Nonetheless, the law assumes that you should not have been deceived by the fantasy in the ad because its claim is patently ludicrous.

The NARB's treatment of the Chicken of the Sea claim that it was the "best" tuna illustrates the bounds of a claim based in fantasy. When Chicken of the Sea made the claim "in a whimsical jingle involving a mermaid" it was acceptable. When the mermaid was eliminated or de-emphasized "thereby diluting the whimsical quality of the claim," and the claim "what's the best tuna—Chicken of the Sea" was juxtaposed with a visual of a government seal, the NARB concluded that the ad had the capacity to deceive. The ad's use of the seal, available to any seafood manufacturer who maintains the required quality, implied that Chicken of the Sea had government endorsement as the "best" tuna.[22]

Limitations Imposed by the Audience

The mass media are available to people of all ages and they address the whole public, not some specialized segment. Therefore, most ads accepted by the media (with the exception of political ads, to be discussed later) will not overstep what the media consider to be the standards of decency and taste of the audience. So, for example, the *Washington Post* rejects sexually explicit ads for X-rated films.

Children in Audiences   The presence of children in the audience also imposes special requirements on advertisers. In 1974, a National Advertising Review Board consulting panel concluded, for example, that "all product advertising must be 'child-proofed,' reviewed and evaluated from the standpoint of a child's interpretation of what he [*sic*] sees and hears."[23] So, for example, the Children's Unit of the NAD recommended that an ad showing a woman inside a dishwasher

21. "News from NAD" (press release), 15 May 1981, p. 10.
22. NARB release, 30 January 1980.
23. "News from NAD," National Advertising Division Council of Better Business Bureaus, 15 April 1981, p. 1.

Ads on Children's Programming

In 1984 the Federal Communications Commission eliminated guidelines on the number of commercials on television programs for children. Nowadays, says Consumers Union, children watch up to 14 minutes of commercials on each hour program on weekdays and as much as 11 to 12 minutes on weekends. About $500 million a year is spent promoting games, toys, foods, and other goodies to young consumers.

In the fall of 1990, Congress passed a bill limiting commercials on children's television programs to $10\frac{1}{2}$ minutes an hour on weekends and 12 minutes on weekdays. The legislation also requires the FCC to evaluate the quality and quantity of children's programs when a broadcaster's license comes up for renewal.[d]

[d]Walter Goodman, "Cautionary Guide for Little Customers," *New York Times*, 3 December 1989, p. 33 H; Nathaniel C. Nash, "White House Gets Bill to Cut Ads on Children's TV Shows," *New York Times*, 2 October 1990, p. A 1 Y.

be discontinued after the Dallas Better Business Bureau reported that a 3-year-old child had allegedly climbed into an automatic dishwasher after viewing the ad.

The realization that children watch television at all hours of the day and night led the NAD to its conclusion that all ads should be child-proofed.

Advertisers are conscious that ads shape children's attitudes by the environments shown in the ads as well as by the appeals made on the product's behalf. In response to the concern of the Children's Unit of the NAD, Dial-a-Story ads were changed to include the caution, "And kids, be sure to ask your parents before you call" to ensure that children would not be encouraged to use the telephone without parental supervision or consent.

The language in advertising directed to children is also subject to special scrutiny. When research indicated that children do not understand the phrase "assembly required," the NAD recommended that advertisers simplify such language. "You have to put it together before you can play with it" was a recommended alternative.

Critics remain dissatisfied with advertising to children. Whittle Communications was widely criticized for making satellite dishes and playback equipment available to elementary and secondary schools that agreed to air its newscast, a newscast that carried advertising. In summer 1990, Consumers Union singled out a number of major advertisers for criticism, among them

Nike and Reebok International for using "emotional sells" in TV spots featuring celebrities; Hershey Foods Corp. and Colgate-Palmolive Co. and Procter and Gamble for candy and toothpaste ads, respectively, that resemble editorial matter; Campbell for giving schools sports equipment in exchange for soup labels; and PepsiCo for donating free products or sports equipment in exchange for vending machine placements."[24]

24. Judann Dagnoli, "Consumers Union Hits Kids Advertising," *Advertising Age*, 23 July 1990, p. 4.

Taboos   If visitors from another planet were to analyze all of our commercials to determine what we are like as a people, they would conclude that we habitually speak in superlatives and view the purchasing of products as a solution to all our problems. Our visitors would also note that, despite our preoccupation with beauty, youth, sex, security, and social acceptability, we are also a remarkably prudish people. This prudery would be documented by ads that suggest a decided discomfort with speaking directly about the human body and its functions, and about the specific functions of products designed for use on taboo areas of the body. For example, why don't ads for brassieres mention breasts? Bras "cross your heart" (they do?), "support" (support what?), "uplift" (perhaps this is a claim about their spiritual quality). Some are designed for the "full-figured woman" (who will certainly wear one only on a portion of her full figure).

Some products are advertised seldom, if at all, on television. For example, there are no nationally televised ads for birth control pills, but such ads do appear in print.

Our visitors could make a strong case for a claim that Americans are uncomfortable discussing bodily functions or specific portions of the anatomy, if televised ads were their only source of information. What would the visitors say when they hear the characters in a soap opera agonizing over whether one of the protagonists should have an abortion? Discussion of abortion in programming but no ads for contraceptives? No ads for abortion clinics? No ads for Planned Parenthood? They would wonder why programmers are more liberal than advertisers, or network censors more liberal about program content than ad content.

One answer is that there is a difference between deliberate exposure to a program and inadvertent exposure to a commercial. A person who tunes in to watch reruns of "Dallas" presumably knows what to expect. We don't anticipate commercials and commercial content in the same way. Also, although many find it hard to believe, advertisers are loath to offend any segment of the consuming public. Because television is a public mass medium, children are watching it at all hours. Advertisers do not want to create ads that will make consuming adults feel awkward about the product. If a child sees an ad for a douche or a contraceptive and asks the adult questions that the adult would prefer not to answer, that adult is not going to respond with great affection to the product or to the product's sponsor.

Why then the treatment of such topics as abortion, incest, homosexuality, and rape on prime-time and afternoon television? In part, because the sponsor is somewhat insulated from that content. It takes a sophisticated consumer to blame the advertiser for the content of the sponsored program. Also, because such content increases audience size, it performs a useful service for the advertiser. In short, the advertiser has more to gain than to lose by such discussion in programming, but more to lose than gain by treatment of taboo parts of the body in ads.

Finally, creating ads that force the knowledgeable audience to invest them with meaning is strategically wise; making the audience an accomplice in the process of persuasion increases the likelihood that persuasion will occur. To decode euphemistic ads, the auditor or viewer is drawn into a participatory process

What Would E. T. Think?

Because of the absence of the word *vagina* in ads, interplanetary guests might mistakenly conclude that a "feminine hygiene deodorant spray" is a room deodorizer.

Because of the absence of the word *anus* in ads, they might conclude that we line, wrap, clean, or write about our toilets on toilet paper.

And what would they make of the oblique references in ads to "disposable, absorbent protection" offered by older actress June Allyson?

And what would Emily Post say when she found them setting dinner forks on our sanitary napkins?

Taboos in Action

In response to protests by those opposing use of condoms as birth control, the Massachusetts Department of Public Health pulled out of a $94,000 transit and outdoor advertising campaign for AIDS prevention because the ads mention condoms.[e]

[e]*Advertising Age*, 16 July 1990, p. 12.

highly advantageous to the advertiser. The viewer cannot resent the implied request to fill in explicit content, because the viewer probably is willing to acknowledge that discussion of the taboo subjects—in at least some of the environments in which people watch television and with at least some of the people with whom one watches television—could prove awkward. So euphemistic ads exist because it is to the advertiser's advantage.

When a broadcast ad campaign speaks directly, the very fact of direct address, free of conventional euphemisms, gains our attention. The radio campaign for OXY 5 and OXY 10 facial cleansers, for example, included the word *zits* in the copy; the ad asked, "Which would you rather have, a few extra cents or a few more zits?" The contrast between the announcer's intonation and the harsh slang word riveted the audience's attention.

Similarly, ads that violate advertising's unwritten rules about what may or may not be the visual focus of an ad may attract attention precisely because of that violation. The ad campaign for Calvin Klein jeans featuring teenage movie star Brooke Shields was rejected by some stations and one of the networks. The ad prompted negative columns in newspapers, negative editorials, and hostile letters to the networks not because of the double entendre in the verbal message—after all, the double entendre with sexual nuances is a staple in "beauty product advertising"—but because its use of a teenage model delivering such lines and the camera angle focusing on her pelvis bluntly acknowledged teenage sexuality. By breaking the rules, the ad campaign gained quick visibility and became the topic of public discussion.

The Power of Multinationals

Multinational manufacturers and multinational advertising agencies now have enlarged power to suppress public messages they do not like. In 1988 Saatchi & Saatchi [the world's largest advertising conglomerate] acquired the Campbell-Mithun agency in the United States. The small agency was servicing anti-smoking ads for the Minnesota Department of Health, but Brown and Williamson Tobacco Company was spending $35 million then with Saatchi to advertise Kool cigarettes. The Minnesota account was only 3 percent of that, so Saatchi dropped the health department. The parent firm had learned its lesson three months earlier when one of the biggest advertisers in the world, RJR Nabisco, dropped another Saatchi subsidiary because it had created a Northwest Airlines television commercial showing passengers applauding the airline's no-smoking policy. RJR Nabisco, besides marketing food products, makes Camel, Winston, and Salem cigarettes.[f]

[f]Ben Bagdikian, "Global Media Corporations Control What We Watch (and Read)," *Utne Reader*, July/August 1990, p. 88.

TO SUM UP

In this chapter, we have examined the complex relationships among government, industry, consumers, and advertising. We have demonstrated the eagerness of industry to regulate itself when faced with the threat of government regulation. Government and industry regulators often are faced with difficulties dealing with claims that exist in the minds of the members of the audience but do not reside explicitly in the advertising content.

Existing regulation of advertising provides a sense of what advertisers may and may not do, but unfortunately efforts to minimize deception have produced an unintended result. Instead of producing ads with accurate but challengeable information, the regulations have prompted many advertisers to minimize informational content and instead emphasize unprovable puffery.

However, audiences are made up of potential consumers; the individuals and groups making up these audiences have the power to influence advertising and other media practices.

Analysis

Analyzing an Ad

In the brief space of three chapters on advertising, we have been able to touch only on a few of the questions that could be asked in a thorough analysis of an ad. Here we provide some of the other questions a person intent on critically analyzing an ad might ask.

What type of ad is it?

1. Public service announcement?
2. Advertising an idea?
3. Advertising a service?
4. Ad designed to engender good will?
5. Political ad?
6. Ad for a product?

If the ad is a p.s.a.

1. Did it appear in a space or time when it was likely to reach its intended audience?
2. Was it sponsored by a nonpartisan source?
3. Why was it aired or printed? What distinguishes it from p.s.a.'s rejected by this media outlet?

If the ad is an idea ad (pro-life or pro-choice, for example)

1. Who is the sponsor?
2. Did the sponsor incorporate for the purpose of sponsoring this campaign or have an identity independent of the campaign?
3. Why did this sponsor sponsor this ad? How does this ad serve the sponsor's self-interest?
4. Did the sponsor pay to air or place the ad?
5. How is the idea particularized or made concrete in the ad?
6. What is the intended audience of the ad? What cues in the copy or visuals reveal the identity of this audience? What does the ad want the audience to do? To think?
7. Does this ad exist to counter other ads or unpaid coverage about opposing ideas? If so, how successful is it in accomplishing this objective?

If the ad advertises a service rather than a product (for example, travel on a certain airline)

1. How is the service made concrete in the ad?
2. What was the intended audience for the service? How did the ad reveal the identity of its intended audience? What techniques did the ad use to increase the audience's desire for its service? What attempts were made to convert this want into a need?

If the ad is a goodwill ad

1. Is there a problem with the image or product that the ad is trying to overcome? If so, what techniques are used to overcome the problem?
2. By what channels did the problem come to public attention?
3. Does the ad explicitly identify the problem it is trying to overcome? If so, did the ad inadvertently make you aware of a problem you were not aware of before?
4. What if anything is the relationship between the product manufactured by the sponsor and the content of this ad (such as, ecology ad sponsored by an oil

company)? If the relationship is nonexistent or minimal, does the sponsor provide a rationale for the existence of the ad in the ad itself?

If the ad is a political ad

1. Is it sponsored by a committee associated with or dissociated from a candidate? By a political party?

2. Is it an attack ad or an affirming ad (attacking an opponent or supporting the candidate)?

3. Does the ad identify the party of the candidate? Why or why not?

4. Does the ad make explicit appeals to get you to register? To vote?

5. How long is the ad? Is it a "lift" taken from a longer ad? If so, what, if anything, is lost in the shorter version?

6. Is the ad consistent with unpaid coverage of the candidate? Has the ad incorporated newslike material about the candidate? Actual news footage of the candidate?

7. Did the ad appear adjacent to content with which it was compatible?

8. Did the ad employ a no-tag tag? If so, what was the tag and how effective was it? If not, what form of disclosure was employed to reveal the sponsorship of the ad?

9. What is the audience for which the ad is intended? How is the audience mirrored in the ad?

If the ad is a product ad

1. Who manufactures the product? Can you learn the identity of the manufacturer from the ad? If so, how? If not, what strategic purpose is served by absence of an identifiable manufacturer in the ad?

2. Is the trademark for the product used in the ad? Is it central to the ad? What does the trademark tell you about the product? How is the trademark integrated into the ad?

3. What is the unique selling point in this ad?

4. What are the redundant elements in the ad? Is this redundancy productive?

5. Is the product shown in the ad? Is it focal to the ad? What is being done with or to the product in the ad? What is this attempting to tell you about the product?

Audience

1. What is the intended audience—age? sex? ethnic background? religion? political affiliation? advertisers? elites? suppliers? distributors?

2. Did the ad appear in a time or place likely to reach the intended audience?

3. How does the ad mirror the intended audience? Does the ad imply special knowledge about wants and needs of this audience?

Ad content (not all points apply to p.s.a.'s)

1. What is the central claim in the ad? Is this claim believable?

2. What evidence is marshaled in support of the claim? Example? Lay testimony? Statistics? Figurative analogy? Literal analogy? Expert testimony? Does the explicit evidence in the ad warrant the claim? What associations are used to prompt inferences about the sponsor or product? What are some of these possible inferences? Are they legitimate?

3. Does the ad position the product (or service, idea, candidate) in relation to others? If so, how?

4. What specific strategies are used to personalize the product (service, idea, candidate)? To adapt message to audience?

5. Does the visual content of the ad support, underscore, echo the verbal content? If not, what is the relationship between the visual and the verbal? Is it a productive relationship?

6. Is the ad trying to reach a new audience (persuade them to buy or support) or is it trying to reinforce belief in those who already own the product or support the candidate?

7. Is anyone likely to be offended by this ad? If so, on what grounds? Does the ad offend publicly accepted standards of decency or taste? If so, why was it aired or printed?

8. How does the ad create recognition, differentiation, association, participation, and repetition?

Assumptions (values presumed in the ad)

1. What assumptions about society are embedded in the ad—about progress, consumption, political participation, racial harmony, multigenerational families, and so on?

2. What assumptions about the role appropriate to various types of persons inhere in the ad—older persons? children? women? men? African-Americans? Hispanics? Native Americans?

3. What assumptions about work or occupation are in the ad—about blue collar workers? professionals? professors? doctors? lawyers? working women as a class?

4. What assumptions about societal structures inhere in the ad? (a) Households: what constitutes the normal family according to the ad? How many people? How many children? Number of boys? Girls? Significant others—grandma? Mrs. Olsen? Milkman? Tony the Tiger? What is their relationship to other characters in the ad? Who gives advice? Who takes advice? Who extends approval? Disapproval? What are the norms for appropriate behavior for different characters in the ad? What types of behavior can be initiated by some characters and not by others? (b) Medical establishment: Is the doctor ever anything other than an authority? Are health care and healing ever separate from consumption of a product? When the physician is female, will she be found in different circumstances and in different relationships than when the physician is male? Is the female doctor ever seen treating a male patient? (c) Religious establishment: If there is a rabbi, priest, or minister, what kind of a role does he or she play? How are religious symbols (or roles) used (nuns, monks, altar, candles, icon, and so forth)?

5. Assumptions about bodily processes—aging; euphemistic terms for parts of the body; body functions that are not identified?

6. What types of communication are legitimized in ads? What sorts of problems are revealed or concealed from other characters in ads? Are there things concealed from adults by children or from children by adults? Is duplicity sanctioned (for example, pretext that product made from mix is really homemade)? Is one generation played off against another (grandma says to mother that if she bought the wrong thing it is granddaughter Susie's fault)? Does the product serve as a substitute for an expression of affection or some other form of communication? Does the ad advocate a particular type of communication, for example, preference for the telephone or writing a letter? If so, what are the special attributes of the preferred communication that are demonstrated in the ad?

7. How are politicians treated in nonpolitical ads?

Programming or content sponsored by an ad

1. Is there a relationship between the content of the ad and the content of the sponsored program, for instance, antidrug ad by a politician in an antidrug documentary or an ad for a beauty product in a woman's magazine?

2. Is the content of the program potentially offensive to any organized interest group? If so, is the advertiser aware of this? If so, why is the advertiser sponsoring the program?

Content surrounding (contextualizing) an ad

1. Do the programs or stories surrounding the ad provide a positive context for the ad? Do the ads surrounding this ad provide a positive context for the ad? Does the unpaid coverage of this product, idea, candidate, if any, provide a favorable context for this ad? If not, how does the ad adapt?

Media mix

1. How much money is being spent on purchases of advertising space and time? How many ads have been purchased? Where? When? To reach what total audience?

2. Does the ad appear in the same form in other media? What changes are made in the ad in other media? How do you account for the changes? Constraints in media? Audience adaptation?

3. Do different ads for this product appear in different media?

4. Is the ad one in a campaign? Related to others in a campaign? What is the relationship?

5. Why did the advertiser choose this medium? What are the advantages and disadvantages in this choice? Are there important claims about this product, idea, service, candidate that cannot credibly be made in this medium?

Pressure on advertiser

1. Has the advertiser or manufacturer been subject to pressure from groups that disapprove of the product or the program/content sponsored by the product's ads? Have ads or sponsorship been altered in response to this pressure?

2. Has the advertiser altered the ad in response to a consent agreement with the FTC?

3. Have the networks, stations, newspapers, or magazines in which the ad appears requested changes in the ad? Were the changes made and how did the changes affect the ad's ability to convey its intended meaning?

Effect

1. Was this ad pretested? Was it altered as a result of pretesting?

2. Does evidence exist to document the effect of this ad or ad campaign on its intended audience? On an unintended audience? Was this effect positive or negative? Is the evidence of effect credible?

3. Can you construct a more effective version of this ad?

Selected Readings

Advertising and Women. National Advertising Review Board, 1975.

Preston, Ivan L. *The Great American Blow-Up.* Madison: University of Wisconsin Press, 1975.

U.S. Congress, Select Committee on Aging, *Hearings on Age Stereotyping and Television,* 99th Cong., 1st Sess., 1977 (available from Government Printing Office).

9

How to Influence the Media

Short of running for political office or joining a congressional staff in order to change the laws, what can individuals or groups do to influence media practices? Here we examine the means of persuasion available to individuals, groups, social movements, and nongovernment organizations to change the content or form of ads or news. We assume that an individual who is aware of all the available means of influence is better able to select and skillfully employ effective means. We proceed from the simplest to the most complex, from the easiest to the most difficult, and from individual action to actions by established organizations.

Individual Complaints

The function of the media is to deliver an audience to advertisers, and advertisers want to persuade the audience to buy their products. Therefore, the media and advertisers cater to their audiences and spend large sums of money analyzing audience preferences. Chapter 5 considered this economic basis of the audience-media relationship; Chapters 2 through 4 on news and Chapters 6 through 8 on advertising discussed the character of this relationship.

The relationship between audiences and the media dictates that something as simple as writing a letter can have an impact on a newspaper or a radio or television station. Because relatively few people write them, each letter to a media outlet has a disproportionate impact. Although media managers and advertisers know that people who write letters are not typical of the entire audience, they tend to assume that each letter represents a large number of viewers or readers. As the number of letters protesting any single item, episode, or ad increases, the tendency to assume there is substantial dissatisfaction increases. When the offending medium or program has provided a mechanism for publishing or airing dissident views, a letter can also publicize one's grievance to the outlet's audience. So, for example, "60 Minutes" airs selected comments from viewers as do the letters-to-the-editor columns in newspapers.

Mail and the Media

In both media [print and television] . . . letters which describe factual mistakes are read carefully; as is critical mail when it arrives in unprecedented numbers or when it is unexpected, dealing with topics that do not usually anger letter writers.[a]

[a]Herbert Gans, *Deciding What's News* (New York: Vintage Books, 1980), p. 231.

In the summer of 1986, NBC created a series of image-enhancing spots that gave television critics a national platform on which to air their grievances. The 30-second spots featured nine citizen-activists speaking their minds about television. These critics included Ralph Nader, National PTA President Ann Kahn, and the founders of Viewers for Quality Television. The spots were NBC's answer to critics' complaints that the networks fail to listen to or to air criticism of their performance. The following comments are among those included in the spots: "If you think television is doing anything wrong or having any kind of negative effect on your child, turn the damn set off for a while. Put the five-year-old in your lap and read him [*sic*] a book." "Even if television had nothing but perfect programs on it, I think it would be important for people to limit the amount of television that young children watch."[1]

The public's lack of awareness of the channels of complaint is criticized by both supporters and foes of the regulatory and self-regulatory processes. For example, only one of 150 persons surveyed in 1976 could, without prompting, identify the NARB as an agency processing complaints from consumers about advertising.[2]

Complaints about material appearing on network programs should be addressed to the network's audience services division in New York and to the community affairs director of the local station airing the material. This procedure pressures the people directly responsible for approving content at the network; at the same time, it magnifies the impact of the dissatisfaction by encouraging the local station, whose license is dependent on serving the local community, not to clear such material in the future. Because the network wants to keep its affiliates happy, expressions of dissatisfaction from local stations to the network are very persuasive.

Networks are responsible for what they air. Most of their programming and all of their advertising is internally prescreened and approved. When these internal checks work, they pre-empt objections. When they fail, and protest is mounted by dissatisfied viewers, the existence of these checks assures the public that the network is conscientious. These checks also provide a bureaucratic structure

---

1. *Washington Post*, 11 June 1986, p. B 2.
2. Eric Zanot, "The National Advertising Review Board: Precedence, Premises, and Performance," Diss. University of Illinois, 1977, p. 189.

Courtesy of National Heart Savers Association.

C A S E   S T U D Y
Phil Sokolof v. McDonald's

In 1966 Phil Sokolof had a heart attack. He was not overweight and considered himself physically fit. How had it happened, he wondered. The culprit turned out to be cholesterol. Sokolof vowed to wage a campaign against the cholesterol we ingest unmindful of its presence.

Sokolof had one asset the ordinary citizen lacks. As a building materials manufacturer, he had become a millionaire. By mid-1990, he had sunk $2.5 million of his own money into his campaign for change. In the process, he founded a group called the National Heart Savers Association.

In October 1988, Sokolof took out newspaper ads in more than a dozen daily newspapers indicting companies that created foods by using cholesterol-rich tropical oils. His targets included such corporate giants as Sunshine Biscuits, Quaker Oats, Nabisco Brands, Procter & Gamble, Keebler Co., Borden, General Foods, and Pepperidge Farms.

Media coverage followed. Public pressure mounted. Eleven of the companies substituted other oils for tropical oil. One company, Nabisco, held out. Sokolof turned his attention to that corporation in his second series of "Poisoning of America" ads. In June 1990, Nabisco too gave in.

By April 1990, Sokolof had settled on another target: the high fat content of fast foods. His focus: McDonald's, the nation's leading fast food marketer. His third phase of ads addressed McDonald's directly. "McDonald's, your hamburgers have too much fat!" said his ads. The ads called on fast food chains to lower the fat content of their hamburgers by 10 percent and urged readers, "If you agree, write or call now!" The ads listed McDonald's address and phone number.

Again he bought ads in the nation's major newspapers, including the *Wall Street Journal* and the *New York Times*. But $500,000 of his budget went unspent when the *Los Angeles Times*, the *Baltimore Sun*, and the *Chicago Sun-Times* rejected the ads. Because newspapers are privately owned, they may reject any ads they want. Presumably these papers did not want to risk the wrath of one of the nation's larger advertisers.

By summer 1990, McDonald's was testing cooking french fries only in vegetable oil and noting that it had added bran muffins and low fat yogurt and shakes to its menu.

In the course of his campaign, Sokolof's message has been magnified by appearances on the major morning talk shows, the news, and in stories in the nation's newspapers.

He explains his success this way, "I got the message to the people, and the people got the message to the food companies."*

*Judann Dagnoli, "Sokolof Keeps Thumping Away at Food Giants," *Advertising Age*, 9 April 1990, pp. 3, 63.

How to Write an Op-Ed

The usual Commentary Page column is about 800 words—certainly it can be shorter, sometimes longer. It should be accompanied by your name, address, daytime phone number and Social Security number. (We pay a small honorarium to most contributors). . . .

Analyze the facts. Give us some insight. Help the reader draw some conclusions. . . .

Consider the piece to be an argument—lay out your central points in the beginning, then back them up with facts, anecdotes and illustrations. The opening few paragraphs must get the reader's attention, indicate what the piece is about, and—if at all possible—make the reader believe that he or she will be better off for having read it to the end.

Having something to say is the main aim: then you must be able to back it up. . . .

One word of caution, however: Pick that ammunition carefully. Don't include every possible example to prove your point. . . .

And now to my final point. Emotion. Even passion. We want it on our pages. . . .

One other thing to keep in mind: Remember the difference between a letter to the editor and a column. In general, if you want to respond to a particular story, editorial or another column—that's a letter. An article for the Commentary Page has to stand on its own.^c

^cJane Eisner, Associate Editorial Page Editor, *Philadelphia Inquirer*, 26 November 1989, p. 7 C.

---

through which complaints can be channeled. Although network news is not formally screened and approved by a separate division, any material that appears on the news programs has been examined by various gatekeepers within the news bureau. Complaints about news content can be sent directly to the anchor or to the program's producer. A carbon copy of each complaint should be sent to the president of the offending media outlet as well, to increase internal pressures for change within the system itself.

A letter from an individual can also trigger industry-sponsored self-regulatory mechanisms. As we have indicated, self-regulatory agencies such as NAD monitor advertising and initiate action against ads that seem deceptive. Similarly, readers' advocates for individual newspapers and the National News Council arbitrate complaints from dissatisfied readers and viewers. These individuals and organizations give the individual consumer the ability to initiate the investigation of a deceptive ad or an unfair news item.

An individual letter can also spur action by government regulatory agencies such as the Federal Trade Commission (FTC) and the Federal Communications Commission (FCC). The FTC monitors ads, calling for proof of questionable claims, and initiates formal proceedings against ads that seem deceptive. The FCC superintends the use of the air waves.

The ability of a single individual to produce change in broadcast content was clearly demonstrated when a young lawyer, John Banzhaf III, argued persuasively to the FCC that the Fairness Doctrine mandated anticigarette ads to counter pro-cigarette ads on television. As Banzhaf's legal training proved, specialized expertise is a definite asset in dealing with either the FTC or the FCC.

An effective letter of complaint presupposes a knowledge of the standards the self-regulatory agency or regulatory agency applies, an understanding of the sorts of complaints it is authorized to handle, and of the avenues of redress it is able to exercise if a complaint is credible. In making a complaint, the audience member must clearly specify the time, location, date, and character of the offensive item.

In addition, such a letter should indicate either that the item violates the standards of the agency or that the standards ought to be broadened to include items of this nature. Three lines of argument are particularly effective when justifying a complaint: (1) the item or ad is inaccurate or deceptive; (2) the item or ad violates community standards or tastes; or (3) the news item is unbalanced or the ad is unfair (for example, it exploits negative stereotypes or capitalizes on the gullibility of children).

Group Pressure

Boycotts

What can a consumer do if the regulatory and self-regulatory mechanisms dismiss the complaint? Because the relationship among the consumer, the advertiser, and the media outlet is an economic one, the consumer can threaten a boycott of the advertised product or the sponsored program or both if the desired change does not take place. To make this threat credible, the consumer must have or be able to marshal a large number of like-minded people willing to carry out the boycott. As we shall see, the threat of a boycott often eliminates the need for an actual boycott.

Advertisers want to avoid boycotts for a number of reasons. First, negative publicity in the news is more believable than advertising and functions as negative advertising. In addition, if an advertising agency produces an ad that triggers a boycott—especially if sales begin to drop off or if the boycott seems so well-organized and widespread that it will create negative associations in the public's mind with the manufacturer's other products—it will lose the client's business. Consequently, the advertising agency is uniquely susceptible to pressure to change offensive ads. Groups of consumers can put pressure on the ad agency that produced the ad, the mass media outlet that carried the ad, or the manufacturer that produced the advertised product.

Similarly, groups can marshal members of the community to cancel subscriptions to an offending newspaper or turn off an offending news program. If this tactic works and the size of the audience declines, the media outlet's profits are

---

"Roe vs. Wade"

Pressure from a fundamentalist religious group prompted several advertisers to withdraw from "Roe vs. Wade," a dramatization of the 1973 Supreme Court decision that legalized abortion, according to NBC executives. Some groups, particularly the American Family Association, led by the Rev. Donald E. Wildmon, urged viewers not to watch the film.

The attack on "Roe vs. Wade" sparked concern within the television and advertising industries because the film was considered to be of high quality and well balanced.

Richard Kostyra, media director for the J. Walter Thompson advertising agency, said some clients had withdrawn from the program, and commented: "I don't believe advertisers have a moral obligation to put their products on the line for the benefit of freedom of speech."[d]

[d]Jeremy Gerard, "Advertisers Withdraw from 'Roe,'" *New York Times*, 11 May 1989, p. 15 Y.

---

threatened; it can no longer deliver the desired audience to the advertisers. Groups also can exert indirect economic pressure by persuading advertisers not to buy space or time from the offending media.

Legal Actions

Our ability to influence the media through legal action is constrained by the laws governing the agencies we seek to influence. Before 1966, only persons who had a clear economic stake in a case were able to intervene in the FCC licensing of a station. This changed with a challenge to the renewal of the license of WLBT, a Jackson, Mississippi, television station. In this case, the court ruled that "civic associations, professional societies, unions, churches, and educational institutions or associations" may contest an application for a station's renewal of license. This decision gave such groups legal standing on the grounds that "the holders of broadcasting licenses [must] be responsive to the needs of the audience."[3]

What is important is that not all individuals or groups have legal standing. To have legal standing, an individual must be a member of a group that represents a substantial portion of viewers or listeners and has a legitimate and genuine interest in the station's performance in the community. The challengers in this case, the Office of Communication of the United Church of Christ, argued that although the city of Jackson was 45 percent African-American, the station was not sensitive to matters of concern to the African-American population.

In response to this decision, a number of groups representing the interests of special segments of the audience focused their attention on the license renewal process. These included not only the pioneering Office of Communication of the

---

3. Office of Communication of the United Church of Christ v. F.C.C., 359 F. 2d 994, 1002 (D.C. Cir. 1966), 425 F. 2d 543 (D.C. Cir. 1969).

United Church of Christ but also the National Association for the Advancement of Colored People (NAACP) Legal Defense Fund in New York, which seeks to increase minority involvement, Action for Children's Television in Newton Centre, Massachusetts, and the Mexican-American Legal Defense and Educational Fund in San Francisco.

Such groups are able to produce change not just through actual transfer of licenses but also by threatening that if change does not occur, they will intervene in the licensing process. For example, in 1969 an African-American coalition reached an agreement with KTAL-TV in Texarkana, Texas, under which news coverage, programming, and employment practices were altered. In return the coalition withdrew its petition to deny the renewal of the station's license.

Group legal action also has produced important changes in advertising. A group of law students calling itself SOUP (Students Opposing Unfair Practices) deserves credit for paving the way for the FTC's use of corrective advertising. In 1969 the students tried to intervene in the FTC case against Campbell Soup. Campbell's advertisers had placed marbles in the bottom of soup bowls to accentuate the solid ingredients in the soup. The students argued that a consent order that would stop the practice was insufficient to remedy the impression created by the false ads. Instead the students proposed corrective advertising.

Although the FTC did not impose corrective advertising to resolve the case, it did acknowledge that it had the right to do so if a case warranted such action. The impact of SOUP testifies to the power of groups that understand the regulatory process. Its understanding of this process enabled SOUP, a group otherwise powerless and underfinanced, to bring about a major change in advertising.

Group action often is more effective than individual action, but group action generally requires specialized legal expertise and the resources to support it. Such groups are better able to establish that they have standing before the FCC. In the case of the FTC, where standing is not a prerequisite for consideration of a complaint, individual action is possible. But even here the ability of a group to establish that it represents substantial sentiment in the community is more compelling than a comparable claim by an individual.

Group legal action is not effective in influencing the press except in the area of advertising. The press is not licensed and has important First Amendment protections from government interference. Nongovernment legal action against the print media is limited almost entirely to the enforcement of the libel laws. In extreme cases, such as the suit brought by Carol Burnett against the *National Enquirer*, this avenue can be very effective; the financial judgment against the tabloid in this case was large. The role of legal action in influencing the news is discussed in Chapter 4.

Those bringing action against a business or government make themselves vulnerable to the possibility of libel suits, however. In Suffolk County, New York, a real estate developer is suing nine civic organizations and sixteen individuals for running an ad in a local paper objecting to the developer's plans. They also produced a leaflet and a flier telling citizens to attend a hearing at the town meeting. When the Town Board rejected the developer's plan, the real estate concern brought suit. Even if the defendants win, their legal costs will have exceeded

National Association of Talk Show Hosts

Taxpayer Action Day was organized by the Council for Citizens Against Government Waste, a Washington lobby that claims 400,000 members.

The National Association of Talk Show Hosts mailed out flyers about the protest to 300 of its members. Some of them supported the protest on the air, such as Bob Grant, the host of "The Bob Grant Show" on WABC radio, New York City, which Arbitron says has 126,000 listeners, and Mary Beal, host of "The Morning Magazine" on WNSS, Wichita, with about 50,000 listeners.

Their reasons for supporting the protest are not entirely public spirited. Neil Myers, a host of NBC's Talknet shows, said: "Some of these people are in a numbers game. They are looking to grab headlines. . . . The campaign against giving Congress a raise was a perfect marriage between public interest and the dramatization of hosts. It got covered in *Time* and *U.S. News & World Report* and seemed to galvanize everyone."

Talk show-driven protests can be effective. A talk station, FM New Jersey 101.5, coalesced voter resentment against Jim Florio, the Governor of New Jersey, because of a record tax increase that he pushed through the legislature in 1990. That protest generated 800,000 signatures on a petition seeking to provide a mechanism for recall of public officials and legislation by initiative and referendum.[c]

[c]Wayne King, "Tax Protest, Fueled by Talk Shows, Is Getting Steamed Voters Organized," *New York Times*, 26 October 1990, p. A 12.

$10,000. University of Denver law professor George Pring notes that such suits are not usually brought with the aim of winning damages. Rather, they are intended to deter such actions in the future.[4]

Promoting Self-Regulation

Groups that understand the relationship between government and industry can also effect change by exploiting industry's desire to avoid government regulation. As we have noted, increased self-regulation of the broadcasting and the advertising industries is often prompted by industry fear of government regulation. By arousing industry fears that the government is about to regulate some facet of their operations, viewers or readers can prod industry to adopt its own preemptive regulations.

For example, the now defunct NAB Television Code allowed as much as 16 minutes of commercials during children's Saturday morning programming, but permitted only $9\frac{1}{2}$ minutes during prime time. The Massachusetts-based organization, Action for Children's Television (ACT), charged that this difference unfairly exploited children. The FCC responded to this charge by hinting broadly that if broadcasters did not limit the amount of children's advertising, the FCC would. Subsequently, the code was amended to set a ceiling of $9\frac{1}{2}$ minutes per hour on the commercials in children's shows.

4. *Washington Post*, 19 July 1986, p. A 23.

Controlling Controversy

Networks appreciate controversy for its ability to attract viewers, but they like it best when the controversy is uncontroversial. When the system works, according to Kathryn C. Montgomery, an assistant professor of film and television at UCLA and author of *Target: Prime Time*, political and social issues are shaped "to conform to the institutional demands of network television. Important societal conflicts are extracted from the public sphere and injected into entertainment programs, where they are reduced to problems for individual characters." The result: "Controversial issues are consistently and carefully balanced within each program so that one clear argument cannot be discerned."[f]

But in the spring of 1989, in response to letters from angry television viewers, such major advertisers as Coca-Cola, McDonald's, Chrysler, General Mills, Campbell Soup, Ralston-Purina, and Sears canceled commercials on television programs because of material cited as offensive in viewer complaints. Typical of such grass-roots protests was a campaign by Terry Rakolta of Michigan who charged that the Fox Network series, "Married . . . with Children" was offensively vulgar and shown at a time when children easily could watch it.

A number of factors have contributed to a climate encouraging grass-roots protest. Under economic pressure, all three networks cut back staff in their standards and practices divisions; the Hollywood writers strike of spring 1989 shortened the time between program production and broadcasting, increasing the chances that potentially offensive material would air; technological improvements allowed viewers to tape broadcasts of offensive programming and cite specifics they find objectionable; and there has been heightened concerned about the vulnerability of U.S. children to violence and drugs.

Montgomery argues that corporate takeovers of all three networks in the past five years created a climate in which a new protest movement could flourish: "The reason the standards and practices divisions were working in the first place is because they were actively managing the advocacy groups," she said. "Then the ownership changed, the staffs were cut back, and all that institutional memory was lost. Of course, the advertisers have that institutional memory."[g]

[f]Walter Goodman, "How the Viewers Work Their Will on Commercial TV," *New York Times*, 24 April 1989, p. 18.
[g]Bill Carter, "Sponsors Heed Viewers Who Find Shows Too Racy," *New York Times*, 24 April 1989, p. 14.

Industry is aware of the power of self-regulation to forestall government regulation. Had the broadcasting or advertising industry regulated cigarette advertising, it might have been spared the anticigarette commercials and ultimately the television ban on cigarette advertising. The FCC actually cited the existence of the newly created National Advertising Review Board to justify dismissing arguments by TUBE (Termination of Unfair Broadcasting Exercises) for an FCC-established Code of Advertising Standards for Television Advertising and an Advertising Advisory Board.[5]

5. *Adoption of Standards Designed to Eliminate Deceptive Advertising from Television*, 32 F.C.C. 2d 360, 372–374.

Pressure from an Established Organization

■   Individuals may persuade advertisers and manufacturers that a sizable part of the audience opposes an ad or news practice by protesting through a respected, legitimate group recognized by the public, the media, and advertisers. The arguments of such an established organization will be widely aired and readily accepted even by people not affiliated with the organization.

The PTA is one example. When the PTA takes a stand on advertising, particularly if the stand pertains to children's advertising or to the effects of ads on children, that stand is likely to bring about the desired change. The PTA is newsworthy according to the criteria described in Chapter 2. It has a track record of being newsworthy and is perceived as speaking for a substantial segment of the news outlet's audience—parents, teachers, taxpayers, children, and other people interested in education.

In August 1976, the national PTA placed television programming on probation for the amount of violence shown, and announced a national effort to monitor televised violence. If the level of violence did not decline significantly, the PTA indicated, it would consider sponsoring a boycott of those products advertised in the violent programs. Kodak, General Foods, General Motors, and Sears were among the companies that announced their support for the efforts to reduce violence in programming, an announcement that piggybacked on the newsworthy PTA statement and that garnered favorable national publicity for these manufacturers. By the end of 1977 a number of "violent" shows had been canceled "in a major concession to anti-violence crusaders."[6] Here it was not an actual boycott of products but the threat of a boycott by a nationally respected organization that produced results. In 1978, the PTA expanded its monitoring to include "offensively portrayed sexuality."

A group will be less effective if its economic self-interest is obvious to the audience. Although the PTA has a self-interest in the quality of education, changes in programming or advertising produce no direct economic benefit to its members. By contrast, efforts by Mobil Oil Company to alter broadcast and print stereotypes of Arab sheiks and efforts by the Tobacco Institute to alter the way the media cover the dangerous effects of smoking have been less effective, because their economic self-interest is apparent.

Financial resources are critical if a group plans to use paid channels (advertising) to influence unpaid channels (news coverage). When, for example, the Tobacco Institute took out ads reprinting news items that, in its judgment, were underplayed in the print press, and placed them in elite media like the *Columbia Journalism Review*, it was attempting to influence media decision makers directly by arguing that journalists had violated their own norms of balance and fair play. When such ads appear in the popular press, they suggest that the audience should be more critical in its consumption of news items on such an issue. This strategic use of paid media is not available to resource-poor groups.

6. "ABC: Laughing All the Way with Its New Schedule for Prime Time," *Broadcasting*, 2 May 1977, p. 23.

It's Not What You Know but Who You Know

Organized letter-writing campaigns are discounted by the journalists, but letters from officers of major national organizations are taken into account and are apt to be answered by an executive. If sent to a magazine, they may be published in the letters section.

Interest-group pressure appears to be effective when it obtains political support, in Congress or elsewhere; when it threatens advertisers and local television stations; and when it is persuasive to the journalists. However, pressure from powerless groups is ignored.[h]

[h]Herbert Gans, *Deciding What's News* (New York: Vintage Books, 1980), p. 265.

Viewers for Quality Television— How Many Letters Are Enough?

"Once upon a time viewers just sat quietly and watched," said one network executive who has been the recipient of tens of thousands of letters in the last few years and who asked, fearing more mail, that his name not be used. "Now they write. They write a lot."

Dorothy Swanson, founder of the Virginia-based Viewers for Quality Television, which coordinates efforts to save television shows, commented: "They believe they can influence what's on their television set. Look at 'Cagney & Lacey.'" She was referring to the first of the grass-roots campaigns to save a series. In 1984 CBS announced cancellation of the program about two women police detectives because of poor ratings. CBS received 20,000 letters over the next three months saying the program had fine writing and realistically portrayed working women. "Cagney & Lacey" was renewed.

But letters alone are not enough to return a show to the air. For instance, the ratings for "Cagney & Lacey" rose sharply during the summer between its cancellation and renewal, partly because it ran in a different time slot and partly because of publicity generated by the write-in campaign.

But Swanson and network executives say an avalanche of letters can influence a close call.

In early 1987, CBS took "Designing Women," a comedy about four partners in an Atlanta decorating firm, off the air indefinitely without actually cancelling it. Harry Thomason, executive producer of the program, asked Swanson to ask the 1,500 members who receive her monthly newsletter to encourage their friends to write to CBS. The network received 50,000 letters, and "Designing Women" went on to become the highest rated CBS comedy. In the winter of 1991, it was still on the air.

"The more common these crusades become, the sooner they will kill the effect," Thomason said. "A mere 50,000 letters isn't as impressive anymore."[i]

[i]Lisa Belkin, "Viewers Pens Can Be Mightier Than the Ax," *New York Times*, 18 June 1987, p. 24 Y.

Pressure from a Social Movement

■ Social movements are more loosely organized than groups such as the PTA. In their early stages, social movements lack the structure to disseminate information efficiently; they often lack identified leaders whose opinions are accepted by the media as representative of the opinions of the movement as a whole.

Social movements seek to produce specific changes in society. They also attempt to create awareness of issues, generate audience identification with their cause, and have their leaders recognized as spokespersons for larger constituencies not formally identified with the movement.

Social movements need to capitalize on journalistic norms and routines to accomplish these objectives. Ideally they become part of someone's beat, their leaders are perceived as newsworthy by the media, their concerns become ongoing news themes, and their spokespersons are quoted on controversial issues affecting their constituencies.

As we have indicated in our discussion of age stereotyping in Chapter 6, the media are powerful purveyors of societal attitudes. African-Americans and women, aware of this power of the media, have sought to increase their representation among newspeople. The civil rights and women's rights movements assume that female and African-American reporters are more sensitive to racism and sexism and also assume that their presence is a symbolic statement of support for these movements.

Changing the portrayal of women and minorities was also seen as a means of altering societal attitudes about these groups. The same arguments were made by the members of the movement for the rights of the elderly, who complained that mandatory retirement and age discrimination had deprived such older reporters and commentators as Pauline Fredericks and Eric Sevareid of their network jobs and that older persons are underrepresented and often caricatured when they do appear in ads.

The potential impact of movements is seen in the dramatic changes in advertising that occurred as a result of the pressure of the women's rights movement, pressure that triggered industry self-regulation. The National Advertising Review Board, an industry-based board set up to monitor truth and accuracy in advertising, issued a report titled *Advertising and Women* in 1975. That report acknowledged that "the more vocal critics of advertising as 'sexist' are younger, better educated, more articulate women who often are opinion leaders. On the average, they have more discretionary income. As their numbers increase (with increasing educational and job opportunities), their challenge to advertising will probably become greater, unless constructive action is taken."[7]

Political pressure and economic self-interest allied to produce ads in which women no longer appeared simply as housewives and mothers but also in their roles in business, the professional world, and community affairs. The board

---

7. *Advertising and Women*, Report of the National Advertising Review Board, 1975, p. 6.

Neighbor to Neighbor Versus Procter & Gamble

Neighbor to Neighbor is a citizen group organized to change the U.S. policy toward El Salvador. In 1989, the group began to focus its attention on coffee producers who use Salvadoran coffee beans.

Neighbor to Neighbor created an ad indicting Procter & Gamble for brewing "misery and death." Narrated by actor Ed Asner, the ad showed an overturned coffee mug spilling blood instead of coffee. Twenty-five stations in New Orleans, Kansas City (Missouri), Cincinnati, and New York rejected the ad. When the CBS affiliate in Boston aired the ad, Procter & Gamble responded by pulling $1 million in commercials from the station.

Neighbor to Neighbor countered by picketing N. W. Ayer, the advertising agency that holds the Procter & Gamble account. "Ayer, there's blood on your hands," read the picket signs.

Although most U.S. coffees use Salvadoran beans, the ad campaign targets Folgers because it is the country's best seller. Neighbor to Neighbor next plans to picket stores that carry the coffee. By May 1990, the boycott begun in November had yielded minimal results. Stores in some college towns had dropped the brand. Red Apple markets in Manhattan agreed that it would not provide Folgers with end of the aisle displays and would not feature Folgers in its ads.

"Boycotts are 'economic blackmail'" says a Procter & Gamble spokesperson. "We can't buy time in New York because of the chilling effect of P & G and Ayer's action," said a Neighbor to Neighbor leader.[1]

[1] Judann Dagnoli and Lauri Freeman, "Coffee Boycott Boils," *Advertising Age*, 21 May 1990, p. 6.

---

offered a checklist of principles to be used by advertisers to determine whether their ads treated women in an appropriate fashion.

The power of both respected institutions such as the PTA and large social movements such as the women's rights movement resides in their ability to speak for a large number of consumers who might be persuaded to boycott products or programming if the demands of the movement or institution are not met.

Creating Legislative Pressure

State Level

Both the state and federal governments exercise considerable control over commerce, including advertising. Action by state governments often precedes federal action and, ironically, creates an incentive for industry to acquiesce to federal legislation. One instance occurred in July 1965 when Governor Nelson Rockefeller signed an act requiring a health warning on all cigarette packages sold in New York State. "If there was anything the cigarette companies wanted less than federal regulation," explains A. Lee Fritschler in *Smoking and Politics*, "it was

Where to Write to Comment or Complain

National Advertising Division
Council of Better Business Bureaus
845 Third Avenue
New York, N.Y. 10022
(212) 754-1320

Federal Trade Commission
Pennsylvania Avenue at Sixth Street, N.W.
Washington, D.C. 20580

Federal Communications Commission
Consumer Assistance Office
1919 M Street, N.W.
Washington, D.C. 20554

Networks and Cable Companies

ABC

Chrm. Thomas S. Murphy
Capital Cities / ABC, Inc.
24 East 51st Street
New York, N.Y. 10022
(212) 421-9595

CBS

Chrm. Laurence A. Tisch
CBS, Inc.
51 W. 52nd Street
New York, N.Y. 10019
(212) 975-4321

NBC

Chrm. John F. Welch, Jr.
General Electric Company
3135 Easton Turnpike
Fairfield, Conn. 06431
(203) 373-2211

Showtime, MTV, Nickolodeon, VH-1, The Movie Channel

Chrm. Sumner M. Redstone
Viacom International, Inc.
1211 Avenue of the Americas
New York, N.Y. 10036
(212) 575-5175

HBO, Cinemax

Chrm. J. Richard Munro
Time, Inc.
Time & Life Building
Rockefeller Center
New York, N.Y. 10020
(212) 512-1000

TBS, TNT, CNN

Chrm. R. E. Turner
Turner Broadcasting System
P.O. Box 105366
Atlanta, Ga. 30328
(404) 827-1700

CBN

Christian Broadcasting Network
CBN Center
Virginia Beach, Va. 23463
(804) 424-7777

ESPN

The Sports Network
355 Lexington Avenue
New York, N.Y. 10017
(203) 585-2000

state requirements that health warnings appear. This could have meant as many different labels as there are states, creating an obvious marketing problem."[8]

Federal Level

Congress can exercise enormous power over the government regulatory agencies, which were created by and can be modified by congressional legislation, are funded by congressional appropriations, and are overseen by congressional committees. In addition, high-level government appointments, including appointments of FCC commissioners, must be confirmed by the Senate.

Actual congressional action is not always necessary to produce change in the media. For example, on February 3, 1971, the FTC asked Congress to require that all print advertising for cigarettes carry a health warning. On April 15, seven of the nine largest cigarette companies began voluntarily including health warnings in all print ads.[9]

But when Congress is affronted by the actions of a regulatory agency, it is capable of strong action. In the mid-1960s, for example, without consulting key members of Congress, the FTC bowed to pressure from anticigarette forces and issued a notice of rulemaking requiring a health warning on all packages of cigarettes and in all cigarette advertising. Both houses of Congress held hearings on the FTC action. The resulting legislation removed the FTC's rulemaking powers concerning cigarette advertising and negated the FTC rule.[10]

T O   S U M   U P

This brief consumer's guide to influencing the mass media describes how otherwise powerless individuals or groups can exploit the complex relationship among government, industry, and audience to influence advertising and news coverage. In some cases individual action is effective; in others, group action is necessary. Established organizations have a distinct advantage over social movements; resource-poor groups also operate at a significant disadvantage.

An understanding of journalistic norms and routines, regulatory and self-regulatory procedures, and the legal process enhance the likelihood that a rhetorically sophisticated but resource-poor group will succeed.

In those instances when change can occur only through legislation, individuals may be forced to gain influence as members of congressional staffs or to run for office. Groups can support candidates for public office sympathetic to their points of view. Therefore, in the following chapters, we focus on the use of media to elect politicians.

---

8. A. Lee Fritschler, *Smoking and Politics: Policymaking and the Federal Bureaucracy* (Englewood Cliffs, N.J.: Prentice-Hall, 1975), p. 121.

9. Ibid., p. 165.

10. PL 89-92 (1965), *United States Code*, section 1331. For a discussion, see Fritschler, *Smoking and Politics*, pp. 118–120.

Analysis

Constructing a Dissemination Strategy

In Chapter 4 we spoke of the principles and processes involved in influencing news media. In the last chapter we noted avenues consumers can use to effect change in media practices. Here we combine the principles of these chapters in a checklist of steps useful in creating strategies to influence the media.

Outlined below are the steps to be followed in constructing a strategy for disseminating a message through the mass media. These steps are appropriate for individuals, citizen groups, news managers, and political consultants.

Step I: Isolating the Message   Distill the essential message to be communicated from the ocean of information, and draw together essential support material (forceful, dramatic evidence in support of your claim or position).

Step II: Defining the Intended Audience   What the audience is expected to do with information often determines target audience. Reach all the essential people but *only* the essential people with the message. (Prepare to answer the questions "Why is this on my desk and not on the desk of the assignment editor?" "Why is this on my desk when I don't write about this subject?") Determine if the message will pass through more than one pair of hands if it accomplishes its objective.

Consider who possible target audiences are for this message—employees of a cabinet department? other government employees? members of Congress? scholars interested in this subject? ordinary citizens affected by this policy? residents of particular localities? anyone else?

Step III: Determining the Newsworthiness of the Message   Consider whether you will have to pay to disseminate this message, and whether it can be communicated as soft news if it will not be used as hard news. Decide if it can be made newsworthy by piggybacking off other news, holding it for a slow news day or for dead news time, releasing it in a newsworthy setting, or releasing it through a newsworthy person.

Step IV: Determining Factors Constraining Release   Factors that may affect release of a news item include a congressional deadline, a public promise by a supervisor, *someone* wanting to see it buried, or *someone* wanting to see it released and heavily publicized.

Step V: Selecting Appropriate Channels   In deciding the channels through which to release information, consider which channels best reach the target audience. Does your media list contain all relevant outlets (all publications reaching target audiences, all specialized publications that cover this subject, all outlets in a particular locality)? Have all possible channels been considered (press releases to county papers, radio feeds to rural America for use in pre-drive time)? Is the form of the message compatible with the selected channels? Different channels may require different forms. Is the language of the message compatible with the channel—popular language to popular channels, technical language to specialized channels?

If the message is transmitted by phone or given in response to phoned inquiries, the information should be stored in a manner that lends itself to quick, clear retrieval. Responses to inquiries by phone or stories that must be transmitted by phone to meet deadlines should be written down.

Is the message to be released to selected outlets or mass-released? Decide if you should use the elite media such as the *New York Times* to draw the attention of the other media, and if you should use one medium (such as radio) to sensitize others (for example, print and television) to your message.

Determine whether your message is part of a larger message.

Step VI: Adapting the Message to the Channel   Each channel imposes constraints on the messages it relays: *format* ("MacNeil/Lehrer Newshour," national network news, "Face the Nation," or *New York Times*); *deadlines* (morning or evening papers, drive-time radio); *content* (weeklies or dailies, audio, print, visual, or audio-visual content); and *cost* (costs in equipment and personnel to carry this message).

These constraints influence message construction. Television news is a *visual* medium (consider the talking head versus the visual aid; the effects of location), and it is an *audio*-visual medium (the brilliant statement might be mumbled, stumbled, and fumbled). Television news deals in 1- to 1½-minute units, so try to write the quotable quote, the single synthetic sentence that digests the debate. It is also a medium favoring the dramatic, the confrontational; it often includes upbeat human interest stories at the end of a program. Also, what is not news today may be recast as news tomorrow (newsworthiness is a function of what else is newsworthy that day).

Television also includes interview shows ("Today," "Face the Nation," "MacNeil/Lehrer Newshour") and televised documentaries. Other appropriate media might be radio news spots or all-news radio, newspapers (chains, national, or county), the wire services, and specialized publications.

Step VII: Monitoring Your Success or Failure   In reviewing the success or failure of your dissemination effort, ask again what was covered and why? Future messages should be adjusted accordingly.

Selected Readings

Fritschler, A. Lee. *Smoking and Politics: Policymaking and the Federal Bureaucracy.* Englewood Cliffs, N.J.: Prentice-Hall, 1975.

Krasnow, Erwin G., Lawrence D. Longley, and Herbert A. Terry. *The Politics of Broadcast Regulation.* 2d ed. New York: St. Martin's Press, 1982.

Sethi, S. Prakash. *Up Against the Corporate Wall: Modern Corporations and Social Issues of the Seventies.* Englewood Cliffs, N.J.: Prentice-Hall, 1971.

Simons, Herbert W. *Persuasion: Understanding, Practice & Analysis.* 2d ed. New York: Random House, 1986.

10

Political Versus Product Campaigns

Conventional wisdom says that candidates for political office are now sold to the electorate like cigarettes or soap. There is some truth to the claim. Both manufacturers and politicians develop mass media campaigns to persuade us to act as they wish. Both manufacturers and politicians seek to create name recognition and employ differentiation, association, audience participation, and repetition to communicate their messages. Both rely on campaigns that are centrally coordinated by people issuing many messages—or a single message to many media—across an extended period of time, in order to accomplish a specific objective. Both condense their messages into slogans.

But politicians are not soap or cigarettes, and the campaigns for products and politicians have contrasting functions, values, regulations, and financing. In this chapter we focus on these differences to indicate the peculiar limitations operating on those who would influence the outcome of a political campaign; we also show the resources available to them. By contrasting political and product campaigns we hope to increase understanding of both.

Using the Media

A political campaign's use of media is more *short-lived and more intense* than a campaign on behalf of a product. We may see the ads for a specific product, such as Ivory Soap, for decades. As long as the product holds a share of the market the manufacturer considers acceptable, the product will stay on the market. We use soap all year, so advertising for soap appears year-round. A political campaign is more akin to an ad campaign for a seasonal product, such as a brand of Christmas tree ornaments.

A political campaign is relatively short. Only rarely does a candidate begin to air commercials more than three months before the election. Usually ads appear in the last four to six weeks, and the number of ads increases as the date of the election approaches. By contrast, a three-month campaign for a product would be a very short campaign. Often producers spend more than three months just testing the product and then spend additional time testing the commercials that will market the product. The short duration of the typical political campaign is one of the campaign's major liabilities, because it is difficult to create or change attitudes in a short period of time. Consequently, candidates are announcing earlier than they once did, and speculation about likely contenders begins the day after each inauguration.

Creating an Image

The image of a product can be created more easily than the image for a politician because politicians bring to office a documentable past. Often the campaign attempts to capitalize on that past by stressing that experience has prepared the candidate in specific ways for the office sought. But the past can be a liability too. A politician with no previous elected experience can attempt to frame that lack of experience as an asset by creating an "outsider" image, but experience that isn't in the record cannot be fabricated. A politician—even a vice president—with a shady past may find that it returns to haunt him or her. By contrast, if the product doesn't taste the way potential consumers would like, the manufacturer will determine that fact in product testing and reformulate the product. The product can be repackaged more easily than the candidate can.

Targeting the Audience

The politician wants to reach potential voters. In most states that audience includes unregistered voters until the registration books close. But once the deadline has passed, the politician can effectively discount those who are not registered to vote. In a primary in which only registered Democrats can vote for a Democratic candidate, the various Democratic candidates will focus their attention on reaching registered Democrats. The politician also focuses on voters who can be swayed to vote for him or her. When it is possible to separate one from the other, the politician is unlikely to target advertising to those committed to an opponent.

The politician often focuses attention on different age groups from those important to the commercial advertiser. For example, children and teenagers are prime audiences for the commercial advertiser. For the politician, these audiences are comparatively insignificant because they can't vote. By contrast, the politician will focus more attention on the older segment of the audience than will the commercial advertiser. As we age, the likelihood that we will vote increases. Persons over 65 cast proportionately more votes than their percentage of the population would suggest. The commercial advertiser is interested in those who are likely to spend money to purchase a product; the politician is interested in those who are likely to cast a vote.

Nonpolitical commercials are rarely broadcast to reach lower-income groups. Although people with lower incomes are less likely than their more affluent counterparts to vote, Democratic politicians, particularly liberal Democrats, routinely aim advertising at these groups. Often this advertising includes appeals to register and to vote as well as messages designed to persuade the audience to vote for the liberal Democrat. So voting power is a great equalizer in political advertising. It means that persons who otherwise are not the focus of product advertising will become the target audience in some sorts of campaigns.

Earlier we noted that the typical commercial was set in an upper-middle-class or upper-class environment. Nonpolitical ads do not show poverty, slums, incorrigible despair. Product ads affirm the basic health of the economic system by creating a world in which people live comfortable, pleasant lives. The only discomforts the people in these ads experience easily can be remedied by purchase of a product.

By contrast, the politician out of power wants to indict the status quo and pin the blame for the ills of the system on the incumbent. These indictments are most effective when they are visually underscored. Consequently, the candidate will tape ads in slum housing to establish that the incumbent's promises of change have been unfulfilled. Political ads will also feature testimony from the disenchanted—those who are unhappy at the way in which government is being run. Political ads are able to feature the poor, the unemployed, those who are ill, and ads attacking incumbents are prone to do just that. Ads for liberal candidates, in particular, will include the disadvantaged, who are otherwise seldom seen on television except on an occasional segment of the evening news.

Political ads are also more likely to include persons with regional dialects because their presence is a signal to the corresponding regional or ethnic group that the candidate has support from their peers. In order to reach the widest audience possible, commercial advertising, by contrast, tends to employ characters who speak standard American English with a general American accent.

Both candidates and manufacturers want to reach their target audiences in a cost-efficient fashion. It is generally easier for the manufacturer to meet this objective than it is for the politician, because the ways in which the electorate is segmented for electoral purposes do not always lend themselves to cost-efficient purchase of media space.

For example, a candidate who is running for governor in Connecticut can only reach viewers in Fairfield County if time is purchased on New York television stations; Fairfield County is part of the Greater New York Metropolitan Area for broadcasting purposes. But over 80 percent of the money spent on New York television advertising will reach New Yorkers who cannot vote in Connecticut. This means that, all things being equal, a candidate who is well known in Fairfield County has an advantage. Such a candidate can focus the media budget on buying television time in the central Connecticut cities of New Haven and Hartford, reaching primarily Connecticut voters. But the candidate who is unknown in Fairfield County must decide whether becoming known there is of sufficient importance to warrant spending 80 cents of every dollar reaching nonvoting out-of-staters (see Figure 10.1).

Such circumstances occurred in 1970 when Lowell Weicker faced Joseph Duffey in a race for the Senate. Weicker was well known in Fairfield County;

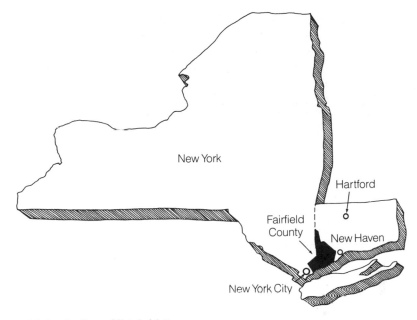

Figure 10.1 Outline of Fairfield County.

Duffey was not. Weicker concentrated media spending in the New Haven and Hartford markets and won the election.

The competition for media time is particularly fierce in those markets that serve many states simultaneously. For example, Philadelphia stations also reach voters in Delaware and New Jersey; Washington, D.C., stations reach Maryland, the District of Columbia, Virginia, and a slice of West Virginia. Because audiences are accustomed to being addressed by those who want them to purchase an accessible product, they run the risk of responding as one Virginia resident did when she told a pollster that she planned to vote for Jay Rockefeller—who was running for the governorship of West Virginia.

Economic Versus Political Values

Ads for products argue that buying is a good thing; ads for politicians argue that voting is good. Ads for products assume that purchasing products makes us as individuals happier. Ads for political candidates assume that involvement in the political process makes the world a better place. In the world of political ads the system works. Ads do not argue for overthrow of those they oppose but for action within the system—voting. In political ads, problems exist but can be solved. Incumbents tell us that they have worked to solve the problems and have actually produced solutions. Those out of office point to problems that remain unsolved and offer solutions. Both types of ads affirm that problems are manageable and ought to be addressed from within the system by voting for one candidate or another. In ads for products, problems exist but these problems too are solvable. Here the solution is found, not in voting, but in purchasing.

Both political ads and ads for manufactured products affirm that we are able to function as agents of change. We can buy the product that produces the whiter smile. We can vote for the politician who will turn the economy around. Consequently, both types of ads are fundamentally optimistic. Their outlook is positive.

Suppose, instead, that the world is filled with unsolvable problems. Suppose, for example, that wars are not winnable, that the federal deficit is intractable, that we are plagued by problems that do not lend themselves to political solutions within the system. If all this were true, then why worry about which candidate ought to be elected? All are equally powerless. Political ads must affirm that we can be agents of change, that voting causes change, that politicians in office can make a difference, that problems are solvable. In the process of affirming these premises, political ads reinforce our belief in our political system.

Regulation

The laws governing political and product ads differ in important ways.

Censorship

Networks are free to recommend changes in ads and often do so when, in their judgment, the ads are inaccurate, are in poor taste, or embody negative stereotypes. In contrast, it is illegal to censor a political ad. Consequently, material that would never be heard or seen in a commercial ad can be included in a political ad. For example, J. B. Stoner, a politician running for state office in Georgia, paid to air a television ad that included the statement, "The main reason why niggers want integration is because niggers want our white women." The NAACP protested the airing of the ad and asked the FCC to ban further airing. The commission refused on the grounds that only a clear and present danger of imminent violence would justify tampering with a political commercial. The ruling was justified by the guarantee of free speech even for claims that are abhorrent.[1]

Similarly, political ads may employ words found to be "obscene, indecent, or profane," although commercial ads and programming may not. In 1978 the Supreme Court upheld the FCC's right to impose sanctions on a radio station that broadcast George Carlin's monologue about words that cannot be used on radio and television.[2] But in 1980, presidential candidate Barry Commoner was allowed to air a political radio commercial that included one of the prohibited words in Carlin's monologue: *bullshit*.

What protects a station, then, from a libel suit claiming that a person or organization was defamed by a political commercial or statement made during access secured as a result of an equal-time request? In Fargo, North Dakota, in 1956 such a situation arose. A candidate for the Senate requested and received equal time

1. "FCC Won't Block Racist Ad in South," *New York Times*, 4 August 1972, p. 37.
2. FCC v. Pacifica Foundation et al., 3 July 1978 in 3 *Med. L. Rptr.* (Washington: Bureau of National Affairs, Inc., 1978), p. 2553.

on WDAY-TV. During the time secured by the equal-time request, the candidate charged that a prominent union, the North Dakota Farmers Union, was controlled by the Communists. The union responded by suing both the station and the candidate. The North Dakota Supreme Court held, and the U.S. Supreme Court affirmed, that stations could not be considered legally responsible for untrue or libelous statements made in such a circumstance. Because Section 315(a) of the Federal Communications Act forbids the censoring of remarks by candidates, the station could not be held accountable.

Equal Time

If stations could effectively deny air-wave access to candidates they opposed, or provide blocks of free time to candidates they supported with no responsibility to other candidates, the broadcast media would become dominant power brokers in the political arena. Section 315 of the Federal Communications Act guarantees that broadcasters who open their facilities to one legally qualified candidate must give equal opportunities to the other legally qualified candidates. To be legally qualified, a candidate must have announced for the office and have met the legal requirements asked of those seeking the office. So, if one candidate is given five minutes of time at no charge, then other legally qualified candidates for the same office must also be given five minutes of equivalent time each. If one candidate has been permitted to buy time on a station, all other legally qualified candidates for the same office also must be permitted to buy time. The equal opportunity provision does not mean that a station must give all candidates free time if one candidate has purchased time; that purchase simply entitles other candidates to purchase equivalent time.

Right to Access

The Supreme Court has also held that candidates have "an affirmative right to access to the broadcast media." This ruling, handed down in July 1981, was the result of a challenge by the Carter campaign to network denial of the right to purchase 30 minutes of prime time in December 1979. ABC and NBC had rejected the request outright. CBS had offered two 5-minute time slots instead. Under the new ruling a broadcaster can deny access only if the requested purchase would substantially disrupt programming. The candidate may then appeal that decision to the FCC, which is empowered to determine whether or not to order that the ad run. If the station refuses an FCC request to air the ad, its license can be revoked.

Prior to this ruling, the FCC simply required stations to discuss controversial issues (the Fairness Doctrine) and to grant equal time to all qualified candidates if any one candidate was given or permitted to purchase time (Section 315). Writing for the Court in 1981, Chief Justice Warren Burger argued that "it is of particular importance that candidates have the opportunity to make their views known so that the electorate may intelligently evaluate the candidates' personal qualities and their position on vital public issues before choosing among them on election day."[3]

---

3. Fred Barbash, "Court Eases Candidates' Access to TV," *Washington Post*, 2 July 1981, pp. 1, 4 A.

How then is it possible for presidential debates among two or three major contenders to take place? The debates between Richard Nixon and John Kennedy in 1960 occurred because Congress had suspended Section 315 to permit them to occur. The debates between Gerald Ford and Jimmy Carter in 1976, between Ronald Reagan and John Anderson and Reagan and Jimmy Carter in 1980, and between Reagan and Walter Mondale and George Bush and Geraldine Ferraro in 1984 were possible under a 1975 ruling of the FCC that held that such debates were bona fide news events and, as such, exempt from the equal opportunity requirement.

To be considered a bona fide news event, the debates must be sponsored by an outside organization (in 1976, 1980, and 1984, the League of Women Voters), must be planned without the involvement of the broadcast media, and must be covered live and in their entirety.

Some other news formats are also exempt from the requirements of Section 315. Bona fide newscasts and interview shows, such as "Meet the Press," are exempt. A news conference scheduled by the candidate and considered newsworthy by the broadcaster is also exempt if it is covered live and in its entirety.

Campaign Objectives

For the politician there is only one day that really counts; for the product one day is as good as another, but sooner is better and often is best. A politician wants us to cast a vote on election day and to cast that vote for him or her. The politician also wants to mobilize that percentage of the electorate that occasionally works in a campaign, if that is possible, and to translate as much support as possible into money and volunteer time.

The manufacturer wants us to buy the product, sooner rather than later, and often—if that is possible. The manufacturer wants those of us who have purchased the product to recommend it to our friends and, when the occasion arises, to purchase it again. In that sense the manufacturer and the politician are alike: both benefit if we become walking advertisements for them.

But "election day" for the manufacturer—the day on which we can vote to buy or not to buy the product—comes more frequently than it does for the politician. This poses a major problem for the politician; in a sense, the politician is trying to persuade us to take action, an important action that will benefit us, but to delay taking the action until a specified day and specified times within that day. It may rain that day. We may be ill. We may be out of town. We may forget to vote. The manufacturer is not plagued by rain, our illness, our business trips, or our forgetfulness in the same way the politician is because we have repeated opportunities to buy the product.

Voting Versus Buying

The manufacturer will make the product available to us in a convenient location, or by phone or mail whenever possible. Ideally, the product intrudes on our normal pattern of activity. We go to the supermarket and there the product is, advertising itself to us from the shelf. But voting occurs in places most of us do not routinely visit—an elementary school or a municipal building. So the facts of a single election day and the special voting place complicate the job of the person who wants us to vote for a certain candidate.

Voting against a product is easier than voting against an elected official. If you buy a product and are dissatisfied, you can complain to the retailer, the manufacturer, and various consumer protection agencies. You can refuse to purchase another, attempt to get your money back, or discourage your friends from buying one. But what can you do when the politician you elect proves to be inept? The next chance you will have to vote "no" will be the next election, unless you are governed by a charter that permits recalls; even then the recall process is time-consuming, costly, and usually unsuccessful.

Criteria for Victory

The criteria for victory are different in elections from those in campaigns for products. If a manufacturer's product is fourth or fifth in the market compared to competing products, that level may be cause for rejoicing. A company can do very well financially by holding 5 or 6 percent of the market for a specific product. Consequently, there are more winners in campaigns to sell products than in elections.

Dove, Dial, and Irish Spring can all make a profit, but George Bush, Jack Kemp, Pierre DuPont, and Bob Dole cannot all be president at the same time. Placing fifth in a field of candidates where the person with the most votes wins means that you have lost. There is no consolation prize. Many manufacturers earn a lot of money with a comparatively small share of the market because the market is large enough to be shared profitably.

In most elections the person who wins the majority of votes cast gets the office, and the rest are losers. But an advertiser can lose entire segments of the audience, even alienate those who won't buy the product, yet the product may make a healthy profit. In contrast, the candidate needs 51 percent plus 1 of the vote in most instances and cannot, as a result, afford to write off as large a percentage of the audience as the manufacturer can.

We refer to "as large a share of the audience" because, like the manufacturer, the candidate does in effect write off a portion of the audience in most cases. It is unlikely that a voter who dislikes Candidate A, is committed to Candidate B, and has a high level of information about both candidates will be persuaded to vote for Candidate A. Such persons are classed as "hostile" and written off in most campaigns. If that class of hostile voters makes up over 51 percent of the electorate, Candidate A is usually advised to withdraw rather than to attempt the impossible.

Unpaid Coverage

A candidate is likely to obtain more unpaid coverage than a product unless the product is in trouble. Candidates both profit and suffer from the media coverage of political campaigns. There is no such thing as an election that is not newsworthy; some elections are simply *more* newsworthy than others. A mayoral contest in a small town is newsworthy to the town paper and may receive coverage in county papers as well. The mayoral contest in a large city like Baltimore will receive coverage not only in the Baltimore media but also in Washington, D.C., because the city is large and because how it is governed has an impact on the area surrounding it.

In the nationwide presidential election, the nominees of the two major parties cannot avoid the attention of the media, and if they attempt to avoid it, their attempts at avoidance will be covered.

On the other hand, it is rare to see much news at all—or favorable coverage when coverage occurs—of a corporation, an industry, a manufacturer, or a product. For example, we read a lot about savings and loans in 1990. Most of the coverage focused on the need for the federal government to come up with billions of dollars to back Federal Deposit Insurance Corporation guarantees. The coverage started from the admitted premise that something was wrong.

However, overall, the news coverage of corporations and their products is almost nonexistent compared to the coverage of the typical political campaign.

Quality

Reporters are assigned to cover specific candidates and become experts in matters pertaining to that candidate; reporters are not assigned to cover specific products unless there is a problem, such as a recall or malfunction. Consequently, there will be more routine investigative reporting about candidates and their campaigns than about products and their campaigns.

Endorsements

The endorsement of a powerful newspaper can save a candidacy, as it did in 1978 when the *Baltimore Sun* endorsed Maryland gubernatorial candidate Harry Hughes and salvaged his foundering campaign. Candidates typically translate endorsements by newspapers into paid advertisements by multicopying the endorsement and distributing it as a flier, paying to have it reprinted as a newspaper ad, reading it in a radio ad, or crawling it across the television screen in a commercial. There are few equivalents for products. When *Consumer Reports* ranks products, for example, it does so with the stipulation that the results may not be used in the products' ads.

Financing

A candidate must not only get you to buy the product—to vote—but also must raise money; a manufacturer has the money to create the product and does not advertise for contributions but rather to get you to buy the product. Presidential candidates who accept matching funds from the government must also accept a ceiling on expenditures. Manufacturers face no such limit.

In 1971 Congress enacted the Federal Election Campaign Act, amended in 1974. The enactment of this law required that candidates running for the presidency or for Congress report campaign contributions and expenditures, "limited the amount of money that could be collected and spent, made public funds available for presidential contenders, and established the Federal Election Commission to administer and enforce the law."[4] Subsequently, the Supreme Court upheld limits on the campaign contributions of individuals and groups other than the candidate and upheld the limits on spending by candidates who accepted public funds. In 1988 both George Bush and Michael Dukakis accepted public funds and the resulting spending ceilings.

The Court also permitted spending on a candidate's behalf by groups independent of the candidate. This provision gave rise in 1988 to such groups as Americans for Bush and the National Security Political Action Committee. The most famous ad of the campaign, the "Willie Horton" ad, was a PAC ad.

In contrast, there is no limit on the amount of money a manufacturer may spend on behalf of a product and no limitations on the sources the manufacturer may tap to raise money—provided, of course, that the money is raised legally.

The Federal Election Campaign Act, as amended, was designed to minimize the influence of large anonymous contributors on government policy. The disclosure requirements were designed to ensure that the public would know to whom the candidates were indebted, personally and economically. The existence of these regulations makes it possible for news reporters to determine which industries are contributing more heavily to one candidate than another and to correlate politicians' voting behavior with the sources of their campaign financing.

Candidates are given a financial break in their purchase of broadcast media time by the Section 315 requirement mandating that, for forty-five days before a primary or for sixty days before a general election, charges for commercial time purchased to air political material may not exceed the lowest rate charged by the station for that class of time. This regulation puts political ads on the same economic footing as the ads of the largest advertisers who purchase huge blocks of time at a discount.

In 1970 the FCC added the Zapple Doctrine to its list of requirements for broadcasters. The Zapple Doctrine gives all legally qualified candidates the right to the same access to purchased time as any one political candidate. If a station sells time to one candidate, comparable time must be made available to opposing candidates who want to purchase it and can afford the purchase.

Many of the regulations we have discussed protect the public's access to political information. Because broadcasters are corporate entities whose existence is predicated on making a profit, they are naturally inclined to limit the amount of time made available to candidates at a rate below the normal selling rate; they are naturally reluctant to pre-empt a show like "L.A. Law" that produces high advertising revenues for a political broadcast that produces minimal revenue. The Zapple Doctrine and the affirmative right-to-access rules are designed to ensure that the corporate desire to maximize profits will not significantly impede the public's right to political information.

4. Herbert Alexander, "Rethinking Reform," in *Campaign Money* (New York: Free Press, 1976), pp. 1–2.

Election Deadlines: Politicians Pay More for Ads

An audit released by the FCC disclosed that during the first half of 1990, television and radio stations in Cincinnati, Dallas-Fort Worth, Philadelphia, San Francisco, and Portland (Oregon) have been charging political candidates significantly more than other customers to broadcast advertisements.

The FCC said that at 80 percent of the television stations and half of the radio stations it had audited, candidates paid more for broadcast time than other customers during virtually every time period of the day, including the vital slots before the evening news programs. At one unidentified station, candidates paid $4,000 for 30-second spots leading into the evening news, while other advertisers paid as little as $575 for such air time; in another city, candidates paid an average of $6,000 for a 30-second spot, while other advertisers paid an average of $2,713.

Broadcasters attacked the report, and television executives said the higher prices paid by political candidates were legitimate. The issue concerns distinctions between rates for "fixed" and for "pre-emptible" air time. Fixed rates, which are higher and are the sort politicians usually demand, guarantee that an advertiser's message will be broadcast at a particular time. A pre-emptible time spot allows a station to replace the scheduled ad at the last minute in favor of another who is willing to pay a higher price.

"Stations overbook time," said Richard Cerucci, vice president and general sales manager for KRON-TV in San Francisco, which is owned by the Chronicle Publishing Company. "All our other advertisers accept pre-emptibility. But the politicians come here and say they don't want to be treated like that. If someone wants to go in and not be pre-empted, they usually pay top of the line."[a]

Fearful that overcharging for political ads would become an issue at license renewal time, stations rolled back their rates in response to FCC findings, dropping their prices for political advertisements by 20 to 30 percent.[b]

[a] Edmund L. Andrews, "F.C.C. Broadcast Data Show Politicians Pay More for Ads," *New York Times*, 8 September 1990, pp. 17, 19 Y.

[b] Randall Rothenberg, "Usual Flurry of Election Ads Becomes Blizzard This Year," *New York Times*, 21 October 1990, p. 20 Y.

TO   SUM   UP

In this chapter we have examined the ways in which the politician's use of media differs from the manufacturer's. In the process we have touched on some of the unique constraints that govern the financing, creation, transmission, and reception of political messages. In the final chapter we will examine the ways in which the political candidate manipulates the media.

11

News and Advertising in the Political Campaign

The U.S. political process has produced few candidates whose images when in office differed shockingly from their campaign images A candidate knows she or he cannot entirely control the news coverage of the campaign. Because differences between the image projected in commercials and the actual behavior of the candidate are likely to be exposed in campaign reporting, commercials cannot stray too far from the truth about the candidate without great risk. Indeed, major campaign goals are creating a positive, electable image of the candidate, ensuring that the image is communicated consistently throughout the campaign, and that it is underscored by news coverage.

To accomplish these ends, the campaign staff attempts to: (1) control news coverage by controlling media access, setting the media's agenda, and creating credible pseudo-events; (2) blur the distinction between news and commercials in order to increase the credibility of the commercial's message; (3) exploit the linguistic categories reflecting criteria for newsworthiness and conventions of news presentations through which journalists view campaigns; (4) insulate the candidate from attack; and (5) enlist the help of journalists in responding to attacks.

Controlling News Coverage

Particularly when a candidate seeks the presidency, it is unlikely that serious character flaws or past misdeeds will evade public scrutiny. If a candidate's commercials create the image of a quiet, reasonable individual but the politician hurls ashtrays when unhappy with staff work, a disgruntled or indiscreet staff member is likely to point out the disparity to journalists. If the candidate is a womanizer but the campaign stresses his image as a good family man, reporters are likely to find out and, in one way or another, convey the contrast to the public.

Journalists have always been aware of discrepancies between image and actuality. Until recently, however, an unwritten journalistic code said that if the private activities of politicians did not affect their conduct in office they ought not be made public. During the 1982 centenary celebration of Franklin Delano Roosevelt's birth, reporters themselves focused attention on this changed standard by telling us that during FDR's four terms as president, news media hid the disabling effects of his polio from the public. An article in the *Washington Post*, for example, noted that in 1932 the press corps made no mention of FDR's fall when, during a speech in Georgia, the podium that was supposed to be bolted to the floor as a brace, slid forward. The same article reminded readers that "although he spent most of his waking hours either in or near a wheelchair, no photograph of this chair ever appeared in the papers or magazines during his lifetime."[1] Nor did newspeople reveal FDR's long-lived involvement with Lucy Mercer.

Similarly, reporters have known which members of Congress drink excessively, but such reports did not appear in the nation's newspapers until a stripper known as the "Argentine Firecracker" leapt from Wilbur Mills's car into the Washington Tidal Basin. This scandal was made public in an era in which investigative reporting revealed that one president lied about the Vietnam War, while another lied about his involvement in Watergate, and in which Theodore H. White's *Making of the President, 1960* legitimized an inside view of campaigns that focused on personal details about the candidates, their families, and the campaign decision-making process.

In this environment Senator Gary Hart's relationship with a young, attractive model became a focus of news coverage in the 1988 presidential primaries. After Hart dared the press to put a tail on him, promising that they'd find that he lived a dull life, the press did just that. Pictures of him aboard a luxury boat followed. On his knee was the model. In his hand, a drink. At an end: his presidential aspirations.

Candidates obviously want to minimize journalistic access to information that might contradict the image their campaigns are trying to convey. Strategies employed in this effort are examined in Chapter 4. Yet candidates are constantly being tripped up by news coverage of events they themselves supposedly controlled.

For example, on a cattle round-up, calculated to stress his masculine, Texas background, 1990 Republican gubernatorial candidate Clayton Williams commented to the assembled reporters that one should treat the advent of poor weather the way one should treat an inevitable rape—just lie back and enjoy it. The remark created a furor and raised questions about Williams' sensitivity to issues of special concern to women.

A candidate can also benefit from the image created by the media. Media focus on the Bushs' dog, Millie, added a dimension of humanity and warmth to

---

1. Hugh Gregory Gallagher, "FDR's Cover-Up: The Extent of His Handicap," *Washington Post*, 24 January 1982, p. D 4.

A Pollster's View

Patrick H. Caddell, pollster for President Jimmy Carter and other Democratic candidates, discussing Ronald Reagan's tightly regulated contacts with the press during the 1980 presidential campaign, said:

> The Reagan campaign has set a model. I would never be involved in another presidential campaign where the candidate was openly accessible to the press. As a campaign operative, this makes it easier for me. As an American citizen, I shudder to think what people like me would do. It's terrible for the country.[a]

[a]From *The Permanent Campaign* by Sidney Blumenthal, cited in the *New York Times*, 3 March 1983, p. 8 Y.

President Bush's persona that would have been denied him if the dog had not become a media favorite.

In order to increase the probability that what we see and hear in the news will be consistent with the campaign theme, politicians employ all available strategies for manipulating the press. We illustrate how these strategies have been used in past campaigns and demonstrate the incumbent's advantage in manipulating media.

Controlling Media Access

As we noted earlier, public officials routinely control press access as best they can. The issue becomes particularly sensitive in times of international crisis or war.

Setting the Media's Agenda

As Maxwell McCombs has argued persuasively, the news media do not tell us what to think as much as they tell us what to think about. From the thousands of events and persons that satisfy basic news norms, some move to the top of the media agenda. For example, from March through May 1990, the story that topped the news agenda with a total of 307 minutes of coverage on the ABC, CBS, and NBC weekday evening news was unrest among the USSR nationalities, including the tension in the Baltic states. The coverage of the Beirut hostages followed with 164 minutes of coverage.[2]

On any given day the president exercises more control over the news agenda than do most other public officials in the United States. An incumbent, particularly an incumbent president, has more control over setting this agenda than a challenger.

---

2. *Tyndall Report*, June 1990, p. 2.

Media focus on one topic can displace others. For example, in summer 1990, the press focus on the unfolding crisis in Iraq displaced headlines about President Bush's nomination of a Supreme Court candidate whose stand on abortion could not readily be discerned.

Creating Credible Pseudo-Events

Politicians routinely create pseudo-events, staged events designed for media coverage. In the last decade, reporters have become more skeptical of politicians—particularly since Joe McGinniss's *The Selling of the President, 1968* revealed the extent to which Richard Nixon had been packaged by media consultants in 1968. As a result, the artificial nature of such events and their explicit goal of media coverage are now pointed out by news people almost as a matter of journalistic honor.

Blurring the Distinction Between News and Commercials

Voters report that their voting decisions are more influenced by what they read, see, and hear in news, documentary, and public affairs programming than by what they gather from commercials. Such research is flawed by its reliance on self-report data. I am not likely to admit that I am influenced by something as crass and manipulative as a commercial when I can say instead that I was influenced by a more socially approved channel—news. In addition, it is likely that most of us are unaware of the primary channels influencing our decisions. In addition, channels influence each other, making it impossible to separate the influence of one from the others. Nevertheless, the mandated disclosure or tag reminds us that the source of the message is self-interested.

As a result, campaign commercials often are made to look as much like news as possible. Commercials may use actual news footage as San Francisco's former mayor Diane Feinstein did in the 1990 California gubernatorial race when her ads included a news clip of her announcing the murder of her predecessor. The news clip underscored Feinstein's theme: Tough and Caring.

Campaign commercials also use production techniques identified with news coverage. Cinéma vérité techniques such as hand-held cameras and natural lighting give the commercials the look of documentaries, for example. Formats we identify as those of public affairs programs also invest commercials with the credibility of news.

Print ads can also capitalize on the credibility of news sources by reprinting and distributing favorable media coverage of the candidate or by reproducing newspaper editorials endorsing the candidate. Alternatively, attack ads feature negative news clips about the opponent.

Slice-of-life commercials also resemble news clips. These commercials walk the viewer through part of the candidate's day, permitting voters to eavesdrop on exchanges with important people, overhear warm human exchanges with constituents or would-be supporters, and see the candidate with family. The difference between such a commercial and a comparable news item is in who controls the editing process. The commercial will not show the candidate making a mistake, being manipulated by staff, or exhibiting characteristics inconsistent with the image being projected in the other paid media. The news clip might well show all three.

In order to blur the distinction between news and commercials, the political ad will often bury its mandated disclosure at the bottom of the last frames, thus minimizing the likelihood that we will recall that what we heard or saw was sponsored by the campaign. In addition, campaign managers encourage us to remember advertised content as news content by placing their ads adjacent to news and public affairs programming. In summary, then, politicians deliberately blur the distinction between news and ads by placing their ads near news and employing newslike formats and newslike or news content in the ads themselves.

A candidate can attempt to obtain news coverage that will serve as advertising as well as news by creating a pseudo-event that plays both in news and as advertising. In 1988, for example, Republican presidential contender George Bush appeared at a rally surrounded by police. At the rally, one officer gave the vice president the police shield of the officer's son, a police officer killed in the line of duty. The scene replayed in news as well as Bush ads.

Exploiting Media Concepts of the Political Process

Like the rest of us, journalists see the world through language that limits what can be seen and how it will be interpreted. Some terminology used to describe the political process illustrates journalistic concepts of political campaigns and political candidates and also illustrates the criteria for newsworthiness discussed in Chapter 2.

The Campaign The media tend to see political campaigns as contests. The contest is described in battle metaphors, sports metaphors, or a combination of the two. If the electoral process is viewed as a game, it has contending sides, rules, and a goal.[3] Sports metaphors enable reporters to describe vividly the stages of the process (early primaries are the first innings or the first quarter), the intensity of the struggle (two outs in the ninth with the runner at bat, third down in the last quarter), the stakes (Super Bowl Sunday, the World Series), and the outcome (touchdown, home run).

Battle metaphors enable reporters to describe the staff and volunteers as troops, the primary as a battleground, the strategy as a process of mapping out options, and the outcome as analogous to such memorable names as Armageddon or Waterloo. Strategic options include a holding action, a retreat, a withdrawal, a first strike, or a pre-emptive strike. The outcome can be defeat, victory, or a rout. Candidates can declare a truce, sign an armistice, sign a peace treaty, declare war, or continue hostilities. Reporters can also dip into the biblical past to resurrect images of David and Goliath or, in the case of feuding among ideological kin, Cain and Abel. In 1988, for the first time in recent history, metaphors of the campaign as war occurred more often than sports metaphors.

---

3. For an excellent analysis of the function of metaphors in press coverage of the 1972 Democratic presidential campaign, see Jane Blankenship, "The Search for the 1972 Democratic Nomination: A Metaphoric Perspective," in *Rhetoric and Communication*, ed. Jane Blankenship and Hermann G. Stelzner (Urbana: University of Illinois Press, 1976), pp. 236–260.

The Candidates   In the linguistic world of the news media, there are front-runners, contenders, minor candidates, and also-rans. The criteria employed by reporters to determine to which category a candidate ought to be assigned vary from campaign to campaign. Before the Campaign Finance Law required that a candidate qualify in twenty states to receive matching funds, the presidential candidate with the most and the earliest "wins" was considered the front-runner. The new finance rules changed the criteria. To be a serious contender and not a minor candidate, a candidate has to qualify for matching funds.

Front-runners and contenders receive more news coverage than minor candidates and also-rans, and the type of coverage they receive differs. Also-rans are treated as human interest oddities. Their stands on issues are not probed; their chances of winning are not pondered. It is assumed they are going to lose.

Once classified a contender, a candidate is subject to comparison to past political figures. Is this candidate glamorous, dynamic, wealthy? Or cold, sneaky, untrustworthy? Like Roosevelt, Kennedy, Reagan, Nixon? Is this a common man like Truman? Or an innovator, a communicator, like FDR? Is this a bookish, intellectual candidate like Wilson or Stevenson? Democrats analogize Republicans to Hoover and Nixon; Republicans respond by tarring Democrats as Carteresque.

Candidates try to act so that journalists will associate their actions with those of admired historical figures such as Lincoln and FDR. They also identify with those people, places, and actions that the intended voters stereotype positively, and divorce themselves from those we negatively stereotype.

So, for example, in his successful 1990 campaign for the Democratic nomination for Cook County Board President, Richard Phelan sits at a "*Cheers*"-like bar, and tells how his parents "*sacrificed*" to enable him to study at *Notre Dame*. He worked at "*a one-lawyer firm*," he says and *built it* into one of the largest in the Midwest. "The *boys in the backroom*" carp about his success, he notes, but adds that that is because he plans to work *for the taxpayers* and not *the professional politicians*.

When a candidate succeeds in sculpting an image consistent with a stereotype, it begins to play out in press coverage. For example, a report in the *Washington Post* described the 1990 Republican Texas gubernatorial nominee this way:

> Williams, a West Texas millionaire oilman, is the most colorful political character to appear on the Lone Star scene in years. He brags about his fistfights, loves to drink beer, rides horses in his TV commercials, designs his swimming pools in the shape of cowboy boots, paints all his possessions, including two airplanes, in the maroon and white colors of his beloved Texas A & M Aggies, says he wants to double the state's prison capacity and get more criminals "pounding rocks," and talks wistfully about Texas the way it was when his Daddy was around.[4]

But stereotypes can cut two ways. When Williams refused to debate Democratic nominee Ann Richards, she told the press, "You can't pretend to be John Wayne and run from a girl."[5]

---

4. David Maraniss, "In GOP Race, Money Takes Lead," *Washington Post*, 10 February 1990, p. A 7.
5. *Dallas Morning News*, 17 August 1990, p. 18 A.

———

C A S E   S T U D Y
Presidential Advertising in the 1984 Campaign

"You have all the characteristics of a popular politician," sneered one of Aristophanes' characters at another, "a horrible voice, bad breeding, and a vulgar manner."

From ancient times, hyperbole has been a mainstay of politics, and humor has played a role as well. In the 1984 campaign some voters found comic relief in the Lyndon LaRouche ads that attacked Henry Kissinger as a Soviet agent and claimed that Moscow endorsed Gary Hart and Walter Mondale but hated LaRouche. Others smiled at Alan Cranston's claim that although he lacked charisma and was bald, he'd make a good president. Those presumed profligates in the other party felt the point of the humor in a Republican party ad. A father, his fist full of bills, was shown lecturing his son: "Son, you owe everybody money. . . . What are you planning to do with your life?" With a grin, the son replied: "Run for the House of Representatives." As a Democrat, of course. Once again, bumper stickers offered one-liners: "Honk If Mondale Promised You Anything" or "Jane Wyman Was Right."

In addition to hyperbole and humor, the campaign produced some intriguing innovations in political advertising. At the same time, the contest in the primaries both confirmed and cast doubt on the conventional wisdom about political advertising. The innovations included use of cable television to reach those most recently enfranchised and least likely to vote. MTV broadcast p.s.a.'s featuring such rock stars as Crosby, Stills, and Nash, Tina Turner, Kool and the Gang, the Pointer Sisters, and Cyndi Lauper. "Are your shoes too tight? Are your feet too small?" asked Lauper. Those surmising that she was selling shoes were in for a surprise. "Well," she concluded, "the answer to this and many other problems is to register and vote." Whether the result of altruism or of a desire to quell criticism of their cutbacks in convention coverage, the networks punctuated their reports of the conventions with appeals to viewers to register and vote. Because those who watch conventions faithfully are more, not less, likely to vote than is the public at large, MTV's campaign probably reached more nonvoters.

Efforts to inspire voting invite the question, Do would-be voters have sufficient information to ballot sensibly? How can we know enough to vote when, for example, "Peyton Place" and "Petticoat Junction" outdrew Barry Goldwater's televised conversation with Ike in 1964 and *Jaws* swallowed a much larger bite of the audience than did Roger Mudd's "Teddy" in 1979?

But although everybody complains about voters' avoidance of meaty messages, in 1984 politicians did something about it. For instance, independent Democrat Lyndon LaRouche used spot ads to promote viewing of his late-night half-hour broadcast on "the coming food shortage in America." And the Ronald Reagan campaign frustrated channel-switchers by launching its general election ad campaign with a half-hour documentary aired simultaneously on all three networks. Ads for Mondale and for the National Conservative Political Action Committee (NCPAC) provided viewers with a number to call for more information or to volunteer time or money.

Lessons also lurk in the use and nonuse of ads in the primaries. When he lost in New York after outspending Mondale two-to-one, Gary Hart confirmed what John

(continued)

Connolly had found in 1980: money can't buy either love or victory if the messages about the candidate in such unpaid formats as news and debates contradict those in ads.

But if some old truths found new validity in Hart's experience in New York, others, such as the belief in the indispensability of advertising in a presidential campaign, were dispatched by Jesse Jackson's campaign. Backed by a smattering of print ads in New York and a handful of broadcast ads in his native Chicago, but blessed with a talent for phrase-making and with the free exposure that came with an unprecedented number of debates, the Reverend Jesse Jackson garnered enough votes in enough states to retain matching funds week after week. Requiring 20 percent of the vote in one of the last five primaries to retain federal funds, Jackson finally mounted an ad campaign. But here, too, he defied predictions. Articulate candidates usually appear in their own ads. In Jackson's, actor Martin Sheen turned the viewers' focus to the message "Jackson Speaks for Me."

Among the ironies of the 1984 primaries was the success with which some ads sabotaged their intended beneficiaries. Mondale's early ads did this by presupposing the inevitability of his nomination and by implying his indebtedness to groups his opponents would characterize as "special interests." In one ad, Mondale declared, "I am ready. I am ready to be president," a conclusion better left to be drawn by the electorate. Among the groups he promised to stand up for were "American workers," a phrase too readily interpreted as "American labor unions."

Hart also was the victim of his own ads. In New York, his ads were critical of Mondale, although in unpaid formats Hart was conciliatory. When paid and unpaid messages conflict, the credibility of the ads is undercut. When news and ads are consistent, the effect of both is magnified.

Walter Mondale gained a second advantage in the New York primary. By framing the central issue of the campaign as "Where's the beef?" he asked a question answered by his ads but not by Hart's. Indeed the form and content of Hart's television spots reinforced Mondale's claims that the Colorado Senator's positions had shifted and that his campaign lacked substance. The high-tech look of Hart's ads, which in the early primaries had effectively differentiated his message from those of his rivals, now hinted that perhaps he was all style and no substance. The futuristic ads showed a computer grid extending from the bottom of the screen toward infinity. Above it, boxed into the center of the screen, was Hart speaking to voters. As he spoke, the boxed image of him peeled back again and again, suggesting visually that there were many different Harts or many different Hart positions on the same issue. The problem was compounded when the spot ads stressed new ideas and new leadership without specifying the substance of either.

In a half-hour speech by the candidate, the Hart campaign finally did supply the beef demanded by Mondale's appropriation of the Wendy's slogan. But because the speech was delivered at 11:30 P.M. with little preliminary fanfare, it couldn't do the job Hart's candidacy required of it. Meanwhile, Mondale's New York ads bathed voters in the sort of detailed information that is the trademark of David Garth, the ads' producer. So, whereas Hart's ads suggested style, Mondale's suggested substance.

The candidates weren't the only ones whose advertising backfired. A NCPAC ad holds the distinction of having failed by succeeding too well. Intending to soften Mondale up for a general election kill, NCPAC, in the final week of the New Hampshire campaign, aired an ad in which viewers were invited to overhear two of Mondale's supposed advisers plotting the strategy that would elect him. After laughing down suggestions that people would vote for him because he owed the special interests nothing or because he could manage the economy, the "advisers" concluded that they might try arguing that he was nice to his mother and his dog. The ad underscored the attacks found in John Glenn's ads and heard in the first debate. By attacking Mondale so effectively, NCPAC succeeded in making Hart the alternative on the Democratic ticket. But Hart was a stronger contender against Reagan than Mondale. NCPAC realized that it might have hurt a weaker contender (Mondale), whom Reagan could readily beat, while helping one who could put up a better fight. The ad was shelved. It was revived later for the general election assault on Mondale.

Again and again the primaries demonstrated how crucial news events are in the political equation. In Illinois, Hart made news by ordering his staff to pull an ad that criticized Mondale's alliance with Chicago alderman Edward Vrdolyak. In the process, of course, he magnified the impact of the mistake and called attention to the inability of his staff to speedily execute his orders. The same sort of situation occurred when Hart attacked Mondale for airing what turned out to be a nonexistent ad that supposedly criticized Hart's changes of age and name. When Hart apologized, that apology dominated the news. In the process the apology reminded voters of the name and age change and underscored a central claim in one of Mondale's ads: that Hart was untested and unsteady.

In recent times, campaigns routinely have previewed their ads for the press. They do this to give the ads wide exposure in a credible news environment at no cost. When reporters panned Reagan's spring run of "feel good" ads, his advisers reconsidered the wisdom of airing them. Accordingly, the half-hour documentary aired in September was not previewed. Free exposure also proved damaging to an independent committee.

Through the use of an ad featuring Anne (Gorsuch) Burford at a press conference, NCPAC secured thousands of dollars of free but probably counterproductive exposure. In the ad, Burford raised questions about Geraldine Ferraro's failure "to disclose her husband's finances even though she is an officer in her husband's company." "Come on, Ms. Ferraro," she asked, "what are you trying to hide?" Only a very few dedicated conservatives viewed Burford as an asset to Reagan. So confident were the Democrats that she was an albatross that they had previously included her photo with those of Charles Wick, James Watt, and others in an ad claiming that the Reagan Administration had produced the "most scandal-tainted officials that we've seen since Richard Nixon and Watergate."

In sum, the interplay between news and ads, "free time" and "paid time," is complex. A student of the 1984 campaign could not understand a candidate's use of one without understanding the other.

CASE STUDY
Campaigns as Seen Through Their Slogans or Themes

The essence of a well-conceived political campaign is distilled in its advertising; the essence of its advertising is distilled in a slogan or theme reflecting the campaign's core by answering the questions, "Why is this candidate running?" and "Why should I vote for this candidate?"

In the 1960 presidential campaign, for instance, Richard Nixon and his vice-presidential running mate Henry Cabot Lodge summed up their campaign in the slogan, "Nixon–Lodge: They Understand What Peace Demands." The advertising slogan revealed that unlike Lyndon Johnson, John Kennedy's running mate, Lodge was a central part of the argument for the election of Nixon. Kennedy's slogan, "Leadership for the 60's," did not mention Johnson and, except for a millisecond glimpse of LBJ's picture on a placard in a televised ad designed both to build name recognition for Kennedy and to create a bandwagon for the Democratic ticket, LBJ was conspicuously absent from national televised advertising.

By contrast, Lodge—his height dwarfing Nixon—not only was featured in the still photograph that closed each Republican ad but also starred in a series of ads. What the 1960 ads reflect is the respective functions of Lodge and Johnson in the campaign. Lodge appeared in nationally aired ads because he strengthened the ticket throughout the country. Johnson's value was primarily regional; consequently, as a campaigner, he concentrated his time on rallying the South behind the Democratic ticket.

The Nixon–Lodge slogan also indicates that the campaign stressed the comparative advantage the Republican ticket offered in foreign policy from Lodge's U.N. ambassadorship and Nixon's vice-presidential experience. Consistent with the campaign theme, televised ads for Nixon translated questions of domestic policy into questions of foreign policy. In one ad, for example, a disembodied voice asked, "Mr. Nixon, what is the truth? Is America lagging behind in economic growth?" Nixon, seated on a desk, assures the viewer that the U.S. economy is healthy, and adds: "This is the kind of economic growth we must have to keep the peace." Each ad closed with the tag "Nixon–Lodge: They Understand What Peace Demands."

Consistent with his theme, Kennedy's opening statement in the first Kennedy–Nixon debate focused the election on domestic questions:

> In the election of 1860, Abraham Lincoln said the question was whether this nation could exist half-slave or half-free. In the election of 1960, and with the world around us, the question is whether the world will exist half-slave or half-free, whether it will move in the direction of freedom, in the direction of the road we are taking, or whether it will move in the direction of slavery. I think it will depend in great measure upon what we do here in the United States, on the kind of society that we build, on the kind of strength that we maintain.

Kennedy asked that we get the country moving again. By contrast, Nixon stressed that we were stronger than ever and that the Republicans had kept the peace:

> There is no question but that we cannot discuss our internal affairs in the United States without recognizing that they have a tremendous bearing on our

international position. There is no question but that this nation cannot stand still; because we are in deadly competition, a competition not only with the men in the Kremlin, but the men in Peking. We're ahead in this competition, as Senator Kennedy, I think, has implied. But when you're in a race, the only way to stay ahead is to move ahead.

Each campaign had created a theme and a slogan consistent with the background and perceived strengths of its candidates. Kennedy's service in the Senate had provided no real foreign policy experience. Consequently, he stressed domestic affairs. Nixon could have stressed domestic affairs, but with the country in a recession, he had a stronger case if he stressed what was, for that ticket, a strength as well as Kennedy's weakness—foreign affairs. The theme chosen by Nixon explains Lodge's importance in the campaign and why he appeared in televised ads. Ads were created that recalled memorable moments from Lodge's U.N. service—his challenge to the Soviets over the presence of bugging devices in a U.S. office, for example.

An effective campaign slogan tells the audience what a vote for the candidate means, and it sums up the content of the candidate's advertising. In addition, an effective campaign slogan cannot be used to attack the candidate, and it is believable to voters.

Telling the Audience What a Vote Means

George Wallace, former governor of Alabama, was a potent force in the 1968 presidential election, where, running as a third-party candidate, he won almost 10 million votes. Wallace might have been a decisive factor in the 1972 presidential campaign had he not been shot and incapacitated during the Maryland primary campaign. His message in each of his tries for the presidency was simple and direct: "Send Them a Message."

A vote for Wallace was a message. But what was the message? In 1968 his commercials asked whether you were satisfied seeing your dollars sent to unsympathetic regimes, whether you were satisfied with crime ridden neighborhoods, whether you were satisfied to see your children bused miles from home in order to attend school? If you were not, a vote for Wallace signaled your dissatisfaction.

Wallace's anti-big government, anti-intellectual, anti-bureaucratic appeals prefigured those that Jimmy Carter would successfully parlay into victory in 1976. In his speeches, Wallace wondered aloud what bureaucrats packed in those big black briefcases and speculated that if you opened one of them you'd probably find the *New York Times* and a peanut butter sandwich. According to Wallace, pointy-headed bureaucrats couldn't even park a bicycle straight, yet dared to meddle in the lives of working people. These statements revealed that the "them" of the slogan were the Washington establishment and federal bureaucrats. By framing the election as a contest of "us" (Wallace and his supporters) against "them" (the Washington establishment), the slogan provided a symbol consistent with the other rhetoric of the Wallace campaign.

Because the press labeled Wallace a spoiler and speculated on whether he would capture enough of the vote to send the 1968 election to the House of Representatives, Wallace needed to insulate himself against the suggestion that a vote for him would be wasted. The slogan accomplished this goal. The reason for supporting Wallace was not necessarily to get him elected but to send a message to the person elected and to other elected officials—that Wallace's constituency must be taken

(continued)

---

seriously and accommodated. A slogan like LBJ's 1964 slogan, "The Stakes Are Too High for You to Stay Home," would not work for a candidate who was not regarded as having a serious chance of winning. LBJ's slogan is the sort useful only to a candidate who has a realistic chance of becoming president. "Send Them a Message" enabled Wallace to redefine the meaning of voting. A vote for Wallace might not elect him (although Wallace never discounted that possibility); rather, the message the vote carried would affect the behavior of those elected.

A campaign slogan can send a subtle, even unintended message. In his campaign for the position of mayor of Los Angeles, Tom Bradley, an African-American former police officer, used the slogan "He'll Work as Hard for His Paycheck as You Do for Yours." The slogan was a message to whites that he would represent both whites and African-Americans and a message to those who feared he would sell out the city to welfare recipients that he believed in the work ethic. According to Jeff Greenfield (one of David Garth's associates and now an ABC news personality), what the media advisor in the Bradley campaign and his associates were trying to say with the slogan was: "(a) Yorty [Bradley's opponent] wasn't working for his salary, (b) Bradley would earn the job of mayor, (c) Bradley understood the premises of the work ethic and was no permissive open-the-treasury welfare enthusiast, (d) Bradley understands how hard you, the typical voter, work for your paycheck because *he is one of you.*"[b]

Bradley won in a landslide. The slogan was a prism through which the campaign could be viewed: it provided a reason to vote against Yorty and a number of reasons to vote for Bradley; it reassured voters who required assurance; and it identified Bradley with an important subsection of his audience—workers. The ads in the campaign were consistent with the slogan. They stressed Bradley's accomplishments and in the process demonstrated that in the past he had worked hard for his paycheck and had worked for things the voters supported.

Summarizing the Campaign's Advertising

The slogans used in the Kennedy and Nixon campaigns of 1960 offered reasons for voting *for* the ticket. Slogans can be directed against the opposing ticket as well. Lyndon Johnson's 1964 presidential campaign slogan was "Vote Johnson November 3. The Stakes Are Too High for You to Stay Home." The slogan implies a special urgency about the 1964 election. If "you" stay home and do not vote for Johnson, catastrophe may result. The slogan also reveals the campaign's concern that projections of a Johnson landslide would lull Johnson supporters into complacency. If all of Goldwater's supporters voted and most of Johnson's supporters stayed home, Goldwater could win the election. In a campaign with a slogan about the urgency of voting, we would expect to find commercials advocating voting. In the Johnson cam-

[b]Jeff Greenfield, *Playing to Win: An Insider's Guide to Politics* (New York: Simon & Schuster, 1980), p. 85.

paign, for example, a commercial showed a man with an umbrella plunging through a downpour to get to the polls. The ad said, "If it rains on November 3, get wet. The Stakes Are Too High for You to Stay Home."

Just as the commercials run on behalf of Nixon and Kennedy in 1960 were summarized by the slogans of each campaign, so, too, the slogan used by the 1964 Johnson campaign previewed and summarized the thrust of the ads run for Johnson. In 5-minute commercials Johnson argued that, like other presidents before him, Republicans as well as Democrats, he was committed to keeping the peace. The implication, of course, was that Goldwater was not.

The famous daisy commercial made that implication explicit in the minds of auditors who read into an otherwise benign ad the conclusion that it was "trigger-happy," "shoot from the hip" Goldwater who would blow the little girl up. The ad did not explicitly make that claim, but simply showed a child in a field picking daisies as she counts from one to ten, slightly out of sequence, a sign of the genius of the ad's creator Tony Schwartz, who realized that children rarely count linearly. As the child reaches "ten," a voice from one of the satellite launch countdowns intones "Ten, nine, eight . . ." When the voice reaches "zero," the girl is replaced on the screen by an exploding bomb, and we hear Lyndon Johnson's voice saying that we must learn to love one another or we will surely perish. The tag then appears as the announcer's voice declares "Vote Johnson November 3. The Stakes Are Too High for You to Stay Home." The tag prompted the audience to read Goldwater into the ad

Other ads more explicitly provided the evidence that the daisy commercial left implicit. One ad for Johnson noted that Barry Goldwater had described the nuclear bomb as "merely another weapon." The announcer's incredulous voice then repeats, "Merely another weapon?" The ads for Johnson also argued that the stakes were too high domestically. One ad showed a Social Security card being torn apart as the announcer informed the audience that even William Miller, Goldwater's running mate, had claimed that electing Goldwater would mean the end of Social Security as we know it. A series of visually compelling production ads insinuated that Goldwater could not be trusted with the presidency. One of these ads purported to show the auction of the Tennessee Valley Authority, a dramatic illustration of Goldwater's suggestion that the TVA be sold. Another showed a model of the map of the United States suspended over water. As a saw loudly severed the eastern seaboard off the map, the announcer reminded the audience of Goldwater's statement that perhaps "we ought to cut off the eastern seaboard and let it float out to sea." "Can a man who would say that really be trusted to serve all the people, justly and fairly?" the ad asked. The Johnson campaign aired ad after ad to reinforce the same claim—that a vote for Goldwater was a risky exercise in a high stakes venture. The ads raised voters' anxiety about Goldwater's stands on issues and then reduced that anxiety by assuring viewers that a victory for Johnson would avert such catastrophes.

Some slogans are too imprecise to accomplish any of these purposes. In 1984, Democrats Mondale and Ferraro campaigned on the slogan "Mondale: Ferraro: Fighting for Your Future." Neither the slogan nor the advertising to which it was attached revealed the nature of that future. The same problem plagued the 1988 Democratic slogan "The Best America is Yet to Come." Not only did that tag fail to define the future America but it also was a slogan equally applicable to the Republican ticket.

Spending by PACs

In 1988 PACs contributed $150 million to political candidates for federal office. Whereas in 1980, 29 percent of the funding for congressional races had come from PACs, by 1988 that figure had risen to 41 percent.[c]

"Charles Keating Jr., principal owner of the failed Lincoln Savings and Loan Association, channeled more than several hundred thousand dollars in campaign contributions to five U.S. Senators. Dubbed the 'Keating Five,' the senators intervened as a group in April 1987 on Keating's behalf with government regulators who were examining alleged violations by Lincoln Savings. It took another two years for examiners to finally seize Lincoln—a delay that will cost taxpayers an estimated $1.3 billion. When Keating was asked whether his contributions influenced political figures to take up his cause, he responded, 'I want to say in the most forceful way I can: I certainly hope so.'"[d]

Common Cause used these instances to lobby for reform. The postcard reproduced on page 277 was part of this campaign.

[c] Federal Election Commission, August 1990.
[d] *Common Cause Magazine*, January/February 1990, p. 43.

Responding to or Preventing Attack

The prime function of an attack is to discredit an opponent. This is usually accomplished by casting suspicion on an opponent's campaign theme or by raising doubts about an opponent that can be corroborated by news channels. The danger in attacking an opponent is that the politician attacking, rather than the opponent, will be discredited.

Fear of backlash limits the attacks in a typical political campaign. A politician who violates our standards of fair play invites the judgment that she or he is not to be trusted with the office sought. But fear of backlash restrains behavior only when the person attacking is identified with the candidate running for office. The rise of independent political action committees, such as the National Conservative Political Action Committee (NCPAC), removes this powerful constraint from the electoral process because, by law, PACs must function independently. Thus it is possible for a PAC to attack one candidate without creating a backlash against the candidate who benefits from the attacks. Consequently, those attacked by an independent political action committee seek to link the PAC to the opponent.

If this can be done successfully, then any backlash resulting from the attack will hurt the opponent. If the reaction hurts only the PAC and not the politician who benefits from the attack, there is no restraining force controlling attacks because no one accountable to the electorate is held responsible for them. So, for example, the most controversial political ads of 1988, those featuring furloughed murderer Willie Horton, were sponsored not by the Bush campaign but by a pro-Republican Political Action Committee.

PLACE
25¢ STAMP
HERE

Name _____
Address _____
City _____ State ____ Zip _____

Representative _____
U.S. House of Representatives
Washington, D.C. 20515

Take the Keating Test.

Dear Representative _____
Will you support the key reforms necessary to clean up congressional campaigns and end influence-money abuses like the Savings & Loan scandal involving Charles H. Keating Jr., the "Keating Five" Senators and $1.3 million in political donations? Take the Keating Test!

YES NO
☐ ☐ **DO YOU AGREE** that "soft money" contributions must be banned to prevent "fat cat" contributors, like S&L owner Charles Keating, corporations and labor unions from making contributions of $100,000 or more to support presidential and congressional candidates?

YES NO
☐ ☐ **DO YOU AGREE** that limits on sky-rocketing campaign spending must be established to stop the never-ending chase for campaign contributions that sends Members of Congress running to private interests like Charles Keating and the PACs for political money?

YES NO
☐ ☐ **DO YOU AGREE** that political action committee (PAC) contributions to congressional candidates must be dramatically reduced to prevent special interests, like the S&L industry, from contributing huge amounts of influence money to Members of Congress?

YES NO
☐ ☐ **DO YOU AGREE** that alternative campaign funds must be provided to ensure that "clean" campaign resources, such as public matching funds and low-cost mailings, are available so Members of Congress aren't dependent on influence-seekers?

YES NO
☐ ☐ Will you support and fight for these reforms necessary to end influence-money abuses like the "Keating Five" Affair and restore the credibility of Congress?

Sincerely,

_____

PRINTED BY COMMON CAUSE · 2030 M STREET NW · WASHINGTON, D.C. 20036

Reprinted by permission of Common Cause.

In general, candidates who are ahead in the polls and who anticipate winning do not attack their opponents. An attack invites reply and media coverage of the reply. This legitimizes the opponent and provides the opponent with media access. Counterattack is a legitimizing strategy that tacitly assumes comparable stature. Why would a politician waste time attacking someone who was totally inconsequential and no real threat to the politician's election?

Last-Minute Attacks

Not surprisingly, the sorts of attacks that have difficulty withstanding journalistic scrutiny tend to appear late in a campaign. In such circumstances the political system works for the attacker and against the candidate attacked. Because stations may not censor political ads, the burden of proof falls on the person attacked. If a lie is carefully worded, the burden of establishing its falsity can divert the time and attention of the attacked candidate's top-level campaign strategists who, in the final days of a campaign, ought to be concentrating on getting out the vote. In such circumstances, a well-financed campaign with a skilled media consultant has at least the chance of placing responsive or counteractive ads on the air. A poorly financed campaign must rely on the investigative tendencies of reporters and the sympathies of columnists.

When the Fair Campaign Practices Committee was still functioning, an injured candidate could appeal to it for a determination of whether an ad was fair or not. Newspeople then reported the complaint and the resolution. No functioning independent national group now exists to police the fairness of campaign tactics.

The difficulty in dealing with last-minute attacks is compounded by the fact that an attack ad can run for a full day or more before the attacked candidate knows about it. Once alerted to its existence, the campaign staff must spend time securing a copy. Additional time is required to document its falsity. If the attack campaign includes many ads, the burden is increased proportionately.

If the candidate decides to use a news conference to expose and reply to the attack ads, schedules must be cleared, an appropriate location secured, and the media alerted—all of which take time. Meanwhile, the candidate's staff must develop a strategy to counter the ads. Under such pressure, strategic errors are likely to occur. Perhaps the candidate will be panicked into refuting ads that have reached few voters. Such a move enlarges the opponent's audience. Perhaps the candidate's rebuttal will seem histrionic and discredit him or her. Finally, given the time pressure, there is a danger that even if they are exposed as false by journalists, the attack ads will have reached more people than the rebuttal. There may not be time for a backlash to build against the attacker, and the sight of two candidates battling it out over the truth of the ads may drive voters to a third candidate not contaminated by the controversy.

Utilizing Blunders

At some point in their political lives, most public figures have said something they regret. These blunders are often newsworthy not only because they reveal a previously unknown fact but also because they express a candidate's position succinctly. In 1976, presidential candidate Reagan made the mistake of attaching a specific figure to the amount of money that could be cut from the federal budget. The gaffe was a headline writer's dream: "The Ninety Billion Dollar Blunder." The statement was newsworthy not simply because Reagan was newsworthy as a candidate but also because it was brief, concise, specific, concrete, and dramatic. It haunted Reagan through the rest of the campaign.

Similarly, when presidential aspirant George Romney returned from Vietnam in 1968 and admitted that he had been "brainwashed," the dramatic, newsworthy nature of the claim, summed up in one word, effectively disqualified Romney from serious consideration. After all, how could we elect a president who had been brainwashed? In retrospect, what distinguished Romney from the other candidates was his ability to see the delusionary process and his forthright admission that he had been susceptible to it. But, for practical purposes, in the 1968 New Hampshire primary Romney was the brainwashed candidate.

When a prominent candidate makes this sort of slip, it receives news coverage. By incorporating reminders of the gaffe in attack commercials, the candidate's opponents can keep the charge alive and make it a focal factor in voting decisions. The "revolving-door prison furlough program" ad that the Republicans aired against Democratic nominee Michael Dukakis drew its power from the furlough of Willie Horton during Dukakis's term and then Dukakis's resistance to public calls for change in the law and his refusal to meet with Horton's victims or apologize to them.

When an attack ad replays an opponent's blunder, it is often to make the mistake concrete for the audiences. For example, in a 1976 commercial Gerald Ford reminded workers gathered around him that Carter had promised to lower taxes for those below the median income and raise taxes for those above the median income. But the median income in this country turned out to be lower than Carter had imagined. Ford then said that he didn't think the people surrounding him needed to have their taxes raised.

When the blunder is not a concise synthetic statement but part of a long rambling answer to a question, it cannot be used as effectively either in news or in an ad. A commercial that opens in the middle of an opponent's sentence or cuts from the sentence before it is finished invites us to conclude that the statement has been taken out of context. This saved Ronald Reagan from hearing replays of his 1976 statement that he might order the use of troops in Rhodesia. (The statement came in the middle of a long, rambling, involved answer that did not lend itself to use in an opponent's commercial.) Instead, the Ford campaign assumed audience familiarity with the statement and created an ad that stated "Governor Reagan couldn't start a war. President Reagan could."

Attacks Legitimized by the Media

News and ads are not the only outlets for, or sources of, attacks in political campaigns. Editorial cartoons, political columns, and comic monologues are among the other sources of attacks over which a candidate exercises no direct control and which are especially difficult for a candidate to counter effectively.

A political attack appearing in a comic strip is effective because it appears in a context that does not ordinarily provoke critical responses in us. We expect to be entertained, so we relax our guard. The same is true of the political humor in Johnny Carson's monologues. Audiences laugh and, in the process, accept the premises underlying the jokes. Occasionally, when a newspaper comic strip becomes too blatantly political, the editors will move it from the comic section to the editorial page. This was done with Al Capp's "Li'l Abner" in the 1960s and with Garry Trudeau's "Doonesbury" in the 1980s. Occasionally newspapers drop "offending" cartoons altogether or selectively delete them when the message proves distasteful or controversial.

The nature of humor is such that a cartoonist or a comedian will tend to reinforce existing attitudes rather than create new ones. When audiences fail to laugh at a certain type of joke, that joke is quickly dropped. This ensures that Johnny Carson will underscore, not initiate, attacks.

Editorial cartoonists have more latitude than any other source in the broadcast or print industry. Because their content is primarily visual, they are not readily subjected to tests for truth that, as we have indicated earlier, are most suited to assessing verbal statements of factual propositions. So, for example, when one editorial cartoonist wanted to make the claim that Reagan's Secretary of the Interior was not interested in protecting wildlife, he showed James Watt at a desk with Bambi's stuffed head decorating the wall. The claim in the drawing, which can be comprehended in seconds, is stronger, clearer, and more damning than any of the columns of ponderous prose that defended a milder version of the same claim in deadly—and probably unread—detail.

The effectiveness of such cartoons poses problems for attacked candidates. If a candidate is attacked in an editorial, a newspaper column, or an opinion editorial (op-ed), he or she may appeal to the newspaper for space to respond. Unlike the broadcast media, newspapers are under no legal obligation to permit reply. Nonetheless, most newspapers will give an aggrieved party who has been directly attacked space in an op-ed or in the letters-to-the-editor column. The controversy adds excitement to the paper and holds readership. Presenting both sides creates a sense that the newspaper is fair and responsive to the interests and needs of the community, so it is in the newspaper's self-interest to permit a person attacked in its pages the opportunity to respond. But there is no effective way to respond to an editorial cartoon.

The national syndication of cartoons and columns means that when an attack occurs or misinformation is published, the impact is widespread. A column by nationally syndicated *New York Times* columnist William Safire will reach some audience in every major city in the country. Someone attacked by Safire who wants to respond to a column and does not have access to the syndication service will have to deal directly with hundreds of op-ed page editors across the country.

Editors occasionally refuse to print a regular column when, in their judgment, it has overstepped professional boundaries. Jack Anderson's free-wheeling columns, on occasion, have failed to appear in the *Washington Post*, for example. Columnists also police themselves. When Anderson learned that vice-presidential candidate Thomas Eagleton had not been convicted of drunken driving as Anderson had claimed, he admitted the error and apologized. It is difficult to determine what damage was done by the false charge.

Enlisting the Help of Journalists

The material used in attacks against a candidate is often culled from the public record. The most accessible channels that preserve the public record are often the print and broadcast media. Consequently, any political figure has a vested interest in accurate reporting about his or her activities. If uncorrected, misinterpretations by journalists can be resurrected for use against a candidate.

Reporters have access to those who have followed the careers of both candidates and to the public record of both candidates' activities, as reported by journalists in past stories and broadcasts. Thus, it is often a reporter or columnist who is in the best position to determine the accuracy of an attack. Because interpreting the meaning of a candidate's voting record is a complex process involving analysis of many substantively meaningless procedural votes, it is often the knowledgeable columnist or reporter who alerts the public that, although an attack is a technically accurate report of a procedural vote, it misrepresents the actual position of the attacked candidate.

So, for example, nationally syndicated columnist George Will evaluated charges made by senatorial aspirant Bruce F. Caputo against incumbent Senator Daniel Patrick Moynihan and concluded: "Caputo asserts that Moynihan 'voted against capital punishment.' Moynihan favors capital punishment for certain crimes. There has been no direct vote on capital punishment since Moynihan entered the Senate. Caputo is referring to procedural votes that reveal more about the parliamentary context at the time than Moynihan's views on the subject."[6]

When candidates believe they have been unfairly attacked, they often attempt to enlist the aid of the media in combating the attack. Journalists can be drawn into the campaign as arbiters of the truth or falsity of attacks by the attacker, the person attacked, or by the interchange itself.

After the 1988 campaign, academic conferences around the country raised the question, "Why had the press not pointed out the distortions and the false inferences invited by the 1988 presidential candidates' ads?" Among these were the implications of a Dukakis ad that George Bush would all but eliminate Social Security, and the implications of a Bush ad that Dukakis had released a large number of first-degree murderers to kill and rape again.

Newspapers responded by printing the texts of 1990 ads in their entirety and then documenting the facts as the reporters knew them. For example, when an ad for Texas Democratic gubernatorial candidate Ann Richards claimed that her opponent had "mountains of debt," the *Dallas Morning News* boxed the following information: "The Midland entrepreneur has borrowed extensively over the years to develop his oil, ranching and long distance telephone enterprises. And he has seen his net worth fall by almost two-thirds since 1982, according to a review of his business dealings by the *Dallas Morning News*. Still, the *News* puts Mr. Williams' net worth at about $116 million, concentrated in oil and gas properties."[7]

Political commercials also reveal their creators' perception that material culled from news reports constitutes credible evidence. Hard-hitting attack spots

6. George Will, "The Things Bruce Caputo Says," *Washington Post*, 28 February 1982, p. B 7.
7. *Dallas Morning News*, 17 August 1990, p. 18 A.

quoting an opponent's stand are often insulated from journalistic attack by their use of actual quotations from newspaper articles or television coverage to document their claims.

Tests of Credibility Applied by Journalists

Journalists are uniquely sensitive to changes in a candidate's position.[8] Consistency is one of the categories reporters use to test a candidate and a campaign. If the candidate is a prominent one or the election an important one, the meaning of the change in position will be probed. Throughout his 1988 presidential bid, George Bush repeated the promise: "Read My Lips: No New Taxes." When in summer 1990, he concluded that new tax revenues were in fact needed, the switch in positions provided fodder for editorial cartoonists and dominated three days of broadcast and print coverage.

Journalists focus so tightly on consistency because it is easy to test and because it lends itself to the behind-the-scenes-of-the-campaign perspective with which reporters are comfortable. By focusing on inconsistency, newspeople provide credible evidence for opponents to use in attacking the inconsistent candidate.

Charges of inconsistency can be damaging for a reason implied in the closing statement of an ad that Democrats for Nixon ran in 1972 against George McGovern. The ad asked, "Last year . . . this year . . . what about next year?" The tactic is commonplace in races at all levels. In spring 1990, Republican gubernatorial contender Clayton Williams aired ads asking how one could know where his fellow Republican aspirant Ken Hance actually stood. The ad opens with blurry pictures. The announcer intones: "There are two candidates for governor who can't seem to agree on anything." The ad proceeds to document their contradictory stands on issues. As the pictures come into focus, the announcer notes: "The trouble is . . . they're both Ken Hance." If a candidate has changed on important issues in the past, what assurance have we that the candidate will not change on those issues that make him or her attractive to us?

How Has Television Changed Politics?

■

Television has changed politics by changing the way in which information is disseminated, by altering the way politics happens, and by changing our patterns of response to politics. By giving the electorate direct access to the candidates, television diminished the role of party in the selection of the major party nominees. By centering politics on the person of the candidate, television accelerated the electorate's focus on character rather than issues.

Television has altered the forms of political communication, as well. The messages on which most of us rely are briefer than they once were. The stump speech of $1\frac{1}{2}$ to 2 hours that characterized nineteenth-century political discourse has given way to the 30-second spot ad and the 10-second sound bite in broadcast

---

8. Donald R. Matthews, "The News Media and the 1976 Presidential Nominations," in *Race for the Presidency*, ed. James David Barber (Englewood Cliffs, N.J.: Prentice-Hall, 1978), p. 67.

news. Increasingly the audience for speeches is not that standing in front of the politician but the viewing audience that will hear and see a snippet of the speech on the news.

In these abbreviated forms, much of what constituted the traditional political discourse of earlier ages has been lost. In 15 or 30 seconds, a speaker cannot establish the historical context that shaped the issue in question, cannot detail the probable causes of the problem, cannot examine alternative proposals and argue that one is preferable to others. In snippets, politicians assert but do not argue.

Because television is an intimate medium, speaking through it required a changed political style that was more conversational, personal, and visual than that of old-style stump oratory. Reliance on television means that increasingly our political world contains memorable pictures rather than memorable words. And words increasingly have been spoken in places chosen to heighten their impact. "We have nothing to fear but fear itself" has given way to "Let them come to Berlin" and "Mr. Gorbachev, tear down this wall." Schools teach us to analyze words and print; in a world in which politics is increasingly visual, informed citizenship requires a new set of skills.

Recognizing the power of television's pictures, politicians craft televisual, staged events called pseudo-events designed to attract media coverage. Much of the political activity we see on television news has been crafted by politicians, their speechwriters, and their public relations advisers for televised consumption. Sound bites in news and answers to questions in debates increasingly sound like ads.

Political managers, termed "handlers" in 1988, spend large amounts of time ensuring that their clients appear in visually compelling settings so that the pictures seen in news will reinforce those seen in ads. In debates, candidates recall those staged pseudo-events.

By focusing on mainstream values, television mainstreams its viewers. Heavy viewers of television differ from light viewers in some politically relevant ways. The likelihood that a character in a prime-time program will be the victim of a crime is higher than it is in real life. Heavier viewers believe that they are more likely to be victims of crime than they actually are. Heavy viewers are also more conservative in their views about the socially appropriate response to crime. They are, for example, more likely than light viewers to favor heavy sentences and use of the death penalty. Heavy-viewing conservatives and heavy-viewing liberals are more likely to agree on how to respond to crime than are heavy- and light-viewing liberals.

But whereas heavy viewing makes liberals more conservative on crime, television's legitimation of government response to social problems draws conservatives closer to a more liberal view of the value of government solutions to social problems.

The quantity, quality, and audience for televised information about politics is changing. In the mid-1980s an increase in the quality of political programming on the Public Broadcasting Service and the rise of cable meant that the amount of substantive political information available on television increased. Until the mid-1980s those who sought extended political contact with candidates would have to give up their careers and become camp followers. Ads, news, and debates had all moved to highly abbreviated forms. By 1988, however, any citizen with a television set could tune to PBS and hear 10-minute excerpts from candidate stump speeches on the "MacNeil/Lehrer Newshour" and watch hour-long biographies on the two major party candidates by prize-winning author Garry Wills; those with cable could attend to the complete stump speeches of the major candidates on C-Span. In other words, in 1988, it was possible for an interested citizen to be more knowledgeable about the national race than in any time in the history of the United States.

The rise of cable meant that specialized audiences could now be addressed directly by candidates. What had been a broadcast medium, reaching a large undifferentiated mass audience, was increasingly becoming a narrowcast medium, reaching smaller, more homogenous audiences. What was once true only of radio and direct mail became true of television in the mid-1980s. Spanish-language cable reached Hispanics in large numbers; MTV reached young voters. Whereas broadcasting dictated that political messages speak to concerns that transcended our differences, the narrowcasting of cable meant that the special concerns of special segments of the audience could now be addressed.

But whereas the limited number of broadcast channels meant that reporters could easily eavesdrop on and critique candidate ads, the narrowcasting available on over 100 cable channels makes this increasingly difficult.

If the good news is that there is an unprecedented amount of televised political information available, the bad news is that the most educated electorate in human history is less disposed than ever to pay attention to it. The trend has been clear for quite a while. In 1964 viewers faced an evening of television that offered three choices. On one channel was that incarnation of high culture, the predecessor of "Dallas" and "Dynasty"—"Peyton Place." On the second channel was "Petticoat Junction." On the third was a paid political program featuring former President Dwight David Eisenhower discussing the future of the world with Republican party nominee Barry Goldwater. The next morning Goldwater's opponent, incumbent President Lyndon Johnson eagerly called reporters' attention to the fact that the audience had overwhelmingly chosen "Peyton Place" and "Petticoat Junction" over Goldwater.

In 1980, voters made an equally memorable choice. On CBS, Roger Mudd's documentary on Edward M. Kennedy. On the other channel *Jaws*. *Jaws* swallowed "Teddy." These examples are simply dramatic expressions of a statistical fact. Viewership for political substance is steadily declining and has been for well over a decade. More people watched the first Kennedy–Nixon debate of 1960 than watched the first Dukakis–Bush debate of 1988. In 1988, convention viewership was down as well. More people tuned in to the speeches of President Gerald Ford than to the speeches of President Jimmy Carter. The drop-off continued in the Reagan presidency. On most evenings, the "MacNeil/Lehrer Newshour" attracts such a small audience that a percent doesn't even appear in the ratings book.

Image versus issues; character versus positions. Scholars have wasted a lot of time trying to distinguish between messages that relate to candidate image and messages that relate to candidates' stands on issues. The problem, of course, is that almost every message says something that can be interpreted as an issue and tries to enhance the candidate's credibility, hence image. It is more useful to recognize that stands on issues produce an image and that such "image" questions as trustworthiness and competence often are issues.

A more useful distinction separates the character or natural temperamental dispositions and relevant biography of the candidate from the specific legislative action the candidate proposes. So a candidate might demonstrate her compassion, a facet of character, by indicating her strong support for Aid for Dependent Children, a policy position or stand on an issue. Since the early seventies, voters have been telling pollsters that the character of the candidates is more important to them than the candidates' policy positions or stands on issues.

The Comparative Relevance of Character and Stands on Issues

In the 1960s and 1970s the electorate learned that judging a candidate on stands on issues was not a reliable predictor of his or her conduct in office. Some candidates acted against voter expectations: Lyndon Johnson, elected in 1964 as the peace candidate, escalated the war in Vietnam. Some presidents proved unable to meet their objectives. John Kennedy did not succeed in translating his campaign promises into law; only after his death did his successor secure passage of some of Kennedy's key initiatives. Jimmy Carter, elected to bring the budget into balance and lower inflation and unemployment, had not accomplished these goals by the end of his first term.

In this period, one campaign stood out for accurately forecasting a president's positions and accomplishments. Ronald Reagan campaigned promising a defense buildup and tax cuts and produced both.

Meanwhile, the character of a candidate seemed increasingly important in judging performance in office. Whether a person was truthful and trustworthy were focal concerns of those probing the failures of Johnson's handling of the Vietnam War and Nixon's handling of Watergate; whether a person was competent was central to those probing the failures of the presidencies of Ford and Carter; whether a person was candid about his health was of concern to those who learned of Kennedy's Addison's disease only after his death.

What can and does television tell us about issues and the character of presidential candidates?

Determining Which Issues Are the Likely Focus of a Campaign

In their own ads, in debates, and in news clips, candidates reveal their popular past positions and conceal their unpopular ones. At the same time, candidates reveal the unpopular past positions of their opponents. Public opinion polls and focus group tests (analysis of the response of small groups to various messages) help campaigns determine which issues will resonate with which voting group.

When an issue is controversial but, nonetheless, beneficial to one side or the other, that issue is more likely to be raised in the ads and news coverage of a Political Action Committee (PAC), not in the candidate's own messages. As we noted in the previous chapter, a PAC is a group of like-minded citizens formed to advance a specific interest and unaffiliated with a party or candidate. A PAC contributes to candidacies and produces messages consistent with the self-interest of its members. Most major corporations have formed PACs as have a number of ideological groups.

When an issue hurts both candidates or both parties, as the savings and loan crisis did in 1988, it will be raised by neither side.

In general, at the presidential level the party affiliation of the contender has accurately predicted the likely positions on certain issues. Republicans will, for example, favor less government intervention and less taxation but will support greater defense spending than will Democrats.

In general, the issues on which news, advertising, and debates will focus are those advanced by major party nominees. Although in 1988 over 100 citizens filed the appropriate papers to be considered bona fide presidential contenders, public discussion focuses, with few exceptions, on the Democratic and Republican parties' nominees and on the issues they consider important.

Issues of general concern will receive treatment in the mass media; issues of less national concern or highly specialized issues will be treated in specialty publications and broadcasts. For example, those interested in a candidate's monetary philosophy are more likely to find such information on "Wall Street Week in Review" or in the *Wall Street Journal* than on the "NBC Nightly News" or in *USA Today*. Specific environmental policies are likely to be treated in magazines devoted to the subject.

Since television is a visual medium, the messages produced on it are more likely to speak to issues that lend themselves to visualization. This means that crime and environmental pollution are more likely to be the subject of political ads and of news coverage than is the national debt or international liquidity.

Determining Which Facets of Character Are the Likely Focus in a Campaign   The character defects of the most recent president are likely to shape the criteria by which the character of the candidates is judged. After Nixon's resignation, Carter won election campaigning as a candidate who would never lie and who would provide a government as good as its people.

Societal norms shape the criteria we set for candidate character. In the 50s and 60s, a divorced candidate was weakened by that fact. During their presidential runs, it was raised as an issue against Adlai Stevenson and Nelson Rockefeller. By the 1980s being divorced no longer carried a social stigma, and the country elected its first divorced president.

The press and public are in the process of determining which facets of character are relevant to governance. In the 1988 primaries we learned that having smoked marijuana in one's youth was not a disqualifier. In the Texas gubernatorial campaign of 1990, we learned that the press and public consider it inappropriate for a candidate for governor to have purchased the services of prostitutes in his youth.

Any form of hypocrisy, any discrepancy between private behavior and public statement of politics, is likely to be scrutinized by the press. Pledging that they would find nothing, Gary Hart challenged the press to tail him. The press took him at his word and reported a weekend tryst with an aspiring actress that cost Hart his credibility as a presidential contender.

The resulting press scrutiny of itself is instructive. The reporting was justified on two grounds: Hart's hypocrisy and reporters' contentions that Hart's behavior showed a disposition toward risk-taking unacceptable in one who would head the country.

The Interplay of Influence: Issues and Character in Ads, News, Debates

Ads

There is more issue content in many ads than in broadcast news. The typical television viewer gets most of his or her political information from ads. A number of factors minimize the ability of ads to convey useful issue information. Conveying useful information is not the goal of the advertising. By stressing issues that will benefit them, candidates' ads attempt to set the issue agenda for the campaign. Because ads are partisan sources of information, they are poor sources of prime political information. Ads suppress information that would hurt their candidate; ads occasionally take evidence out of context; ads occasionally invite false inferences.

Political ads for bona fide candidates for federal office are not subject to tests of fairness or accuracy by those broadcasting them. A political ad for a bona fide candidate for federal office must meet only four tests: (1) it must have a discernible disclaimer disclosing its sponsor; (2) it must fit the time purchased; (3) it must meet the technical standards of the broadcast outlet; (4) it may not be obscene.

If a station has sold advertising time to one candidate in a race, it must make comparable time available for sale to all other bona fide candidates for that race. Since candidates must pay for most ad time, we are more likely to see ads for those who are wealthy or able to raise more money than their opponents. At the presidential level, in the general election, this advantage is muted by equal federal financing of both major party candidates.

Ways to Compensate for or Counter These Limitations

1. The best way to protect oneself from distortions in advertising is seeking out alternative forms of information. The best-informed voters are those who combine television viewing with newspaper and magazine reading. Since candidates often respond to the distortions of ads in press conferences, viewing news helps obtain the "other side."

2. In debates candidates are directly accountable to a press panel and to their opponents. Some questions of accuracy can be resolved by attentive debate viewing.

3. Concern about the distortions in attack advertising has prompted calls for legislation. Opponents of these proposals argue that they violate the Constitution's protections of free speech. Proposals include: (a) requiring that attacks be

made by a candidate in person speaking in an ad; (b) providing free response time for a candidate attacked by a PAC ad; (c) requiring that shortly after an ad begins airing, the sponsoring candidate hold a press conference to respond to questions about it.

News

Viewers tell pollsters that their voting choices are more influenced by print and broadcast news than by ads. This finding, however, may be the by-product of our human tendency to report that we are influenced by approved sources and uninfluenced by presumably manipulative sources. There is no dispute over the fact that when news coverage of a candidate is consistent with that candidate's ads and debate performance, the power of the candidate's message is magnified.

Several factors may minimize the ability of news to communicate useful issue information. For over a decade, scholars have consistently found that broadcast and print journalism focus not on issue content of campaigns but on strategic intent of the candidates, the outcome of their strategies, and on who is winning or losing. This focus on the "horse race" and "game plan" displaces discussion of other matters.

In addition, candidates attempt to control the news agenda. When they succeed, the news agenda and their ads are similarly focused, employ similar pictures, and repeat much of the same language.

When network newscasts do focus on issues, some of their news norms minimize the impact of their discussion. For instance, news is only news once. Once a story on an issue has aired or been printed, it is unlikely to be re-aired. The problem occurs when a distortive ad repeatedly makes a false claim that is only corrected or contextualized a single time in news. A problem occurs as well when the attention of parts of the public has not yet focused on the campaign at the time at which the issue is covered.

Another news norm problem is that it is the job of reporters to cover the story, not to make it. Accordingly, reporters focus on the issues preselected by the candidates. However, reporters are willing to set the agenda for discussion of character and to probe any discrepancies between candidate character and accepted social norms.

Ways to Compensate for or Counter These Limitations

1.   Gather information from multiple news sources and multiple media.
2.   Determine what issues are relevant to you and seek out forms in which those issues are likely to be addressed.
3.   Begin paying attention to news and debates in the early presidential primaries when news coverage is likely to treat emerging issues in depth.
4.   Use computer-based retrieval in libraries or at home to retrieve early news stories of importance in contextualizing candidate claims. Often newspapers carry careful studies of the biography and record of a candidate early in the primaries.

Debates

In a national election, debates are the single most useful form of information available to voters. In debates, a large viewing audience has the opportunity to compare the candidates and their positions. Debates provide the only direct comparison available in most campaigns. The results are beneficial to every segment of the viewing audience from the least to the best educated. After each presidential debate, surveys have shown that viewers could more accurately identify and report the candidates' positions on the major issues debated.

There are several factors that minimize the ability of debates to communicate useful information on issues. First, the candidates' desire to protect themselves from gaffes leads them to (1) seek a panel of reporters on the expectation that reporters will ask predictable questions; (2) negotiate a format that includes only short candidate answers on the assumption that all possible questions can be anticipated and short answers prepared; and (3) negotiate a format that denies reporters the ability to follow up their questions on the assumption that inconsistencies and inaccuracies are less likely to be exposed if there are no follow-up questions.

Second, the press panelists tend to ask questions of more interest to a knowledgeable reporter than to an information-seeking voter.

Third, press coverage tends to reduce debates to a single decisive moment. This focus distracts from information about the candidates and their positions contained in the debate. These supposedly decisive moments include "There you go again." "Do you remember when you said, 'There you go again?'" and "Senator, you are no John Kennedy."

Fourth, the press focuses on the strategic intent of the candidates and on who won or lost the debate. There is no intelligent way to judge a win or loss. More important is that the focus on winning and losing displaces other more useful discussion of what could be and should be learned from debates.

Ways to Compensate for or Counter These Limitations

1. The well-informed voter will be able to spot errors and inconsistencies.

2. The well-informed voter need not rely on commentators to determine what was and was not significant in the debate.

3. The well-informed viewer will not let debate coverage determine what is useful but will instead ask what issues and traits of character are important and will seek out that information systematically.

T O   S U M   U P

In this chapter we have examined the complex interaction among the candidates and the media in campaigns. One medium can be used to contextualize the content carried by another; for example, a print reporter may determine the accuracy of charges contained in a broadcast ad. Alternatively, an ad such as the anti-Nixon Watergate ads run by McGovern may take articles published in a print form and employ them in a televised ad.

We also noted the interplay of news and advertising across the various media. Ads become the subject of analysis in news, and items in the news become the content of ads. In the process, the well-financed candidate has the ability to take his or her case directly to the American people in ads, but even as this right is exercised, it is subject to the scrutiny of the news media.

Finally, we have shown some of the ways in which politicians manipulate the news in their attempts to impose a consistent image of themselves and their campaigns on all media outlets. This chapter illustrates the systemic and commercial character of United States mass media. Political communication includes both news and advertising. As news, political activities are shaped by the criteria for newsworthiness and the conventions of news presentation. In advertising, candidates, like products, must achieve name recognition, differentiate themselves from their competitors, create identification with and participation by target audiences, associate themselves with admired persons, activities, and values, and use repetition to overcome audience resistance.

In political communication, news and advertising interact in an unusually significant way. News coverage can make a candidate credible, reinforce the messages in political ads, and protect her or him against certain kinds of attacks. As a result, politicians seek to blur distinctions between news and advertising; campaign managers create pseudo-events to attract media coverage; and news footage or newslike content and formats are used in political advertising.

Journalists, with their special access to information and their credibility as investigators, evaluate the claims in political ads and serve as a corrective to deceptive and misleading advertising. Conversely, through ads candidates can respond to news coverage and influence how audiences react to news items.

National and state political candidates cannot be elected without the credibility conferred by news coverage or without the images created through advertising. As a result, the costs of political campaigning have increased. Political advertising is expensive, as are the services of professionals with the expertise to influence news coverage. In one sense, mass media have made political communication more efficient—the cost of reaching each voter has decreased—but they have also made politics a game successfully played primarily by the affluent and the media-savvy.

Analysis

Political Ads and News

Many of the questions found at the end of the chapters on news and advertising can be asked also of political use of ads and news. Here we include some additional questions that pertain more specifically to advertising and news in political campaigns.

Determining Who Is Newsworthy   What criteria are governing which candidates are receiving news coverage? Are some candidates receiving more coverage than others? Are some candidates receiving more coverage in one medium than in others? If so, why? How are the candidates using the conventions and routines of news coverage to secure news coverage? Are some candidates doing this with greater skill than others? Are reporters reporting these efforts at manipulation?

Determining What Is Covered   Are the candidates' ads a subject of news reporting? If so, what is the focus of such stories? (cost? claims? evidence? fairness? image? media consultants?) Is one candidate more clearly setting the agenda for the media than others? What agenda is being set for voters by the media? Are they focusing on issues that favor one candidate over the others? Are the media focusing on some primaries and not others? If so, why? Which candidates are benefiting from this focus? Has the nature of coverage changed during the campaign? Has the quantity of the coverage increased, decreased, or remained the same as the campaign has progressed? What interpretation has been placed on each announcement of candidacy and each statement of withdrawal? Are journalists acting to determine the truth or falsity of charges in the campaign? If so, to what effect? Has any candidate invoked the Fairness Doctrine, equal opportunity, or right to access? If so, to what effect? If this is a statewide campaign, a congressional or senatorial campaign, has it received coverage in the national media? If so, what of significance or interest to a national audience is being credited to this campaign?

Relationship of Candidates and Reporters   Compare the treatment of reporters by each campaign. Are they better fed and housed, more courteously treated in one campaign than others? If so, what effect, if any, is this having on media coverage? Are some journalists being given preferential treatment? If so, to what effect? Are some reporters being punished by the campaign for unfavorable coverage? If so, what form of action is the punishment taking? Restricted access? Undesirable accommodations? What are the ongoing themes in the coverage of this campaign? (horse race? appearance versus reality? consistency?)

The Image of the Candidate   Is the image projected by the candidate consistent? If not, what are the discrepancies and what accounts for them? Is the image projected in person consistent with the image in ads? In news? Are some of the candidates more visually appropriate for televising than others? If so, what impact is that having on the campaign? On reports about the campaign? Has the image of the candidate altered over time? If so, why and to what effect? Is the presence of a media consultant an issue in this campaign? If so, what is the consultant saying about his or her role in the campaign? Is the media consultant helping or hurting the candidate? What are the adjectives used most often by the media to describe this candidate? Is an independent political action committee running ads to create a positive or negative image about one of the candidates? If so, to what effect? How are the candidates reacting to the PAC?

Candidates' Ads   Are candidates using ads to contextualize news? Are materials from news reports functioning as evidence in ads? Have ads been a subject of news reports? If so, did the coverage help or hurt the candidate? Is the candidate using attack ads? If so, are they truthful and fair? If so, are they airing throughout the campaign, at specific points in the campaign, or at the end of the campaign? How does the pattern of airing attack ads affect their impact in this campaign? Will these ads provoke a backlash? If so, why? If not, why not? Are these attack ads responding to other attacks? If so, is the response legitimizing the attack of the opponent? How are the ads creating recognition, differentiation, association, participation, and repetition?

Selected Readings

Barber, James D., ed. *Race for the Presidency: The Media and the Nominating Process*. Englewood Cliffs, N.J.: Prentice-Hall, 1978.

Blumenthal, Sidney. *The Permanent Campaign: Inside the World of Elite Political Operatives*. Boston: Beacon Press, 1980.

Blumenthal, Sidney. *Pledging Allegiance: The Last Campaign of the Cold War*. New York: Harper Collins, 1990.

Cannon, Lou. *Reporting: An Inside View*. Sacramento: California Journal Press, 1977.

Crouse, Timothy. *The Boys on the Bus*. New York: Random House, 1972.

Edelman, Murray. *Politics as Symbolic Action: Mass Arousal and Quiescence*. New York: Academic Press, 1971.

Edelman, Murray. *The Symbolic Uses of Politics*. Champaign: University of Illinois Press, 1967.

Graber, Doris A. *Verbal Behavior and Politics*. Champaign: University of Illinois Press, 1976.

Hart, Roderick P. *The Sound of Leadership*. University of Chicago Press, 1988.

Herbers, John. *No Thank You, Mr. President*. New York: W.W. Norton, 1976.

Jamieson, Kathleen Hall. *Eloquence in an Electronic Age*. New York: Oxford University Press, 1988.

Jamieson, Kathleen Hall. *Packaging the Presidency*. New York: Oxford University Press, 1984.

Nelson, Michael. *The Presidency and the Political System*. Washington, D.C.: Congressional Quarterly, 1984.

Patterson, Thomas E. *The Mass Media Election: How Americans Choose Their President*. New York: Praeger, 1980.

Sherrill, Robert. *Why They Call It Politics*. New York: Harcourt Brace Jovanovich, 1979.

Windt, Theodore O. *Presidential Rhetoric: The Imperial Age 1961–80*. Dubuque, Iowa: Kendall-Hunt, 1980.

Windt, Theodore O. *Presidents and Protestors: Political Rhetoric in the 1960s*. Tuscaloosa: University of Alabama Press, 1990.

Afterword

We considered entitling this book *Manipulating Media* because the deliberate ambiguity of that phrase reflects the dual perspective we have taken: the mass media manipulate their publics; publics, in turn, manipulate the mass media. We do not condemn newspeople, advertisers, or politicians for the sheer fact of influence, nor do we condemn those who seek to influence news, advertising, or political communication.

Instead, we presume that rhetoric is an essential part of human action. No one can avoid imposing a perspective when selecting what is to be communicated; no one can avoid making arguments and appeals; no one can avoid shaping content to reach and affect a desired audience. In this book we have examined some of the techniques available to the mass media and to those who would use the mass media to achieve their ends.

We emphasize the close, reciprocal relationship between the mass media and their publics. In fact, when individuals, groups, or government agencies attempt to manipulate the media, media decision makers are, for them, an audience of sorts. Because audiences participate in creating the messages by which they are influenced, they can influence those who create messages. Because of the associative and participatory processes by which messages prompt inferences in audiences, no regulation based on a simple truth criterion can be an effective response to the rhetoric of political or product advertising.

Although we argue that all can manipulate the mass media, we recognize that resource-poor individuals and groups are at a severe disadvantage. Under most circumstances, in order to be newsworthy those lacking resources are forced to engage in acts that violate social norms, acts likely to provoke social condemnation. Thus, media access is achieved by such groups at incalculable social costs to them and to us. Similarly and with few exceptions, political candidates who are not skilled fund-raisers will not be elected to public office, whatever their qualifications; such candidates will be unable to purchase sufficient access to media time and space.

This book emphasizes the commercial character of U.S. mass media. We presume that the news media cannot be understood apart from their intense need to attract audiences and advertisers. Similarly, advertising cannot be understood without analyzing the programming and print materials sponsored by advertisers to attract audiences. Finally, political communication requires an understanding of the complex interrelationship between news coverage and political advertising.

We assume that the tendency of any mass media system is to affirm establishment values. A system that failed to do so would not attract audiences or government or private sponsorship. News, advertising, and political communication in the United States reflect this ideological reality.

Index

295